SUCCESSFUL
BLACK
ENTREPRENEURS

SUCCESSFUL BLACK ENTREPRENEURS

HIDDEN HISTORIES, INSPIRATIONAL STORIES, AND EXTRAORDINARY BUSINESS ACHIEVEMENTS

CASE STUDIES BY HARVARD BUSINESS SCHOOL

STEVEN S. ROGERS

HARVARD BUSINESS SCHOOL, RETIRED

WILEY

For general information on our other products and services or for technical support, please contact our Customer Care Department within the United States at (800) 762-2974, outside the United States at (317) 572-3993 or fax (317) 572-4002.

Wiley publishes in a variety of print and electronic formats and by print-on-demand. Some material included with standard print versions of this book may not be included in e-books or in print-on-demand. If this book refers to media such as a CD or DVD that is not included in the version you purchased, you may download this material at http://booksupport.wiley.com. For more information about Wiley products, visit www.wiley.com.

Library of Congress Cataloging-in-Publication Data is Available:

ISBN 9781119806738 (Hardcover)
ISBN 9781119806813 (ePDF)
ISBN 9781119806806 (ePub)

Cover Design: Wiley

SKY10032245_122821

Contents

Preface   vii

Introduction   xi

Chapter 1   History of Black Entrepreneurship   1

Chapter 2   Importance of Black Entrepreneurs   37

Chapter 3   Black Start-Up Entrepreneurs   43

Chapter 4   Entrepreneurship Through Acquisitions   75

Chapter 5   Entrepreneurship Through Franchising   125

Chapter 6   Access to Capital for Black Entrepreneurs   157

Chapter 7   Black Turnaround Entrepreneurs   203

Chapter 8   Entrepreneurial Exits: Selling the Company   235

Chapter 9   Black Intrapreneurs   285

Epilogue	311
Appendix	313
Acknowledgments	317
About the Author	321
Index	323

Preface

ALL OF THE case studies included in this book were taught as part of my course at Harvard Business School. This course, "Black Business Leaders and Entrepreneurship," was historic as it represented the first course, in any business school, devoted singularly to the challenges, efforts, and accomplishments of Black entrepreneurs. The course description and syllabus is included in the Appendix.

The primary objective of the course was the same as one of the objectives of this book—to identify, recognize, and celebrate the brilliance of Black men and women who achieved success as entrepreneurs. Of particular note, these people were and are not athletes or entertainers.

Rarely will you see the inclusion of athletes or entertainers on any list identifying successful entrepreneurs. The exception that nearly makes the rule is when such a list identifies Black entrepreneurs. This is problematic for the Black community because it implies that non-Blacks can achieve entrepreneurial success through their intellect and vision, but Blacks rely on their athletic accomplishments or entertainment skills to achieve similar success. It is unfair because it ignores the fact that these Black entertainers typically pursued entrepreneurial endeavors AFTER they had successfully established a brand. Establishing a brand allowed them to then use their names, financial resources, and hired management teams to extend the range of their impact to areas of new products or services. There is absolutely nothing wrong with this business model when it is applied to the universe of entrepreneurial recognition. But achieving entrepreneurial success through branding alone is only applied to Blacks generally. Therefore, it sends a message to the Black community that if a person aspires to be a successful entrepreneur, then the pathway requires becoming a successful athlete or entertainer first.

Therefore, the mission of this book and all of the case studies that I published is to fight the stereotypic conviction that there is a narrow Black entrepreneurial archetype. My fervent belief is that it is imperative for Blacks to embrace something broader, to know that their entrepreneurial role models should be and are other Black men and women who have used their intellect, problem-solving skills, and business acumen to become successful entrepreneurs.

The case studies in this book also differ from the typical Harvard Business School case studies with the inclusion of Black history. Every case reviewed has a section devoted to teaching the reader something historical about the Black community. All of the supplemental information covered was tangentially related to the protagonist covered. For example, the case study on Otis Gates included a section about the Pullman porters, after it was mentioned that Gates's father held that occupation. A similar historical vignette about Tuskegee Airmen was included in the case study on John Rogers because his father was one of those distinguished military pilots.

Finally, I am most proud of the fact that a distinguishing aspect of every case is that the Black entrepreneurs are shown to be more than just symbols of monetary success. These men and women made tangible, public contributions to the Black community. To illustrate my point, you may note that Valerie Daniels-Carter created a community center in the heart of the Black community in Milwaukee, while Otis Gates not only increased housing opportunities but funded after-school programs, adult education, and job coaching in community centers in Boston's Black community.

The inclusion of the community contributions of these Black entrepreneurs was intentional. My intent was to define Black entrepreneurial success as being more than an individual with the ability to make a lot of money. There is a legacy that our Black entrepreneur ancestors have left us that is highlighted throughout this book that the true measure of a successful Black entrepreneur requires a positive answer to the question, "In addition to your financial success, what have you done to help the Black community?"

One couple who had financial success and helped the Black community was Willa and Charles Bruce, mentioned in Chapter 3. Their successful beach resort was closed after the city government took their land. This was done because they were Black and their customers were Black. On April 6, 2021, the Manhattan Beach City Council voted to begin the process of righting the wrong inflicted on the Bruce family. Their objective is to return the land ownership to the descendants of Willa and Charles. This effort to transfer the land was accompanied by the following statement from a government official, "The Bruces had their California dream stolen from them. . . . And this was an injustice inflicted not just upon Willa and Charles Bruce but generations of their descendants who almost certainly would have been millionaires if they had been able to keep this property and their successful business."[1] I strongly believe the right thing to do is for the county to return this property to the Bruce family.

Hopefully the publicity about this injustice will also teach people about Willa and Charles, two successful Black entrepreneurs who were not athletes or entertainers, but great business people! While I am making you aware of the crimes against these two entrepreneurs, this book also recognizes and celebrates their brilliance, as well as the effulgence of other Black entrepreneurs.

---

[1] John Antczak, "Plan Would Return California Beachfront Taken from Black family in '20s." ABC10. April 9, 2021. https://www.abc10.com/article/news/nation-world/los-angeles-county-beachfront-property-black-family-return/507-a1e2a4d6-5e1d-4cc3-a09b-47e44b0b8316

Introduction

As STATED IN the Preface, a few years ago, while serving as a professor at Harvard Business School (HBS), I created a new course titled "Black Business Leaders and Entrepreneurship." After hearing about the new course, a White professor asked, "Why do we need this course? What is the difference between Black and White entrepreneurs?" In response, I identified the following:

1. Black entrepreneurs do not have the same access to capital from traditional financial institutions, including banks and private equity firms.
2. Many Black entrepreneurs who want to sell to White customers must practice "racial concealment" to be successful.
3. Successful Black entrepreneurs who are not athletes or entertainers are virtually invisible in the minds of the mainstream public.

All of these forces have a negative impact on Black entrepreneurship, which, in turn, hurts the Black community and the entire country. For centuries, Black entrepreneurs have contributed to the growth of the American economy. That is the reason why all of America should care about the success of Black entrepreneurs. Therefore, this book is not only for Black readers but for every person interested in learning about great entrepreneurs who have made the U.S. a better country.

This book leverages the rich data learnings from HBS coursework and case studies (included in almost every chapter) and applies them to the current social justice and political movements in the world at large. My belief is that the world needs more Black leaders in business generally, and more Black entrepreneurs in particular.

Successful Black entrepreneurs create jobs for Black, White, and other racial groups. They have created companies that provide products and services that have benefited society at large. To emphasize that point, the following list includes Black entrepreneurs who invented or made major improvements to everyday products that remain in common use:

- Sarah Boone – the ironing board
- Lydia Newman – the hairbrush
- Thomas Stewart – the string mop
- George Sampson – the automatic clothes dryer
- John Burr – the lawn mower
- Richard Spikes – the automatic gear shift
- Garrett Morgan – the traffic light
- John Standard – the refrigerator

As significant as these products may be in your life, the real question is, how many of these people had you heard of? More than likely, the answer is "none," even if you are Black. Most of you, of course, will have heard of Steve Jobs, Bill Gates, Thomas Edison, Henry Ford, Sam Walton, and Charles Schwab, I will wager. Why such a disparity in our awareness, and appreciation?

The largely, heretofore, hidden history of Black entrepreneurship motivated the creation of my course at HBS. Initially, I combined lesser-known facts and stories, along with an HBS case study that I wrote about a Black entrepreneur. I only wrote about successful Black entrepreneurs. My definition of success includes their monetary accomplishments as well as their contributions back to the Black community. These contributions were comprised of jobs for Blacks and/or philanthropic donations to the Black community. I published 24 case studies before retiring from HBS in 2019, which comprises the most case studies with Black protagonists written by a single author in this country, and some of them will be included in this unique book.

HBS has an inventory of over 10,000 case studies that generate over $100 million in annual revenue for the university. Over 80% of all case studies used by business schools throughout the world are from this HBS inventory. I have written over 50% of all HBS case studies that have a Black protagonist. This book will bring many of them together in a collection for the first time. While such a large collection of case studies regarding Black entrepreneurs makes this book distinctively different, the addition of content about the history of Black entrepreneurship, with related issues and materials, will make it substantially more than a simple collection of case studies.

Every chapter will end with one of my case studies, preceded by a brief description of the case and at least two questions that can help you structure your analysis and determine your answers. The case study topic will be directly related to the title of the chapter. Each case was taught at Harvard Business School to MBA students. You will now get the exact same opportunity to read the case, analyze it, identify the problems, and recommend solutions.

The objectives of this book are multifold, including the following:

- Provide you with history that you are not likely to have ever heard before.
- Kill stereotypes that only athletes and entertainers are successful Black entrepreneurs.
- Raise the profile of Black entrepreneurs so that, hopefully, it improves their access to capital.
- Help all entrepreneurs see themselves solving problems currently addressed only by Black entrepreneurs.
- Inform you that more Black entrepreneurs are needed.
- Inspire Black people through entrepreneur role models who look like them.
- Promote the idea that entrepreneurship is a skill that can be learned and is not a quality that is defined by race.

By the way, the White professor mentioned earlier is Jeff Bussgang. After learning about the realities of Black entrepreneurship, he decided to be part of the solution. He partnered with a Black woman, Donna Levin—a former entrepreneur who took her company, Care .com, public—to co-teach his popular course "Launching Technology Ventures." He also added my case study, "Mented Cosmetics," to his course. Finally, he has partnered with two Black HBS professors to create and co-teach a new course titled "Scaling Minority Businesses" that has a focus on Black-owned companies. Jeff's initials are J.B. One of his course co-creators mentioned above, Henry McGee, stated with pride that J.B. stands for "John Brown," the famous White abolitionist.

This book is for Whites, Blacks, and every other race and ethnicity. The facts, stories, and importance of Black entrepreneurs are topics that should be known to all Americans and people throughout the world. I know that you will learn something new and enjoy reading this book!

1

History of Black Entrepreneurship

IN A SINGLE word, entrepreneurship has meant *freedom* to the Black community. Freedom to command their own destinies, to serve their own communities, to live out their own dreams through entrepreneurship, and the freedom to free enslaved people. However, to be clear, Black entrepreneurship did not begin in 2019 when Kim and Jim Lewis, founders of CurlMix Inc., pitched their company on *Shark Tank* and rejected a $400,000 offer.[1] It also did not begin in 1991 when Bob Johnson, the founder of Black Entertainment Television (BET), took the company public, raising $72 million and becoming the first Black-owned company on the New York Stock Exchange (NYSE).[2] Nor did it begin in 1969, when Parks Sausage Company became the first Black-owned company to complete an initial public offering.[3] It did not begin in 1942 when John H. Johnson started the *Negro Digest*, which later became *Ebony* magazine, to, in his words, "tell the swell story about the Negro."[4] Nor did it begin in 1910 when Sarah Breedlove Walker, who we all know as Madam C. J. Walker, built a hair care manufacturing plant with over 3,000 employees in Indianapolis and became the country's first Black millionaire.[5] It did not begin in 1905 when Robert Abbott began the *Chicago Defender* newspaper, a major publication of the Black press, which grew to be one of the most influential national newspapers of the time.[6] Finally, it did not begin

1

in 1903 when Maggie Walker became the country's first female bank president with the establishment of the St. Luke Penny Savings Bank in Richmond, Virginia.[7] Black entrepreneurship began in 1651 when Anthony Johnson, formerly enslaved, purchased 250 acres of land in Virginia, and experienced enormous success as a tobacco farmer.[8]

Before the Emancipation Proclamation, free Blacks in the South and North had an insatiable appetite for business ownership, such that on the eve of the Civil War, their collective wealth was conservatively estimated to be over $50 million.[9] Assuming an interest rate of 4% over 150 years, the present value of that $50 million would be approximately $15 billion! Among those Black entrepreneurs was James Forten, who, in the late 1700s, owned a manufacturing company in Philadelphia that made sails for ships.[10] He employed more than 40 Black and White workers.

A recurring theme of Black entrepreneurship in the nineteenth century was job creation. In 1838, free Black women created jobs for themselves and others through their domination of the dress-making and wig-making industries. In 1840, free Blacks in New York also created jobs through their ownership of a clothes cleaner, a hairdressing salon, a confectionary, a fruit store, two coal yards, two dry goods stores, two restaurants, three tailor shops, and six boarding houses.

Surprisingly, Black entrepreneurship was not limited to free Blacks. While enslaved in the early 1800s, Frank McWorter started a company that produced saltpeter, the main ingredient in gun powder. With the company's profits, he purchased his freedom and the freedom of 16 family members. John Berry Meachum, among his several accomplishments, owned a carpentry business.[11] With the earnings from his carpentry, he purchased his own freedom and that of his family and 20 friends. In 1794, Robert Renfro started a restaurant in Nashville, Tennessee, where he served food as well as liquor.[12] He purchased his freedom and that of his friend in 1801.

Yes, my friends, Blacks have always been entrepreneurs. I applaud and celebrate those brave Black men and women who used entrepreneurship, literally, as a tool for freedom. As recounted earlier, a recurring theme of Black entrepreneurs is their use of their business earnings to purchase their own and the freedom of family and friends.

However, as laudatory as these Black entrepreneurs were in their use of the profits from their businesses, there were members of the American community who were not so enamored of Black entrepreneurship.

In fact, one of the worst incidents of violence ever visited upon Blacks was directly related to successful Black entrepreneurship. In Tulsa, Oklahoma, on June 1, 1921, a terrorist event occurred that some have referred to as the "Black Holocaust in America."[13] In the early twentieth century, the most affluent Black community in America was not found in New York or Chicago, but in Tulsa, Oklahoma, a community well known as the "Black Wall Street." With 15,000 Blacks residing in the city, occupying a 36 square block area, they owned and operated over 600 businesses.[14] Among those many businesses, they owned 30 grocery stores, 31 restaurants, 8 doctor's offices, 6 private airplanes, 4 drug stores, 2 movie theaters, 1 hospital, 1 bank, and a bus system. One way to appreciate the vitality of this community is to note that the dollar of a Black person would circulate 36 to 1,000 times, taking up to a year to leave the Black community.

The main thoroughfare of these 36 square block areas was Greenwood Avenue, intersected by Archer and Pine streets. The first letter in each of those street names is a G, A, and P, which spells GAP, and that is where the GAP band, who jammed with "Burn Rubber on Me," got its name.[15]

Don't these acts just warm you with pride and admiration? Well, the pride and admiration that you, I, and those 15,000 Black people had was equaled by the jealously and disdain of a group of Whites. Overnight, on May 31 and June 1, 1921, in a period of fewer than 12 hours, Black Wall Street was gone.[16] A horde of Whites, angry, envious, and/or resentful of this Black success, burned down all of the Black businesses, 1,100 homes, and a dozen churches, and killed over 300 Black Americans living in Tulsa.

Eldoris McCondichie vividly recalled being awakened by her mother on that June morning. Eldoris, who was nine years old, remembers her mother's exact words as she said, "Eldoris, wake up! We have to go! The white people are killing the colored folks!"[17] This massacre, which represented a clear act of domestic terrorism against Blacks included the ingenious evil of dropping Molotov cocktail bombs from airplanes, carried out by Whites who were former World War I pilots. This constituted the first aerial attack on Americans on American soil, 20 years before the Japanese bombing of Pearl Harbor on December 7, 1941, or the attacks against the Twin Towers of the World Trade Center on September 11, 2001. It is not surprising, but unfortunate, that Tulsa's Black community has never recovered from this little-known major tragedy.

Today, only one block houses Black-owned businesses. Most of the Greenwood Avenue area, once bustling with Black-owned businesses, has very few, and almost every piece of real estate is White owned. The headlines of *The Washington Post* call this "The 'whitewashing' of Black Wall Street."[18]

The story of Black entrepreneurship is the story of American history. It spans every memorable period of our country's existence including slavery, Jim Crow, the Civil Rights Era, and the pre/post Black Lives Matter Era.

Even as the COVID-19 pandemic has driven 40% of Black businesses to close,[19] the story of Black entrepreneurship was bittersweet. The sweet was that there were over 3 million Black-owned businesses out of the 22 million companies in America. The fastest-growing entrepreneurial group was Black women. From 1997 to 2015, the number of female-owned businesses grew 74%.[20] During that time, Black female–owned businesses grew 322%![21] But the bitter ingredient in the story of Black entrepreneurship today is the fact that only 4% of Black businesses have at least one employee, compared to 20% of White-owned businesses, and that the average Black company has $915,000 of annual revenue compared to $2.4 million for White-owned companies.[22] The primary factor driving these disparities is the lack of capital available to Black entrepreneurs required to develop and grow.

Chapter 6 will deal with this topic more substantively, identifying the problem, the root causes, and recommended solutions. As explained in the introduction, the disparity in access to capital hurts the Black community and the entire country.

The Black community and no other community can thrive, be healthy, and prosper without a meaningful foundation of private enterprises; namely entrepreneurial ventures. Therefore, an ever-increasing number of successful Black entrepreneurs are desperately needed. And as the following chapters demonstrate, they can achieve their entre-preneurial aspirations via a start-up, where they create something from nothing; via franchising as a franchisor or franchisee; or via an acquisition, whereby they purchase an ongoing concern, that is independent and not a franchise.

As the next chapter shows, these pathways to entrepreneurial success for Black men and women are burdened with unique financial challenges. But as you will see from the plethora of success stories, Black entrepreneurship has always been, and will always be, alive! The best phrase to describe Black entrepreneurship comes from the great poet laureate, Maya Angelou, who famously said, "And still I rise!"[23]

Introduction to the Case Study

John Rogers Jr. is one of the country's most successful entrepreneurs in the financial services industry. This case looks at the challenges he faces as the leader of Ariel Investments Co. as he pursues exponential growth that he expected to occur from being at a top performing asset management firm.

HARVARD | BUSINESS | SCHOOL

9-318-099

JANUARY 2, 2018

STEVEN ROGERS

GREG WHITE

John Rogers, Jr. - Ariel Investments Co.

John Rogers, the CEO of Chicago-based Ariel Investments ended a 15 minute phone call with his board member without a commitment to "toning down" his strong public advocacy for corporations hiring African American owned professional services firms. His board member had called John in a panic after reading a highly controversial article in Chicago's most subscribed business magazine. This article was about the local corporate and non-profit community's unwillingness to spend and invest with minority owned companies. In reference to institutional investors, John had asserted, "you guys have a commitment to working with black businesses, but it's all a big charade. Things are substantially worse than they were 40 years ago." (See **Exhibit 1**.)

The board member was concerned that John's critical, blunt, and public criticism of institutional investors would undermine Ariel Investments' attempt to manage money for these organizations. "John, be smart and don't bite the hand that feeds you", he was advised. These large institutional managers were a tight-knit club and could be highly sensitive to public criticism. Furthermore, many in Chicago's corporate community felt they were making good progress by increasing business relationships with minority owned companies over the last few years. "We are very committed and headed in the right direction" is how one corporate CEO characterized his firm's actions.

This Crain's article was not the first time John or his company had publicly criticized Chicago's corporate community. Over the last several years, John had become increasingly disappointed and vocal about the lack of action by the business community to give African American companies a fair opportunity to contractually perform professional services for multibillion dollar corporations, foundations, and pension funds. Recently, one of Ariel's executives had criticized one of Chicago's largest hedge funds for its failure to do business with minority companies. What began as discreet complaints to a few people had now escalated into a public confrontation with Ariel's potential clients.

The Industry – Money Management

Institutions with large amounts of financial assets to invest (foundations, pension funds, university endowments, etc.), often elect to hire outside managers, known as money management companies. In the U.S., there are thousands of money management companies, managing over $71 trillion in assets, and generating billions of dollars in annual management fees. The top 25 largest Chicago Money

HBS Senior Lecturer Steven Rogers and independent researcher Greg White prepared the original version of this case "John Rogers and Ariel Investments" HBS No. 318-015. This version was prepared by the same authors. Funding for the development of this case was provided by Harvard Business School and not by the company. HBS cases are developed solely as the basis for class discussion. Cases are not intended to serve as endorsements, sources of primary data, or illustrations of effective or ineffective management.

Managers are listed in **Exhibit 2**. In total, they manage over $2 trillion in assets. This list includes hedge funds, private equity and mutual fund managers.

Compensation structures for money managers vary depending on the type of investments being made and can include both an annual asset fee-typically .5% to 2% of assets under management (AUM) and, in some cases, a percent of the profits generated. As a result, this tends to be a high margin business with the potential to create significant personal wealth for the firm's owners and employees.

The institutional investor's selection process for hiring a money manager can be complex, subjective and greatly influenced by long-standing relationships. Established institutional investors typically have a maximum number of money managers to whom they are willing to allocate their investable assets. In theory, money management firms are selected based on their track record in delivering superior financial returns for a certain level of risk and/or within a specific asset class.

In many cases, firms will hire Consultants to help them identify money managers who meet their investment criteria. They manage the screening process on behalf of the institution to identify prospective money manager, winnowing the list down to a final recommendation. These Consultants can make introductions and significantly influence the final selection of the money manager. (See **Exhibit 3**.)

In select cases, institutional investors have elected to allocate a certain percentage of their assets to be managed by minority or emerging money management firms. A minority firm is defined as a company owned and led by an ethnic minority and an emerging fund is typically any fund with less than $2 billion assets under management and may or may not be minority owned. This special allocation is done for several reasons including the opportunity to: 1) identify new emerging managers; 2) meet certain corporate diversity goals; 3) invest in marketplaces typically overlooked by mainstream funds; 4) comply with local government mandates; 5) respond to the criticism that the investment industry has systematically excluded non-whites from participating; and/or 6) find the truly outstanding future or ignored money managers. (See **Exhibits 4 – 7**.)

The CEO

John Rogers is the Founder, CEO, and Chief Investment Officer for the country's largest minority owned money management firm - Ariel Investments. The firm launched in 1983 with $200,000 in investable funds from family and friends. Over time it has grown to almost $12 billion in investable assets and 85 employees. In a recent publication about the world's 99 greatest investors, John was featured with legendary investors Sir John Templeton and Warren Buffet.

John Rogers' passion for investing started when he was 12 years old when his father bought him stocks every birthday and every Christmas instead of toys. His interest grew while majoring in economics at Princeton University. After graduation, he worked as a stockbroker for 2½ years at William Blair & Company, LLC - a regional investment banking firm. In 1983, John founded Ariel Investments to focus on investing in undervalued small and medium-sized publicly traded companies.

Ariel manages assets on behalf of institutions (endowments, unions, and pension funds) and individuals (mutual funds). The firm is considered a "value investor" as it invests in undervalued companies that the marketplace has overlooked or underpriced. This investment approach requires extensive due diligence, rigorous analysis, patience and highly sophisticated and disciplined fund manager.

Ariel has become a leading mutual fund company by delivering strong financial returns to its investors. Since its inception, Ariel-Fund and the Ariel Appreciation Fund had delivered 11.34% and 10.75% compounded annualized returns, respectively. John Rogers' Ariel Fund has the best performance of any fund in its peer group (more than 200 funds) since market bottom in March 2009. A comparison of Ariel's performance versus comparable benchmarks is listed in **Table 1** below.

Table 1

ARIEL FUND PREFORMANCE
INVESTOR CLASS | ARGFX
As of June 30, 2017

	1 Year	5 Years	Market Bottom 03/09/09	Since Inception 11/06/86
Ariel Fund (Investor Class)	+ 15.76%	+ 14.75%	+ 24.25%	+ 11.34%
Russell 2500 Value Index	+ 15.75	+ 13.25	+ 20.27	+ 11.34
Russell 2500 Index	+ 17.79	+ 13.86	+ 20.70	+ 10.86
S&P 500 Index	+ 18.61	+ 14.22	+ 19.09	+ 10.32
Lipper mid-cap core rankings	47% (170/365)	9% (22/250)	1% (1/189)	15% (1/6)
Morningstar mid-cap value absolute rankings	41% (144/410)	14% (36/319)	1% (3/233)	33% (2/6)

ARIEL APPRECIATION FUND PERFORMANCE
INVESTOR CLASS | CAAPX
As of June 30, 2017

	1 Year	5 Years	Market Bottom 03/09/09	Since Inception 11/06/86
Ariel Appreciation Fund (Investor Class)	+ 12.41%	+ 13.10%	+ 21.76%	+ 10.75%
Russell Midcap Value Index	+ 13.37	+ 14.33	+ 21.45	+ 11.56
Russell Midcap Index	+ 15.32	+ 14.26	+ 20.93	+ 11.34
S&P 500 Index	+ 18.61	+ 14.22	+ 19.09	+ 9.66
Lipper multi-cap value rankings	89% (313/353)	36% (99/278)	8% (17/239)	6% (1/17)
Morningstar mid-cap value absolute rankings	77% (308/410)	53% (153/319)	6% (15/233)	30% (3/10)

Source: Ariel Investments, https://www.arielinvestments.com/performance-mf/.

According to John Rogers, not only was he proud of the financial returns achieved and the growth in assets over the last 34 years, but he was equally proud that he had built a highly successful and profitable company with diverse talents in the money management industry; an industry that rarely, if ever, allowed African Americans to participate or succeed.

In addition to leading Ariel Investments, John Rogers serves on many influential boards of directors including University of Chicago, McDonald's Corporation and Exelon. Previously, he served on four other corporate boards (Aon Corporation, GATX, Bank One and Bally Total Fitness). He believes that board members must push organizations to live their values when it comes to diversity and inclusion. "As a board member, I ask the management team for data on the organization's spending with minority and women owned professional services firms. I am not a passive board member who checks my personal values and beliefs at the door. I believe that diversity and inclusion are good business practices that bring value. As a board member, I use my position to coach, advocate, and push the senior management teams to live their values."

Understanding the unique power and leverage of corporate boards of directors, John Rogers launched The Black Corporate Directors' Conference in 2002 to encourage attendees to address the civil rights agenda from the board room, including a call to action to push companies to measure their spending and investments with minority professional services firms. This premiere annual conference attracts and trains nearly 200 African American corporate board directors on how to maximize their contribution to their respective board and how to use their power and influence to positively impact the African American community. John was inspired to pursue economic empowerment of the African American community by the Rev. Dr. Martin Luther King, Jr. who in 1967 wrote, "I cannot see how the Negro will totally be liberated from the crushing weight of poor education, squalid housing and economic strangulation until he is integrated, with power, into every level of American life". [1]

John Rogers was the only child of his parents, Jewel LaFontant and John Rogers, Sr. (See **Exhibit 8**.) "My mother was the first African American woman to graduate from the University of Chicago's law school and was very active in the civil rights movement. She participated in sit-ins, protests, and historically significant legal cases". Her passion and commitment to the African American community came from her father, J.B. Stafford, a highly successful business leader who owned the Stafford Hotel, one of the finest hotels in Tulsa, Oklahoma. In 1921, it was intentionally burned down in the Tulsa domestic terrorist attacks, most commonly known as, "The Race Riot that Destroyed Black Wall Street".

In the early 1900s, African Americans migrated to Tulsa attracted by the booming oil economy. By 1921 there were over 15,000 black residents and over 600 prosperous businesses, all owned and operated by blacks and patronized by both whites and blacks. This tight knit and highly successful community subscribed to the belief that they had the best chance of economic success by pooling their resources and supporting one another's businesses.

This community's economic and social success was destroyed on June 21, 1921 when an envious white mob torched all these businesses and murdered almost 300 black residents. Even more were injured, became homeless or held in internment camps by local law enforcement. John Rogers' grandfather lost his business but bequeathed to John's mother a fearless spirit to fight injustice and always protect the Black community.

John Rogers' father, John Rogers, Sr., was also a civil rights pioneer having served as a Tuskegee Airman, a group of the first African Americans allowed to train and fly military airplanes. Historically African Americans were denied military leadership roles and skilled training because many believed they lacked sufficient intellect. The Tuskegee Airmen overcame segregation and racism to become one of the most highly respected fighter groups in World War II.

At John's father's funeral, Reverend Jessie Jackson gave the eulogy. He told the story about John's father returning from World War II and applying to the University of Chicago's law school. The day after he received a rejection letter, he went to the school dressed in his full decorated military uniform to speak to the dean and left a few minutes later as an accepted student. During the course of John's father's esteemed career, he became a Juvenile Court Judge to help families in distress. "Both of my parents worked diligently to help others and expected me to do the same. My parents made it clear that courageous advocacy for others was not something you do after you are successful but expected your entire lifetime".

One example of John following his parents mandate was the 1996 launch and ongoing support of the Ariel Community Academy (ACA), an elementary Chicago Public School serving over 500 students

---

[1] Martin Luther King, Jr., *Where Do We Go from Here: Chaos or Community?* (Beacon Press, 1967).

on Chicago's south side. Ninety-eight percent of the student body is African-American and over 85 percent of the students qualify for subsidized lunches. The school offers an enhanced financial literacy curriculum including an investments program in which 7th and 8th graders invest real money portfolios in the stock market. In fact, one of John's proudest moments was hiring two recent Ariel Community Academy graduates to work fulltime for his company. According to John, "I have learned that helping others pays dividends in ways you can't imagine or anticipate. It is the right thing to do and it benefits our company".

The Controversy

"If I don't speak out, who will?" John asked himself. Too many CEO's of African American firms are afraid they will be ostracized or blacklisted if they express their frustration with being excluded from opportunities they are qualified to perform. White CEOs of large corporations have been allowed to express their controversial views on a variety of issues without repercussion. These leaders have become personally involved in social issues; they have leveraged their public platform, authority and influence to advocate for social and business issues that are important to them. Why can't African American CEOs exercise these same rights?" (See **Exhibits 9 & 10**.)

The resistance to John's advocacy came not only from his board but, in some cases, from minority led companies. Some minority CEO's have told John that their obligation and allegiance are only to their shareholders and employees and they do not have the time or interest to advocate for social change. One very prominent money manager said to John, "my job is to deliver the best possible return to my shareholder and not to become distracted with issues that do not directly impact these returns. I only have so many hours in a day and they are best used outperforming my competitors and exceeding my customers' expectations. When I create significant wealth, I can more positively impact society with my philanthropy than trying to persuade a handful of firms to change their investment allocation to include minority firms. Minority money managers need to stay focused and be more patient. I am confident that over time these corporations will judge us by our results."

John disagreed with being patient. "We have given mainstream organizations more than enough time to match their rhetoric with our reality. Although many firms publicly proclaim they value diversity and inclusion, far too many systematically exclude African American owned companies. When firms do elect to retain black-owned firms, it is for the low margin "catering and construction" work and not the high margin professional services work where wealth is created. The old boys' network is alive and well and continues to exclude African American owned business owners from the mainstream." Many of these companies are willing to make donations to address social problems but are unwilling to do business that will lead to African American empowerment. This behavior reminded John Rogers of Dr. Martin Luther King's statement that, "Philanthropy is commendable, but it must not cause the philanthropist to overlook the circumstances of economic injustice which makes philanthropy necessary."[2]

"We are not asking for special treatment" says John Rogers, "I just want to be able to fairly compete based on my firm's track record and capabilities. This would be a win for the organizations that hire me to invest their funds and the African American community who benefit when African American companies are successful". As an illustration of the multiplier effect that occurs when an African American company is successful, John Rogers points to the Chicago-based Johnson Product Company.

At its peak and before its sale to Ivax Corp. this company employed over 500 people (overwhelming African American) and helped launch many of the most successful African American owned companies in the country (Burrell Advertising, Ebony & Jet Magazine, Soul Train, Independence Bank, and Lafontant, Wilkins, Jones & Ware) and financially supported the most impactful African American advocacy organizations (Chicago Urban League, Southern Christian Leadership Conference, and Operation Breadbasket). See **Exhibit 11** for a visual representation of the impact and multiplier effect of an African American successful business on other African American organizations.

The Decision

John had to decide if he should take the advice of his board member and many others, who advised him to "tone down" his criticism of institutional investors, or remain a vocal and fierce advocate for African American professional services firms seeking more opportunities.

---

[2] Martin Luther King Jr., *Strength to Love*, (Stanford, 1963).

Exhibit 1   Ariel Investments' John Rogers is on a Mission: Opening Doors for Minorities

John Rogers has been to the mountaintop . . . and now he wonders why it's so lonely there. How this black finance exec aims to open doors for others.

All too often when Ariel Investments Chairman and CEO John Rogers Jr. calls Chicago universities, museums and foundations seeking business, he comes away frustrated. He moves in the city's top business circles, has ties to President Barack Obama and has built the largest African-American-led money management firm in the country. And yet his firm, which manages $10.4 billion in assets, just can't make inroads with some of the city's biggest nonprofits.

Why? Rogers strongly suspects his race has something to do with it. In spite of his personal success, his industry's lily-white status largely remains. And changing it has become a primary mission for him.

"I say, 'I understand that your institution has a commitment to diversity and inclusion, but I'm looking at your professional services spend, and I've talked to my friends that are part of the Business Leadership Council, and all of us say we can't get anywhere with your institution,' " he says during an interview. " 'You guys have a commitment to working with minority business, but it's all a big charade.' "

Rogers, a mild-mannered Chicago native, is distraught that blacks are backsliding in business. Taking on the nonprofits' disinterest is simply the latest step in his broader campaign to bolster African-American-owned enterprises, especially in professional services, like investment management, law and accounting, where he says meaningful wealth and power are created. His leadership of Ariel is increasingly intertwined with a quest for black opportunities in business.

Rogers is a "race man," says Bruce Gordon, formerly CEO of the NAACP and an ex-Verizon executive. He has "always been attuned to the issues around diversity and inclusion, not just in business but in the broader community."

Rogers, 58, whose parents divorced when he was 3, grew up on the South Side, shuttling between his Tuskegee Airman father's studio apartment in Prairie Shores and his civil rights lawyer mother's mansion in Hyde Park. His Democrat father, John Rogers Sr., who later became a Cook County judge, ignited a love of financial markets in his son by giving him stocks for his birthdays. His gregarious and politically active Republican mother, Jewel Stradford Lafontant-Mankarious, taught him the power of networking.

That mix of privilege and prominence set Rogers on a path to Princeton University after he graduated from the private University of Chicago Laboratory Schools. His smarts helped him last three days on "Wheel of Fortune" during college but, more important, landed him a stockbroker job after he graduated, at Chicago-based William Blair in the 1980s.

In 1983, at age 24, he left to start Ariel with $200,000 in capital from his parents and friends. Early on he realized he would have to reach out to friends' parents and former William Blair clients for business because most people in his African-American community didn't have the "multigenerational wealth" or "the same exposure and comfort with the markets," he says.

His flagship Ariel Fund launched in 1986, and several more followed, in addition to his winning institutional investor money to separately managed accounts. By 2007, he had $20 billion under management. Then the recession struck, wrecking returns nationwide and slashing his firm's assets to just $3.3 billion in 2009.

Still, his main fund's performance swung back with 63 percent gains the next year, contributing to what are now benchmark-matching 11 percent returns annually over the life of that fund. Half of Ariel's funds have also performed at or above their index benchmarks, allowing Rogers to rebuild Ariel's assets to about half of their peak.

Ariel was the biggest black-led money management firm in the U.S. last year, based on its assets, according to Black Enterprise magazine. It has 85 employees, mainly in Chicago.

Exhibit 1 (continued)

Surviving three decades is no small feat in the asset management world, and Rogers celebrated the milestone this month by gathering money managers who also launched funds in 1986 for a Chicago reception.

"A lot of what happens in the money management space is based on relationships," says Marty Nesbitt, a friend who runs Chicago private-equity firm Vistria Group. "John has been a real trailblazer in opening those doors."

'HE HAS LIVED IT'

And not just for his own benefit. In 1996, Rogers' firm sponsored a North Kenwood public school that became Ariel Community Academy to focus on financial literacy. He has also locked arms with black professionals in the Business Leadership Council, a Chicago-based organization that promotes black leadership in business and politics, and with the Rev. Jesse Jackson to chip away at discrimination. And every year, Ariel hosts the Black Corporate Directors Conference to encourage outspokenness in boardrooms.

Still, Rogers laments a lack of progress in business. "Things are substantially worse than they were 40 years ago," he says. African-Americans, like Independence Bank Founder George Johnson, once used their wealth to back other black businesses, startups and philanthropy, he says. That faded as other companies came calling for black customers. "The spinoff benefits of a successful George Johnson were so powerful for our community. . . .We lost all of that. We don't have those types of businesses of scale, and it's such a challenge."

His knock on nonprofits follows on earlier efforts. In the 1990s, he supported legislation mandating that Illinois and Chicago pensions track and disclose allocations to minority-owned money managers. He also needles private companies over their shortcomings in hiring minority-owned firms. "He has championed this initiative because he has lived it," says Monica Walker, CEO of Chicago-based asset manager Holland Capital Management. "In living it, you obviously understand what others may be experiencing."

Rogers dismisses the flight to index funds as a passing trend that won't affect Ariel's business, but Walker says it's taking a toll on small boutique firms, with Holland's assets only half their $5 billion peak.

Documenting the discrimination is part of the challenge. There are few statistics substantiating the dearth of minority-owned money management firms and their uphill battle to win allocations. So, Ariel, Exelon, the Service Employees International Union, the Knight Foundation and others formed the Diverse Asset Managers Initiative in 2014 and hired a Harvard Business School professor, Josh Lerner, to research the issue. Lerner declines to comment, deferring to the release early next year of his results.

Similarly, Ariel is part of a coalition of Chicago financial services companies that launched the Financial Services Pipeline Initiative in 2013. A study they commissioned last year by consulting firm Mercer found that African-Americans and Latinos are underrepresented in the industry relative to their numbers in the Chicago population and acutely so at C-suite levels. Those groups won't see any improvement in leadership levels even by 2019 if current practices stay the same, Mercer says.

Nationwide, the picture was similar.

"Until we're able to really address some of the unconscious biases that clearly are having a negative impact on the retention of professionals of color in the industry, we're going to continue to see that outflow of talent," says Valerie Van Meter, a senior vice president at the Federal Reserve Bank in Chicago and co-chair of the pipeline project's steering committee.

CHEERS AND JEERS

Rogers is proud that Illinois and Chicago pensions have become leaders nationally in the percentage of dollars they direct to minority money managers. The Illinois Teachers' Retirement System, the state's biggest pension fund, now invests about $4 billion with minority-owned firms, or 9 percent of its overall $45 billion fund (see the PDF).

Exhibit 1 (continued)

"We just need a chance to be on the playing field to compete and to be in the room, and often you just can't get in the room if you don't have the relationships, or you're hurt by this stereotype of how people perceive you as, maybe, less than," he says.

Rogers also appreciates big Chicago companies, like Exelon (where he is a board member), Boeing and McDonald's, seeking to be more inclusive in their investing and spending, while some, like Walgreens, are still "impossible," he says.

Walgreens dismisses the criticism. "Walgreens is strongly committed to supplier diversity," says spokesman Phil Caruso. The company has a program that "fosters vendor diversity" with ties to 2,500 such businesses, including Chicago financial firm Loop Capital, he adds.

Foundations, universities, museums and hospitals are worse, and it's not just a Chicago problem, Rogers says, citing even his own alma mater, Princeton. He estimates that less than 5 percent of nonprofits work with minority firms.

And Rogers, who peppers conversations with lessons learned from Princeton basketball, is not unfamiliar with how nonprofits operate, having served on the boards of Princeton, the University of Chicago, Rush University Medical Center and the Chicago Urban League.

"It's a national phenomenon," says Thurman White, who leads San Francisco-based money manager Progress Investment Management. Whether it's unfairness, ignorance or indifference, they don't have policies of inclusion, he says.

Nonprofits may contract with black firms for physical labor or commodity work, but not the more lucrative professional services work, Rogers says. "You get that sort of modern-day Jim Crow feeling—it's white men (who) can apply for those opportunities, and the people of color, you should be happy over here with the construction and catering."

Nonprofits represent an important potential source of business because they rely heavily on outside professionals to invest sizable endowments. They accounted for about $1 trillion, or 2 percent, of the $58 trillion in U.S. investable assets in 2010, according to McKinsey Global Institute.

Ariel attracts 9 percent of its assets from nonprofits, while it pulls 40 percent from retail investors in its mutual funds, 23 percent from public pensions and 3 percent from union pensions and high-net-worth individuals.

Chicago-based Forefront, an association of 1,200 foundations and nonprofits, including some universities and hospitals, does not dispute shortcomings, but its CEO, Eric Weinheimer, says the organization began addressing them last year. It is sponsoring events to introduce foundations to minority managers, says Weinheimer, who notes that research shows minority managers can deliver superior returns. "There is more momentum building toward action," he says. (The organization doesn't have such an effort for its other members.)

The Chicago Community Trust, Rush and University of Chicago are some of the few local nonprofits Rogers credits for giving minority-owned firms a chance. The Trust has 14 percent of its $2.3 billion portfolio invested with minority-owned firms. It stuck with Ariel when the firm's returns crashed and was rewarded on the upswing, says CEO Terry Mazany, who lauds Rogers' commitment to inclusion. "As he gets older, I think, he's becoming impatient with the slow pace of change in the business world," Mazany says.

Rogers says he hopes nonprofits will be more responsive in an upcoming round of meetings with the Business Leadership Council.

Source: Crain's Chicago Business/Lynne Marek, http://www.chicagobusiness.com/article/20161112/ISSUE01/311129990/
           ariel-investments-john-rogers-is-on-a-mission-opening-doors-for-minorities, accessed November 12, 2016.

Exhibit 2   Crain's List Chicago's Largest Money Managers

CRAIN'S LIST CHICAGO'S LARGEST MONEY MANAGERS

Ranked by total assets managed

Rank	2016 rank	Company / Head of Chicago office	Total assets managed as of 12/31/16 (millions); % change from 2015	Minimum required for separate accounts (millions)	No. of portfolio managers in the Chicago office	No. of analysts in the Chicago office
1	1	NORTHERN TRUST ASSET MANAGEMENT; 50 S. LaSalle St., Chicago 60603; 312-630-6000; NorthernTrust.com — Stephen N. Potter, President, asset management	$715,483.7 / 5.9%	NA	72	42
2	2	NUVEEN LLC; 333 W. Wacker Drive, Chicago 60606; 800-257-8787; Nuveen.com — Robert G. Leary, CEO	$226,000.0 / NC	$0.1	29	42
3	3	GUGGENHEIM INVESTMENTS; 227 W. Monroe St., Chicago 60606; 312-827-0100; Guggenheiminvestments.com — Mark R. Walter, CEO, Guggenheim Partners	$206,000.0 / 4.0%	NA	NA	NA
4	5	LEGAL & GENERAL INVESTMENT MANAGEMENT AMERICA; 71 S. Wacker Drive, Suite 800, Chicago 60606; 312-585-0300; LGIMA.com — John Bender, Interim CEO	$140,070.9 / 17.2%	$100.0	22	8
5	4	HARRIS ASSOCIATES LP; 111 S. Wacker Drive, Suite 4600, Chicago 60606; 312-646-3600; HarrisAssoc.com — Kevin G. Grant, Anthony P. Coniaris, Co-chairmen	$108,528.7 / -11.5%	$10.0	17	11
6	7	INVESCO POWERSHARES; 3500 Lacey Road, Suite 700, Downers Grove 60515; 630-933-9600; InvescoPowerShares.com — Dan Draper, Managing director, global exchange-traded fund	$105,636.6 / 9.8%	NA	18	8
7	6	PPM AMERICA INC.; 225 W. Wacker Drive, Suite 1200, Chicago 60606; 312-634-0050; PPMAmerica.com — Mark Mandich, CEO	$100,829.6 / 1.5%	$100.0	25	41
8	8	LSV ASSET MANAGEMENT CO.; 155 N. Wacker Drive, Suite 4600, Chicago 60606; 312-460-2443; LSVAsset.com — Josef Lakonishok, CEO, chief investment officer, portfolio manager	$97,043.1 / 15.0%	$25.0	6	5
9	10	WILLIAM BLAIR; 222 W. Adams St., Chicago 60606; 312-236-1600; WilliamBlair.com — John R. Ettelson, President, CEO	$74,800.0 / 5.5%	$2.0	NA	NA
10	9	HARBOR CAPITAL ADVISORS INC.; 111 S. Wacker Drive, 34th floor, Chicago 60606; 800-422-1050; HarborFunds.com — David G. Van Hooser, Chairman, CEO	$69,200.0 / -12.4%	NA	4	5
11	11	GCM GROSVENOR; 900 N. Michigan Ave., Suite 1100, Chicago 60611; 312-506-6500; GCMGrosvenor.com — Michael J. Sacks, Chairman, CEO	$49,000.0 / NC	NA	NA	NA
12	12	BMO ASSET MANAGEMENT U.S.; 115 S. LaSalle St., 11th floor, Chicago 60603; 312-461-5370; BMO.com/gam — Phillip E. Enochs, Head of global asset management U.S.	$34,556.1 / -5.6%	$5.0	22	16
13	14	MESIROW FINANCIAL HOLDINGS INC.; 353 N. Clark St., Chicago 60654; 312-595-6000; MesirowFinancial.com — Richard S. Price, Chairman, CEO	$31,338.1 / 0.4%	$1.0	115	115
14	15	ADAMS STREET PARTNERS LLC; 1 N. Wacker Drive, Suite 2200, Chicago 60606; 312-553-7890; AdamsStreetPartners.com — Jeff Diehl, Managing partner, head of investments	$28,987.0 / 6.6%	$50.0	17	10
15	13	HIGHTOWER ADVISORS LLC; 200 W. Madison St., Suite 2500, Chicago 60606; 312-962-3812; HightowerAdvisors.com — Elliot S. Weissbluth, CEO	$27,500.0 / NA	NA	NA	NA
16	16	CITADEL LLC; 131 S. Dearborn St., Chicago 60603; 312-395-2100; Citadel.com — Kenneth C. Griffin, CEO	$26,236.0 / 5.1%	NA	20	60
17	17	CALAMOS ASSET MANAGEMENT INC.; 2020 Calamos Court, Naperville 60563; 630-245-7200; Calamos.com — John Koudounis, CEO	$18,278.0 / -16.6%	NA	12	28
18	19	ASSET ALLOCATION & MANAGEMENT CO.; 30 W. Monroe St., 3rd floor, Chicago 60603; 312-263-2900; AAMCompany.com — John L. Schaefer, President	$18,305.0 / 9.4%	$25.0	9	6
19	18	COLUMBIA WANGER ASSET MANAGEMENT LLC; 227 W. Monroe St., Suite 3000, Chicago 60606; 312-634-9200; ColumbiaThreadNeedleUS.com — P. Zachary Egan, President, global chief investment officer	$13,800.0 / -32.0%	NA	11	8
20	20	MAGNETAR CAPITAL; 1603 Orrington Ave., 13th floor, Evanston 60201; 847-905-4400; Magnetar.com — Alec Litowitz, CEO	$13,300.0 / NC	$100.0	10	30
21	22	WINTRUST WEALTH MANAGEMENT; 231 S. Lasalle St., 13th floor, Chicago 60604; 312-431-1700; WintrustWealth.com — Thomas Zidar, Chairman, CEO	$12,490.0 / 10.8%	$0.1	17	6
22	21	MCDONNELL INVESTMENT MANAGEMENT LLC; 18W140 Butterfield Road, Suite 1200, Oakbrook Terrace 60181; 630-684-8600; McDonnellInvestments.com — Mark J. Giura, CEO, chief investment officer	$11,462.0 / 1.2%	$1.0	9	10
23	23	ARIEL INVESTMENTS LLC; 200 E. Randolph St., Suite 2900, Chicago 60601; 312-726-0140; ArielInvestments.com — John W. Rogers Jr., Chairman, CEO, chief investment officer	$11,000.0 / 8.9%	$10.0	6	5
24	New	ZIEGLER CAPITAL MANAGEMENT LLC; 70 W. Madison St., 24th floor, Chicago 60602; 312-368-1442; ZieglerCap.com — Scott Roberts, President, CFO	$10,664.9 / 8.8%	$10.0	36	35
25	New	PRIVATEBANCORP INC.; 120 S. LaSalle St., Chicago 60603; 312-564-2000; ThePrivateBank.com — William Norris, Chief investment officer	$9,700.0 / 32.9%	$1.0	10	0

Includes firms that are based or have a branded asset management division in the seven-county area (Cook, DuPage, Kane, Lake, McHenry and Will in Illinois and Lake County in Indiana). Does not include asset managers mainly working in real estate, private equity or venture capital. Minimum for some separate accounts requirements may be higher. Crain's estimates are shown in gray. NA: Not available. NC: No change. 1. Corresponds to total assets managed in Chicago. 2. Parent company is New York-based TIAA-CREF. Nuveen's AUM has been estimated here because the firm declined to break out figures for individual brands. 3. For equity strategies. For municipal separate accounts, minimum is $250,000. 4. Parent company Guggenheim Partners has had headquarters in Chicago and New York. 5. Parent company is Paris-based Natixis Global Asset Management SA. 6. Parent company is Atlanta-based Invesco Ltd. 7. Parent company is London-based Prudential PLC. 8. Does not include non-security assets managed by PPM Finance Inc. 9. Includes regulatory AUM of William Blair & Co. LLC and William Blair Investment Management LLC. 10. Parent company is Rotterdam, Netherlands-based Robeco Groep NV. 11. Fiscal year ends in October. 12. Parent company is Toronto-based BMO Financial Group. 13. Fiscal year ends in March. 14. Corresponds to the equity management team's small-mid cap value and small cap value vehicle. 15. Includes all investment professionals. 16. As of this ranking, HighTower's AUM excludes $9 billion managed by independent teams with access to HighTower services. 17. Citadel does not have Illinois state/local government pension clients. 18. As of Jan. 1. 19. Company estimate. Excludes employees within Citadel Securities. 20. Parent company is Minneapolis-based Ameriprise Financial Inc. 21. Parent company is Toronto-based CIBC.

Researched and edited by Sabrina Gasulla

Source: Crain's Chicago Business. Accessed March 6, 2017.

Exhibit 3   "New Report Finds Opportunities for Investment Consultants to Promote Diversity; Create Long-term Financial Value for Institutional Investors"

Investments consultants are failing to promote minority men and women to management roles

Date: October 12, 2016

WASHINGTON, D.C.–Although research shows that diversity yields positive performance and returns in capital markets, minorities remain underrepresented in this industry. A new joint report from The ReFund America Project, Roosevelt Institute and Service Employees International Union finds promoting diversity may not be a priority for major consulting firms managing our nation's pensions, largely due to their lack of diversity to identify and promote emerging managers.

"Casting a wider net: Increasing opportunities for minority and women owned asset managers in institutional investments" findings are based on a survey of investment consultants representing more than $1.3 trillion in assets under management. This report aims to explore the reasons why these disparities exist and what industry leaders can do to address them. Consulting firms often serve as gatekeepers between pension funds and asset management funds and therefore play a critical role in promoting diversity.

The basic findings of this report are:

- There is a lack of diversity at major consulting firms, especially at the senior management level. Minorities–especially Blacks and Latinos–are vastly underrepresented at pension fund consulting firms; making up less than 6 percent of the consultant workforce. The representation of Black and Latinos employed at consulting firms falls even below percentages in other occupations in the financial industry and represent approximately 4% of all management within the firms surveyed.

- Promoting diversity may not be a priority for consulting firms where there are no systems to identify and promote emerging managers. Only five of the surveyed firms tracked data on the number of minority asset managers that were ultimately selected to manage investors' funds.

- Several themes emerged repeatedly when firms identified challenges to recommending minority and women asset managers. Beliefs — such as there being a lack of qualified minority-owned asset managers or that emerging managers deliver subpar performance — remain barriers to diversity throughout the investment field.

"As in much of the financial industry, there is a lack of diversity in asset management and the broader capital market that leaves communities of color underrepresented," said Saqib Bhatti, Director of the ReFund America Project and Fellow at the Roosevelt Institute. "This weakens the worldviews of decision-makers and it is our hope that this report, combined with our recommendations, will serve as a starting point for further research on diversifying the capital markets."

"Our nation's public, corporate, faith-based and labor union pension funds have long provided innovative thinkers with the financial clout to bring about a more equitable and sustainable economic growth," said Carrie Sloan, Senior Research Analyst at the ReFund America Project. "By promoting diversity in the financial services industry, we will help ensure the most informed possible decisions from the fullest array of voices are being developed."

"Diversity has been shown to create long-term value for investors," said SEIU International President Mary Kay Henry. "What this report shows us is that investment consultants can identify new and innovative strategies to both promote women and men of color as asset managers and create that long-term financial value."

Source: SEIU   website.   http://www.seiu.org/2016/10/new-report-finds-opportunities-for-investment-consultants-to-promote-diversity-create-long-term-financial-value-for-institutional-investors.

Exhibit 4   Women, minorities are still nearly shut out of this $71 trillion industry

Women, minorities are still nearly shut out of this $71 trillion industry

By Renae Merle, May 3

Women and minorities are locked out of some of Wall Street's most lucrative positions, managing just 1.1 percent of the $71.4 trillion of the industry's assets, according to a report released Wednesday.

The difficulty in attracting investments comes as firms with diverse leadership teams match, and sometimes exceed, the profits of their competitors, found the study commissioned by the John S. and James L. Knight Foundation and the Bella Research Group.

"This study, and our experience, confirm that there is no legitimate reason not to invest with diverse asset managers in the 21st century," said Alberto Ibargüen, president of the Knight Foundation, which has an endowment of more than $2 billion.

Wall Street has long fought its reputation as a place where women and minorities struggle to succeed. In the complex world of asset management, where firms are given billions of dollars to invest by pensions, endowments and wealthy investors, the disparity is particularly stark. Only 5.2 percent and 3.8 percent of all mutual funds are owned by women and minorities, for example. The figures are similar in the hedge fund industry, where women and minorities manage less than 1 percent of the industry's assets, the report found.

Exhibit 4 (continued)

The industry's diversity has improved in recent years, but women and minorities remain woefully underrepresented, the study found. Only one woman appeared on Institutional Investor's Alpha magazine's annual ranking of highest-paid managers last year. Leda Braga, who founded Systematica Investments in January 2015 and made $60 million in 2015, ranked 44th among the top 50 hedge fund managers listed by the magazine. The highest-ranked managers made more than $1 billion that year. A recent report by Morningstar Research found that only 1 in 5 mutual funds has at least one manager who is a woman, a figure that has not improved since the global financial crisis of 2008.

The disparity is likely rooted in a perception that investing with women or minorities is riskier, industry officials say. When a company or university is looking to increase its diversity, it may reflexively hire an African American-owned firm for construction work but not to manage its money, said John Rogers, founder of Ariel Capital Management, the largest minority-run mutual fund firm in the United States.

"Close your eyes and picture an investment banker and what comes back is a white male that looks like George Clooney," Rogers said.

Women and minorities are also less likely to have the connections to raise enough money to start their own firms, industry officials said.

"People do business with people who they have built relationships with. People of color have had less opportunities to build these multigenerational relationships that lead to business opportunities," Rogers said. "Our community hasn't been as exposed to the financial services careers. ... We don't have the grandfather to leave us money and to talk about the stock market at the dinner table."

The lack of diversity also contributes to women not receiving the proper attention when investing money or planning for retirement, said Wall Street veteran Sallie Krawcheck.

"The truth is that Wall Street has done a poor job for women forever. So much so that it calls women a niche market," said Krawcheck, who owns the Ellevate Network, a professional women's group. "We don't invest to the same extent that men do and Wall Street has been laser focused on its core client — a middle-aged male — and women have not been well served."

The Knight Foundation began looking into the issue in 2010 when its managers realized that just $7 million of its $2 billion in assets were being managed by executives who were not white males, in this case an African American-owned private equity fund. "I was shocked," Martinez said.

The foundation has since moved about $472 million of its endowment, or 22 percent of its assets, to firms owned by women and minorities.

"We made a conscious decision to change our approach — and we urge our colleagues to do the same," he said. "Our managers have performed very well. There is no discount associated with minority and women managers."

Source: https://www.washingtonpost.com/news/business/wp/2017/05/03/women-minorities-are-still-nearly-shut-out-of-this-7-trillion-industry/?utm_term=.42bb66c1212a.

Exhibit 5   Illinois State Board of Investment Diversity Policy

Objective

The Illinois State Board of Investment ("ISBI" or the "Board") has adopted this Diversity Policy (the "Policy") to increase access and opportunities for emerging managers and brokers who are minorities, women and persons with a disability as those terms are defined in the Business Enterprise for Minorities, Females, and Persons with Disabilities Act1 and the Illinois Pension Code.

A. Emerging and Minority Investment Managers

It is the primary goal of ISBI to develop and maintain an investment program that will help secure the retirement benefits of the participating retirement plans. In order to achieve this objective, investment advisers are selected based on their long-term records of performance, depth of investment staff and consistency of approach among other characteristics.

However, the Board recognizes that even large, experienced and successful investment organizations were once small, start-up firms with few assets under management. Today many such firms are owned by minorities, women and persons with a disability. These firms are often started by experienced investment professionals, who show great promise, but find it difficult to compete with large majority owned organizations. The firms typically do not meet the minimum standards set for investment advisers by large investment programs such as ISBI. Consequently, they are not considered.

In order to take advantage of these emerging organizations, the Board has established an aspirational goal to use emerging investment managers for no less than 20% of the total portfolio funds under management within ISBI's investment program. Furthermore, the Board goes beyond the utilization of emerging managers and has adopted goals for the utilization of minority investment managers. The Board has established an aspirational goal to have no less than 20% of its investment advisors be minorities, females, and persons with a disability.

<u>Goals for Utilization of Emerging and Minority Investment Managers Minority-Owned Businesses, Female-Owned Businesses, and Businesses Owned by Persons with a Disability</u>

It is the goal of the Board that, subject to its fiduciary responsibility, the use of emerging investment managers shall be significant in each of the broad asset classes in which ISBI is invested and not concentrated in any particular asset class.

The Board has adopted the following minimum goals for the utilization of emerging and minority investment managers:

<u>Goals for Utilization of Emerging and Minority Investment Managers By Investment Manager Classification</u>

Classification	Percent of Total Portfolio	
	Emerging	Minority
Minority-Owned	5% - 7%	5% - 7%
Female-Owned	3% - 5%	3% - 5%
Disabled	0% - 1%	0% - 1%

Exhibit 5 (continued)

Goals for the Utilization of Emerging and Minority Investment Managers by Asset Class

Asset Class	Percent of Asset Class	
	Emerging	Minority
Equities	8% - 10%	8% - 10%
Fixed Income	10% - 12%	10% - 12%
Alternatives*	1% - 5%	1% - 5%

* Alternative investments are not subject to the requirements set forth in Public Act 96- 0006.

These goals will be reviewed annually by Investment Staff and the Board.

For purposes of this Policy, the emerging and/or minority investment manager must provide to the Board documentation of a current State of Illinois certification or documentation of a current state-issued certification. For emerging and/or minority investment manager without a state issued certification, an attestation by the investment manager or General Partner stating that the investment manager or advisor is a "minority owned business", "female owned business" or "business owned by a person with a disability", as those terms are defined by the Illinois Business Enterprise for Minorities, Females and Persons with Disabilities Act must be provided. The emerging and/or minority investment manager is required to immediately notify ISBI as to any change in the matters covered by any such attestation. On an annual basis, the emerging and/or minority investment manager must certify to ISBI that its state-issued certification is in good standing or, alternatively, that nothing in its attestation stating that the investment manager or advisor is a "minority owned business", "female owned business" or "business owned by a person with a disability", as those terms are defined by the Illinois Business Enterprise for Minorities, Females and Persons with Disabilities Act, has changed. ISBI and the Board are relying on certifications and/or investment manager attestations for reporting purposes. In the event it is discovered an investment manager has misrepresented information to ISBI, such misrepresentation shall be grounds for termination of the relationship.

Minority investment managers may represent any asset class within ISBI's asset allocation. Allocations of the Board's assets to minority investment managers will be made in accordance with the fiduciary standards under which all ISBI investment advisers operate.

Asset Management

1. Investment Staff will review the statistical requirements for investment adviser searches as needed to provide better access to minority investment managers that have appropriate products.

2. Investment Staff will seek to include at least one minority investment manager in final Investment Staff interviews. Investment Staff will inform the Board of all minority investment manager candidates.

3. Investment Staff will regularly meet with Illinois-based minority investment managers on-site, and learn more about the Illinois-based minority investment manager community.

4. Investment Staff will encourage ISBI Consultants to be proactive and use creative approaches in achieving the Board's objectives with respect to the use of minority investment managers.

Source: PDF Document from Illinois.gov website, https://www.illinois.gov/isbi/Documents/Diversity%20Policy.pdf.

Exhibit 6   "Public Pensions Have a Ton of Leverage. They Should Use It"

Who's managing (and profiting from) trillions of pension dollars? Mainly white men. But some Illinois funds are trying to change that.

Date: December 10, 2016

Whether you're talking about retirement dollars for teachers or firefighters, their pensions are a treasure trove—some $40 trillion, or more than twice the U.S. GDP—socked away for people who worked in the public sector. That's a big number, but the discussions about which firms invest the money and who stands to benefit from the lucrative fees earned are small-scale.

In short, it's mainly men who invest the money, and they reap the rewards despite plenty of well-intentioned pledges to route more pension business to women- and minority-led firms. "There's a huge, obvious, glaring, painful, terrible, embarrassing problem," says Illinois Democratic state Sen. Daniel Biss, pointing to the white men who dominate money management, particularly in private equity and hedge funds. "We (as public pensions) have very real leverage to take it on—let's go do that."

All year Crain's has been examining women's role in finance, from those exiting private equity to the rise of women in one division of Chicago-based CME Group. Here's our latest installment.

DIVERSITY IS 'GOOD BUSINESS'

The $9.5 billion Chicago Teachers' Pension Fund invests just 15 percent with firms owned by women. That might seem like a paltry amount, but it's double what most pensions muster, and a feat in a field where women lead less than 10 percent of firms. With a state mandate to consider and track their investments at women- and minority-owned firms, some Illinois and Chicago public pensions are among a small group leading the way in such investing and giving fledgling firms a fighting chance in a consolidating industry.

The nascent nationwide trend is driven partly by an attempt to better mirror the interests of pension stakeholders—like the overwhelmingly female teachers who are members of many of the biggest pensions in the country. Of the 10 biggest U.S. pension funds, three are for teachers—in California, Texas and New York—with more than $100 billion at each. While California is prohibited by law from allocating based on gender, they all have programs aimed at bolstering minority- and women-owned firms.

In the past 20 years, the Chicago teachers' pension has posted benchmark-beating returns of 7.12 percent for its members, and in the past five years, it's an even better 9.98 percent, net of fees. "It turns out that diversity is absolutely good business," says Jay Rehak, a Whitney Young Magnet High School teacher who has been president of the teachers' pension fund board for five years. "The numbers have borne us out."

The fund overhauled manager hiring after the Illinois Senate started annual public hearings in 2003 to press pension leaders to adhere to a 1993 state law that encourages state and local pensions to invest with women and minorities.

Its allocations to women and minority firms have jumped to a collective 35 percent of its assets, from 6.5 percent when the Senate started the hearings. The pension remade its manager list by revamping its seven-person investment staff so that it's now mainly women and half African-American. Its board also has open monthly meetings to hear from prospective managers.

Exhibit 6 (continued)

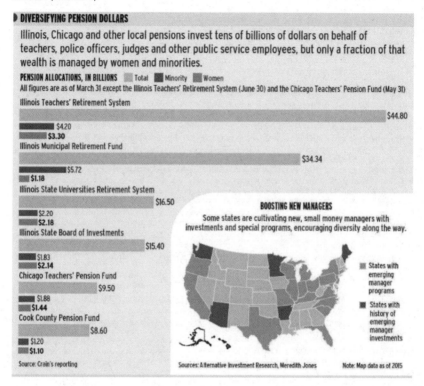

▶ DIVERSIFYING PENSION DOLLARS

Illinois, Chicago and other local pensions invest tens of billions of dollars on behalf of teachers, police officers, judges and other public service employees, but only a fraction of that wealth is managed by women and minorities.

PENSION ALLOCATIONS, IN BILLIONS   ▢ Total   ▇ Minority   ▇ Women
All figures are as of March 31 except the Illinois Teachers' Retirement System (June 30) and the Chicago Teachers' Pension Fund (May 31)

Illinois Teachers' Retirement System
$44.80
$4.20
$3.30

Illinois Municipal Retirement Fund
$34.34
$5.72
$1.18

Illinois State Universities Retirement System
$16.50
$2.20
$2.18

Illinois State Board of Investments
$15.40
$1.83
$2.14

Chicago Teachers' Pension Fund
$9.50
$1.88
$1.44

Cook County Pension Fund
$8.60
$1.20
$1.10

Source: Crain's reporting

BOOSTING NEW MANAGERS
Some states are cultivating new, small money managers with investments and special programs, encouraging diversity along the way.

▇ States with emerging manager programs

▇ States with history of emerging manager investments

Sources: Alternative Investment Research, Meredith Jones   Note: Map data as of 2015

Still, Illinois pension leaders—who are some of the most progressive in the country—say a dearth of female firms curtails opportunities. Illinois Teachers' Retirement System Executive Director Dick Ingram confesses that there likely remains an "unconscious bias" favoring men. "Whether a person of color or female, it's different historically from the norm," he says. "We're still walking uphill to break out of that."

Pension fund officers suggest there's a tension between fulfilling their fiduciary duty to seek top returns and meeting goals to hire women- and minority-owned firms. But others in the industry increasingly say there's no trade-off between returns and policy. "Everybody from Wall Street to Main Street loses out financially because there aren't more women in the asset management industry," says Meredith Jones, author of "Women of the Street: Why Female Money Managers Generate Higher Returns." Jones, who also works for Aon Hewitt from Nashville on diversity in asset management issues, says women invest differently than men, pointing to research that shows men are more likely to be overconfident and overtrade their positions while women are more consistent in applying strategies.

Exhibit 6 (continued)

In her book, Jones interviews a dozen female managers, including several in the Chicago area. They include Leah Joy Zell, real estate magnate Sam Zell's younger sister, who heads Chicago hedge fund firm Lizard Investors, as well as Thyra Zerhusen, co-founder and CEO of what may be the biggest woman-owned money manager in the city, Fairpointe Capital, with $5 billion under management.

A STUBBORN STATUS QUO

In the U.S., only 1 in 10 mutual fund managers is a woman, according to a report last month from Morningstar. That's even lower than the 1-in-5 average across 56 countries, the report says. Female fund managers who lead their own firms are even more rare, says Laura Pavlenko Lutton, a Morningstar researcher who worked on the report. Some big financial companies are trying to create more leadership opportunities for women, especially in expanding areas like passive investing, Lutton says.

"The most enduring principle of sound investment management is diversification, yet it is remarkably absent from team construction across all spectrums of the investment profession," says a CFA Institute Research Foundation report this year (here's the PDF) that also laments the lack of female managers.

Pension industry organizations couldn't provide nationwide statistics on assets managed by women and minorities. "It's not self-serving to maintain that information because it's so disappointing," says Lauren Mathias, a senior vice president at industry consultant Callan Associates. Other institutional investors — such as foundations, corporate pensions, nonprofits and high-net-worth individuals — have shown even less interest in changing the status quo. "It tends to be the public funds that are really pushing the initiative forward," Mathias says.

The Teachers' Retirement System, the biggest pension in Illinois, directs $3.3 billion, or 7.4 percent of the fund's $44.8 billion, to women-led firms. Two other major state funds, the Illinois State Universities Retirement System and the Illinois State Board of Investments, are nearly double that percentage.

Source: Crain's   Chicago   Business/Lynne   Marek,   http://www.chicagobusiness.com/article/20161210/ISSUE01/ 312109993?template=printart.

Exhibit 7   "Diversity Pressed for Illinois Pension Managers"

Illinois pensions have boosted investments with women- and minority-owned money managers in the 13 years since the General Assembly began tracking allocations, but the job isn't done, policymakers say.

At its annual hearing on the topic last week, members of the Illinois Special Committee on Pension Investments lauded the state's leadership on the effort, but also grilled pension executives and their consultants about seeking and hiring more diverse financial advisers.

Illinois and City of Chicago pension funds report annually to the committee on a long list of questions regarding the ethnicity and gender of the members of their own staffs and boards as well as money managers they hire to invest pension dollars for teachers, firemen, and thousands of other state and city workers. The thrust is that holding pensions accountable for their hiring and airing their performance publicly will advance more diverse choices.

Sen. Kwame Raoul, who co-chaired the hearing on Aug. 11 and 12 in Chicago, says he's pleased with progress, but stops short of saying he's satisfied. "I don't want to send the message that we've arrived," the Democrat from Chicago said after the hearing.

Though state law doesn't dictate percentages, it encourages pension investments with women- and minority-owned firms.

The Illinois Teachers' Retirement System, the state's largest pension, had allocated $7.86 billion to women- and minority-owned businesses as of the end of June, more than twice as much as the $3.27 billion in 2009 (when the recession was weighing down assets generally). It reached a peak last year of $7.93 billion, and dropped off this year because one firm was purchased by another that wasn't minority-owned, TRS said.

Those assets last year and this year represent 17 percent to 18 percent of the $43.8 billion that TRS oversees. That was above the TRS goal of 16 percent, but still inadequate from the point of view of Sen. Daniel Biss, a Democrat from the North Shore.

"That's a real problem," he said during the hearing, offering a "blunt" interpretation that the lion's share of assets being managed by white men smacked of a "boys club" and "institutionalized racism." He said the public pensions had the opportunity to "push back against those patterns."

Other pensions, including the Illinois State Board of Investments, the Illinois Municipal Retirement Fund and the Chicago Policemen's Annuity and Benefit Fund, also presented data from thick reports that listed firms in various ethnic and gender categories.

"We should be making more progress," said Sen. Iris Martinez, a Democrat from Chicago who has attended almost all of the hearings since they began in 2003, though she was absent last week. "There are a lot more minority firms out there that want the opportunity."

Consultants in the industry point to Illinois as one of the leaders in programs to shift investments to these typically smaller, and often less experienced firms. San Francisco-based Callan Associates said that half of the $20 billion that its clients have invested with such firms nationwide derive from pensions in Illinois.

"I work with other state plans where it's not a factor," said Ryan Ball, a senior vice president at Callan who is a consultant to Illinois pensions.

Exhibit 7 (continued)

The Illinois initiative helps fledgling managers get the additional exposure, assets under management, and track record they need to win more business, Ball said. That helps spread the Illinois approach to other states, he added.

Chicago-based Ariel Investments is one firm that got a lift from the state's effort to direct pension dollars to minority-owned firms. It received its first million-dollar investment from the Municipal Employees' Annuity and Benefit Fund of Chicago in 1984 and today it manages $123 million for the pension. It also manages money for a number of other state and local pensions.

"Illinois is doing a terrific job in this area," said Ariel Chairman, CEO and Founder John Rogers, noting just a few exceptions among local pension funds that "don't get it."

Illinois could use some help from other states to advance the cause, Raoul said. "Illinois shouldn't carry that burden," he said. "We're not the only diverse state in the country."

Source: Crain's Chicago Business/Lynne Marek, http://www.chicagobusiness.com/article/20160817/NEWS01/160819885/diversity-pressed-for-Illinois-pension-managers.

Exhibit 8   "John W. Rogers Jr. Honors his Trailblazing Parents, who Started their Careers at the Law School"

John W. Rogers Jr. stood behind his father's wheelchair and pointed up to a plaque on the wall.

"Everyone's here to honor you," the prominent businessman told his father, John W. Rogers Sr., '48. The plaque affixed to the wall in the main classroom hallway of the Law School features a photo and biographical information of both the elder Rogers and his first wife, the late Jewel C. Stradford Lafontant, '46.

The Law School held a lunchtime banquet on October 19 to honor the family, after Rogers Jr., who is a University Trustee, made a significant donation to name the Director of Admissions Office after his parents. Rogers Jr. is the Founder, Chairman, and CEO of Ariel Investments, which manages assets of $4.7 billion, and Chair of the Board of Directors of the University of Chicago Laboratory Schools, which he attended through high school.

John Rogers Sr. was one of the original Tuskegee Airmen, the first squadron of African-American pilots in the U.S. military. As an Airman, he flew 120 successful combat missions. He is a retired Cook County Juvenile Court judge and founding partner of the law firm Rogers, Rogers and Strayhorn. He earned the Congressional Gold Medal in 2007.

Lafontant, who died in 1997, was the first black woman to graduate from the Law School and the first woman and the first African American to hold the post of U.S. Deputy Solicitor General. She held leadership positions in the Department of State, as Ambassador at Large and Coordinator for Refugee Affairs, and was U.S. representative to the United Nations in 1972. She was the first black woman on several corporate boards and lead attorney before the Supreme Court for *Beatrice Lynum v. Illinois,* which set the case law for the famous 1966 *Miranda* case. When she died, a *New York Times* obituary noted her leadership of civil rights groups like the Congress of Racial Equality and the sit-ins she participated in during the 1940s to fight racial discrimination at restaurants in the Loop.

Both Judge Rogers and Lafontant encountered racial discrimination throughout their careers, and the Law School was not always the easiest place for them in the 1940s, their son said, because of the attitudes of some professors and students. Even so, they loved the Law School and recognized its importance in their lives.

Lafontant was initially discouraged from attending the Law School by administrators, but would not take no for an answer, said her niece, Leslee Stradford, who flew in from California to attend the event.

"This is the school she wanted to go to, and this is where she was going."

Stradford was one of several members of the Rogers extended family who came to the event. The head table included Judge Rogers, Rogers Jr., Judge Rogers's wife Gwendolyn Rogers, AM '53, who helped orchestrate the event, and Rogers Jr.'s daughter Victoria, a 2008 graduate of the Lab Schools.

"This is an honor, particularly because when I was growing up, we had so few individuals of African-American descent who were honored in any way, or even acknowledged," Stradford said.

Besides relatives, the room was filled with various leaders and dignitaries who wanted to honor Judge Rogers and Lafontant. U.S. District Court Judge Rebecca Pallmeyer, '79, called Lafontant a personal hero.

Exhibit 8 (continued)

Many years ago, "I learned she was a University of Chicago graduate," Pallmeyer said. "That made me really proud." As a public servant herself, Pallmeyer "loved the fact that she was a government official at a time when there were relatively few women of any race, especially African -Americans" in those positions.

The roster of attendees demonstrated how connected the family is to those who are in leadership positions today. For example, U.S. District Court Judge Sharon Johnson Coleman, who was in attendance, worked with Judge Rogers in juvenile court before he retired, met Lafontant in the early '90s, and in 2010 received the Cook County State's Attorney's Stradford Award, named for Lafontant's father, a prominent attorney. She knows Rogers Jr. through mutual friends, including U.S. Secretary of Education Arne Duncan, and both are Leadership Greater Chicago fellows.

Many others in the Green Lounge on Friday knew the family much better, Coleman said, but "I'm equally sure my admiration for their achievements and service to the community is as high as anyone in the room."

The program included a conversation between Rogers Jr. and Dean Michael Schill, who told the crowd that, "the more I've read about John Rogers's parents, I'm just in awe of their achievements." It also featured a videotaped message from Secretary Duncan, who said, "Congratulations to my best friend, John Rogers."

In the conversation between Schill and Rogers, Rogers explained that both his parents talked their way into the Law School, where they met on the first day of class.

"They wanted to go to the best school," he said. "They knew this was one of the greatest institutions in the world."

He remembered his mother as a world traveler and an optimist, someone who thought everything was possible and wanted to see what the world had to offer. His dad, he said, smiling at his father, seated just a few feet away, was respected as a "tough but fair" judge, one who taught him that "you show up on time, and you do what you say you're going to do."

Schill asked Rogers how institutions, both in education and business, can increase diversity. Rogers said these "anchor institutions" in a city – such as the University of Chicago – must go out of their way to do business with minority firms and suppliers, thereby creating wealth in those communities.

Schill even squeezed in a few questions about the upcoming presidential election. Rogers is a well-known friend of President Barack Obama. He predicted Obama will be reelected, and said he thought he'd face less opposition for his policies in his second term.

After the program and lunch concluded, the extended Rogers, Lafontant, and Stradford families lingered to spend time together and enjoy the moment. Now, whenever they're near the Law School, they can come see the plaque honoring their loved ones, hung between two other very important plaques: one for Sophonisba Breckinridge, Class of 1904, the first female graduate, and another for Earl Dickerson, '20, the first African-American graduate.

Source: The University of Chicago Law School Office of Communications/ Meredith Heagney, http://www.law.uchicago.edu/news/john-w-rogers-jr-honors-his-trailblazing-parents-who-started-their-careers-law-school.

Exhibit 9   "Corporate Activism and the Rise of the Outspoken CEO"

Corporate chieftains have historically adhered to a golden rule when it comes to Washington and the political world: It is better to be seen than heard.

But those days of silence appear to be long gone.

Just in the past week, a handful of corporate executives managed to place themselves front and center in hot-button political debates ranging from gay rights to government snooping to income inequality.

On Tuesday, e-commerce giant PayPal announced it was shelving a planned North Carolina expansion project that would have garnered millions of dollars in capital investment and generated more than 400 local jobs. The move came in response to a religious freedom bill passed by the North Carolina state government, which prohibits individual cities and municipalities from expanding their own anti-discrimination policies in a move that opponents say effectively restricts protections to people who identify as gay, lesbian, bisexual or transgender. PayPal President and CEO Dan Schulman said the legislation "perpetuates discrimination" and "violates the values and principles that are at the core of PayPal's mission and culture."

Only a day later, Allergan pharmaceutical company CEO Brent Saunders told CNBC that he believes a new Treasury Department regulation "was designed very specifically to target" Allergan's proposed merger with U.S.-based Pfizer, criticizing the Obama administration's new policy. Pfizer was set to acquire Dublin-based Allergan in a multi-billion deal that would have allowed Pfizer to move its base of operation to Ireland to avoid steep U.S. corporate and foreign earnings taxes.

"For the rules to be changed after the game has started to be played is a bit un-American," Saunders said Wednesday. "But that's the situation that we're in."

And on Thursday, General Electric Chairman and CEO Jeffrey Immelt penned an op-ed in The Washington Post, suggesting Democratic presidential candidate and Vermont Sen. Bernie Sanders was "missing the point" by criticizing GE for being a global company in a recent interview with the editorial board at the New York Daily News. Immelt implied that Sanders' criticisms of GE's trade practices were nothing more than "hollow campaign promises" and "cheap shots."

For what it's worth, Goldman Sachs chairman and CEO Lloyd Blankfein has previously said that Sanders' campaign has the "potential to be a dangerous moment" in U.S. politics.

But this public dialogue is atypical behavior for executives with employee- and customer-bases that hold potentially conflicting sets of interests and values. Business leaders have historically remained tight-lipped when it comes to controversial or politically charged subject matter – preferring instead to keep business matters strictly professional. That way they don't offend any employees or customers, and their business structure remains intact.

There are exceptions to this rule, of course. Former Mobil oil company CEO Rawleigh Warner Jr. made waves in the 1970s when he bought up advertising space in newspapers to profile his political stances related to the oil industry. Marketing and media analysis company Advertising Age dubbed Warner's efforts "advocacy advertising" and were impressed enough to name him Adman of the Year in 1975.

Exhibit 9 (continued)

Outliers excluded, though, the majority of CEOs have avoided being too outspoken when it comes to political and social issues. But if this past week is any indication, that script seems to have been flipped as business leaders are increasingly looking for opportunities to make their voices heard on issues they'd previously shied away from.

"We haven't made the specific claim that it's on the rise, but I suspect it is," says Michael Toffel, a professor at Harvard Business School who has researched what many perceive to be a rise in CEO activism. "We had observed in the past that when CEOs spoke out on public issues, whether they're testifying in Congress or being posted in the newspaper, it's for issues that really seem very self-serving – issues related to their bottom line."

For example, Toffel says he wouldn't be surprised to see a coal CEO speak out against carbon taxes or an executive in the solar industry advocate for renewable energy subsidies. By that same token, Allergan's response to the Obama administration's new trade policies and GE's response to Sanders' direct criticisms make sense. Both instances show an executive addressing an issue directly related to his industry.

"But it's interesting that [Starbucks CEO] Howard Schultz is speaking out on race relations," Toffel says. "That doesn't seem like it would obviously promote sales at Starbucks."

Indeed, social issues that aren't directly connected to a company's individual industry seem to have attracted attention from corporate executives of late. The religious freedom bills in North Carolina and Mississippi [and previously Georgia and Indiana] are good examples. More than 100 business leaders recently wrote a letter to lawmakers in North Carolina voicing their disapproval, and a handful of companies like PayPal and Lionsgate films have pulled certain operations from affected areas.

"I think that CEOs today and business leaders are as important as political leaders and that they have a role like political leaders, which is that they have to stand for something," Marc Benioff, CEO of Salesforce, said in an interview in December with Bloomberg News.

Benioff adamantly opposed religious freedom bills in both Georgia and Indiana, heaping pressure on state lawmakers who ultimately opted to either terminate or revise the controversial legislation in their respective states.

"When things happen in the world that you don't agree with, as a CEO, you have a responsibility to come forward and say, 'Hey, I don't agree with that because it doesn't support my employees, or it doesn't support my customers,'" he said.

Toffel said, though, that there's anecdotal evidence of outspokenness being a "double-edged sword" for corporate executives, using Chick-fil-A as an example. Isolated efforts to boycott the company cropped up back in 2012 when current CEO Dan Cathy made comments in opposition to same-sex marriage.

At the same time, however, former Arkansas Gov. Mike Huckabee helped organize a Chick-fil-A Appreciation Day to support Cathy's business.

"That's a good example of that polarization," Toffel says. "With the growing political divide and the idea that, if you compromise, that's a terrible thing, I think you're seeing this schism."

Exhibit 9 (continued)

Toffel's own research, conducted with Duke business school professor Aaron Chatterji, found that CEO positioning on particular issues can ultimately help sway public opinion. Toffel surveyed nearly 3,400 respondents and found that support for Indiana's religious liberty bill ultimately declined when subjects were told that Apple CEO Tim Cook opposed the piece of legislation. Cook has also been outspoken over efforts by the FBI to break the encryption in the company's signature iPhone, resulting from the investigation into the terror shooting in San Bernardino, California, earlier this year. That case, however, arguably directly affects the company's bottom line.

But the ability to help potentially sway public discourse should not be taken lightly, Toffel says. He believes the immediate corporate backlash from Georgia's and Indiana's religious liberty bills played significant roles in their respective state governments' eventual decisions to backpedal.

"If [corporate executives] hadn't themselves chimed in, it's possible that the framing wouldn't have reached as many people. And so the backlash might have been smaller," he says. "If they're early movers, they have the opportunity to shape some of the conversation."

His research also found that, at least in Apple's case, that double-edged sword dynamic didn't come into play. Knowing that Apple's CEO opposed the Indiana bill didn't noticeably deteriorate the company's standing in the eyes of those he surveyed.

"We didn't find people who were less likely to buy Apple products among gay marriage opponents," he says, though he noted that Apple "has huge brand loyalty" and that these particular results may not hold steady for less prominent businesses.

It's worth noting, though, that even Chick-fil-A's earnings managed to avoid taking too much of a hit immediately following its same-sex marriage controversy. That same year, Chick-fil-A sales hit $4.6 billion (up 12 percent over the year), and sales last year eclipsed $6 billion. So Cathy's comments, which were viewed negatively by many same-sex marriage proponents, haven't prevented the company from continuing to expand.

So certain high-profile executives leading powerful companies may not have much to lose by taking a stand nowadays – and they could ultimately help shape discourse around an issue to better align with their own or their company's views.

Toffel also says executives may now have to voice their opinions out of necessity – silence in today's politically polarized society can be just as telling as outspokenness.

"I think that is indicative of sort of the culture wars. You have people trying to make statements and defend certain positions as a political statement rather than actually remedying an actual societal problem," Toffel says. "I think silence is also political. I think people are starting to interpret that."

Source: U.S. News and World Report / Andrew Soergel, https://www.usnews.com/news/articles/2016-04-08/corporate-activism-and-the-rise-of-the-outspoken-ceo.

Exhibit 10   "Gun Brutality Emboldens CEOs to Speak out about Race"

Having spoken out in increasingly vocal fashion on issues such as gender equality, gun control and gay rights, a few tech leaders and companies are making their voices heard on social media in the aftermath of the fatal shootings of two black men and five police officers, expressing grief for the victims and their families or calling out divisiveness amid escalating racial tensions.

In a series of tweets, Apple CEO Tim Cook lamented Thursday night that the "senseless killings this week remind us that justice is still out of reach for many," sharing a tweet from civil rights activist Rep. John Lewis (D-Ga.) and saying "We can and must do better." On Friday, he again took to Twitter to express sympathy for the officers' families and the Dallas community, adding that "justice cannot be gained through violence" and sharing a Martin Luther King, Jr. quote: "We must all learn to live together as brothers, or we will all perish together as fools."

On its official Twitter account, Google wrote Thursday that "#AltonSterling and #PhilandoCastile's lives mattered. Black lives matter. We need racial justice now," adding a statement that the company is "devastated by the senseless deaths" of the two men and held vigils in their memory.

Other CEOs known for being active on social issues -- or who lead social media companies -- also commented on the events. Salesforce.com CEO Marc Benioff, known as a leader of corporate America's fight against bills that would diminish gay rights, shared tweets about gun violence and (twice) quoted Martin Luther King: "We learned to fly like birds, & swim like fish, and yet we haven't learned to walk the earth as brothers & sisters." Mark Zuckerberg issued a statement of his own, part of which referred to a video shot by Castile's girlfriend, Diamond Reynolds: "while I hope we never have to see another video like Diamond's, it reminds us why coming together to build a more open and connected world is so important -- and how far we still have to go."

As companies and business leaders become more engaged in social issues, it's possible such comments could prompt more business leaders outside technology to speak out on a topic -- racial tension -- that has gotten much less public attention from corporations than other issues, such as gay rights. More than 200 companies, for instance, have signed a position letter from the Human Rights Campaign opposing North Carolina's HB2. Some, such as PayPal and Deutsche Bank, took further action, abandoning investments or freezing planned expansions in local areas.

As author and advocate Janet Langhart Cohen wrote in an op-ed in the Washington Post in April, "the corporate titans who issued their démarche may truly have been offended by the denial of basic human rights to a historically oppressed segment of our society," referring to efforts by business leaders to defeat bills in states such as Arizona and Georgia that threatened to erode gay rights. "Regrettably, this corporate zeal has yet to be extended to people of color."

Communication experts say that may be because the issue of racial justice has become more divisive and politically charged. "There are people who are going to complain you're siding with one group -- supporting the police or supporting Black Lives Matter," said Paul Argenti, a professor at Dartmouth's Tuck School of Business who studies corporate communication strategy, in an interview. "It's a lot more dangerous for companies to take a [stand] on this."

Exhibit 10 (continued)

One CEO who has tried to bring attention to racial tension, of course, is Starbucks' Howard Schultz, whose #RaceTogether campaign -- part of which involved getting baristas to write a hashtag on coffee cups and talk with customers about race -- was met with spectacular backlash. Watching that reaction may have given other CEOs pause. "I think [Schultz] had his heart in the right place for sure, but I think it kind of trivialized the issue," Argenti said. "It angered people who were white. It angered people who were black. It's a really good example of what can happen." (A Starbucks spokeswoman said in an email that she was not aware of any statement the company was planning to make following this week's events, but pointed to remarks Schultz made at the company's annual shareholder meeting in March, when he said "our reservoir is running dry -- depleted by cynicism, despair, division, exclusion, fear and yes -- indifference.")

Tom Andrews, president of consulting for SYPartners who has worked with leaders on public responses to social issues, says another reason companies may not be as active on race could be a lack of guidance on how to talk about it. "We have a language for the LGBT community -- there's been such a movement around creating that language you can trace right back to the [gay rights advocacy group] Human Rights Campaign," he said in an interview. "A lot of CEOs feel so awkward about race diversity and how to address it. They can't go there. They don't have a language for it."

Still, some are sure to try. Leslie Gaines-Ross, chief reputation strategist for Weber Shandwick, said in an e-mail that she expects to see more CEOs speak out on this week's events in coming days, though she warns "they need to carefully consider their influence on all their stakeholders, particularly employees and customers who are personally impacted by these events in different ways."

Meanwhile, Andrews thinks when CEOs do find the words, putting them in a tweet may seem short of taking real action. Andrews thinks moves like the one by JetBlue to offer free airfare to family members following the mass shooting in Orlando and to police officers wishing to attend the funeral last year of slain New York police officer Brian Moore, come off with real authenticity. He thinks it could take longer -- perhaps even into the next generation of CEOs -- before race becomes a "productive dialogue" among corporate leaders. In the very near term, those who do speak out face the difficult challenge of seeming genuine in the face of horrific tragedy.

"What do any of us say when something horrible happens?" Andrews said. "You can only grieve."

Source: Washington Post/ Jena McGregor, https://www.washingtonpost.com/news/on-leadership/wp/2016/07/09/gun-brutality-emboldens-ceos-to-speak-out-about-race/?utm_term=.86c13dd4e308.

Exhibit 11   The Importance of Black Economic Empowerment: Johnson Products Case Study

Source: Company documents.

Exhibit 12 Population of the United States by Race and Hispanic/Latino Origin, Census 2000 and 2010

Race and Hispanic/Latino origin	Census 2010, population	Percent of population	Census 2000, population	Percent of population
Total Population	308,745,538	100.0%	281,421,906	100.0%
Single race				
White	196,817,552	63.7	211,460,626	75.1
Black or African American	37,685,848	12.2	34,658,190	12.3
American Indian and Alaska Native	2,247,098	.7	2,475,956	0.9
Asian	14,465,124	4.7	10,242,998	3.6
Native Hawaiian and other Pacific Islander	481,576	0.15	398,835	0.1
Two or more races	5,966,481	1.9	6,826,228	2.4
Some other race	604,265	.2	15,359,073	5.5
Hispanic or Latino	50,477,594	16.3	35,305,818	12.5

Source: U.S. Census Bureau: National Population Estimates; Decennial Census.

Note: Percentages do not add up to 100% due to rounding and because Hispanics may be of any race and are therefore counted under more than one category.

Population of Illinois by Race Number of People Receiving Illinois State Pensions by Race

	Illinois
African American	1,813,447
Latino	2,171,988
Asian	669,595
Caucasian	7,948,431

Source: U.S. Census Bureau: National Population Estimates; Decennial Census.

John Rogers Case Study Assignment Questions

1. Are John's outspoken views right or wrong?
2. Is John being reckless?
3. What type of leader is John?
4. What things should a leader consider before speaking out?

Notes

1. Crudup, Devin. "CurlMix Raises $1.2M After Rejecting 'Shark Tank' Offer." Afro Tech. March 27, 2020. https://afrotech.com/these-black-founders-rejected-a-shark-tank-deal-because-they-were-worth-more.
2. McKinney, Jeffrey. "45 Great Moments in Black Business – No. 3: BET Holdings $72.3M in IPO." Black Enterprise. January 12, 2019. https://www.blackenterprise.com/45-great-moments-in-black-business-no-3-bet-holdings/.
3. McKinney, Jeffrey. "45 Great Moments in Black Business – No. 26: Parks Sausage Returns to Black Ownership with $4 Million Buyout." November 7, 2017. https://www.blackenterprise.com/45-great-moments-in-black-business-no-26-with-parks-sausage-4-million-buyout-iconic-company-returns-to-black-ownership/.
4. "John H. Johnson Biography." The History Makers. Accessed March 19, 2021. https://www.thehistorymakers.org/biography/john-h-johnson-40.
5. "Madam C.J. Walker Biography." History.com. January 26, 2021. https://www.history.com/topics/black-history/madame-c-j-walker#:~:text=Sources-,Madam%20C.%20J.,care%20products%20for%20black%20women.
6. "On This Day: May 05, 1905, Chicago Defender Publishes First Issue." Calendareji.org. Accessed March 19, 2021. https://calendar.eji.org/racial-injustice/may/5#:~:text=On%20May%205%2C%201905%2C%20the,Black%20newspapers%20of%20the%20time.
7. Levins, Sandy. "America's First Female Bank President: Maggie Lena Walker." Wednesday's Women. October 2, 2019. https://wednesdayswomen.com/americas-first-female-bank-president-maggie-lena-walker/.
8. "Race and Belonging in Colonial America: The Story of Anthony Johnson." Facing History. Accessed March 19, 2021. https://www.facinghistory.org/reconstruction-era/anthony-johnson-man-control-his-own.
9. Spriggs, William E. "Here's Some History to Help Understand the Racial Wealth Gap." American Federation of Labor Congress of Industrial

Organizations. January 22, 2016. https://aflcio.org/2016/1/22/heres-some-history-help-understand-racial-wealth-gap.

10. "James Forten Historical Marker." Explore PA History. Accessed March 19, 2021. https://explorepahistory.com/hmarker.php?markerId=1-A-28C.

11. Brenc, Willie. "John Berry Meachum (1789–1854)." Black Past. July 29, 2014. https://www.blackpast.org/african-american-history/meachum-john-berry-1789-1854/.

12. Ellis, Larry Michael. "Robert "Black Bob" Renfro: Tennessee's First Black Entrepreneur." *Nashville History*. February 20, 2020. https://nashvillehistory.blogspot.com/2020/02/robert-black-bob-renfro-tennessees.html.

13. "On This Date In History, May 31, 1921: The Tulsa Race Riot." America's Black Holocaust Museum. June 1, 2013. https://www.abhmuseum.org/on-this-date-in-history-may-31-1921-the-tulsa-race-riot/.

14. Elliott, Dominique. "Remembering the Excellence in Black Wall Street." Fayetteville State University Press, *The Voice*. February 24, 2017. https://www.fsuthevoice.com/remembering-the-excellence-in-black-wall-street/.

15. "The Gap Band Name Has Ties to the Tulsa Massacre of 1921." 107.3 Kiss FM. June 25, 2020. https://1073kissfmtexas.com/til-the-gap-band-name-has-ties-to-the-tulsa-massacre-of-1921/.

16. Merelli, Annalisa. "We Still Don't Know Just How Much Was Lost in the Tulsa Massacre of 1921." *Quartz*. June 18, 2020. https://qz.com/1870188/what-happened-to-tulsas-black-wall-street/#:~:text=Overnight%20on%20May%2031%20and,Greenwood%20district%20of%20Tulsa%2C%20Oklahoma.

17. Madigan, Tim. "Remembering Tulsa." *Smithsonian Magazine*. April 2021. https://www.smithsonianmag.com/history/tulsa-race-massacre-century-later-180977145/

18. Jan, Tracy. "The 'Whitewashing' of Black Wall Street." *The Washington Post*. January 17, 2021. https://www.washingtonpost.com/business/2021/01/17/tulsa-massacre-greenwood-black-wall-street-gentrification/.

19. Brooks, Rodney, A. "More Than Half of Black-Owned Businesses May Not Survive COVID-19." *National Geographic*. July 17, 2020. https://www.nationalgeographic.com/history/2020/07/black-owned-businesses-may-not-survive-covid-19/#:~:text=One%20report%20found%2041%20percent,percent%20of%20white%2Downed%20businesses.&text=For%20Monique%20Greenwood%2C%20this%20year,Inns%2C%20and%20business%20was%20good.

20. Haimerl, Amy. "The Fastest-Growing Group of Entrepreneurs in America." *Fortune*. June 29, 2015. https://fortune.com/2015/06/29/black-women-entrepreneurs/.

21. Dickerson, Penny. "Small Business Is Big for Blacks." *The Miami Times*. January 8, 2020. https://www.miamitimesonline.com/business/small-business-is-big-for-blacks/article_6c44653a-3237-11ea-94bf-4fb1b2ffb30c.html#:~:text=Reports%20show%20that%20from%202012,of%20entrepreneurs%20at%20that%20time.

22. "What Will It Take to Build More Black-Owned Businesses?" McKinsey & Company. October 15, 2020. https://www.mckinsey.com/about-us/new-at-mckinsey-blog/what-will-it-take-to-build-more-black-owned-businesses.

23. Angelou, Maya. "Still I Rise." Poetry Foundation. Accessed March 31, 2021. https://www.poetryfoundation.org/poems/46446/still-i-rise

2

Importance of Black Entrepreneurs

TODAY, ENTREPRENEURSHIP FOR the Black community is just as important as it was 200 years ago. It is one of the main ingredients for the development of Black self-sufficiency and healthy, safe, Black communities. Before the COVID pandemic, there were 2.6 million Black-owned firms in the country, which equaled 7% of all companies in the U.S.[1] The American Black community makes up 13% of the country's population. This is not enough! Our country desperately needs more Black entrepreneurs who can build significant wealth for themselves and others. In the book *The Millionaire Next Door*, the authors cite the fact that 80% of the country's millionaires got their wealth through business ownership, and the other 20% did it the old-fashioned, hard way – they inherited it![2]

As Eugene Lang, founder of the I Have a Dream Foundation, said, "There is nothing wrong with becoming rich, as long as one enriches others along the way." Wealthy Black entrepreneurs do just that—they enrich minorities by giving them jobs. Yes, like all other entrepreneurs, Black entrepreneurs, do good for society by doing well for themselves.

An article by the *Chicago Tribune* columnist Clarence Page really magnifies the need for more Black entrepreneurs. He cites that the fact in a recent study, it was shown that Black males in their twenties committed four violent crimes for every one crime committed by White males in the same age category. But when the study was controlled for employment, there were no significant differences in the crime rates.

Who are the most likely employers of Black males and other minorities? Black entrepreneurs! Research has shown that like their ancestors, Black entrepreneurs, regardless of their company's location, in the city or suburbs, create jobs for minorities. A study by Dr. Timothy Bates in his book *Banking on Black Enterprise*, shows White-owned companies located in minority communities have workforces that are 32% minority, while Black-owned companies in minority communities have a workforce that is 85% minority. Then he moved the study out of the minority communities and found that White-owned companies located in White communities have workforces that are 15% minority. Conversely, Black-owned companies in White communities have a workforce that is at least 75% minority.[3]

Obviously, these facts show that more Black entrepreneurs will help solve the problem of providing jobs for minorities. In fact, Black-owned companies are the largest private employer of Black people in the country.[4] The government is the largest public employer.[5] We need more Black entrepreneurs. Simply placing companies in minority communities does not create jobs for minorities. The company's ownership is more important than the company's location. For example, the Austin community on the West side of Chicago, has a population of approximately 100,000 people. In 2006, a time of low national unemployment, 11% of the Austin community was unemployed; 23% received food stamps; and 98% were minorities. The same community had one of the densest populations of small manufacturing companies. These 4,000 companies, which were primarily White-owned, employed 90,000 people. Only 8% were minorities.

It would be too simple to blame this entirely on racism. Instead, the reality is that a lot of this has to do with how people get jobs—especially in small companies. It is primarily based on employee referrals by friends and family. The companies' initial employees tend to come from the owner's same communities, because that is who they know. Therefore, that is who gets referred and hired for new openings. Let me repeat, we need more Black entrepreneurs. This would benefit the Black community and the country as a whole. America is strongest when all of its citizens are employed.

A fantastic example of Black entrepreneurs employing minorities is Radio One, a NYSE company owned and operated by Cathy Hughes and her son Alfred Higgins. They own 53 radio stations and employ more than 680 people, of which 74% are minorities.

Black-owned companies have made major contributions in ways other than job creators. For example, if we look at the communications industry, we see that Black-owned newspapers such as *The California Eagle*, *Pittsburgh Courier*, *Chicago Defender*, and *New York Freedom Journal*, have always been a voice against Black injustices. One of the leaders of the 1800s abolitionist movement was the *New York Freedom Journal*, whose headline read "No Longer Shall Others Speak For Us."[6]

Black newspapers such as the *Chicago Defender* also helped Blacks find new employment opportunities in the North. During the 1920s, the *Defender*, through its "Northern Workers Campaign," informed poor Southern Black sharecroppers of the abundance of high-paying industrial jobs in Northern cities such as Pittsburgh, Detroit, and Chicago.[7] These papers were also the training grounds for some of America's greatest writers, poets, and artists, including Langston Hughes, Gwendolyn Brooks, and Romare Bearden.[8]

And finally, Black entrepreneurs have been instrumental in creating new products or improving old products that have improved the quality of life of all Americans. Following is the story of a little boy named Theo, who woke up one morning and asked his mother, "Mom, what if there were no Black entrepreneurs in the world?"[9]

Well, his mother thought about that for a moment, and then said, "Son, follow me around today and let's just see what it would be like; now go get dressed and we will get started."

Theo ran to his room to put on his clothes and shoes. His mother took one look at him and said, "Theo, where are your shoes, and those clothes are all wrinkled, son; I must iron them." But when she reached for the ironing board, it was no longer there. You see, Sarah Boone, a Black woman, got a federal patent #473,563 to improve the ironing board, and Jan E. Matzeliger, a Black man, invented the shoe-lasting machine, which automated shoe making from 50 pairs per day made by hand to over 700 per day.

"Oh well," she said, "please go and do something to your hair." Theo ran in his room to comb his hair, but the comb was not there.

You see, Walter Sammons, a Black man, invented the hot comb. Theo decided to just brush his hair, but the brush was gone. You see, Lydia O. Newman, a Black woman, invented the durable hairbrush.

Well, this was a sight – no shoes, wrinkled clothes, hair a mess, even Mom's hair, without the hair care inventions of Madam C. Walker – well, you get the picture. Mom told Theo, "Let's do our chores around the house and then take a trip to the grocery store." Theo's job was to sweep the floor.

He swept and swept and swept. When he reached for the dust pan, it was not there. You see, Lloyd P. Ray, a Black man, invented the stand-up dust pan. So, he swept his pile of dirt over in the corner and left it there. He then decided to mop the floor, but the mop was gone. You see, Thomas W. Stewart, a Black man, invented the removable string mop head and the device attached to the mop that could be used to wring water from the mophead without getting the hands wet.

Theo yelled to his Mom, "Mom, I'm not having any luck." "Well, son," she said, "let me finish washing these clothes and we will prepare a list for the grocery store." When the wash finished, she went to place the clothes in the dryer, but it was not there. You see, George T. Sampson, a Black man, invented the clothes dryer.

Mom asked Theo to go get a pencil and some paper to prepare their list for the market. So, Theo ran for the paper and pencil but noticed the pencil lead was broken. Well, he was out of luck because John Love, a Black man, invented the portable pencil sharpener. Mom reached for a pen, but it was not there because William Purvis, a Black man, invented the fountain pen. As a matter of fact, Lee Burridge invented the portable typewriting machine, and W. A. Lovette the advanced printing press.

Theo and his mother decided to head out to the market. Well, when Theo opened the door, he noticed the grass was as high as he was tall. You see, John Burr, a Black man, made patented improvements to the lawn mower.

They made their way over to the car and found that it just wouldn't go. You see, Richard Spikes, a Black man, invented the automatic gear shift and Joseph Gammel invented the supercharge system for internal combustion engines. They noticed that the few cars that were moving were running into each other and having wrecks because there were no traffic signals. You see, Garrett A. Morgan, a Black man, invented the traffic signal.

Well, it was getting late, so they walked to the market, got their groceries and returned home. Just when they were about to put away the milk, eggs, and butter, they noticed the refrigerator was gone. You see John Standard, a Black man, invented the refrigerator. So, they just left the food on the counter.

By this time, Theo noticed he was getting mighty cold. Mom went to turn up the heat, and what do you know. Alice Parker, a Black woman, invented the heating furnace. Even in the summer time they would have been out of luck, because Frederick Jones, a Black man, invented the air conditioner.

It was almost time for Theo's father to arrive home. He usually takes the bus. But there was no bus, because its precursor was the electric trolley, which had patented improvements by another Black man, Elbert R. Robinson. Dad usually takes the elevator from his office on the 20th floor, but there was no elevator because Alexander Miles, a Black man, invented the elevator automatic system to open and close the doors. Dad also usually dropped off the office mail at a nearby mailbox, but it was no longer there because Philip Downing, a Black man, invented the letter drop mailbox, that he called the "street letter box," and William Barry invented the postmarking and canceling machine.

Theo and his mother sat at the kitchen table with their head in their hands. When the father arrived, he asked, "Why are you sitting in the dark?" Why? Because Lewis Howard Latimer, a Black man, invented the filament within the light bulb.

Theo quickly learned what it would be like if there were no Black entrepreneurs in the world. Not to mention if he were ever sick and needed blood. Charles Drew, a Black scientist, found a way to preserve and store blood, which led to his starting the world's first blood bank. And what if a family member had to have heart surgery? This would not have been possible without Dr. Daniel Hale Williams, a Black doctor, who performed the first open heart surgery.

So, if you ever wonder, like Theo, "Where would we be without us?" Well, it's pretty plain to see. We would still be in the dark!

Notes

1. "Black Owned Businesses." Black Demographics. Accessed April 1, 2021. https://blackdemographics.com/economics/black-owned-businesses/
2. Stanley, Thomas J. & Danko, William D. "The Millionaire Next Door: The Surprising Secrets of America's Wealthy." *The Washington Post.* Accessed April 1, 2021. https://www.washingtonpost.com/wp-srv/style/longterm/books/chap1/millionairenextdoor.htm
3. Bates, Timothy. *Banking on Black Enterprise: The Potential of Emerging Firms for Revitalizing Urban Economies* (University Press of America, 1993).
4. Stoll, Michael A., Raphael, Steven, & Holzer, Harry J. "Why Are Black Employers More Likely than White Employers to Hire Blacks?" Institute for Reach on Poverty. August 2001. https://www.irp.wisc.edu/publications/dps/pdfs/dp123601.pdf
5. Mead, Walter R. "Blacks Need to Look to the Private Sector." *The New York Times.* August 2, 2016. https://www.nytimes.com/roomfordebate/2011/07/25/how-budget-cuts-will-change-the-black-middle-class/blacks-need-to-look-to-the-private-sector
6. "No Longer Shall Others Speak for Us." *Freedom Journal.* Accessed April 1, 2021. http://newsreel.org/guides/blackpress/overview.htm.
7. "Founder Editor – Robert S. Abbott." *The Chicago Defender.* Accessed April 1, 2021. https://www.pbs.org/blackpress/news_bios/defender.html
8. "A Separate World." PBS. Accessed April 1, 2021. https://www.pbs.org/blackpress/educate_event/separate.html
9. Johnson, Simeon W. *Romw vs Ramb* Reveals God Adam and Creation: What Would Grandma and Grandpa Adam, and Eve Say? If They Could See Us Now. Xlibris Corporation. Pg. 22–24. https://books.google.com/books?id=Lbfl1iEbuq0C&printsec=frontcover&source=gbs_ge_summary_r&cad=0#v=onepage&q&f=false

3

Black Start-Up Entrepreneurs

"None of my inventions came by accident. I see a worthwhile need to be met and I make trial after trial until it comes. What it boils down to is 1 percent inspiration and 99 percent perspiration. A "genius" is often merely a talented person who has done all of his or her homework."[1]

—*Thomas Edison*

THERE WAS A time when it seemed that almost all the start-ups of Black entrepreneurs were focused on servicing needs that were ignored due to racism. These motivated and inspiring men and women were creating businesses that provided products or services heretofore denied to the Black community as a direct result of laws and practices that empowered Whites established specifically to discriminate against Blacks.

An excellent example of entrepreneurial ingenuity meeting harsh reality was *The Green Book*, which Victor Hugo Green originated and published in 1936 to identify accommodations, restaurants, and gas stations where Black travelers could get services given that most White-owned restaurants and hotels in the country barred or refused service to Blacks.[2] More expansively, many places in the country were "sundown towns," where not only was it illegal for Blacks to be in that town after the sun went down, but they would be at risk of suffering physical violence.[3] There were over 10,000 such towns in every

43

part of the country by 1960, including, but not limited to, California, New York, North Carolina, Michigan, and Illinois. A Black person found guilty of violating this law in these towns could be and were lynched. *The Green Book* was published annually and had tens of thousands of buyers; Black travelers reaped the dual benefit of a more pleasant traveling experience and the safety of avoiding "sundown towns."

A rather famous person in the Black community who began as a start-up entrepreneur was John H. Johnson. He founded *Ebony* magazine at a time when it was a common practice and an unwritten rule of the White media that the photo of a Black person was shown in a newspaper or on television only if that Black person had committed a crime. Johnson created his magazine to counter the negative images and one-dimensional portrayal of Black people. Insightfully, he believed that the Black community desired to see positive images of themselves in the media. As he proclaimed when he founded the magazine, "Not enough is said about all the swell things we Negroes can do and accomplish."[4]

Fundamentals of a Start-Up

As demonstrated in these two success stories, start-up entrepreneurs are problem solvers who identify unmet market needs (problem) and develop ways to address them (solution). Customers' demands are always evolving. They want new and better products, lower prices, faster delivery, increased safety, more delivery options, more information about the products or services, and easier access to the services. All of this provides opportunities for entrepreneurs who want to create something from nothing. In addition, there is the opportunity not only of profits for the entrepreneur but also for the creation of service for the greater community.

As noted, once a problem has been identified, a start-up must identify a solution and then execute a plan. Often, such plans require innovation. When most people think of *innovation*, they believe that the term is synonymous with *technology*. However, this is narrow thinking. Innovation, or more specifically, innovative thinking applies to the solution of *any* problem in a different and inventive approach. To think innovatively, the entrepreneur must apply strategy, which means being different. Often, being different is more important than being first. For example, Google was not the first search engine. Speed of the search is what made it different from other search engines. Users loved that difference, which led to its popularity.

In response to an identified market gap, an entrepreneur could start a company to offer lower prices, provide faster service, make a search for information easier, enable customers to order merchandise from home, provide higher-quality products, or communicate information in different languages. In the world of entrepreneurship, investors typically ask start-up entrepreneurs, "What is your strategy?" What they are really asking is, "How are you (your idea or approach) different from what is already in the market?"

One of the easiest ways to think strategically, or differently, is to identify a competitor's or an industry's "value chain" and then either compress or elongate it to better meet customer demands. The value chain is all of the steps required in a process to complete a task. Every business has a value chain, where each link in the chain represents a step in the process. Each subsequent link adds value to the chain because it sets closer to the completion of the task. The stories of Blockbuster Video and Netflix illustrate how a company can compress a value chain and, by so doing, create a less costly and simplified process for customers.

A brief history would be helpful for those who are too young to know what a VHS tape is and cannot visualize what a video rental store looked like. In the 1980s, the only way a person could watch a movie that was no longer playing in movie theaters was by either buying the video home system (VHS) cassette format of the movie or renting one from video rental stores. For the most part, these stores had limited inventories of a few hundred titles with only a single or few copies of each, resulting in customers frequently being frustrated with the movie selection available to them.

In 1985, Blockbuster, a video rental store, responded to this "unmet" demand and differentiated itself from its competitors by offering customers a selection of over 8,000 movie titles.[5] Customers were charged a rental fee for a fixed period and daily late fees were applied when videos were not returned on time. Within one year of starting its operations, Blockbuster opened three additional stores, and in

1987 secured $18.5 million from three investors and began expanding by acquiring local video stores and opening new ones. Within a year, the chain had 800 locations and went public in 1999.[6] In addition to rental revenue, Blockbuster made a significant amount of money by charging customers a daily late fee for video rentals that were not returned by the due date.

Customers hated the late fee! Two entrepreneurs responded to this "unmet" demand. Netflix was founded in 1997 with the idea of giving customers a more convenient way to rent and watch movies without the anxiety of late fees, solving the problem by changing the distribution channel. In 1999, Netflix began offering a movie rental subscription service through its website—customers could order movies from Netflix's extensive movie catalog, receive them in DVD format along with prepaid return envelopes in the mail. There were no limits on the number of movies a customer could rent and no charge for late returns. Netflix partnered with Warner Brothers Studios, Columbia Pictures, and others to increase their movie offerings to tens of thousands of movie titles that were available exclusively on its website. They established over 100 distribution centers across the U.S. to expedite delivery to customers and eventually provided an overnight delivery option. Netflix also utilized algorithms that allowed customers to rate the movies they saw and receive recommendations for similar movies that they might be interested in watching. Although this feature is common among video streaming applications today, Netflix adopted this technology earlier than most, understanding that enhancing customer experience would build brand loyalty that would distinguish Netflix from its competitors.[7]

Following are the value chains for Blockbuster and Netflix. Blockbuster's business model included 10 steps. By reducing the number of steps it took for customers to rent a movie from 10 to 4 (suppressed the value chain), Netflix found a way to become a successful entrepreneurial start-up.

Blockbuster: Value chain steps

Netflix: Value chain steps

In 2000, Blockbuster had the opportunity to buy Netflix for $50 million but decided not to do so. Blockbuster was presented with several synergistic opportunities between the two companies; however, its senior management, unable to either understand or properly value Netflix's strategy, rejected the deal.[8] As the video rental industry began to change because of technology and the desire of customers to find easier ways to rent movies, Blockbuster refused to change its strategy and, instead, reinforced its commitment to its vast network of over 6,000 chain stores to grow their business, failing to understand that customers no longer wanted nor needed to rent movies from stores. Unable or refusing to think innovatively, Blockbuster failed to meet its customers' evolving needs and saw its business revenue decline as the nature of its industry changed and its competitors, especially Netflix, exploited the burgeoning opportunities.

In 2010, after several years of failed attempts to revive its business, Blockbuster filed for bankruptcy protection. The last corporate Blockbuster store closed in 2014. Netflix, on the other hand, continued to adapt to changes in the movie industry and has moved to a subscription-based streaming service offering online streaming from a vast library of films and television series, including those produced in-house. As of April 2020, the company's market value is $196 billion, with over 160 million subscribers worldwide.[9]

Another example is Uber's successful start-up amid a highly established, successful, and mature taxi industry. Taxicabs have been a staple mode of transportation for decades, and in many large cities like New York where a significant number of residents do not own a car and choose not to take public transportation, they are the fastest and most convenient way to get around. However, using a cab can be a Frankenstein's monster of a process—the wait time, the unknown condition of the cab and the skill of the cabdriver, the process involved in getting to your destination, the cumbersome and/or untrustworthy nature of the fee/payment, can often be a frustrating experience.

In 2008, two individuals were left stranded on the streets of Paris unable to find a taxi to get to an annual tech conference they wanted to attend. Born out of this experience, they became start-up entrepreneurs with the idea of an app for a timeshare limo service. After several design iterations they developed UberCab, a ride-sharing app that allowed riders to order a car to their desired location and automatically charge the fare to a credit card on their user account. In 2010, after a cease-and-desist order from the San Francisco Municipal Transportation Agency, they dropped the "cab" from the name.[10] Uber drivers are individuals who work as independent contractors using their own cars and get paid a percentage of the fare plus any tips.

Uber disrupted the taxicab industry by offering a ride service that is cheaper, easier to access and pay for, with the result of an enhanced overall customer control of the ride experience. As opposed to hailing a taxi from the sidewalk, or phoning a taxi, a rider simply presses a button on the Uber app and a driver, using GPS to determine a customer's location, comes to a destination of the rider's choosing, and the rider makes a payment through the application. The following illustration highlights how Uber compressed the value chain of calling a taxi and made the process of getting a ride seamless and less stressful. The entrepreneurial opportunity was found in reducing the value chain from eight to four steps.

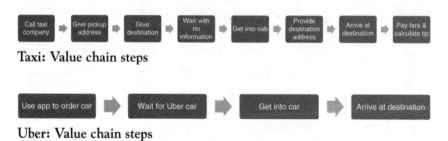

Taxi: Value chain steps

Uber: Value chain steps

Black Business Models

By popularizing ride-sharing, Uber has had an enormous impact on how people travel every day. However, it is important to note that Uber was not the pioneer of this mode of transportation—jitneys were the original rideshares. Jitneys were unlicensed cabs (personal cars) or buses in the Black communities throughout the country. This inexpensive ride-sharing system emerged in the early twentieth century. They were an essential, oftentimes only, mode of transportation within many Black neighborhoods where licensed cabs refused to serve or bus service was considered uneconomical for the city. As most taxi companies refused to hire Black drivers, jitney cab operations became a source of income for many Black drivers. In fact, they inspired other ridesharing variants in many cities across the US. The life of jitney cab drivers is memorialized in a play by August Wilson, *Jitney*, which premiered on Broadway in 2017.[11]

Another popular entrepreneurial venture today that has its origins in the Black community is the Airbnb. This home-sharing business model dates back to the late 1800s when Black homeowners would rent rooms to Black travelers who were not permitted to rent rooms in White hotels. Black start-up entrepreneurs have always had a presence in virtually every industry ranging from technology, financial services, health care, transportation, and media to manufacturing. The difference today, compared to 50 years ago, is the greater likelihood that Black entrepreneurs can have White customers. But, as stated in this book's introduction, the Black identity of an entrepreneur is still viewed by many Black entrepreneurs as a potential challenge to their ability to adding or keeping White customers.

Therefore, as the following stories show, many Black entrepreneurs pursued Black customers and some who pursued White customers had success doing so.

Thomas Jennings

Thomas Jennings was a Black entrepreneur who was able to procure White customers. He did so by identifying the problem of chemicals that damaged clothes during the cleaning process and founding a company to address that problem.

Born a free man in 1791, Thomas Jennings started his career as an apprentice to one of the most prominent tailors in Manhattan. His renowned skills as a tailor and clothier helped him develop a large customer following, and by the age of 19 he had opened what would become a phenomenally successful clothing shop on Williams Street in New York City. In response to customer complaints about stains on clothing caused by cleaning products, he developed a "dry scouring" method of removing dirt and stains from clothing without causing damage. In March 1821, at the age of 29, he was granted a patent for his "dry scouring" process, becoming the first Black person in America to receive a patent.[12] Jennings received this legal recognition for his invention because he was born a free man, an acknowledgment denied Black enslaved inventors for whom patents were unobtainable because the inventions of an enslaved person legally belonged to his or her master. The patent was not only a recognition of Jennings's work but also provided him the legal standing and recourse to respond when rival tailors illegally used his invention. Jennings's *dry scouring* method is a forerunner of the dry-cleaning process used today. With the wealth from his successful tailoring and dry-cleaning business Jennings supported abolitionist efforts, founded and supported philanthropic organizations, and promoted social justice and civil rights organizations. He served as assistant secretary for the First Annual Convention of the People of Color in Philadelphia in 1831 and helped organize the Legal Rights Association in 1855, raising challenges to discrimination, while funding and organizing legal defenses for court cases. He was a co-founder of the *Freedom's Journal*, the first African American owned and operated newspaper published in the United States, and a founder and trustee of the Abyssinian Baptist Church in New York. He was also an ardent supporter of the Anti-Colonialism Movement.[13]

Michael Hollis

Another Black start-up entrepreneur who had a customer base of Whites was Michael Hollis, the founder of Air Atlanta airlines. Michael started the company to address the problem of expensive first-class quality air travel.

Michael Hollis was born in Atlanta, Georgia, on October 22, 1953, the youngest of five children of Flem H. Hollis, a Pullman porter, and Virginia R. Hollis, an official with the Atlanta Housing Authority. He grew up in a family that valued education, stressed financial independence, and promoted excellence. His upbringing helped him develop a strong sense of confidence and a desire to excel at an incredibly young age.

Hollis was elected president of the Atlanta Youth Congress at the age of 15. Through this organization, he met influential Atlanta political and civil rights leaders, including Andrew Young, Julian Bond, Vernon Jordan Jr., H.J. Russell, and Maynard H. Jackson, many of whom would be lifelong friends and mentors. When he was 16, he began working in the public relations department of the Atlanta Braves and was selected as a Georgia delegate to the White House Conference on Youth. He spearheaded the organization of Young Atlantans for Maynard Jackson, when he ran for the U.S. Senate in 1969, before he successfully ran to become the first Black mayor of Atlanta.

Hollis attended Dartmouth College where he graduated with honors. While a student at Dartmouth, he served as student advisor to and later mentee of John George Kemeny, the college president. Hollis became interested in mass transportation and transportation finance while he was studying political science at Dartmouth and was particularly interested in the airline industry. After college, he attended the University of Virginia law school where he was elected the first African American President of the Law Student Division of the American Bar Association, which had 30,000 student members.

Soon after graduating from law school, he was appointed associate chief counsel by then President Jimmy Carter to investigate the legal ramifications of the Three Mile Island nuclear power-plant accident near Middletown, PA. In 1979 he moved to New York to take a position as Vice President of Public Finance with Oppenheimer and Company and helped establish their public finance department. This experience provided Hollis many valuable lessons about deal structuring. The deregulation of the airline industry during the Carter administration made Hollis think that his plans to create an airline were timely.

In 1981, Hollis returned to Atlanta to turn his dream into reality. One of his mentors, Maynard Jackson, arranged an introduction to Robert L. White, president of the National Alliance of Federal and Postal Employees, a predominantly Black labor union. White agreed to invest $500,000 of the union's pension fund as seed capital for the airline. Jackson then introduced Hollis to William J. Kennedy, the chairman of the Black-owned North Carolina Mutual Life Insurance Company, which ultimately invested approximately $2.5 million to finance the start-up. Hollis was then introduced to UNC Ventures Inc., a Black-owned venture firm based in Boston that invested in minority-owned businesses; UNC Ventures provided $2.75 million. UNC Ventures helped enlist Equitable Life Insurance, which provided $15 million as initial seed financing but invested a total of $35 million in the venture. Hollis was able to get Aetna Life and Casualty Company to commit $7.7 million. After an introduction made by one of his mentors, Mayor Andrew Young, Hollis was able to convince CSX Corporation to invest $8 million into his venture.[14]

Hollis purchased an initial fleet of Boeing 727 airplanes and reconfigured them with wider, roomier seats, similar to the accommodations for first class in other airlines. At its peak, Air Atlanta had 400 employees. Hollis's vision of good airplane service was different from that of his competitors. With the slogan "born to serve business," the airline catered to business travelers, the majority of whom were White, but charged standard prices while offering many innovative amenities, including gourmet meals, free gate-side and onboard telephone service, and free newspapers. Air Atlanta's route included New York, Memphis, and Miami and during its three years of operation, flew approximately 3 million passengers. The carrier began flights in February 1984 and Hollis became the first African American to start and operate an airline.

Annie Turnbo Malone

Another Black entrepreneur who achieved an historic first was Annie Turnbo Malone. While she was one of the first Black female millionaires in America, she also mentored another, Madame C.J. Walker. The basis of Ms. Malone's wealth was the creation of products that filled the void reflecting the lack of hair and beauty products specifically designed for Black women.

Annie Turnbo Malone was born in Metropolis, Illinois on April 9, 1869, to former enslaved parents. Malone grew up during the "Great Migration" when millions of Black people left the South and relocated to the North. This was a period in which the transplanted Southern

Black woman was adjusting to the urbanized Northern lifestyle. For them, part of that transition meant developing a more modern and sophisticated look that included new ways of grooming and styling their hair. Malone had been fascinated with hair styling and grooming from a young age, often testing her designs on her sister. An avid observer of hair fashions and trends, Malone noticed the absence of products available to Black women seeking remedies to itchy scalps and stunted hair growth. With the assistance of her aunt, an herbalist, she began to experiment with chemicals in her kitchen (once using her sister as her trial subject) to develop hair care products for Black women specifically. Her efforts also resulted in an improved way to straighten hair without damaging the scalp and follicles. Her first product was the Wonderful Hair Grower, but she would proceed to develop an extensive line of hair care products.

In 1902, with the goal of reaching a larger market, Malone decided to relocate her business to St. Louis, Missouri, a city that had the fourth largest population of African Americans at that time. She copyrighted her Poro brand of beauty products and opened her first store. She hired and trained three assistants and began selling her products door-to-door, implementing an innovative marketing strategy of offering free hair care treatments to potential customers to showcase the capabilities of her products. As her business grew, Malone began to recruit and train Black women to serve in her Poro network of sales agents, giving them an opportunity to earn income for themselves and leave low-paying jobs. As a result of this option, many of these women were able to start their own micro-businesses. Decades later, the sales agent network that Malone created would become the model that companies such as Mary Kay and Avon followed.

A brilliant and highly successful entrepreneur who continuously innovated, Ms. Malone did not limit her impact to product creation or sales. In 1917, she established Poro College, the first educational institution in the United States dedicated to the study and instruction of Black cosmetology. The aim and purpose of Poro College was to contribute to the economic betterment of "Race Women." The training center provided cosmetology and sales training for women interested in joining the Poro agent network as well as classes on proper deportment and etiquette. Students, who were mostly women between the ages of 16 and 80, were taught how to care for hair, manufacture hair pieces, and perform beauty care services. Training was provided to Poro sales agents, who were independent contractors, who were trained to sell her custom products and use the Poro system of scalp cleaning and hair nourishing. Through franchising, Malone was able to expand her business across the U.S. and abroad. Black beauticians came from across the country for instruction in Black hair and skin care, training they would use to establish their own beauty care businesses. Among the graduates of the program were future beauty care entrepreneur Madam C.J. Walker—who worked as a Poro Agent for about one year before starting her own hair care product business—and future Rock and Roll Hall of Famer Chuck Berry. By 1926, the college employed 175 people, had approximately 75,000 sales agents, and franchised outlets in North and South America, Africa, the Caribbean, the Philippines, and Canada. *The Philadelphia Tribune* reported that in 1923 Annie Malone paid the highest income tax of any African American in the country and in 1924 it was estimated that her net worth was $14 million.[15]

Built for an estimated $350,000, the three-acre Poro College campus was a multipurpose complex that housed classrooms, beauty shops, laboratories, an 800-seat auditorium, conference rooms, cafeteria, dining halls, ice cream parlor, bakery, emergency hospital, theater, gymnasium, chapel, roof garden, general office, shipping department, manufacturing plant, laundry, seamstress shop, dormitories, and guest rooms. It served as a gathering place for the city's African American citizens who were denied access to other entertainment and hospitality venues. In 1920, the campus was expanded even more extensively with the addition of an annex.

Malone was renowned as a generous benefactor, and throughout her life donated to many causes around the greater St. Louis area, in addition to making donations to several educational institutions including prominent HBCUs Howard University and the Tuskegee Institute. During the 1920s, this amazing entrepreneur financed the education of two full-time students at every historically Black college and university in the country. Her contribution of $25,000 to Howard University constituted one of the largest gifts the university had received from a private donor of African descent. Malone served as the board president of the St. Louis Colored Orphan's Home from 1919 to 1943 and raised most of the orphanage's construction costs. She was president of the Colored Women's Federated Clubs of St. Louis, an executive committee member of the National Negro Business League and the Commission on Interracial Cooperation, and a member of the African Methodist Episcopal Church. Her generosity also extended to family members and employees. She paid for the education of several nieces and nephews and bought homes for her brothers and sisters. She awarded employees with gifts for attendance, punctuality, and years of service.

Like Malone, Willa and Charles Bruce started a company that specifically targeted Black patrons. In 1912, they purchased beachfront property and built a resort on it. At that time, almost every beach resort in the country denied admission to Blacks. Therefore, this Black couple built a beautiful facility in Manhattan Beach, California, where Black customers could comfortably enjoy themselves. In 1929, the property was taken from Willa and Charles by the city government via an eminent domain lawsuit, which is used by governments to seize private property. The Manhattan Beach City Council successfully argued to the courts that the property was needed for public use. The City alleged that they were going to build a park on the land. That park was not built until 1960.[16] These Black entrepreneurs lost their successful, profitable business through no fault of their own. This book would be incomplete if devastating stories like this one were not included.

Introduction of the Case Study

In the case study, *Amanda and Kristen: Mented Cosmetics*, co-founders Amanda E. Johnson and Kristen Miller encounter the challenge that all start-ups ultimately face—now that an unmet need has been identified, an untapped market delineated, and a strategic plan articulated, how do we tell our story convincingly enough to compel others to invest in our vision?

HARVARD | BUSINESS | SCHOOL

9-318-093

DECEMBER 13, 2017

STEVEN ROGERS

ALTERRELL MILLS

Amanda and Kristen: Mented Cosmetics

In August 2016, after more than a year of researching viable business opportunities and working to develop their own set of proprietary products, Amanda E. Johnson and Kristen "KJ" Miller sat in the meeting room of their Harlem, New York working space determined to attract investors to their newly founded company, Mented Cosmetics. Mented, derived from the word "pigmented" and initially focused on bringing nude color lipsticks to the market, is intended to service women of all shades. Amanda and KJ believed that every woman deserved to see herself in the world of beauty. They felt that the beauty industry was largely ignoring them and an entire market segment that also included other Black, Latina and Indian women.

Amanda and KJ still had a long way to go in order to successfully launch their enterprise: neither of the co-founders were working on their venture full-time, they had yet to produce or sell a single unit of their finished product, and money was becoming tight given the fact that the venture was entirely self-funded. The co-founders knew they would have to address some very immediate challenges to move from testing the market and prototyping to launching a consumer-ready product to the public. Was now the right time to begin seeking outside investment or did they still need more time to prove their concept? If it was the right time, how much should they seek and how could they best make their case to investors? If it wasn't the right time what more could they do with their limited resources?

Identifying Opportunity

History

Black entrepreneurs have a long history of tapping into unmet needs, creating companies in virtually every industry including advertising, media and technology. The most prominent Black-owned advertising firm was founded by Carol Williams, the woman who created the famous tagline "strong enough for a man, but made for a woman" for Secret deodorant. In 2017, Carol was the second African-American woman inducted into the Advertising Industry Hall of Fame. The first was Cathy Hughes who founded Radio One (NYSE), a media company with radio stations throughout the country.[1]

Cathy Hughes purchased her first radio station in 1980 on the path to founding Radio One. The network was built by acquiring underperforming stations in big cities and changing their format to cater to black listeners. In 1999, she became the first black woman in the United States to Chair a

HBS Senior Lecturer Steven Rogers and independent researcher Alterrell Mills prepared this case. It was reviewed and approved before publication by a company designate. Funding for the development of this case was provided by Harvard Business School and not by the company. HBS cases are developed solely as the basis for class discussion. Cases are not intended to serve as endorsements, sources of primary data, or illustrations of effective or ineffective management.

publicly traded company.[2] Hughes' son, Alfred C Liggins III, became the new CEO of Radio One and the Chair of TV One. The new television network was developed in part because he believed the Black Entertainment Television (BET) network was not serving all of the Black market.[3]

BET, which was co-founded by Sheila Johnson, primarily targeted Black youths, 16-25 years old. The company was sold to Viacom in 2000 for $3 billion.[4] Sheila used some of the money to endow and create the Sheila Johnson Fellowship at Harvard University. The graduate students selected to receive this two-year fellowship (covering tuition, healthcare fees, and a stipend) were chosen for their work in uplifting the Black community.[5]

Within the beauty industry, Madam C.J. Walker (regarded as America's first self-made female millionaire) earned her fame and fortune developing hair care products for Black women. She also created beauty schools, salons and instructional facilities.

Would Amanda and KJ follow in the footsteps of so many successful black female founders and entrepreneurs?

Foundations of Partnership

Amanda and KJ met in 2012 while working on *The HBS Show*, an annual theatrical production put on by the students at Harvard Business School. The two became fast friends and bonded over their interest in entrepreneurship while working together on a number of different projects ranging from a final paper for a marketing class to planning Sankofa, the African dance show organized by the African American Student Union. They knew they worked well together and wanted to start something after school, however, they weren't sure what it would be. As graduation came, they both accepted full time positions in New York: Amanda with Barney's working in e-commerce business development and KJ with Deloitte focusing on retail strategy consulting (**Exhibit 1**). They had yet to come up with an idea they felt passionate enough about to strike out on their own and they both felt they needed to earn an income for a while, in order to pay back student loans, cover living expenses, and save some start-up capital that could be invested once they identified an opportunity.

Once in New York, the two met regularly to discuss ideas. "In the fall after graduation we started purposefully meeting, maybe once a week to talk about startup ideas. In between meetings, we would send each other articles about interesting things we saw happening. It was very brainstormy" Amanda recalled. Amanda and KJ knew they needed to identify a problem in the market, develop a product as the solution, and then find customers willing to purchase their products. But they weren't sure which of those aspects to focus on first when trying to come up with a start-up idea.

KJ recalled having some basic guidelines to their meetings. "Foremost it was 'what were we interested in?' And then, I think the second question was 'is it something that *we* could do?' Because I had attempted other start ups before, I felt pretty adamant that I didn't want to do anything that we couldn't get off the ground with just us. I didn't want to upset our dynamic, because the thing that makes a startup work is the team. At the end of the day if you have someone you're working with who you really respect, and who even when you disagree with them, that disagreement leads you to more progress instead of hitting a wall, that's what is precious. It wasn't just that it had to be something in our wheelhouse, or it had to be something where there's a need, those things weren't enough. It needed to be us as a team and something that we were absolutely excited about."

Based on their backgrounds they decided that they were best suited for the creation of a consumer goods company. KJ would focus on production and Amanda would focus on marketing. Amanda majored in Finance at Howard University, a historically Black university in Washington D.C. After graduation she worked for two years in investment banking. While she liked the analytical rigor of finance she wanted to work with real products that impacted everyday people so she transitioned into digital marketing at a multinational mass media corporation for two years before enrolling at Harvard Business School. KJ graduated from Harvard University in 2008 and worked for four years in fashion and apparel merchandising for a national department store chain and a New York based urban apparel retailer with a global online footprint. While their backgrounds narrowed down the universe of possible opportunities there was still a seemingly infinite stream of ideas that fit within those broad parameters.

It wasn't until Amanda lamented that she had been looking for the perfect nude lipstick – without any luck for the past three years – that the two felt they had stumbled across a problem that they were both passionate about and well suited to solve. After a weekend spent buying and trying over 100 different nude lipsticks, Amanda and KJ were convinced that the product they needed simply did not exist. They began to look into developing and producing a line of nude lipsticks designed for and marketed to African American women and other women of color. Their first step was to learn everything about the beauty industry.

The Beauty Industry

Overview

The cosmetics and beauty industry amassed $49 billion of revenue in 2015. Roughly a third of the industry is devoted to cosmetics (20%) and fragrances (10%), with the balance split nearly equally between skincare, hair care, and nail products. While the four largest firms have about thirty percent (combined) market share, the majority of firms have fewer than 20 employees.[6]

Raw Materials

Nearly half of high-end cosmetics and skin care products sold in the United States are imported from France, Italy, the United Kingdom and Canada. Products from China and Mexico are mostly sold through mass retailers and drug stores. Imports accounted for nearly 17% of all cosmetics and skin products in 2015 (**Exhibit 2**). Trade agreements such as the North American Free Trade Agreement (NAFTA) influence exports and imports. [7]

The Trade-Weighted Index (TWI)[a] fluctuations and global oil prices influence consumption of beauty and cosmetic products. US companies located in New York (7.8% of industry headquartered here) and New Jersey benefit from access to shipping ports and chemical producers. Crude oil is a key input for many cosmetic and beauty products.[8]

Consumer Behavior

The industry sees a direct relationship between demand for "nonessentials" and the share of households earning more than $100,000 in annual revenue. [9] Beauty customers are over weighted towards those in the top quintile of the population based on income. While this group represents 20% of the population, they generate nearly 40% of all retail beauty industry revenue, which is more than the combined revenue generated by consumers in the bottom three quintiles. [10]

Interestingly, as consumer confidence increases, volume does not shift as much as a preference toward higher quality products. Some examples include the increased popularity of natural and

---

[a] The trade-weighted index (TWI) is a measure of US dollar strength against the currencies of its trading partners.

organic products that carry a premium price tag. Higher cost goods as well as perceived quality positively impact brand financials: US brands are often considered high quality and desirable to international consumers. Other measures of perceived quality include metallized packaging.[11]

Redefining Nude

According to *British Vogue*, the conventional concept of "nude" – "something of a pinky beige colour" – is no longer relevant.[12] Nude is a shade that is muted and resembles a natural shade. Such shades are critical for working women who require understated makeup in professional settings. Some Black women have lips that are different colors with one deeply pigmented and the other a more pink color. In addition, many Black women and women of color have fuller lips that require a moisturizing element absent in most products designed for thinner lips.

British Vogue experts say the key to identifying the perfect nude lipstick is based on the skin's undertones though most consumers are unaware of their undertones, which can be blue, yellow or red. Often trial and error is the only path as visual inspection in the tube or applications to the back of the hand provide imperfect matches. The fuller bottom lip can be two-toned which requires a lipstick with better coverage in order to give a uniform appearance when applied.

Demographic Shifts

In 2012, the US Census Bureau noted that births of non-Hispanic Whites for the first time in US history accounted for less than fifty percent. Hispanics are projected to account for nearly 85% of population growth by 2050. In fact, each generation of the US is becoming more multicultural (**Exhibit 3**). Of the top 25 most populated counties in the US, 21 are more than 50% multicultural. Life expectancy increases for multicultural populations have positive impacts on marketing spend return of investment (ROI).[13]

Fad or The Future?

For many, the question remains whether these forays into the market for Black beauty products will be successful. Maya Brown, the vice president of marketing for Black Opal, a makeup and skincare company, believes that while targeting Black consumers more effectively could help to better serve this community, understanding the needs and concerns of the Black community and building products for them is critically important. "[The recent] changes are done from a standpoint of not taking in some of the cultural factors and understanding the nuances that relate to people of color and recognizing that we're not homogenized," Brown says. "Brands are trying to come out with something that's a brief introduction into the marketplace without really looking at the formulas and how they're going to market, and making sure that the products are customized and tailored."[14]

The Business of Diversity

The Black Female Dollar

Black women outspend their non-Black counterparts on beauty products, accounting for $7.5 billion of spend annually in that industry alone. Black women spend 100% more on skin care and 80% more on cosmetics than their non-Black counterparts.[15] According to the "Our Science, Her Magic" Nielsen Report, the black female population is 24.3 million, which is 14% of the total female population and 52% of the black population within the United States.[16] The same report projects the overall buying power (all industries) for both black men and women to rise from $1.2 trillion in 2016 to $1.5 trillion in 2021 with a majority (about 62%) concentrated in 10 states (**Exhibit 4**). Despite significant purchasing power and willingness to spend a greater proportion of it on health and beauty products companies are not developing and targeting products for this segment. According to a Nielsen Report on Black consumers, 81% of Blacks believed that products advertised using Black media are more relevant to them yet only three percent of advertising dollars spent is with media focused on Black audiences.[17]

The Faces in the Room

The beauty industry is well known for its lack of diversity in its employees, models and products. This lack of diversity has had lasting impacts to the profits of Fortune 500 brands. For example in the 1990s, Maybelline CEO Robert Hiatt stated it "is not the makeup of our management that is important; it is paying attention to the market and customers" in response to consumer criticism for their Shades of You product (geared towards black women). Prior to this comment, the now defunct product was said to have 35% share of a $100 million ethnic cosmetics market. The CEO added that the company does not keep track of the minorities employed within the organization.[18]

In 2015, L'Oreal launched its first diversity report to highlight the organization's progress from the prior five years across several areas of diversity including their marketing departments. In contrast to Robert Hiatt, Jean-Paul Agon, Chairman and CEO of L'Oreal stated, "A diverse workforce in all functions and levels of a company enhances our creativity and our understanding of consumers, thus allowing us to develop and market products that are relevant to their expectations."[19] The report further asserts that the management of diversity is a strategic lever for the organization.

But diversity at cosmetic manufacturers is simply one piece of the puzzle. Advertising agencies are often responsible for developing the concepts, choosing the models and executing the marketing campaigns. In 2005, Blacks represented 7.1% of the employees in advertising, public relations and related services (Blacks accounted for 11.7% of the overall workforce). In 2015, the number of Blacks in advertising, public relationships and related services declined to 5.3%.[20]

Consumers Speak Up

The Internet has played a significant role in shifting the landscape of the market by providing a voice to the previously unheard. An executive at IMAN Cosmetics believes "it's not that these consumers were silent before, but companies didn't have to listen."[21] Within the last decade several notable brands have faced significant customer backlash for tone deafness, poor execution in advertising, and not fully understanding its customers or market.

In 2008, L'Oreal was accused of lightening the skin of Beyoncé Knowles in its advertisement. In 2015, Black Opal, whose company's mission statement reads, "Created in 1994 to celebrate the nuances of black skin," faced online criticism for perceived alienation by its black customers.[22][23] The company response to the criticism was that they were a brand for every shade and had "never issued any 'non-inclusive' statements about our product offerings nor any statements about our sales objectives." Some consumers noted the abrupt transition in the brand's positioning away from its origins and "the professional woman of Jamaican descent, who embodied the Black Opal customer" that was listed as the brand's muse.[24]

In 2016, BareMinerals was criticized for a lack of options for darker shades of its Complexions Rescue concealer. In the same year, Maybelline featured black British model Jordan Dunn in an advertisement for its Dream Velvet foundation launch. However, Dunn's shade of foundation was not included in the available products; after significant customer complaints, the company spokesperson discussed plans for a future release of Dunn's shade.[25]

Diversity as a Winning Formula

Sam Fine, a makeup artist and Cover Girl's and Revlon's first African American spokesperson, believes the problems some companies face extends beyond marketing as cosmetic companies have "failed to create colors, formulas and marketing initiatives" targeted to Black and other women of color. Fine, who counts Naomi Campbell, Halle Berry and Oprah among his clients, believes some companies who have tried to appeal to Black women have tried to darken existing products without accounting for balancing undertones or the additional coverage required.[26]

In addition, Balanda Atis, L'Oreal chemist, described the scientific challenges in creating foundations for medium and darker skin tones as both poorly optimized formula architecture and poorly balanced pigments for Black skin.[27] Atis, a Haitian woman who grew up in the United States, started at L'Oreal as a researcher in the mascara lab and conducted research on skin color as a side project. Several years and product patents later, executives at L'Oreal created and named her the head of its new Women of Color Lab. The goal of the lab is to ensure women in each of the countries L'Oreal products are sold can find a color match. [28]

As part of its research aims, the lab measured women's skin tones from 57 countries and used that data to identify a new, rare pigment, Ultramarine Blue, to create new foundations for women of color.[29] Interestingly, L'Oreal named Lupita Nyong'o[b] as a Brand Ambassador for their high-end brand Lancôme before they had a foundation to match her skin tone.[30] It was Atis' lab that created the foundation for the Academy Award-winning actress.

A Set of Dilemmas

Once products intended for Black women are created, distribution in appropriate channels, store placement and effective marketing are essential. For example, Sam Fine lamented the lack of IMAN Cosmetics products in stores like Sephora, a prestige retailer with 2,300 stores in over 30 countries around the world.[31] Sephora is a subsidiary of Louis Vuitton Moet Hennessy.[32] While the IMAN brand, named for the iconic Somali model Iman (**Exhibit 5**), considers itself prestige, it's licensing and distribution agreements are with mass retailers like Wal-Mart, Target and Walgreens.[33]

Placement and retail space is a highly competitive business: companies with products geared toward Blacks and other women of color face a placement dilemma. Opting into a separate aisle could limit brand growth to a wider consumer base in the future, while later shifting into the general cosmetics aisle may alienate loyal customers. Not all companies want to be relegated to the "ethnic aisle" (the actual aisle category often reads "Ethnic Hair & Beauty Products") as Carol's Daughter founder, Lisa Price, proclaims "the room for improvements is in breaking the cycle of thinking that there needs to be a separate shopping section" for Blacks and other people of color.[34]

At the same time, many consumers face the dilemma of choosing between popular brands that other women use and potentially feeling criticized for choosing a specialty brand made for Black women.[35] Black women and other women of color want to be considered part of the industry. Desiree Reid, an executive for IMAN Cosmetic's line, warns of the dangers of ignoring market segments, noting that "[customers] will move on and find brands that do speak to them and service them." [36]

---

[b] Lupita Nyong'o was born in Mexico (raised in Kenya) to Kenyan parents. She was the first Kenyan to win an Academy Award (Oscar) in 2003's *12 Years a Slave* in addition to the 27 other awards for her role. She was also named *People Magazine*'s Most Beautiful Woman in 2014.

Creating Mented

Developing the Product

Personal experience suggested that color, coverage, and branding were the most important characteristics of their new lipstick line. There were many other characteristics that they could have tested from the quality of the lipstick to packaging, but Amanda and KJ made the conscious decision to get feedback on the highest priority items first. Part of their decision involved financing and a desire to create a cost efficient product sample. KJ leaned on her experience in buying and sourcing to contact major cosmetic manufacturers.

Manufacturers make a variety of products for different brands and typically allow customers to either: create a derivative shade from mixing stock colors or produce an entirely custom shade if the customer provides a proprietary formula. The drawback to a custom color was cost: manufacturers require a commitment to purchase a large volume of product, as an entire vat of a single color could not be used with other clients. In addition, independent R&D companies are often needed to develop new shades. Using a derivative product from stock colors would require their brand to rely entirely on marketing for product differentiation.[37]

As a self-funded start-up, manufacturing a custom color for product samples added significant additional costs. Amanda agreed with KJ's insistence on making the test colors themselves. KJ bought a lipstick mold, some basic ingredients of wax and oil, and a number of different pigments to mix into prototypes.

Amanda developed a targeted strategy, in line with the modest scale of their current operations, that would provide enough data per shade. Product samples were sent to social media influencers with significant influence in the beauty space that catered to Black women and other women of color. Influencers like KingMaliMagic (126K followers) and BlackMakeUpBrands (17K followers) built their following by knowing what Black women wanted and what products worked best for their beauty needs.

Outreach to prominent influencers aggregated the opinions of hundreds of thousands of potential customers on the product itself as well as the company name. Within nine months of identifying the problem they wanted to solve, Amanda and KJ had come up with and tested a name for the company and perfected six lipstick shades. Their color Mented #5 was actually the first shade the company settled on but named it #5 because it took them five iterations before arriving at the color influencers truly embraced. In April 2016, Amanda and KJ officially incorporated Mented Cosmetics.

Going to Market

With a brand created and a product line solidified, Amanda and KJ needed to develop and execute a go to market strategy in order to turn Mented Cosmetics into a revenue generating company. In addition, they would have to transition from handmade samples to professional quality finished goods before making their lipsticks commercially available.

To maintain complete control of the brand and keep costs low, the co-founders decided to focus on their online strategy by going to market as a direct to consumer brand. A primarily online presence would require creative thinking to stand out from their brick and mortar competitors (where consumers can try on products before purchasing). In comparison to most brands that only feature pictures of the products, Mented included pictures of their products on models of different complexions to give buyers a clearer idea of the shade on their skin (**Exhibit 6**). In addition to their incredibly active social media presence, their brand awareness strategy included paying for social media advertising and hosting events in local markets.

Amanda and KJ agreed that they should position their product as a luxury/mass-teige (a portmanteau for mass-market and prestige) good in the $15 - $20 per lipstick range. This positioning aligned with their brand image and small batch manufacturing, while at the same time filling a hole in the current competitive landscape (**Exhibit 7**). Typical lipsticks can range in price from $5 for capsules available at convenience stores such as Duane Reade, to $15 for the baseline products sold by mass-teige brands such as MAC cosmetics, all the way up over $30 for luxury products by brands such as Lancome, Estée Lauder, and Dior.

KJ contacted several manufacturers across New England to determine production cost at scale including minimum order amounts per shade as well as the cost of producing custom colors, raw materials and packaging. She chose a manufacturer willing to produce their custom shades at a price and volume that matched closely their first year sales projections. Familiar with buying beauty products directly from China via Alibaba for personal use, she negotiated directly with Chinese packaging suppliers by cutting out intermediaries who liaise with foreign suppliers on behalf of many American companies, often at significant mark ups.

Amanda and KJ created a personnel plan: they planned to leave their jobs once they had secured funding. Amanda would run Marketing, Digital Experience, & Finance while KJ would focus on Product and Business Development. In addition to the co-founders coming on full time, their plan included provisions for entry-level help to manage their day-to-day content production, order fulfillment, and online presence.

Attracting Investors

Mented needed money to produce and bring their products to market at scale. In order to raise money from outside investors, the co-founders knew that they would have to prove to demand for their products. At the same time, they needed seed capital to actually produce and sell their lipsticks. They faced a causality dilemma: how could they prove demand without product, how could they sell product without financing and how could they secure financing without providing demand.

To solve this "chicken or egg problem", Amanda and KJ spent the next four months leveraging all of the resources available to them. Reaching back out to the community of influencers, Mented requested product reviews and reposted influencer reviews to Mented's social media pages along with original Mented content (**Exhibit 8**). During this "soft launch" period, the website mostly served to collect email addresses – featuring a "coming soon" banner – before customers were able to sign up to pre-order products.

As Amanda and KJ collected email addresses and product reviews, they continued to do their primary research by conducting focus groups and customer surveys to demonstrate demand. Fifty seven percent of those surveyed indicated a dissatisfaction with their current cosmetics options. Over 100 women provided opinions and thousands of social media followers across Instagram and Facebook indicated a strong interest in Mented's products.

Understanding the Odds

According to the "Project Diane" report by Digital Undivided, of the 10,238 startups that secured venture funding between the years of 2012 and 2014, only 24 (0.2%) were headed by a Black woman. The same report states that Black women represent the fastest-growing group of entrepreneurs in the United States, accounting for $44 billion in revenue annually. The same report found the average amount raised from the already small number was $36,000 – compared to an average of $1.3 million by white men. Over half of the black female founders who received any funding received less than $100,000.[38]

Project Diane is an initiative of Digital Undivided, a company founded in 2012 by Black female entrepreneur Kathryn Kinney to create a pipeline of Black entrepreneurs in the technology sector. The initiative sought to identify and quantify the challenges facing black female entrepreneurs, reviewing over 50,000 entries in TechCrunch Magazine's startup database in addition to surveying organizations within Digital Undivided's network. As of February 2016, only 11 startups led by Black women had raised over $1 million in outside funding.[39] Of the 11 startups to raise over $1 million in outside funding, Joanne Wilson of Gotham Gal Ventures has invested in three.[40]

Wilson's investment represents a major contrast from the majority of the venture capital industry. According to analyses reported in TechCrunch in a study of 71 venture capital firms with an excess of $160 billion in assets under management, there were several prominent firms without any women or any minorities on their investment leadership teams. For example, women represented 8% of the senior investment teams analyzed but represented 60% of non-investment roles. The same analysis indicated just 1% of senior investment team members in are black.[41]

What Next?

Amanda and KJ were certain that they had a product that met a need and a customer base willing to pay for it. In order to fully execute on their master plan, they needed to determine how much money to raise and craft a convincing story to take on a roadshow to potential investors. The co-founders thought about how far they had come, putting pen to paper as they projected the first five years of sales (**Exhibit 9**).

Exhibit 1   Founders' Background

Kristen Jones (KJ) Miller
Title: Co-CEO
Education:
- MBA, Harvard
- BA, Harvard
Background:
- Spent four years as an apparel and fashion buyer for Sears and DJ Networks
- Spent two years consulting in Deloitte's retail practice focused on assortment planning, merch planning and inventory

Amanda Johnson
Title: Co-CEO
Education:
- MBA, Harvard
- BA, Howard
Background:
- Spent two years in investment banking at Goldman
- Spent two years in digital marketing at Time
- Spent two years at Barney's in e-commerce business development

Source: Mented Cosmetics company documents.

Exhibit 2a   Cosmetics & Beauty Industry Data 2010 – 2015

	2010	2011	2012	2013	2014	2015
Revenue ($M)	42,644	46,027	43,746	43,286	46,979	49,125
Employment	50,772	53,286	50,294	52,332	53,089	55,229
Exports ($M)	7,838	8,065	8,580	9,015	9,285	9,239
Imports ($M)	6,001	6,668	7,191	7,791	8,234	8,316
Wages ($M)	3,071	3,206	2,899	2,966	2,977	3,114
Domestic Demand ($M)	40,807	44,630	42,358	42,062	45,928	48,201
Consumer Confidence Index	54.5	58.1	67.1	73.6	87.1	97.1

Source: Anya Cohen, "Cosmetic & Beauty Products Manufacturing in the US," IBISWorld Industry Report No 32562 (May 2017), IBISWorld, accessed November 9, 2017.

Exhibit 2b   2015 Industry Cost Breakdown (as % of Revenue)

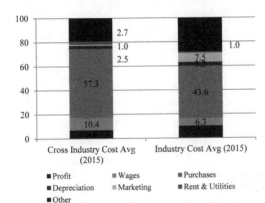

Profit   Wages   Purchases
Depreciation   Marketing   Rent & Utilities
Other

Profits: Larger companies keep cost low with supplier relationships and investing in distributer networks. Crude oil prices directly influence this category.

Wages: High-end goods require quality control which can increase overall employee expense.

Purchases: Manufactures' inputs include chemicals, dyes and essential oils. Packaging can be done internally or through a third party. **Marketing**: Promotional samples and add-on samples with the purchase of other brand goods. Large retailers often outspend the industry average in this category.

Other costs: Accounting, legal fees, R&D and other expenses fall into this category.

Source: Anya Cohen, "Cosmetic & Beauty Products Manufacturing in the US," IBISWorld Industry Report No 32562 (May 2017), IBISWorld, accessed November 9, 2017.

Exhibit 5   Partial History of Cosmetic Brand Launches Aimed at Black Women

Launch	Brand	Additional Information
1967	Flori Roberts Cosmetics	Founded by publicist Flori Roberts after listening to the concerns of black models during New York fashion shows. Along with the expertise of her plastic surgeon husband with knowledge of the chemistry of black skin, products enjoyed department store success ($25M global revenues in 1988).
1973	Fashion Fair	Founded by John Johnson, owner and of Johnson Publishing (*Jet* and *Ebony*). Originally started as mail-order product, The Capsule Collection, in 1969. 1988 global revenues of $60M.
1975 (1982)	Polished Ambers	Developed by Revlon with a marketing campaign, "Carving Out a Niche." Marketing problems were cited as a "cause of the line's demise."
1984	M-A-C	Founded by Frank Toskan, makeup artist and photographer, and Frank Angelo, beauty salon owner, in Toronto. Initially sold in hair salons to makeup artists and models, then launched in a department store with its staff made up of professional makeup artists.
1986	Gazelle International / Cosmetics	Founded by Patricia French, former model and makeup consultant. A native of Georgia (US), she moved to Paris to open a research lab focused on dark-skinned women that launched after 5 years and $4M in investments.
1986 (1988)	Juin Rachele	Founded by Juin Rachele and husband Pat Cooper, both natives of Jamaica. The brand was in Saks and Nordstrom with $1M in sales in first 3 months. Closed in August 1988 filing for bankruptcy with losses of $2.5M.
1990	Shades of You	Developed by Maybelline.
1994	IMAN Cosmetics	Founded by Iman, Somali model who began her modeling career in 1975 and was honored by the Council of Fashion Designers (CFDA) in 2010 with the Fashion Icon Award. In 2004, IMAN licensing agreement granted distribution in Target, Wal-Mart, Walgreens and Duane Reade.
2011	Beauty Bakerie	Founded by Cashmere Nicole. The company known for its smudge-free "lip whip" had revenues of $3.3 million in 2016 (up from $475K in 2015).
2013	Women of Color	Lab developed by L'Oreal.

Sources: Compiled from these sources: Patricia O'Toole, "Battle of the Beauty Counter," New York Times Magazine, December 3, 1989, http://www.nytimes.com/1989/12/03/magazine/battle-of-the-beauty-counter.html?pagewanted=all, accessed November 15, 2017; "Anne-Marie Schiro, "For Skins of All Shades, New Cosmetics," New York Times Magazine, May 15, 1987, http://www.nytimes.com/1987/05/15/style/for-skins-of-all-shades-new-cosmetics.html, accessed November 15, 2017; Fashion Fair, "About Us," http://www.fashionfair.com/aboutus.php, accessed November 15, 2017; MAC Cosmetics, "Our History," http://www.maccosmetics.jobs/mac/our-history.html, accessed November 30, 2017; IMAN Cosmetics, "About IMAN," http://www.imancosmetics.com/aboutiman, accessed Nov 9, 2017; Amy Feldman, "A Single Mom Battle Breast Cancer Built Beauty Bakerie To A $5M Brand, Got Unilever to Invest," Forbes, December 3, 2017, https://www.forbes.com/sites/amyfeldman/2017/12/03/how-a-single-mom-battling-breast-cancer-built-beauty-bakerie-to-a-5m-brand-got-unilever-to-invest/#7a79953a43f8, accessed December 27, 2017.

Notes: (1) Dates in parentheses indicates year product was discontinued (if known).

(2) Beauty Bakerie states that it is an inclusive brand and "fifty-five percent of our customer base is Caucasian."

Exhibit 6   Mented Cosmetics Nude Colors on Models of Different Shades

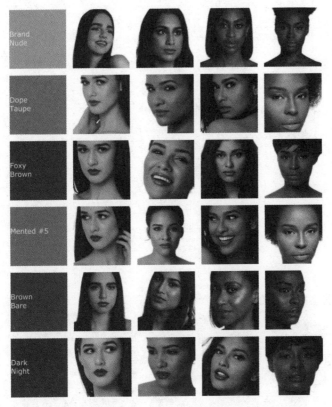

Source: Mented Cosmetics website.

Exhibit 7   Competitive Landscape

Source: Mented Cosmetics company documents.

Exhibit 8   Mented Content

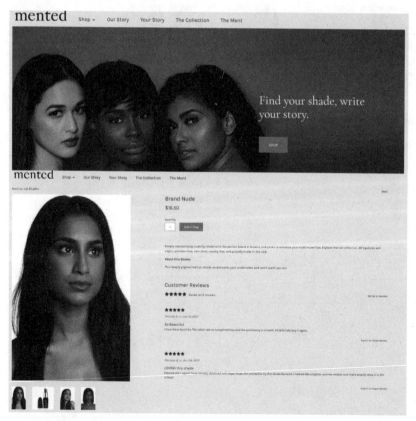

Source: Mented Cosmetics company website.

Exhibit 9   Excerpt from Mented Investor Pitch Deck, 5 Years of Projected Sales

Pro Forma Income Statement	Year 1	Year 2	Year 3	Year 4	Year 5
Revenues					
Unit Growth Rate		*100%*	*100%*	*100%*	*100%*
Number of Products Sold	26,466	52,932	105,864	211,728	423,456
Direct Ecommerce					
Channel % of Sales	*60%*	*60%*	*70%*	*70%*	*70%*
Number of Products Sold	15,880	31,759	74,105	148,210	296,419
Average Price	$19	$31	$31	$31	$31
Direct Ecommerce	$301,712	$984,535	$2,297,249	$4,594,498	$9,188,995
Revenues					
Specialty Retailer					
Channel % of Sales	*40%*	*40%*	*30%*	*30%*	*30%*
Number of Products Sold	10,586	21,173	31,759	63,518	127,037
Average Price	$12	$18	$18	$18	$18
	$130,742	$386,404	$579,605	$1,159,211	$2,318,422
Retailer Revenue					
	$432,454	$1,370,939	$2,876,854	$5,753,708	$11,507,417
Total Revenues					
Total Cost of Goods Sold	$79,663	$196,378	$392,755	$785,511	$1,571,021
	$352,791	$1,174,561	$2,484,099	$4,968,197	$9,936,396
Gross Profit					
Operating Expenses					
Marketing % of Sales	*30%*	*30%*	*30%*	*30%*	*30%*
Retailer Marketing % of	*10%*	*10%*	*10%*	*10%*	*10%*
Sales					
Product Development	$10,000	$80,000	$100,000	$100,000	$100,000
Rent		$60,000	$60,000	$72,000	$72,000
Employee Compensation	$235,000	$350,000	$500,000	$750,000	$750,000
Employee Benefits	$70,500	$105,000	$150,000	$225,000	$225,000
Number of Employees	3	5	7	10	10
Legal Fees	$24,000	$24,000	$24,000	$24,000	$24,000
General and Administration	$8,649	$19,691	$45,945	$91,890	$183,780
Website	$16,000	$16,000	$16,000	$16,000	$16,000
Warehouse & Distribution	$17,280	$34,560	$51,840	$69,120	$86,400
	$490,448	$980,973	$1,676,270	$2,852,980	$4,539,121
Total Operating Expenses					
	($137,657)	$193,588	$807,829	$2,115,217	$5,397,275
Operating Profit					
Taxes (40%)	($55,063)	$77,435	$323,132	$846,087	$2,158,910
	($82,594)	$116,153	$484,698	$1,269,130	$3,238,365
Net Income					

Source: Mented Cosmetics company documents.

Exhibit 10   Investment Matrix (Illustrative Example)

	Year 1	Year 2	Year 3	Year 4	Year 5
Projected Net Income	-$30M	-$50M	-$70M	$500M	$500M
Cumulative Projected Net Income	-$30M	-$80M	-$150M	$350M	$850M

Source: Casewriter.

Note: Some entrepreneurs raise capital based on operating expense rather than net income.

Endnotes

[1] Sapna Maheshwari, "An Ad Woman at the Top of an Industry That She Thinks Still Has Far to Go," The New York Times, April 24, 2017, https://www.nytimes.com/2017/04/24/business/carol-williams-advertising-hall-of-fame.html, accessed December 8, 2017.

[2] "The comeback queen," Forbes Magazine, September 20, 1990, https://www.forbes.com/forbes/1999/0920/6407086a.html#2d3d306677cf, accessed December 6, 2017.

[3] Felicia R Lee, "A Network for Blacks With Sense of Mission, The New York Times, December 11, 2007, http://www.nytimes.com/2007/12/11/arts/television/11one.html?pagewanted=print, accessed December 6, 2017.

[4] V Dion Haynes, "The empire of Sheila Johnson," The Washington Post, July 5, 2010, http://www.washingtonpost.com/wp-dyn/content/article/2010/07/02/AR2010070204911.html, accessed December 8, 2017.

[5] Leslie Milk, "The 2015 Washington Business Hall of Fame," The Washingtonian, November 9, 2015, https://www.washingtonian.com/2015/11/09/washington-dc-business-hall-of-fame-what-it-takes-to-build-strong-companies-communities/, accessed December 8, 2017.

[6] Anya Cohen, "Cosmetic & Beauty Products Manufacturing in the US," IBISWorld Industry Report No 32562 (May 2016), IBISWorld, accessed November 9, 2017.

[7] Ibid

[8] Ibid

[9] Ibid

[10] Ibid

[11] Ibid

[12] Funmi Fetto, "The Quest For A 'Nude' Lipstick That Works On Black Skin, British Vogue, April 12, 2017, http://www.vogue.co.uk/gallery/best-nude-lipsticks-for-black-women, accessed November 15, 2017.

[13] "The Multicultural Edge: Rising Super Consumers," Nielsen (March 2015), the-multicultural-edge-rising-super-consumers-march-2015.pdf, accessed November 15, 2017.

[14] Taylor Bryant, "How the Beauty Industry Has Failed Black Women," Refinery29.com, February 27, 2016, http://www.refinery29.com/2016/02/103964/black-hair-care-makeup-business, accessed November 15, 2017.

[15] Ibid

[16] "African-American Women: Our Science, Her Magic," Nielsen (September 2017), http://www.nielsen.com/us/en/insights/reports/2017/african-american-women-our-science-her-magic.html, accessed November 15, 2017.

[17] "Resilient, Receptive, and Relevant: The African-American Consumer," Nielsen (September 2013), http://www.nielsen.com/us/en/insights/reports/2013/resilient--receptive-and-relevant.html, accessed November 15, 2017.

[18] Faye Rice, "How to Make Diversity Pay," Fortune, August 8, 1994, http://archive.fortune.com/magazines/fortune/fortune_archive/1994/08/08/79604/index.htm, accessed November 15, 2017.

[19] "L'Oreal's 1st Worldwide Diversity Report," press release, December 17, 2015, on L'Oreal website, http://www.loreal.com/media/press-releases/2015/dec/loreals-1st-worldwide-diversity-report, accessed December 6, 2017.

[20] Nathalie Tadena, "Why the Picture of Diversity on Madison Avenue Is So Murky," The Wall Street Journal, March 18, 2016, https://www.wsj.com/articles/why-the-picture-of-diversity-on-madison-avenue-is-so-murky-1458332278, accessed November 15, 2017.

[21] Clover Hope, "The Makeup Industry's Frustrating Cycle of Struggle and Progress for Women of Color," Jezebel.com, August 23, 2016, https://jezebel.com/the-makeup-industrys-frustrating-cycle-of-struggle-and-1782880385, accessed November 15, 2017.

[22] Ibid

[23] Black Opal Beauty, "About Us," https://www.blackopalbeauty.com/about-us/about-black-opal-beauty, accessed December 8, 2017.

[24] Portia, "Black Opal Claims It Was Never A Cosmetics Line for Black Women," Black Girl With Long Hair, October 22, 2015, http://blackgirllonghair.com/2015/10/black-opal-claims-it-was-never-a-cosmetics-line-for-black-women/, accessed December 8, 2017.

[25] Clover Hope, "The Makeup Industry's Frustrating Cycle of Struggle and Progress for Women of Color," Jezebel.com, August 23, 2016, https://jezebel.com/the-makeup-industrys-frustrating-cycle-of-struggle-and-1782880385, accessed November 15, 2017.

[26] Corina Zappia, "The Big Cover-Up," *The Village Voice*, May 23, 2006, https://www.villagevoice.com/2006/05/23/the-big-cover-up/, accessed November 15, 2017

[27] Clover Hope, "The Makeup Industry's Frustrating Cycle of Struggle and Progress for Women of Color," Jezebel.com, August 23, 2016, https://jezebel.com/the-makeup-industrys-frustrating-cycle-of-struggle-and-1782880385, accessed November 15, 2017.

[28] Elizabeth Segran, "The L'Oreal Chemist Who's Changing The Face of Makeup," Fast Company, October 1, 2015, https://www.fastcompany.com/3050173/the-loreal-chemist-whos-changing-the-face-of-makeup, accessed Dec 6, 2017.

[29] Andrea Arterbery, "Meet Balanda Atis, L'Oreal's Women of Color Lab Manager," *Essence*, April 5, 2016, https://www.essence.com/2016/04/05/meet-balanda-antis-loreals-women-color-lab-manager, accessed November 15, 2017.

[30] "Meet Balanda Atis. The Chemist Behind Lupita Nyong'o's Lancôme Foundation," SUPERSELECTED, April 4, 2016, http://superselected.com/meet-balanda-atis-the-chemist-behind-lupita-nyongos-lancome-foundation/, accessed December 6, 2017.

[31] Corina Zappia, "The Big Cover-Up," *The Village Voice*, May 23, 2006, https://www.villagevoice.com/2006/05/23/the-big-cover-up/, accessed November 15, 2017.

[32] Sephora, "About Us," https://www.sephora.com/about-us, accessed December 6, 2017.

[33] IMAN Cosmetics, "About IMAN," http://www.imancosmetics.com/aboutiman, accessed November 9, 2017.

[34] Taylor Bryant, "How the Beauty Industry Has Failed Black Women," Refinery29.com, February 27, 2016, http://www.refinery29.com/2016/02/103964/black-hair-care-makeup-business, accessed November 15, 2017.

[35] Jennifer Scanlon, "The Gender and Consumer Culture Reader," (NYU Press, 2000), p. 173.

[36] Taylor Bryant, "How the Beauty Industry Has Failed Black Women," Refinery29.com, February 27, 2016, http://www.refinery29.com/2016/02/103964/black-hair-care-makeup-business, accessed November 15, 2017.

[37] Anya Cohen, "Cosmetic & Beauty Products Manufacturing in the US," IBISWorld Industry Report No 32562 (May 2017), IBISWorld, accessed November 9, 2017.

[38] Davey Alba, "It's Embarrassing How Few Black Female Founders Get Funded," Wired Magazine, February 10, 2016, https://www.wired.com/2016/02/its-embarrassing-how-few-black-female-founders-get-funded/, accessed December 27, 2017.

[39] Ibid

[40] Clare O'Connor, "Inside One Woman Investor's Plan To Get Black Female Founders Funding," Forbes Magazine, February 17, 2016, https://www.forbes.com/sites/clareoconnor/2016/02/17/inside-one-woman-investors-plan-to-get-black-female-founders-funding/2/#65848351406a, accessed December 27, 2017.

[41] Kim-Mai Cutler, "A Detailed Breakdown of Racial and Gender Diversity Data Across U.S. Venture Capital Firms," TechCrunch Magazine, October 6, 2015, https://techcrunch.com/2015/10/06/s23p-racial-gender-diversity-venture/, accessed December 27, 2017.

Mented Cosmetics Case Study Assignment Questions

1. Where is there evidence of an underserved market?
2. Would you invest in Mented Cosmetics?
3. How much money do they need?

Notes

1. Spoken Statement by Thomas Edison. *Harper's Monthly*, September 1932. Accessed March 14, 2020. https://quotepark.com/quotes/1857696-thomas-edison-genius-is-one-percent-inspiration-ninety-nine-per/
2. Andrews, Evan. "The Green Book: The Black Travelers' Guide to Jim Crow America." History.com. March 13, 2019. https://www.history.com/news/the-green-book-the-Black-travelers-guide-to-jim-crow-america
3. Sullivan, Tim and Nasir, Noreen. "AP Road Trip: Racial Tensions in America's Sundown Towns." Associated Press. October 14, 2020. https://apnews.com/article/virus-outbreak-race-and-ethnicity-violence-db28a9aaa3b800d91b65dc11a6b12c4c
4. Dennis, Carolyn. "The Growth and Development of the Johnson Publishing Company." Michigan State University, p. 41. 1971. file:///Users/darlene_le/Downloads/MSU_31293000683338.pdf
5. Olito, Frank. "The Rise and Fall of Blockbuster." *Business Insider*. August 20, 2020, www.businessinsider.com/rise-and-fall-of-blockbuster.
6. Ibid.
7. Newman, Rick. "How Netflix (and Blockbuster) Killed Blockbuster." *U.S. News & World Report*. September 23, 2010, www.money.usnews.com/money/blogs/flowchart/2010/09/23/how-netflix-and-blockbuster-killed-blockbuster.
8. Zetlin, Minda. "Blockbuster Could Have Bought Netflix for $50 Million, but the CEO Thought It Was a Joke." *Inc.*, September 20, 2019. www.inc.com/minda-zetlin/netflix-blockbuster-meeting-marc-randolph-reed-hastings-john-antioco.html.
9. "Netflix Now Worth More than ExxonMobil as Value Reaches $196bn." *The Guardian*. April 16, 2020, www.theguardian.com/media/2020/apr/16/netflix-now-worth-more-than-exxonmobil-as-value-reaches-187bn.
10. Blystone, Dan. "The Story of Uber." Investopedia. August 28, 2020. www.investopedia.com/articles/personal-finance/111015/story-uber.asp.
11. McCabe, Noelle. "A Brief History of Jitneys." *Seattle Rep.* March 20, 2020.   www.seattlerep.org/about-us/inside-seattle-rep/a-brief-history-of-jitneys/.
12. Matchar, Emily. "The First African-American to Hold a Patent Invented 'Dry Scouring.'" Smithsonian Institution. February 27, 2019. www.smithsonianmag.com/innovation/first-african-american-hold-patent-invented-dry-scouring-180971394/.
13. Mikorenda, Jerry. "A Bold Man of Color: Thomas L. Jennings and the Proceeds of a Patent." The Gotham Center for New York City History.

January 21, 2016. www.gothamcenter.org/blog/a-bold-man-of-color-thomas-l-jennings-and-the-proceeds-of-a-patent.

14. Schwartz, Jerry. "After Three Years of High Hopes, Air Atlanta Is out of Cash." *The New York Times*. April 12, 1987. www.nytimes .com/1987/04/12/business/founding-father-michael-r-hollis-after-three-years-high-hopes-air-atlanta-cash.html.

15. Wetli, Patty. "Annie Malone Was A Millionaire Black Hair Icon Whose Mansions Were Listed In The Green Book - But Her Legacy Is Often Overlooked." *Block Club Chicago*. February 21, 2019. www.block clubchicago.org/2019/02/21/annie-malones-poro-college-a-green-book-ghost-overshadowed-by-madam-cj-walkers-hair-care-empire/.

16. Antczak, John. "Plan Would Return California Beachfront Taken from Black family in '20s." ABC10. April 9, 2021. https://www.abc10.com/ article/news/nation-world/los-angeles-county-beachfront-property-black-family-return/507-a1e2a4d6-5e1d-4cc3-a09b-47e44b0b8316

4

Entrepreneurship Through Acquisitions

"Wayne doesn't like start-ups. Let someone else do the R&D. He prefers to buy and pay a little more for a concept that has demonstrated some success and may just need help in capital and management."[1]

ONE OF THE most popular courses at Harvard Business School and other graduate business schools is "Entrepreneurship via Acquisition" (EVA). Its popularity over the past decade rivals that of courses about entrepreneurial start-ups. This practice of becoming an entrepreneur through the acquisition of a company has also increased in popularity with Black entrepreneurs.

Davonne Reaves and Jessica Myers are two brilliant Black women who represent the successful use of this entrepreneurial model. In January 2021, as part of a collective, these women paid over $8 million to acquire a hotel.

Reaves and Myers met and became college roommates at Georgia State University in 2006. After graduation, they went their separate ways to pursue professional careers.

Reaves worked in various positions in the hospitality industry starting as a front desk manager at the Hyatt Regency Atlanta, progressing through various event planning, hotel operations, hotel development, and consulting positions. In 2015, she moved to Boston to work as an associate for CHMWarnick, the country's largest third-party hotel asset management company, where she managed portfolios totaling over $1 billion in hotel assets.[2] After working with CHMWarnick for two years, Reaves returned to Atlanta.

Myers worked as a communications and advertising industry professional for CBS and Outfront Media. In 2017, she ventured into real estate investment by buying and selling single-family homes. In 2017, Myers and Reaves reconnected to pursue their lifelong dream of owning commercial real estate in the hotel industry. In 2019, they formed Epic Collective, a commercial real estate investment firm that focuses on investments in multifamily and hotel projects.

According to the National Association of Black Hotel Owners, Operators, and Developers (NABHOOD), African American women own less than 1% of all hotels.[3] Reaves and Myers were acutely aware of this underrepresentation in the hotel and hospitality industry. As Reaves recounted of her personal experience, "I would often see other hotel owners, but they didn't look like me. So that's when I started on a 14-year mission to make a change."[4] The duo set ambitious goals for their company, noting, "Our goal is to own at least 1,000 'doors' and create 221 hotel owners in 2021."[5]

In January 2021, partnering with Nassau Investments, Reaves and Myers made their first investment through Epiq Collective— the $8.3 million acquisition of Home2 Suites by Hilton El Reno, Oklahoma, located about 30 miles west of Oklahoma City. At the age of 33, they earned the distinction of being the youngest African American women to co-own a property in a major hotel chain.

Pros and Cons

There are several advantages in pursuing entrepreneurship via an acquisition. The advantages include the following:

- It may be easier to procure bank or other institutional financing because the acquired company has a history of revenues and profits;
- The company has a known brand, established customers, a financial and operating system in place, trained managers and employees— all tools with which to grow and build value;

- An existing business can be updated and improved more easily to promote faster growth and enhanced value; and
- The potential for higher rates of return and lower relative risk compared to a startup; startups tend to have relatively high failure rates, while approximately 80% of acquisitions show profitability within a few years.[6]

The disadvantages of acquisition entrepreneurship include the following:

- The buyer must invest 10–20% of the total purchase price if she is to get seller and bank financing;
- Coming into an already established organizational culture could lead to disagreements and clashes regarding management approach or style;
- Potential for staff defections as key management and employees may leave after a company is acquired;
- Expected synergies may not come to fruition;
- Expected assets valuations may be less than forecasted;
- Costs, particularly during the leadership transition and the years following, may rise rather than fall as planned; and
- Customers may leave.

The Acquisition Process

Acquiring a business involves the following steps:

1. Raising capital to finance the search phase;
2. Identifying acquisition prospects;
3. Deal negotiation and closing the deal; and
4. Transitioning into new ownership.

Financing the Search Phase

The first step in acquiring a business is the search to identify prospects for acquisition. This involves identifying and vetting potential buying opportunities. An entrepreneur needs to decide whether to partner or do the search alone, where to base the search geographically, which industries to target, what will be the acquisition criteria (such as manufacturing, service, or distribution company), and how much money to raise for the search and the acquisition. During the search phase, which can last 6 to 12 months, an entrepreneur needs to cover living expenses and other search costs such as office space, travel, and due diligence costs. These costs can vary from $300,000 to $400,000 for a single entrepreneur and $600,000 to $700,000 for a partnership.[7] Entrepreneurs can finance the search themselves or through a search fund.

Self-Financed Search Entrepreneurs may choose to self-finance a search, using their own resources to pay for all the costs incurred during the search phase. These resources may incorporate the recruitment of friends and business acquaintances to serve as an informal advising network to help with the vetting of potential acquisition targets, due diligence, and deal negotiation. Self-funding a search provides more control over and flexibility with the decision-making process as the entrepreneur does not have investors to answer to when making decisions concerning the location, industry, business size, or other elements of the target acquisition. A self-funded search means that an entrepreneur may be able to retain a higher percentage of ownership of the acquired business, as they do not have to give up preferred equity had there been investors involved in the search. On the downside, entrepreneurs face the risk of losing their entire investment if an acquisition falls through.

Traditional Search Fund A search fund is a financial vehicle established to raise funds from advising investors (usually 5–15) to finance the identification, acquisition, and management of a company.[8] These investors provide initial capital to cover the entrepreneur's salary and other expenses incurred during the search. In return for their financing, the investors receive preferred equity in the acquired company based on their contribution to the fund and the right of first refusal to invest additional funds in the company during the acquisition stage.

They serve as an advisory group providing the entrepreneur with expertise and access to a professional network to assist with the sourcing of potential deals. The entrepreneur faces minimal financial risk as all the expenses incurred during the search phase are financed by outside investors. However, for this funding, the entrepreneur not only gives up equity ownership in the company but also potential control over key decisions. The investors may demand the power to make most of the important decisions, such as management compensation or the level of credit extended to customers.

Sponsored Search Fund[9]   This type of search fund involves an exclusive arrangement between an entrepreneur and the firm that provides all the required search and acquisition capital and becomes the controlling shareholder. In addition to financial resources, the sponsoring firm provides the entrepreneur with office and infrastructure support to conduct the search.

Crowdfunded Search   These types of searches are undertaken on an online platform that connects entrepreneurs looking for capital to accredited investors seeking to make an investment. Investors receive preferred equity and/or convertible debt in return for their search capital contribution and common and/or preferred for acquisition capital.[10]

Identifying Potential Acquisition Prospects

Once financing for the search is secured, the next phase involves identifying (sourcing) potential acquisition targets. In addition to using their own networks—investors, professional, and personal acquaintances—entrepreneurs can use business brokers and intermediaries to identify acquisition opportunities. Another option is searching for proprietary deals, that is, opportunities that are not being marketed actively. This search process is time-consuming and can be quite grueling, possibly necessitating contacting hundreds or thousands of business owners to identify the right business to buy. This process could take from 12 to 24 months.

Deal Negotiation and Closing the Deal

Once a potential acquisition is identified, in most cases, an investment memorandum is sent to investors prior to a letter of intent (LOI) being signed. The entrepreneur, with assistance from advisors and investors, undertakes the due diligence process to confirm the accuracy of all data and information, and to ensure that all outstanding questions and issues are answered and addressed. A purchase agreement is negotiated and agreed upon, while funding for the transaction is finalized. Investors in the search fund have first right of refusal to contribute additional capital for acquisition of the company. The entrepreneur is responsible for securing additional capital from the existing investor base or from new sources to secure all the funding needed to make the acquisition.

There are several financing options available to entrepreneurs to buy a company including:

- Use of personal funds such as savings, or any other funds that an entrepreneur has available;
- Seller financing where a loan is provided by the seller of the business to the buyer to purchase the company;
- Loans from traditional banks or lending services that specialize in acquisitions in a particular market or industry;
- Loans from the Small Business Administration (SBA), including the 7A loan program, which are available for buyers that meet size and other requirements;
- Private Equity (P/E) investment funds from P/E firms; and
- Investments from high-net-worth individuals.

Reginald F. Lewis

Reggie Lewis is arguably the most successful Black entrepreneur to use the acquisition model. His net worth in 1993 was $1.4 billion, making him one of the wealthiest people in the country.[11] His primary success came from the purchase of Beatrice International Foods, the largest overseas leverage buyout in 1987. This acquisition resulted in his company, TLC Group, becoming the first Black-owned business to exceed a billion dollars in revenue.

Reginald F. Lewis was born in Baltimore, Maryland, and grew up in a middle-class suburb outside the city. He started his first business at the age of 10—a delivery service for a local African American newspaper—which he grew by hiring other children to work for him. Within two years, he increased his customer base and revenue and sold the business at a profit.[12] He attended the Dunbar High school in Baltimore, where he proved to be an exceptional athlete—he was a shortstop for the varsity baseball team, a forward on the basketball team, and quarterback of the football team, serving as captain of all three teams.[13] He won a football scholarship to attend the Virginia State University (VSU), a historically Black college/university (HBCU).

During his senior year at VSU, Lewis was admitted to a summer program at the Harvard Law School funded by the Rockefeller Foundation, aimed at introducing Black students to the legal profession. He performed so well that at the end of the program Harvard invited him to attend the law school the following fall semester, making him at that time the only person in the school's 148-year-history to be admitted before applying.[14] Upon graduation from law school, Lewis started work as a corporate lawyer at a New York law firm. After working for two years and realizing that he would not make partner, Lewis, with a few partners, established the first African American law firm on Wall Street. The law firm specialized in corporate law and developed expertise in structuring investments in minority-owned businesses.

Wanting to be more directly involved in deals, Lewis established TLC Group, L.P. in 1983. After several unsuccessful acquisition bids, he was able to purchase his first company with a $22.5 million leveraged buyout of McCall Pattern Company, a sewing and pattern publishing firm. He streamlined operations and increased marketing. These actions led to two of the most profitable years in its history. In 1987, he sold the company for $90 million, making a 90-to-1 return on his investment.[15]

Lewis was frustrated with the lack of publicity and credit that he received for his work on the McCall deal, so he sought public relations help to increase his exposure in the financial sector. Rene "Butch" Meily, who would become Lewis's PR manager, recalls:

> Reg told me his problem. He'd recently sold an old-line home sewing pattern company, McCall Pattern, but in *The New York Times* article about the sale, the current managers never acknowledged the work he'd done turning the company around and even disparaged him. So, Reg being the kind of guy he was, looked up the reporter's number in the phone book, which was something you could do in those days, and woke him up at 6 a.m. to yell at him. The reporter's name was Dan Cuff and I happened to know him. Accordingly, I reassured him, "Don't worry Reg, I know the guy. I'll set up an interview for you and we'll get your version of McCall out . . . Reg had been painfully precise about what he wanted—the message was a 90-to-1 return for his investors, no mention about his being African American, just a photo.[16]

Meily was able to get an article published on the front page of the *New York Times*, with the headline "90-to-One Return for Investors" and a photo of Lewis smiling confidently. The *Times* article made Lewis a celebrity on Wall Street and was instrumental in getting him the attention that was crucial for his next deal. According to Meily:

> The *Times* piece turned Reg into a minor celebrity in Wall Street circles. But at that time, I had no idea what it would eventually lead to. Reg had met Michael Milken a few times and discussed doing the McCall acquisition with him but nothing had materialized. Yet according to Loida (Lewis's wife), Milken called Reg early that morning after reading the Times story to congratulate him and invite him to Drexel's Beverly Hills office for a meeting. The timing was fortuitous. It happened that Reg was already working on a much bigger deal. A billion-dollar bid for one of the largest corporations in the world, Beatrice International.[17]

Beatrice Holding Corporation was looking to sell its international unit comprised of 64 companies operating in 31 countries throughout Europe, Canada, Latin America, Asia, and Australia. Several large financial firms, including Citicorp and Shearson & Lehman, were interested in participating in the auction. The sheer size of the deal and the fact that Lewis was a relative unknown in the investment community made it important for him to partner with a large, established, and well-known firm to ensure that the TLC deal had a significant shot at succeeding. Lewis partnered with Michael Milken, the legendary junk bond king and partner with Drexel Burhnam Lambert, to arrange financing for a leveraged buyout.

Charles Clarkson, Lewis's law partner, recounted the deal that TLC structured: "We were talking about how much we should bid for Beatrice. We made a first bid of $950 million and then increased it to $985 million. We may have been bidding against ourselves, but Reg had put his whole life into the auction, and if he hadn't pulled it off, it's hard to tell what would have happened."[18]

After a meeting at which Lewis presented the TLC bid, Milken noted, "From that point on, all of our interaction convinced me that he was the right person for the transaction. . . . My feeling was that he knew Beatrice better than I knew Beatrice. In fact, he knew it better than the people who ran it."[19]

With the backing of Drexel Burham Lambert, TLC Group presented a $985 million leveraged buyout bid and won the auction, beating out major competitors, including Citicorp and the huge French food company BonGrain. At the time, the Beatrice deal was the largest leveraged buyout of off-shore assets in history and made the TLC Group the biggest Black-owned business in the country. After taking over TLC Beatrice International, Lewis paid down approximately $430 million of the company's debt. Five years later, the company had over $1.8 billion in revenue, making it the largest snack food, beverage, and grocery conglomerate in the country.

Lewis became an inspiration and role model for generations of Black entrepreneurs and business leaders. His biography, *Why Should White Guys Have All the Fun?*, was published in 1995, becoming a best seller. It is still considered a must read for aspiring entrepreneurs and business leaders. One of his admirers is Kenneth Chenault, the former chairman/CEO of American Express, who observed, "There is no doubt that Reginald Lewis's success paved the way for me and many others, and I think that really is the test and demonstration of real leadership."[20]

Reginald Lewis died of a brain tumor on January 19, 1993, at the age of 50.

His legacy speaks volumes. The Reginald F. Lewis International Law Center was the first building at Harvard University named after an African American. The Reginald F. Lewis Foundation is among the largest African American private foundations in the world. According to its website, the organization has given $30 million in grants since its inception.

He began his philanthropy with a $1 million donation to Howard University, the same year that he closed the Beatrice deal. Five years later, his donation to Harvard Law school of $3 million was the largest in the school's history. His undergraduate alma mater, VSU, received their largest donation of $1.5 million from his foundation. VSU is now the home of the Reginald F. Lewis School of Business.

Introduction of the Case Study

This case follows an African American entrepreneur through the process of sourcing a potential acquisition, valuing a company, and securing the funding to purchase the company. This entrepreneur must decide if he should close the deal and which financing term sheet to accept.

HARVARD | BUSINESS | SCHOOL

9-317-061
REV: AUGUST 3, 2017

STEVEN ROGERS

GREG WHITE

Earl Gordon - Eastern Circle

It was approaching midnight on Sunday and Earl Gordon had to a make a final decision before going to bed. Should he proceed with the purchase of Eastern Circle? It had taken him several months to source, evaluate, negotiate, and structure the acquisition and raise financing for this company, and now he had to make a go or no-go decision.

Was this the right deal and was this the right time? Was he really ready to purchase and lead a company as the CEO? Was Eastern Circle really worth $11.0 million? What could go wrong and how could these risks be mitigated? Which term sheet should he accept? If he successfully executed his strategy despite the risks, was there enough upside to this transaction?

Background

The seeds of entrepreneurship were planted early in Earl's life but a powerful inspiration came during his sophomore year in college while reading Reginald Lewis' autobiography, *"Why Should White Guys Have All the Fun?"* Reginald Lewis was a highly successful deal maker who made history as the first African American to purchase an almost billion dollar company. It was the Beatrice International LBO. Mr. Lewis' success inspired many other African Americans, including Earl Gordon, to pursue entrepreneurship through the acquisition of an existing company.

In college, Earl majored in Finance and International Business at the Stern School of Business at New York University. Unlike most of his classmates, he had no long term desire to work in a large corporation. Instead he had a burning desire to be the CEO and owner of his own company, where he could exercise his leadership skills, grow an enterprise, employ people and create personal wealth.

Post College

Immediately after college, he worked in both investment banking and private equity for several years where he gained first-hand experience evaluating, structuring, and closing complex deals. He found the work challenging and intellectually fulfilling but he wanted to be more than an investor or broker. "The best part of my job in private equity was working with the portfolio companies after the investment was made. I noticed that while the firm's partners made the decision as to whether the firm invested in a specific company, ultimately, they relied on the entrepreneurs to develop the growth plan,

HBS Senior Lecturer Steven Rogers and independent researcher Greg White prepared this case. It was reviewed and approved before publication by a company designate. Funding for the development of this case was provided by Harvard Business School and not by the company. Certain details have been disguised. HBS cases are developed solely as the basis for class discussion. Cases are not intended to serve as endorsements, sources of primary data, or illustrations of effective or ineffective management.

make the key operational decisions, and hire and motivate the right team". Earl developed his entrepreneurship plan so that he could transition from a finance role to an operating role. He purposely built a strong business network and lived frugally in order to save money and build his capital base.

After six years on Wall Street, Earl matriculated to Harvard Business School where he was an active member of the African American Student Union and excelled academically. During his first year, he finished in the top 10% of his class garnering first year honors. During his second year he volunteered as a tutor in Finance to 1st year students, and strategically selected classes to expand and maximize his learning. "When I went to business school, I knew that I wanted to be prepared to take on an operational role in the future so I selected elective classes and other activities in order to expand my skillset beyond finance and increase my knowledge of marketing, operations and leadership". One of his most valuable leadership roles at Harvard Business School was serving as Co-President of the African American Student Union.

After Business School

After business school, Earl chose not to return to the financial services industry and turned down several potentially lucrative offers. He decided not to return to Wall Street because of his long term entrepreneurship plan. He understood that this career path was far riskier than traditional post-MBA career paths and it could result in complete failure. He was willing to accept this risk and the potential downside. "If I failed, I thought that I could always find a job. I was not going to starve. Regret is much harder to live with than failure" is how he explained his decision to his friends and family.

He knew this pivotal decision meant that he had to be comfortable with the possibility that he would, in the short run, make less money and hold a less prestigious career position. He often joked with his friends that this path would not allow him many bragging rights at his 5th HBS reunion, however he was convinced this was the right path for his long term happiness and career fulfillment.

Based on an honest assessment of his skills and his desire to one day run a company he knew he had to gain hands-on operational experience managing people, improving processes, growing sales, having direct involvement in a firm's strategic direction, and managing a P&L.

Between 2008 and 2014 Earl worked at four different start-up companies, Kidrobot, Quidsi, Kikin, and littleBits. He was fortunate that one of those companies, Quidsi, was sold to Amazon.com and he experienced a liquidity event. However, one of the lessons he learned through that experience was that unless you are on the founding team of your company when it goes public or sells to a major strategic buyer, the potential upside may be limited and while lucrative it was not "life changing". One of his future goals was to achieve financial independence by buying, leading and eventually selling.

While building up his operational experience he also served for several years on the board of exalt youth, a Brooklyn-based non-profit that helps juveniles (primarily minorities) between 15-19 years of age who've been involved in the criminal justice system.

The Search Fund Decision

In March 2014, Earl decided to leave his job at littleBits and pursue his purchase of a company on a full-time basis. His first key decision was whether he should raise money from investors to capitalize his search fund. If raised, this capital would be used to pay costs associated with pursing potential acquisition opportunities, due diligence costs, and potentially funds for Earl to pay himself a modest salary until he closed a deal. In exchange for their investment, Earl would grant these investors the first right to invest in Earl's deal and final approval over the transaction.   In order to weigh the pros and cons of raising a search fund, Earl spoke to several entrepreneurs who had used both funded and unfunded search fund vehicles to pursue an acquisition.

The feedback from these entrepreneurs was mixed.   On one hand, entrepreneurs who had raised "funded search" funds valued the guidance, financial support, and discipline offered by their investors. Having funds to invest in due diligence and being able to draw a modest salary allowed the entrepreneurs to more patiently pursue a deal and having committed investors enabled them to have more credibility with business brokers and company owners.   Especially for entrepreneurs with spouses and/or kids, having some form of predictable income was often a requirement to making the decision to become a search fund entrepreneur.   The entrepreneurs with funded searches also shared the major drawbacks with being sponsored -- they tended to have very narrowly prescribed deal criteria which limited the type of opportunities they could pursue.   Sometimes search fund investors prevented entrepreneurs from buying companies because of their size, location, industry, and a myriad of other reasons.

After careful consideration, Earl decided to pursue an acquisition without a funded search fund.   "I had stashed money away for years and had saved enough to give myself some time to find a deal and pay for the due diligence (legal, accounting, etc.) and also cover my day-to-day overhead.   At the time I was making this decision I wasn't married, I didn't have any kids, and didn't own any real estate -- so my commitments and fixed overhead were minimal.   In addition, through my professional and personal network pre- and post-HBS I had developed a group of trusted advisors and mentors who could not only act as my de facto search fund board but could also be potential investors in future deals.   Also, I was optimistic that if I spent a year diligently pursuing a deal and was unsuccessful, I would hopefully still be in a strong position to raise a traditional funded search fund later on if I could demonstrate to investors what I was able to achieve on my own with limited funds."   He concluded that although it was the riskier path, he still had a good probability of getting a deal done with an unfunded search fund because he would be highly motivated to be efficient with both his time and money by putting his own capital at risk and also be able to expand the universe of potential deal opportunities without the limitations inherent in traditional search fund investors' strict, narrow, and sometimes inflexible deal criteria   He wanted the flexibility to pursue a good deal regardless of size, geography, and industry.

The Hunt Begins

In June 2014, he established Fenton Avenue Capital and began his search to buy a company.   His first step was to develop his deal criteria (**Exhibit 1**) followed by proactive action to generate deal flow. Based on his conversations with other entrepreneurs who had successfully purchased companies, he assumed it would take him between 12 to 24 months to find the right deal.   These entrepreneurs shared with him the importance of networking and developing broad deal networks to identify an attractive deal.   In July 2014, he attended a conference for M&A Advisors in Chicago with the hope of developing relationships with business brokers who would in the future show him opportunities that met his criteria.   He was concerned about the amount of time it would take to find a deal and was eager to begin the process of connecting with business owners looking to sell their companies.   "I considered the conference in Chicago a 'practice run', but I got lucky and found a compelling deal from one of the brokers I met there".

The Opportunity - Eastern Circle

At the conference, after being shown a deal, Earl always responded with a list of insightful and thoughtful questions about the industry, the market, the financials, etc. His initial due diligence checklist for Eastern Circle is found in **Exhibit 2**. He thinks the brokers treated him as a serious buyer because of the thoroughness of his due diligence questions as well as the fact that he made a credible case that he could secure financing and close the deal.

In August 2014, a broker that he met at the Chicago conference brought Earl a deal (Eastern Circle) that seemed to meet his criteria and, based on preliminary due diligence, was worth aggressively pursuing. After meeting with the company's owner and describing his background and plan to finance the purchase, the seller agreed to accept a term sheet and an $11.0 million purchase price for 100% of the company's stock. The Seller also agreed to accept a $2.2 million seller note as part of the financing deal. Earl had found a deal, negotiated a term sheet; and now he had to secure financing.

Search for funding

In order to secure $8.8 million in funding, Earl knew he had to prepare a detailed and compelling investment memorandum that highlighted the attributes of the deal and allowed potential investors to understand and quantify the potential return and risks of the deal. Earl spent four weeks researching and drafting this memorandum that described the company, industry, and outlined his financial projections. A summary of his investment memo is attached. His investment banking and private equity experience were invaluable as he had previously prepared similar deal books for his clients and investment committees.

Earl's second major step was identifying potential investors. He relied on extensive research and discussions with his network of entrepreneurs to generate a target list of investors to contact. Whenever possible, he secured an introduction from a trusted source. However, in many cases he made cold calls to investment firms on this list. Over the next three months, Earl circulated his investment memorandum to over 30 institutional investors and high net worth individuals. Whenever a potential investor declined to invest, Earl always asked for a referral to another investor who might be interested. At the same time, he continued his due diligence on the company and verified the information he received from the Seller and other sources.

Several investors requested additional information and, after four months of multiple meetings and conference calls, Earl secured two term sheets to invest in Eastern Circle. A copy of these two term sheets from Investor Group A and Investor Group B are found in **Exhibit A-3a** and **Exhibit A-3b**. Earl struggled to compare the two term sheets because the structure and terms were very different. There were aspects of each term sheet he found attractive and conversely both term sheets had conditions and terms he did not like. However, after extensive negotiations, both investors made it clear, that the current term sheets were their best and final offer and he had to accept or reject the financing terms as offered.

It was time for Earl to a make a final decision. Should he proceed with purchasing Eastern Circle? If yes, which investor should he partner with to launch his entrepreneurial career?

Exhibit 1   Deal Criteria

Fenton Avenue Capital is an entrepreneurial investment firm seeking to acquire and grow one high-quality U.S. based private company.

> $1.5MM+ EBITDA
> 10%+ Operating Margins
> History of Profitability
> Significant Recurring Revenue
> Headquartered in the U.S.

> Healthcare & Healthcare Services
> Niche Manufacturing
> Consumer Products & Services (incl. Ecommerce)
> Business Services & Outsourcing

Source: Company documents.

Exhibit 2   Preliminary Information Request List

Financials

1. Audited financial statements for the fiscal years ended 2012, 2013 and 2014 (draft version if that is all that is available)
2. Management Letters from accountants for the last 3 years
3. Monthly financial statements (Income Statement, Balance Sheet and Cash Flow Statement) for fiscal years ended 2013 and YTD 2014 (in electronic format, if available)
4. Financial projections for 2015 - 2017 (and beyond, if available) on a monthly basis
5. Details on any material changes in accounting policies over the last three years
6. List of all assets and liabilities on the books but not related to the business (including all non-operating assets to be written off)
7. Detail of any off-balance sheet liabilities
8. Detail of any expenses of a non-recurring nature for 2012, 2013 and YTD 2014
9. Detail of other income and expense for 2012, 2013 and YTD 2014
10. List of material acquisitions or divestitures
11. Detail on payroll/wages & salaries and bonuses for 2012, 2013 and YTD 2014
12. Details on marketing/sales expense line items for 2012, 2013 and YTD 2014
     a. Advertising
     b. Auto Expense
     c. Commissions
     d. Meals & Entertainment
     e. Seminars
     f. Telephone
     g. Trade Shows
     h. Travel

Revenue

1. Sales and gross profit by product for 2005, 2006, 2007, 2008, 2009, 2010, 2011, 2012, 2013 and YTD 2014
2. Sales and gross profit by customer for 2005, 2006, 2007, 2008, 2009, 2010, 2011, 2012, 2013 and YTD 2014
3. Unit sales by product line for 2005, 2006, 2007, 2008, 2009, 2010, 2011, 2012, 2013 and YTD 2014
4. Schedule of sales returns, discounts, and other customer credits for 2005, 2006, 2007, 2008, 2009, 2010, 2011, 2012, 2013, and YTD 2014
5. Detail on booked orders for 2014 and pipeline customers for 2015 – 2017
6. Detail of any sales made under license or royalty agreements
7. Descriptions of policies for pricing, sales returns, discounts, allowances and rebates

Indebtedness and Liabilities

1. Copies of bank agreements and all amendments/waivers, if any
2. Copies of shareholder/employee note agreements and all related documentation
3. Schedule of accounts payable and accrued liabilities
4. Description of any rebate or commission arrangements

Inventory and COGS

1. Schedule of inventory by type (raw materials, WIP, finished goods) for 2012, 2013 and YTD 2014
2. Description of inventory on consignment or consigned to others

Management, Labor, Benefits

1. Details of existing employment agreements, bonus and other compensation plans for Eastern Circle senior management (including amounts paid in 2013 and 2014 and expected for 2015)
2. Details on incentive compensation for marketing/sales groups
3. Customer coverage list by salesperson for 2005, 2006, 2007, 2008, 2009, 2010, 2011, 2012, 2013 and YTD 2014

Fixed Assets and Real Estate

1. Schedule of real estate owned or leased, including address, age, square footage, lease termination date, extension provisions and lease payments
2. Schedule of all vehicles owned or leased, including age
3. Detailed schedule of all capital expenditures for 2012, 2013 and 2014

Other

1. Copies of product brochures and marketing materials
2. Detailed organizational chart and list of employees, including date of hire
3. List of current officers and directors
4. Resumes of senior management team

Legal

1. Separate due diligence list will be forthcoming

Source: Company documents.

Appendix A

Confidential

Eastern Circle Industries

Manufacturer & distributor of a diverse range of niche fabricated steel products

CONFIDENTIAL INVESTMENT MEMORANDUM

DECEMBER 2014

FENTON AVENUE CAPITAL

Company Overview

Eastern Circle is a manufacturer and distributor of a diverse range of niche fabricated steel products and was founded in 1978 in California. The initial primary focus of Eastern Circle was manufacturing two products, steel gates and corrals, which filled a need for the agricultural and livestock industries that were thriving in the Central Valley region of California. Over the past 36 years, the Company has added wine barrel racks, harvest bins and vineyard trailers to its product assortment to meet the demands of the wine industry. Today, Eastern Circle is the leading U.S. manufacturer of barrel racks and other steel equipment used in winemaking. The Company's agricultural products, water bottle rack and warehouse/storage businesses offer significant growth potential.

Steel Barrel Racks (Wine, Beer and Spirits)

Ownership and Reason for Sale

Tony Michaelson (65 years old) acquired Eastern Circle in 1995 along with other shareholders. Since buying out his partners, Tony has been the sole shareholder of Eastern Circle, which is registered as a C-Corporation in California. He would like to sell the Company in order to spend more time with his family. He also believes Eastern Circle would benefit from more sophisticated management. Tony has indicated he is open to and interested in helping with various projects to help grow the Company on a regular consulting basis as well as adequate transition support after the closing of the transaction. The letter of intent includes a three (3) year consulting and non-compete agreement as part of the transaction.

Business Description

Customers

In FY 2014, approximately 90% of Eastern Circle revenue came from wine related products (wine barrel racks and vineyard equipment). The Company has over 600 customers, including a significant number of the top wine producers in the United States. In most cases, Eastern Circle is the exclusive barrel rack supplier to these wine producers. In addition, 75% of Eastern Circle revenue is generated by customers in California and significant opportunities exist to expand into other states. There are over 4,000 vineyards located outside of California and the beer and whiskey/bourbon industries are headquartered in Illinois, Missouri and Kentucky.

Sales and Marketing

Eastern Circle sells its products primarily through a network of sales representatives. The Company employs several full-time sales representatives assigned to specific territories (with the Key Accounts Manager covering specific customers across geographies) and independent manufacturer representatives that cover territories outside of California. The Company's website directs potential customers to contact the sales representative for their geographic territory, and provides a picture, email and a phone number for each sales representative.

Despite Eastern Circle's strong revenue growth, the Company lacks a well-conceived sales, marketing and business development program. In conversations with the current owner, it was very evident that he is stretched between managing the day to day operations of the Company, managing marketing as well as acting as Sales Manager.

Competitors

The steel barrel rack industry is relatively small and Eastern Circle is the dominant manufacturer of new steel barrel racks (the Company does not participate in the refurbished barrel rack market). Most of the Company's competitors either sell both new and refurbished barrel racks or the barrel rack business is a smaller portion of a multi-product steel fabrication portfolio. Eastern Circle is a very small player in the agricultural products industry. An overview of Eastern Circle's competitors is presented in **Table A-1**.

Table A-1   Competitors

Primary Competitors	Products
Titan Rack	Barrel Racks (New)
Rack & Maintenance Source	Barrel Racks (New + Refurbished)
Topco	Barrel Racks (New + Refurbished)
Bonar Plastics (Snyder Industries)	Barrel Racks (New)
Rackit	Barrel Racks (New)
Behlen Country	Agricultural Products
Powder River	Agricultural Products
Priefert Manufacturing	Agricultural Products

Source: Sponsor interviews as part of due diligence.

Information Technology

Eastern Circle uses QuickBooks for its accounting and financial reporting system, Sage ACT! for sales contact and CRM management and Microsoft Excel for data entry and analysis. All entries into QuickBooks are manual. Inputs on the revenue side come from customer invoices, paper checks, credit cards and wired funds. Inputs on the cost side come from paper bills from suppliers, corporate credit card expenses and payroll processing.

The Company is in the process of installing a Salesforce-based CRM and order-taking database. Historically, the Company used email, paper print outs and manual data entry into QuickBooks for tracking customer orders.

Management and Employees

Eastern Circle currently has 15 full-time and 25 part-time non-union employees. Eastern Circle's employees have significant experience with niche steel fabrication and the winemaking and agricultural industries. The Company has a strong core management team with long term commitment to the Company. On average, each member of the management team has been at Eastern Circle for over 19 years. Many of the production workers have also been with the Company for over 13 years.

The management team has developed and implemented the Company's expanded product line and increased sales footprint. Each member of management takes a great deal of pride in the growth and accomplishments of Eastern Circle and is committed to maintaining the growth of the business going forward. The culture that management has created, of fabricating superior products and providing excellent customer service, has had a positive impact on all employees.

Post-closing, the current Eastern Circle management team, with the exception of the current owner who will work to transition out of the business, will be joined by Earl A. Gordon, the Managing Partner of the Sponsor. Earl A. Gordon will become CEO of Eastern Circle, responsible for business development, marketing, finance and HR. See **Exhibit A-2** for a copy of Earl's resume.

The Company has experienced very low personnel turnover. Eastern Circle provides stable employment with comprehensive benefits and has maintained a loyal, hardworking staff. Benefits offered to employees include healthcare insurance, a 401(k) plan, paid holidays and family/maternity leave. Management expects to be able to hire the workforce necessary to support its projected growth.

Litigation

Eastern Circle is not a defendant in any material litigation, nor is management aware of any material claims pending or which may be asserted against the Company.

Financial Review

Financial Summary

In FY 2014, approximately 82% of revenue came from wine barrel racks sales with the balance of revenue from vineyard equipment (8%), agricultural products (5%), brewery and distillery racks (4%) and water bottle racks (1%). The Company has nearly tripled wine barrel rack revenue since 2011 and has increased vineyard equipment revenue more than tenfold.

From FY 2010 to FY 2014 the Company's revenue grew at a cumulative annual growth rate ("CAGR") of 26%.

Figure A-1   Eastern Circle Revenue and EBITDA (dollars in millions)

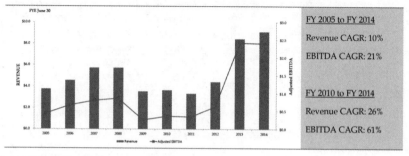

Source: Company documents.

Historical and Forecasted Financial Performance

The following statements of operating results provide an overview of the historical and projected financial performance for Eastern Circle for the fiscal year ended June 30, 2012 through the fiscal year ending June 30, 2019. Also included are LTM results through September 30, 2014. Note that the financials presented for the periods ending September 30, 2014 and earlier come directly from the Company and the financials for the periods ending June 30, 2016 and later, along with pro forma June 30, 2015 results, were prepared by the Sponsor.

Table A-2   Eastern Circle Historical and Forecasted Financial Performance (dollars in thousands)

	For The Fiscal Year End June 30,			LTM 9/30/14	For The Fiscal Year End June 30,				
	2012	2013	2014		Pro Forma 2015	Projected 2016	Projected 2017	Projected 2018	Projected 2019
Net Revenue	$ 4,422	$ 8,450	$ 9,115	$ 8,662	$ 9,109	$ 9,733	$ 10,696	$ 12,126	$ 14,051
Growth %	*32.9%*	*91.1%*	*7.9%*	*n/a*	*(0.1%)*	*6.8%*	*9.9%*	*13.4%*	*15.9%*
Cost of Goods Sold	$ 2,223	$ 3,995	$ 4,166	$ 3,906	$ 4,270	$ 4,562	$ 5,014	$ 5,684	$ 6,586
Gross Profit	2,198	4,455	4,949	4,756	4,839	5,171	5,682	6,442	7,465
Gross Margin %	*49.7%*	*52.7%*	*54.3%*	*54.9%*	*53.1%*	*53.1%*	*53.1%*	*53.1%*	*53.1%*
Operating Expenses	$ 2,073	$ 3,738	$ 4,297	$ 4,440	$ 2,935	$ 2,883	$ 3,117	$ 3,370	$ 3,643
% of Net Revenue	*46.9%*	*44.2%*	*47.1%*	*51.3%*	*32.2%*	*29.6%*	*29.1%*	*27.8%*	*25.9%*
EBITDA	$ 125	$ 717	$ 651	$ 317	$ 1,904	$ 2,287	$ 2,565	$ 3,073	$ 3,822
% of Net Revenue	*2.8%*	*8.5%*	*7.1%*	*3.7%*	*20.9%*	*23.5%*	*24.0%*	*25.3%*	*27.2%*
EBITDA Adjustments	509	1,701	1,748	1,778	195	-	-	-	-
Adjusted EBITDA	**$ 634**	**$ 2,418**	**$ 2,399**	**$ 2,095**	**$ 2,100**	**$ 2,287**	**$ 2,565**	**$ 3,073**	**$ 3,822**
% of Net Revenue	*14.3%*	*28.6%*	*26.3%*	*24.2%*	*23.1%*	*23.5%*	*24.0%*	*25.3%*	*27.2%*
Capital Expenditures	$ 78	$ 388	$ 160	$ 164	$ 100	$ 300	$ 100	$ 100	$ 100
% of Net Revenue	*1.8%*	*4.6%*	*1.8%*	*1.9%*	*1.1%*	*3.1%*	*0.9%*	*0.8%*	*0.7%*

Source: Company documents.

Discussion of Financial Results and Projections

Revenue – Eastern Circle experienced significant growth beginning in FY 2012. Growth has been driven by increasing wine and agricultural industry demand for barrel racks and vineyard equipment as well as a renewed Company focus on customer relationship management which has yielded positive results, with more prospective customers motivated to upgrade older equipment in their warehouses.

Revenue growth in FY 2012, FY 2013 and FY 2014 was driven both by existing and new customers

Gross Profit – Gross margins increased steadily from FY 2012 to FY 2014. The Company targets keeping steel costs below 40% of revenue and direct labor costs below 20% of revenue. The Sponsor believes that a small amount of margin expansion is possible through better inventory management and through supplier negotiations.

Operating Expenses –Historical operating expense as a percentage of net revenue is overstated because of owner-related expenses and bonus distributions. Operating expenses are expected to reduce to 32% of net revenue in FY 2015 because of the removal of owner's expenses.

Capital Expenditures – With the exception of an investment in an ERP system, the Sponsor anticipates capital expenditures will remain at relatively low levels, as they have historically.

Adjustments to Operating Results

The Company has incurred specific expenses related to the current owner. These items have been added back to the historical and forecasted operating results of Eastern Circle to better present the true historical financial performance of the Company and illustrate the results under the Sponsor's ownership. These expenses are being reviewed and verified by a third party accounting firm as part of the quality of earnings due diligence review of the Company

Working Capital

Eastern Circle's business model exhibits favorable working capital characteristics. Approximately 70% of orders are paid with credit card and 25% paid via checks. Payment is usually received within 30 days of shipment.

Valuation Creation Opportunities

The Sponsor plans to grow Eastern Circle by optimizing its sales and manufacturing functions. Eastern Circle's brand name, customer database, and sales/marketing capabilities can be leveraged to expand into related niche markets. Similarly, as the Company grows, the Sponsor plans to make investments in sales staff to establish market positions in new product/industry segments, which may also include buying small businesses that have customer lists or manufacturing expertise in a particular category. The Sponsor's goal is to have the wine, beer and spirits industry's best-in-class steel fabrication facility with the ability to be a one-stop-shop for products related to winemaking and storage as well as beer and distilled spirts production and storage.

Growth Initiatives

Going forward, the Sponsor has identified a number of initiatives that could increase revenue beyond the Company's current projections. Additional revenue and operational efficiency can be obtained from:

- Expanding the Company's geographic sales footprint;

- Developing a formal database and sales process for barrel racks;

- Exploring sales of other niche fabricated steel products;

- Emphasizing vineyard equipment sales by promoting the Company as a one-stop-shop to wineries and vineyards;

- Increasing sales in the Company's other product categories (agricultural products, water bottle racks and warehouse/general storage) by targeting customers outside of wine, beer and spirits; and

- Expanding sales to international markets.

Investment Analysis

The Sponsor believes an investment in Eastern Circle will offer an investor superior financial returns, as discussed below.

Scenario Analysis

To help investors understand the return expectations for Eastern Circle, the Sponsor has developed three sets of projections: base case, upside case, and downside case.

Base Case

The base case scenario envisions the Sponsor being able to drive double digit revenue growth via increased sales across several categories. Margins improve slightly over time. The base case projections are presented in **Table A-3**.

Table A-3   Eastern Circle Base Case Projections and Returns (dollars in thousands)

	Fiscal Year Ending June 30,				
	2015	**2016**	**2017**	**2018**	**2019**
Net Revenue	$ 9,109	$ 9,733	$ 10,696	$ 12,126	$ 14,051
Growth %	*(0.1%)*	*6.8%*	*9.9%*	*13.4%*	*15.9%*
Gross Profit	$ 4,839	$ 5,171	$ 5,682	$ 6,442	$ 7,465
Gross Margin %	*53.1%*	*53.1%*	*53.1%*	*53.1%*	*53.1%*
EBITDA	$ **2,100**	$ **2,287**	$ **2,565**	$ **3,073**	$ **3,822**
% of Net Revenue	*23.1%*	*23.5%*	*24.0%*	*25.3%*	*27.2%*
Capital Expenditures	$ 100	$ 300	$ 100	$ 100	$ 100
% of Net Revenue	*2.1%*	*5.8%*	*1.8%*	*1.6%*	*1.3%*

	Exit Multiples				
	4.5x	**5.0x**	**5.5x**	**6.0x**	**6.5x**
Total Invested Cash IRR	**29.2%**	**32.4%**	**35.3%**	**38.0%**	**40.5%**

Source: Company documents.

The Sponsor's key assumptions for the base case include:

- Revenue grows modestly for the next five years, driven by growth across multiple product categories (wine racks, brewery and distillery racks, agricultural products, vineyard equipment, water bottle racks and storage racks);

- Gross margins reduce to 53.1% in FY 2015 and stay constant through FY 2019;

- EBITDA margins expand from 23.1% in FY 2015 to 27.2% in FY 2019;

- Capital expenditures increase to $100,000 per year;

- A new ERP system is implemented in FY 2016, which requires $200,000 of additional capital expenditures;

- Working capital metrics remain consistent

Upside Case

The upside case envisions the Sponsor being able to maintain a double digit growth rate across all product categories other than wine barrel racks, while increasing margins. Additional capital will be reinvested in the business and it is likely a portion of the profits would be distributed to investors.

The Sponsor's key assumptions for the upside case includes:

- Revenue grows across all categories for the next five years and the Company increases each product category outside of wine barrel racks to at least approximately $1,000,000 in revenue per year by FY 2019;

- Gross margins expand and remain consistent through FY 2019;

- EBITDA margins expand through FY 2019;

- Capital expenditures reduce to $75,000 per year;

- A new ERP system is implemented in FY 2016, which requires $150,000 of capital expenditures;

- Working capital metrics remain consistent

Downside Case

The Downside case scenario envisions a significant slowdown in growth and margin erosion. Additional capital will be reinvested in the business.

The Sponsor's key assumptions for the downside case include:

- Revenue grows at 3.0-4.0% for the next five years, which is less than one-fourth of the Company's 5-year CAGR;

- Gross margins decline modestly

- EBITDA margins decline to around 19%;

- Maintenance capital expenditures increase to $125,000 per year;

- A new ERP system is implemented in FY 2016, which requires $200,000 of capital expenditures;

- Working capital metrics are stable

Exit Strategies

The Sponsor will run the business with the objective of providing an outstanding product and service experience, which should translate into maximizing shareholder value. Investors may achieve liquidity for their investment through one or more of the following events: 1) distribution of profits, 2) recapitalization or 3) sale. The Sponsor intends to pursue a capital event in a five to seven year period, depending on the performance of the business, the outlook of the industry, and the state of the M&A market. The preference would be an outright sale to a strategic acquirer or financial group with experience in the industry sector or in manufacturing. The Sponsor may also explore a recapitalization in year three or four, depending on the performance of the business and the state of the debt markets, in order to return a portion or all of the investors' invested capital.

If a sale is pursued, there are three likely potential categories of buyers:

- Makers or distributors of wine, beer and spirits

- Makers or distributors of storage solutions and/or other niche manufacturers

- Industry related investment groups

Next Steps

The Sponsor is targeting a March 2015 close, which is achievable assuming due diligence remains on track. To date, due diligence completed includes:

- Business and operational review conducted by the Sponsor, including meetings with the CEO and Key Accounts Manager;

- Customer site visits conducted by the Sponsor; and

- Industry and market review conducted by the Sponsor.

Exhibits:

Exhibit A-1: Financial Models (Base Case, Upside Case, Downside Case)

Exhibit A-2: Resume for Earl A. Gordon Managing Partner of Fenton Avenue Capital

Exhibit A-3: Investor Group A and B

Exhibit A-1a   Financial Models – Base Case

Project Vino
Income Statement - Base Case
($ in millions)
Fiscal Year Ending June 30,

	2013	2014	LTM 9/30/14	Pro Forma 2015	2016	2017	2018	2019
Wine Racks Revenue	7.1	7.5	7.0	7.5	7.8	8.3	8.8	9.3
% Growth		4.8%		(0.1%)	5.0%	6.0%	6.0%	6.0%
Agricultural Products Revenue	0.4	0.5	0.5	0.5	0.6	0.7	0.8	1.1
% Growth		13.3%		(0.1%)	15.0%	20.0%	20.0%	30.0%
Vineyard Equipment Revenue	0.4	0.7	0.8	0.7	0.7	0.8	0.9	1.0
% Growth		86.8%		(0.1%)	8.0%	10.0%	10.0%	10.0%
Bottle Racks Revenue	0.1	0.1	0.1	0.1	0.2	0.3	0.5	0.8
% Growth		(2.6%)		(0.1%)	60.0%	60.0%	70.0%	75.0%
Brewery & Distillery Racks	0.4	0.3	0.3	0.3	0.4	0.5	0.6	0.7
% Growth		(21.0%)		(0.1%)	10.0%	20.0%	25.0%	25.0%
All Other Revenue	(0.0)	0.0	0.0	0.0	0.0	0.2	0.6	1.2
% Growth		(150.8%)		(0.1%)	200.0%	350.0%	250.0%	100.0%
Total Revenue	$ 8.4	$ 9.1	$ 8.7	$ 9.1	$ 9.7	$ 10.7	$ 12.1	$ 14.1
% Growth		7.9%		(0.1%)	6.8%	9.9%	13.4%	15.9%
Steel	2.2	2.3	2.2	2.7	2.8	3.1	3.5	4.1
% Margin	25.6%	25.1%	24.9%	29.3%	29.3%	29.3%	29.3%	29.3%
Other Material	0.6	0.7	0.6	0.5	0.5	0.6	0.7	0.8
% Margin	7.1%	7.8%	7.5%	5.6%	5.6%	5.6%	5.6%	5.6%
Labor	1.0	1.0	0.9	0.9	1.0	1.1	1.2	1.4
% Margin	12.4%	10.4%	10.5%	10.2%	10.2%	10.2%	10.2%	10.2%
Manufacturing Overhead	0.2	0.2	0.2	0.2	0.2	0.2	0.2	0.3
% Margin	2.2%	2.4%	2.2%	1.8%	1.8%	1.8%	1.8%	1.8%
Total Cost of Goods Sold	4.0	4.2	3.9	4.3	4.6	5.0	5.7	6.6
% Margin	47.3%	45.7%	45.1%	46.9%	46.9%	46.9%	46.9%	46.9%
Total Gross Profit	$ 4.5	$ 4.9	$ 4.8	$ 4.8	$ 5.2	$ 5.7	$ 6.4	$ 7.5
% Margin	52.7%	54.3%	54.9%	53.1%	53.1%	53.1%	53.1%	53.1%
Sales & Marketing	0.1	0.1	0.1	0.1	0.2	0.2	0.2	0.2
% Margin	1.6%	1.5%	1.7%	1.5%	1.5%	1.5%	1.5%	1.4%
G&A	3.6	4.2	4.3	2.8	2.7	3.0	3.2	3.4
% Margin	42.6%	45.6%	49.6%	30.7%	28.1%	27.6%	26.3%	24.5%
Total Operating Expenses	$ 3.7	$ 4.3	$ 4.4	$ 2.9	$ 2.9	$ 3.1	$ 3.4	$ 3.6
% Margin	44.2%	47.1%	51.3%	32.2%	29.6%	29.1%	27.8%	25.9%
Base EBITDA (Pre-Adjustments)	0.7	0.7	0.3	1.9	2.3	2.6	3.1	3.8
% Margin	8.5%	7.1%	3.7%	20.9%	23.5%	24.0%	25.3%	27.2%
EBITDA Adjustments								
Owner's Salary/Bonus	1.7	1.7	1.7	0.2	-	-	-	-
Owner's Payroll Taxes	0.2	0.2	0.2	0.0	-	-	-	-
Related Party Rents to Owner	0.0	0.0	0.0	0.0	-	-	-	-
Other Owner's Expenses (Travel, Vehicle, etc.)	0.0	0.1	0.1	0.0	-	-	-	-
Replace CEO Position	(0.2)	(0.2)	(0.2)	(0.1)	-	-	-	-
Total EBITDA Adjustments	1.7	1.7	1.8	0.2	-	-	-	-
Adjusted EBITDA	$ 2.4	$ 2.4	$ 2.1	$ 2.1	$ 2.3	$ 2.6	$ 3.1	$ 3.8
% Margin	28.6%	26.3%	24.2%	23.1%	23.5%	24.0%	25.3%	27.2%
Net Inc. Avail. to Common				$ 0.9	$ 0.5	$ 0.8	$ 1.2	$ 1.7

Exhibit A-1a (continued)

Project Vino

Balance Sheet - Base Case
($ in millions)
Fiscal Year Ending June 30,

	Pro Forma 2015		2016		2017		2018		2019
				Projected					
ASSETS									
Cash	$ -	$	-	$	-	$	-	$	-
Accounts Receivable	1.0		0.8		0.9		1.0		1.2
Inventory	1.4		1.2		1.3		1.4		1.7
Prepaid Expenses	0.1		0.1		0.1		0.1		0.1
Other Current Assets	0.0		0.0		0.0		0.0		0.0
Total Current Assets	$ 2.6	$	2.1	$	2.3	$	2.6	$	3.0
Net Plant and Equipment	0.7		0.7		0.7		0.6		0.5
Old Goodwill	-								-
Intangibles	0.4		0.4		0.4		0.4		0.4
Prepaid Fees and Expenses	0.3		0.2		0.2		0.1		0.0
Other Current Assets	0.0		0.0		0.0		0.0		0.0
Employee Loans & Advances	-				-		-		-
Total Long-Term Assets	$ 1.4	$	1.4	$	1.2	$	1.1	$	0.9
TOTAL ASSETS	$ 4.0	$	3.5	$	3.5	$	3.6	$	3.8
LIABILITIES & EQUITY									
Accounts Payable	0.5		0.4		0.5		0.5		0.6
Accrued Expenses	0.1		0.2		0.2		0.2		0.2
Customer Deposits	0.0		0.0		0.0		0.0		0.0
Accrued Income Taxes	0.3		0.3		0.3		0.3		0.3
Total Current Liabilities	$ 1.0	$	0.9	$	1.0	$	1.1	$	1.2
Revolver	1.5		1.4		1.4		1.0		0.1
Senior Debt / Term Loan A	5.3		4.3		3.3		2.3		1.3
Capital Lease	0.0		0.0		0.0		0.0		0.0
Term Loan B	-		-		-		-		-
Sub Debt	-		-		-		-		-
Seller Note	2.2		2.2		2.2		2.2		2.2
Total Debt	$ 9.1	$	8.0	$	6.9	$	5.5	$	3.7
Total Liabilities	$ 10.1	$	8.9	$	7.9	$	6.6	$	4.8
Redeemable Preferred Stock	-		-		-		-		-
Convertible Preferred Stock	3.1		3.4		3.6		3.8		4.1
Common Equity	(9.3)		(8.8)		(8.0)		(6.8)		(5.1)
Total Equity	$ (6.2)	$	(5.4)	$	(4.4)	$	(3.0)	$	(1.0)
TOTAL LIABIL. & EQUITY	$ 4.0	$	3.5	$	3.5	$	3.6	$	3.8
	-		-		-		-		-

Exhibit A-1a (continued)

Project Vino

Cash Flow Statement - Base Case
($ in millions)
Fiscal Year Ending June 30,

	Pro Forma	Projected			
	2015	2016	2017	2018	2019
Net Income Available to Common	$ 0.9	$ 0.5	$ 0.8	$ 1.2	$ 1.7
Depreciation	0.2	0.2	0.2	0.2	0.2
Amortization	0.0	0.0	0.0	0.0	0.0
Accretion of Convertible Preferred	0.1	0.2	0.2	0.2	0.2
Non-Cash Interest Expense	-	-	-	-	-
Amortization of Financing Fees	0.0	0.1	0.1	0.1	0.1
Working Capital	(0.2)	0.4	(0.1)	(0.2)	(0.3)
Change in Other Current Assets & Current Liabilities	-	0.0	0.0	0.0	0.0
Operating Cash Flow	$ 1.1	$ 1.4	$ 1.2	$ 1.5	$ 2.0
Capital Expenditures	(0.1)	(0.3)	(0.1)	(0.1)	(0.1)
Purchase of Intangible Assets	-	-	-	-	-
(Increase)/Decrease in Other Long Term Liabilities	-	-	-	-	-
Free Operating Cash Flow	$ 1.0	$ 1.1	$ 1.1	$ 1.4	$ 1.9
Option/Warrant Exercise	-	-	-	-	-
Issuance of Common Equity	-	-	-	-	-
Additional Issuance of Convertible Preferred	-	-	-	-	-
Total Mandatory Debt Retirements	-	(1.0)	(1.0)	(1.0)	(1.0)
Total Debt Automatically Added/(Retired)	0.4	(0.1)	(0.1)	(0.4)	(0.9)
Redemption of Convertible Preferred	-	-	-	-	-
Excess Cash	$ 1.4	$ -	$ -	$ -	$ -

Source: Company documents.

Exhibit A-1b   Financial Models – Upside Case

Project Vino

Income Statement - Upside Case
($ in millions)
Fiscal Year Ending June 30,

	2013	2014	LTM 9/30/14	Pro Forma 2015	Projected 2016	2017	2018	2019
Wine Racks Revenue	7.1	7.5	7.0	7.5	7.9	8.5	9.2	10.1
% Growth		4.8%		(0.1%)	6.0%	8.0%	8.0%	10.0%
Agricultural Products Revenue	0.4	0.5	0.5	0.5	0.6	0.7	0.9	1.2
% Growth		13.3%		(0.1%)	20.0%	20.0%	25.0%	30.0%
Vineyard Equipment Revenue	0.4	0.7	0.8	0.7	0.7	0.8	0.9	1.1
% Growth		86.8%		(0.1%)	8.0%	10.0%	15.0%	15.0%
Bottle Racks Revenue	0.1	0.1	0.1	0.1	0.2	0.3	0.5	0.9
% Growth		(2.6%)		(0.1%)	60.0%	75.0%	75.0%	80.0%
Brewery & Distillery Racks	0.4	0.3	0.3	0.3	0.4	0.5	0.6	0.9
% Growth		(21.0%)		(0.1%)	10.0%	25.0%	35.0%	35.0%
All Other Revenue	(0.0)	0.0	0.0	0.0	0.1	0.3	0.7	1.5
% Growth		(150.8%)		(0.1%)	600.0%	250.0%	150.0%	100.0%
Total Revenue	$ 8.4	$ 9.1	$ 8.7	$ 9.1	$ 9.9	$ 11.1	$ 13.0	$ 15.7
% Growth		7.9%		(0.1%)	8.5%	12.8%	16.3%	20.9%
Steel	2.2	2.3	2.2	2.7	2.7	3.0	3.5	4.2
% Margin	25.6%	25.1%	24.9%	29.3%	27.0%	27.0%	27.0%	27.0%
Other Material	0.6	0.7	0.6	0.5	0.6	0.6	0.7	0.9
% Margin	7.1%	7.8%	7.5%	5.6%	5.6%	5.6%	5.6%	5.6%
Labor	1.0	1.0	0.9	0.9	1.0	1.1	1.3	1.6
% Margin	12.4%	10.4%	10.5%	10.2%	10.2%	10.2%	10.2%	10.2%
Manufacturing Overhead	0.2	0.2	0.2	0.2	0.2	0.2	0.2	0.3
% Margin	2.2%	2.4%	2.2%	1.8%	1.8%	1.8%	1.8%	1.8%
Total Cost of Goods Sold	4.0	4.2	3.9	4.3	4.4	5.0	5.8	7.0
% Margin	47.3%	45.7%	45.1%	46.9%	44.6%	44.6%	44.6%	44.6%
Total Gross Profit	$ 4.5	$ 4.9	$ 4.8	$ 4.8	$ 5.5	$ 6.2	$ 7.2	$ 8.7
% Margin	52.7%	54.3%	54.9%	53.1%	55.4%	55.4%	55.4%	55.4%
Sales & Marketing	0.1	0.1	0.1	0.1	0.2	0.2	0.2	0.2
% Margin	1.6%	1.5%	1.7%	1.5%	1.5%	1.5%	1.5%	1.4%
G&A	3.6	4.2	4.3	2.8	2.7	3.0	3.3	3.6
% Margin	42.6%	45.6%	49.6%	30.7%	27.7%	27.0%	25.5%	23.2%
Total Operating Expenses	$ 3.7	$ 4.3	$ 4.4	$ 2.9	$ 2.9	$ 3.2	$ 3.5	$ 3.9
% Margin	44.2%	47.1%	51.3%	32.2%	29.2%	28.5%	27.0%	24.6%
Base EBITDA (Pre-Adjustments)	0.7	0.7	0.3	1.9	2.6	3.0	3.7	4.8
% Margin	8.5%	7.1%	3.7%	20.9%	26.2%	26.9%	28.4%	30.8%
EBITDA Adjustments								
Owner's Salary/Bonus	1.7	1.7	1.7	0.2	-	-	-	-
Owner's Payroll Taxes	0.2	0.2	0.2	0.0	-	-	-	-
Related Party Rents to Owner	0.0	0.0	0.0	0.0	-	-	-	-
Other Owner's Expenses (Travel, Vehicle, etc.)	0.0	0.1	0.1	0.0	-	-	-	-
Replace CEO Position	(0.2)	(0.2)	(0.2)	(0.1)	-	-	-	-
Total EBITDA Adjustments	1.7	1.7	1.8	0.2	-	-	-	-
Adjusted EBITDA	$ 2.4	$ 2.4	$ 2.1	$ 2.1	$ 2.6	$ 3.0	$ 3.7	$ 4.8
% Margin	28.6%	26.3%	24.2%	23.1%	26.2%	26.9%	28.4%	30.8%
Net Inc. Avail. to Common				$ 0.9	$ 0.7	$ 1.1	$ 1.6	$ 2.4

Exhibit A-1b (continued)

Project Vino

Balance Sheet - Upside Case
($ in millions)
Fiscal Year Ending June 30,

	Pro Forma	Projected			
	2015	2016	2017	2018	2019
ASSETS					
Cash	$ -	$ -	$ -	$ -	$ -
Accounts Receivable	1.0	0.9	1.0	1.1	1.4
Inventory	1.4	1.2	1.3	1.5	1.9
Prepaid Expenses	0.1	0.1	0.1	0.1	0.1
Other Current Assets	0.0	0.0	0.0	0.0	0.0
Total Current Assets	$ 2.6	$ 2.1	$ 2.4	$ 2.7	$ 3.3
Net Plant and Equipment	0.7	0.7	0.6	0.5	0.4
Old Goodwill	-	-	-	-	-
Intangibles	0.4	0.4	0.4	0.4	0.4
Prepaid Fees and Expenses	0.3	0.2	0.2	0.1	0.0
Other Current Assets	0.0	0.0	0.0	0.0	0.0
Employee Loans & Advances	-	-	-	-	-
Total Long-Term Assets	$ 1.4	$ 1.4	$ 1.2	$ 1.0	$ 0.8
TOTAL ASSETS	$ 4.0	$ 3.5	$ 3.5	$ 3.7	$ 4.1
LIABILITIES & EQUITY					
Accounts Payable	0.5	0.4	0.5	0.5	0.6
Accrued Expenses	0.1	0.2	0.2	0.2	0.3
Customer Deposits	0.0	0.0	0.0	0.0	0.0
Accrued Income Taxes	0.3	0.3	0.3	0.3	0.3
Total Current Liabilities	$ 1.0	$ 0.9	$ 1.0	$ 1.1	$ 1.2
Revolver	1.5	1.2	0.9	0.2	-
Senior Debt / Term Loan A	5.3	4.3	3.3	2.3	0.1
Capital Lease	0.0	0.0	0.0	0.0	0.0
Term Loan B	-	-	-	-	-
Sub Debt	-	-	-	-	-
Seller Note	2.2	2.2	2.2	2.2	2.2
Total Debt	$ 9.1	$ 7.8	$ 6.4	$ 4.7	$ 2.3
Total Liabilities	$ 10.1	$ 8.7	$ 7.4	$ 5.8	$ 3.5
Redeemable Preferred Stock	-	-	-	-	-
Convertible Preferred Stock	3.1	3.4	3.6	3.8	4.1
Common Equity	(9.3)	(8.6)	(7.5)	(5.9)	(3.5)
Total Equity	$ (6.2)	$ (5.2)	$ (3.9)	$ (2.1)	$ 0.6
TOTAL LIABIL. & EQUITY	$ 4.0	$ 3.5	$ 3.5	$ 3.7	$ 4.1
	-	-	-	-	-

Exhibit A-1b (continued)

Project Vino

Cash Flow Statement - Upside Case
($ in millions)
Fiscal Year Ending June 30,

	Pro Forma	Projected			
	2015	2016	2017	2018	2019
Net Income Available to Common	$ 0.9	$ 0.7	$ 1.1	$ 1.6	$ 2.4
Depreciation	0.2	0.2	0.2	0.2	0.2
Amortization	0.0	0.0	0.0	0.0	0.0
Accretion of Convertible Preferred	0.1	0.2	0.2	0.2	0.2
Non-Cash Interest Expense	-	-	-	-	-
Amortization of Financing Fees	0.0	0.1	0.1	0.1	0.1
Working Capital	(0.2)	0.3	(0.2)	(0.3)	(0.4)
Change in Other Current Assets & Current Liabilities	-	0.0	0.0	0.0	0.0
Operating Cash Flow	$ 1.1	$ 1.6	$ 1.4	$ 1.8	$ 2.5
Capital Expenditures	(0.1)	(0.2)	(0.1)	(0.1)	(0.1)
Purchase of Intangible Assets	-	-	-	-	-
(Increase)/Decrease in Other Long Term Liabilities	-	-	-	-	-
Free Operating Cash Flow	$ 1.0	$ 1.3	$ 1.3	$ 1.7	$ 2.4
Option/Warrant Exercise	-	-	-	-	-
Issuance of Common Equity	-	-	-	-	-
Additional Issuance of Convertible Preferred	-	-	-	-	-
Total Mandatory Debt Retirements	-	(1.0)	(1.0)	(1.0)	(1.0)
Total Debt Automatically Added/(Retired)	0.4	(0.3)	(0.3)	(0.7)	(1.4)
Redemption of Convertible Preferred	-	-	-	-	-
Excess Cash	$ 1.4	$ -	$ -	$ -	$ -

Source: Company documents.

Exhibit A-1c   Financial Models – Downside Case

Project Vino
Income Statement - Downside Case
($ in millions)
Fiscal Year Ending June 30,

	2013	2014	LTM 9/30/14	Pro Forma 2015	Projected 2016	2017	2018	2019
Wine Racks Revenue	7.1	7.5	7.0	7.5	7.7	8.0	8.3	8.6
% Growth		*4.8%*		*(0.1%)*	*3.0%*	*4.0%*	*4.0%*	*4.0%*
Agricultural Products Revenue	0.4	0.5	0.5	0.5	0.5	0.5	0.6	0.6
% Growth		*13.3%*		*(0.1%)*	*3.0%*	*4.0%*	*4.0%*	*4.0%*
Vineyard Equipment Revenue	0.4	0.7	0.8	0.7	0.7	0.7	0.8	0.8
% Growth		*86.8%*		*(0.1%)*	*3.0%*	*4.0%*	*4.0%*	*4.0%*
Bottle Racks Revenue	0.1	0.1	0.1	0.1	0.1	0.1	0.1	0.1
% Growth		*(2.6%)*		*(0.1%)*	*3.0%*	*4.0%*	*4.0%*	*4.0%*
Brewery & Distillery Racks	0.4	0.3	0.3	0.3	0.4	0.4	0.4	0.4
% Growth		*(21.0%)*		*(0.1%)*	*3.0%*	*4.0%*	*4.0%*	*4.0%*
All Other Revenue	(0.0)	0.0	0.0	0.0	0.0	0.0	0.0	0.0
% Growth		*(150.8%)*		*(0.1%)*	*2.0%*	*2.0%*	*2.0%*	*2.0%*
Total Revenue	$ 8.4	$ 9.1	$ 8.7	$ 9.1	$ 9.4	$ 9.8	$ 10.1	$ 10.6
% Growth		*7.9%*		*(0.1%)*	*3.0%*	*4.0%*	*4.0%*	*4.0%*
Steel	2.2	2.3	2.2	2.7	3.0	3.1	3.2	3.4
% Margin	*25.6%*	*25.1%*	*24.9%*	*29.3%*	*32.0%*	*32.0%*	*32.0%*	*32.0%*
Other Material	0.6	0.7	0.6	0.5	0.6	0.6	0.6	0.6
% Margin	*7.1%*	*7.8%*	*7.5%*	*5.6%*	*6.0%*	*6.0%*	*6.0%*	*6.0%*
Labor	1.0	1.0	0.9	0.9	1.0	1.1	1.1	1.2
% Margin	*12.4%*	*10.4%*	*10.5%*	*10.2%*	*11.0%*	*11.0%*	*11.0%*	*11.0%*
Manufacturing Overhead	0.2	0.2	0.2	0.2	0.2	0.2	0.2	0.2
% Margin	*2.2%*	*2.4%*	*2.2%*	*1.8%*	*2.0%*	*2.0%*	*2.0%*	*2.0%*
Total Cost of Goods Sold	4.0	4.2	3.9	4.3	4.8	5.0	5.2	5.4
% Margin	*47.3%*	*45.7%*	*45.1%*	*46.9%*	*51.0%*	*51.0%*	*51.9%*	*51.0%*
Total Gross Profit	$ 4.5	$ 4.9	$ 4.8	$ 4.8	$ 4.6	$ 4.8	$ 5.0	$ 5.2
% Margin	*52.7%*	*54.3%*	*54.9%*	*53.1%*	*49.0%*	*49.0%*	*49.0%*	*49.0%*
Sales & Marketing	0.1	0.1	0.1	0.1	0.1	0.2	0.2	0.2
% Margin	*1.6%*	*1.5%*	*1.7%*	*1.5%*	*1.5%*	*1.5%*	*1.6%*	*1.6%*
G&A	3.6	4.2	4.3	2.8	2.7	2.8	2.9	3.0
% Margin	*42.6%*	*45.6%*	*49.6%*	*30.7%*	*29.1%*	*28.9%*	*28.6%*	*28.0%*
Total Operating Expenses	$ 3.7	$ 4.3	$ 4.4	$ 2.9	$ 2.9	$ 3.0	$ 3.1	$ 3.1
% Margin	*44.2%*	*47.1%*	*51.3%*	*32.2%*	*30.7%*	*30.4%*	*30.1%*	*29.6%*
Base EBITDA (Pre-Adjustments)	0.7	0.7	0.3	1.9	1.7	1.8	1.9	2.0
% Margin	*8.5%*	*7.1%*	*3.7%*	*20.9%*	*18.3%*	*18.6%*	*18.9%*	*19.4%*
EBITDA Adjustments								
Owner's Salary/Bonus	1.7	1.7	1.7	0.2	-	-	-	-
Owner's Payroll Taxes	0.2	0.2	0.2	0.0	-	-	-	-
Related Party Rents to Owner	0.0	0.0	0.0	0.0	-	-	-	-
Other Owner's Expenses (Travel, Vehicle, etc.)	0.0	0.1	0.1	0.0	-	-	-	-
Replace CEO Position	(0.2)	(0.2)	(0.2)	(0.1)	-	-	-	-
Total EBITDA Adjustments	1.7	1.7	1.8	0.2	-	-	-	-
Adjusted EBITDA	$ 2.4	$ 2.4	$ 2.1	$ 2.1	$ 1.7	$ 1.8	$ 1.9	$ 2.0
% Margin	*28.6%*	*26.3%*	*24.2%*	*23.1%*	*18.3%*	*18.6%*	*18.9%*	*19.4%*
Net Inc. Avail. to Common				$ 0.9	$ 0.2	$ 0.3	$ 0.4	$ 0.6

Exhibit A-1c (continued)

Project Vino

Balance Sheet - Downside Case
($ in millions)
Fiscal Year Ending June 30,

	Pro Forma	Projected			
	2015	2016	2017	2018	2019
ASSETS					
Cash	$ -	$ -	$ -	$ -	$ -
Accounts Receivable	1.0	0.8	0.8	0.9	0.9
Inventory	1.4	1.1	1.2	1.2	1.3
Prepaid Expenses	0.1	0.1	0.1	0.1	0.1
Other Current Assets	0.0	0.0	0.0	0.0	0.0
Total Current Assets	$ 2.6	$ 2.0	$ 2.1	$ 2.2	$ 2.2
Net Plant and Equipment	0.7	0.8	0.7	0.6	0.5
Old Goodwill	-	-	-	-	-
Intangibles	0.4	0.4	0.4	0.4	0.4
Prepaid Fees and Expenses	0.3	0.2	0.2	0.1	0.0
Other Current Assets	0.0	0.0	0.0	0.0	0.0
Employee Loans & Advances	-	-	-	-	-
Total Long-Term Assets	$ 1.4	$ 1.4	$ 1.3	$ 1.1	$ 0.9
TOTAL ASSETS	$ 4.0	$ 3.4	$ 3.3	$ 3.3	$ 3.2
LIABILITIES & EQUITY					
Accounts Payable	0.5	0.4	0.5	0.5	0.5
Accrued Expenses	0.1	0.2	0.2	0.2	0.2
Customer Deposits	0.0	0.0	0.0	0.0	0.0
Accrued Income Taxes	0.3	0.3	0.3	0.3	0.3
Total Current Liabilities	$ 1.0	$ 0.9	$ 1.0	$ 1.0	$ 1.0
Revolver	1.5	1.7	2.0	2.3	2.3
Senior Debt / Term Loan A	5.3	4.3	3.3	2.3	1.3
Capital Lease	0.0	0.0	0.0	0.0	0.0
Term Loan B	-	-	-	-	-
Sub Debt	-	-	-	-	-
Seller Note	2.2	2.2	2.2	2.2	2.2
Total Debt	$ 9.1	$ 8.2	$ 7.6	$ 6.8	$ 5.9
Total Liabilities	$ 10.1	$ 9.2	$ 8.6	$ 7.8	$ 6.9
Redeemable Preferred Stock	-	-	-	-	-
Convertible Preferred Stock	3.1	3.4	3.6	3.8	4.1
Common Equity	(9.3)	(9.1)	(8.8)	(8.4)	(7.8)
Total Equity	$ (6.2)	$ (5.8)	$ (5.2)	$ (4.5)	$ (3.7)
TOTAL LIABIL. & EQUITY	$ 4.0	$ 3.4	$ 3.3	$ 3.3	$ 3.2
	-	-	-	-	-

Source: Company documents.

Exhibit A-1c (continued)

Project Vino					
Cash Flow Statement - Downside Case					
($ in millions)					
Fiscal Year Ending June 30,					
	Pro Forma	Projected			
	2015	2016	2017	2018	2019
Net Income Available to Common	$ 0.9	$ 0.2	$ 0.3	$ 0.4	$ 0.6
Depreciation	0.2	0.2	0.2	0.2	0.2
Amortization	0.0	0.0	0.0	0.0	0.0
Accretion of Convertible Preferred	0.1	0.2	0.2	0.2	0.2
Non-Cash Interest Expense	-	-	-	-	-
Amortization of Financing Fees	0.0	0.1	0.1	0.1	0.1
Working Capital	(0.2)	0.5	(0.1)	(0.1)	(0.1)
Change in Other Current Assets & Current Liabilities	-	0.0	0.0	0.0	0.0
Operating Cash Flow	$ 1.1	$ 1.2	$ 0.8	$ 0.9	$ 1.1
Capital Expenditures	(0.1)	(0.3)	(0.1)	(0.1)	(0.1)
Purchase of Intangible Assets	-	-	-	-	-
(Increase)/Decrease in Other Long Term Liabilities	-	-	-	-	-
Free Operating Cash Flow	$ 1.0	$ 0.9	$ 0.7	$ 0.8	$ 0.9
Option/Warrant Exercise	-	-	-	-	-
Issuance of Common Equity	-	-	-	-	-
Additional Issuance of Convertible Preferred	-	-	-	-	-
Total Mandatory Debt Retirements	-	(1.0)	(1.0)	(1.0)	(1.0)
Total Debt Automatically Added/(Retired)	0.4	0.1	0.3	0.2	0.1
Redemption of Convertible Preferred	-	-	-	-	-
Excess Cash	$ 1.4	$ -	$ -	$ -	$ -

Source: Company documents.

Exhibit A-2   Resume for Earl A. Gordon Managing Partner of Fenton Avenue Capital

EARL A. GORDON

Experience

2013 – 2014	**LITTLEBITS, INC.** **Director of E-Commerce and Digital Marketing**	NEW YORK, NY

2012 – 2013	**KIKIN, INC.** **Vice President of Business Development**	NEW YORK, NY

2010 – 2012	**QUIDSI, INC. (AN AMAZON.COM COMPANY)** **Director of Marketing (Wag.com)** Part of the launch team for Wag.com, a direct to consumer e-commerce site in the Pet Products market. **Associate Director of Merchandising, Household Products and Personal Care (Soap.com)** Part of the launch team for Soap.com, a direct to consumer e-commerce site in the Health & Beauty market.	JERSEY CITY, NJ

2008 – 2010	**KIDROBOT** **Director of Strategic Planning** Reported directly to CEO of fast-growing manufacturer, retailer, and distributor of designer toys and apparel.	NEW YORK, NY

2004 – 2006	**ALTARIS CAPITAL PARTNERS** **Senior Associate –Healthcare Private Equity Fund**	NEW YORK, NY

2002 – 2004	**UBS PRIVATE EQUITY** **Associate Director (Promoted from Senior Investment Analyst)**	STAMFORD, CT

2000 – 2002	**GOLDMAN SACHS** **Financial Analyst – Mergers & Strategic Advisory Group (Consumer Products and Retail Industries)**	NEW YORK, NY

Education

2006 – 2008	**HARVARD BUSINESS SCHOOL** Master in Business Administration, June 2008. Awarded First-Year Honors.	BOSTON, MA

1996 – 2000	**NEW YORK UNIVERSITY** Bachelor of Science degree in Finance and International Business, May 2000.	NEW YORK, NY

Source: Company documents.

Exhibit A-3a   Investor Group A

Investor Group A
February 1, 2015

Earl Gordon
Fenton Avenue Capital, LLC
Via email

Dear Earl:

Investor Group A is pleased to submit this proposal to provide $7.8 million of subordinated debt and equity financing to Eastern Circle Industries, Inc. (the "Company") in support of a transaction sponsored by Fenton Avenue Capital, LLC (the "Sponsor").

This letter (the "Proposal Letter") is presented for discussion purposes only, and except for the obligations of the Company set forth in the paragraphs of this Proposal Letter labeled "Fees," "Expenses," and "Confidentiality; No-Shop" which are binding commitments of the Company and the Sponsor, this Proposal Letter does not constitute a binding commitment of either of Investor Group A, the Company, or the Sponsor. Except as provided above, a binding commitment will only be evidenced by executed definitive legal documentation that will include customary events of default, representations, warranties and affirmative and negative covenants.

Subject to the foregoing, the principal terms and conditions on which Investor Group A proposes to provide financing to the Company are as follows:

Issuer:	The Company
Investment:	$6.7 million senior subordinated note (the "Note"), a warrant (the "Warrant") to purchase 10.0% of the fully diluted equity interests in the Company which shall apply to all equity regardless of preference or option pools and have a nominal exercise price. Equity investment of $1.1 million (the "Equity")
Closing:	March 31, 2015 or such other date mutually agreeable to the Company and Investor Group A.
Use of Proceeds	To finance the acquisition of the Company. Estimated sources and uses of funds at Closing are shown below:

Estimated Sources & Uses of Funds at Closing

($ in 000s)

Sources		Uses	
Investor Group A Subordinated Debt	$6,700	Cash Purchase Price	$8,800
Unsecured Seller Note	2,200	Seller Note	2,200
Investor Group A Preferred Equity	1,100	Estimated Fees & Expenses	500
Sponsor Preferred Equity	1,500		
Total	$11,500	Total	$11,500

Exhibit A-3a (continued)

Interest Rate: 13.0% per annum fixed.

Fees: 2.0% of the Note, which will be due at Closing.

Equity: We anticipate that all equity invested by Investor Group A or raised by sponsor will be participating preferred equity with an accruing dividend and pro-rata participation in common equity pool, subject to dilution from a carried interest to Sponsor and from an option pool to be granted at the discretion of the Board.

Maturity and Amortization: The Note shall have a five (5) year term, with interest and principal payable as follows:

(i)   Interest payable monthly for five years.

(ii)   Balloon principal payment, representing all unpaid principal, plus accrued interest, payable at the end of month sixty.

Notwithstanding the foregoing, mandatory redemption of the Note will be required, at the option of the noteholder, upon certain events, such as an initial public offering, material sale of Company assets, and change of control.

Prepayments: The Note is prepayable in whole or in part at any time in any amount, provided that any prepayments are subject to the following prepayment premium schedule:

Principal Prepaid in Year:	Premium on Principal Paid:
1	3.0%
2	2.0%
3	1.0%
Thereafter	None

Subordination: The Note will be junior in right of payment to a working capital line of credit that shall be undrawn at Closing (the "Permitted Senior Debt"). The Note will be senior in right of payment to all other equity and debt of the Company, and cash payments on such subordinated securities will automatically suspend if there is an event of default under the Note.

Collateral: The Note shall be secured by:

(i)   Liens and security interests encumbering all of the tangible and intangible assets of the Company and its current and future subsidiaries. Such liens and security interests shall be junior and subordinate only to first priority liens in favor of the senior lender(s) securing the Permitted Senior Debt.

(ii)   A pledge of all stock in the Company's current and future subsidiaries. A non-subordinated collateral assignment of key man life insurance on key management (TBD in diligence) in the aggregate amount of $6.7 million. This will be a best efforts requirement to be put in place within 100 days after Closing.

Exhibit A-3a (continued)

Guaranty: The obligations of the Company under the investment documents will be guaranteed by all current and future subsidiaries of the Company.

Representations and Warranties: The definitive legal documentation will include representations and warranties of the Company which are usual and customary for transactions of this type

Financial Covenants: The definitive legal documentation will include certain financial covenants binding upon the Company so long as the Note is outstanding, including the following:

(i)   The ratio of total debt (excluding seller notes) to trailing EBITDA for any 12 month period shall not exceed the levels below, measured on a quarterly basis with the first measurement period ending June 30, 2015.

Closing – June 2016	4.00x
July 2016 – June 2017	3.75x
After June 2017	3.50x

(ii)   Fixed Charge Coverage shall be at least 1.50x for any 12 month period, measured on a quarterly basis with the first measurement period ending June 30, 2015. Fixed Charge Coverage will be defined as the ratio of EBITDA to all cash payments for interest, capital expenditures, taxes or tax distributions, and scheduled principal payments.

(iii)   Liquidity shall be at least $700,000 on a monthly basis, with Liquidity defined as unrestricted cash plus undrawn line of credit availability.

Other Covenants and Events of Default: The definitive legal documentation will include customary negative and affirmative covenants and events of default for transactions of this type

Warrant Provisions: The Warrant may be exercised at any time and from time to time until six years after closing.

Put Option: At any time following the earlier of (a) the prepayment of the Note in full; (b) an event has occurred which requires prepayment of the Note, (c) an event of default which has not been cured (if at such time the Note is outstanding), or (d) maturity of the Note, the holder of the Warrant or shares issued or issuable upon exercise of the Warrant (the "Warrant Shares") shall have the right (the "Put Right") to cause the Company to purchase the Warrant or the Warrant Shares at a price equal to the percentage of the shares in the Company represented by the Warrant Shares multiplied by the greater of (a) the fair market value of the Company as determined in accordance with an independent appraisal procedure; or (b) an amount equal to 5.0 times the Company's consolidated EBITDA for the preceding 12 month period, less outstanding indebtedness for borrowed money plus cash on hand. The put price will be payable in cash. This option will expire upon a qualified initial public offering of the Company's stock. Any determination of value of the Warrant or Warrant Shares will be made without giving effect to any discount for minority interests or lack of liquidity.

Exhibit A-3a (continued)

Other Rights:	Investor Group A will be granted customary rights of first refusal and co-sale rights, preemptive rights, piggy-back registration rights and other rights that are usual and customary for this type of transaction.
Board and Voting:	As long as Investor Group A owns the Equity, then Investor Group A shall be entitled to appoint 1 of the 5 members of the board of directors of the Company (the "Board") which shall meet at least once per quarter. As long as the Note is outstanding or Investor Group A owns the Equity, Investor Group A will also be allowed to bring one guest to all Board meetings which shall also occur at least once per quarter. The Company will pay reasonable expenses for such Investor Group A designees and guests.

Conditions to Closing:

(i)   completion of due diligence acceptable to Investor Group A

(ii)   approval by the Investor Group A investment committee

(iii)   negotiation, execution, and delivery of definitive legal documentation in form and substance acceptable to Investor Group A

(iv)   no material adverse change in the condition (financial or otherwise) or prospects of the Company

(v)   closing of the Permitted Senior Debt and an intercreditor agreement between Investor Group A and the senior lenders thereunder, all on terms and conditions acceptable to Investor Group A

(vi)   confirmation of trailing 12 month adjusted EBITDA of at least $2,000,000 including the pro forma impact of all planned cost increases to be incurred post-closing (such as management additions)

(vii)   confirmation of liquidity at closing of at least $700,000

(viii) minimum equity investment of $1,500,000 by Sponsor and/or its affiliates

Expenses:	At Closing, the Company shall pay or reimburse Investor Group A and the Sponsor for all out of pocket expenses incurred by each party in connection with the transaction contemplated herein, including, without limitation, the fees and expenses of legal counsel. In the event that the transaction doesn't close, each of Investor Group A and the Sponsor shall be responsible for their own out of pocket costs. Shortly following a successful management meeting, Investor Group A will work with Sponsor to come to a written agreement on the sharing of approved third party expenses between Investor Group A and Sponsor. We expect that such expenses may include accounting/tax, legal, insurance, environmental, and background check due diligence expenses.

Exhibit A-3a (continued)

Confidentiality:	This Proposal Letter is delivered to the Sponsor and the Company with the understanding (to which the Sponsor and the Company hereby agree) that neither it nor its substance, nor the fact that Investor Group A is interested, shall be disclosed to any third party except those in a confidential relationship with the Sponsor or the Company, such as directors, senior executive officers, legal counsel, accountants, and financial advisors.
No-Shop:	Disclosure to other investment banking firms, mezzanine funds, private equity funds, commercial banks and other financial institutions or principal investors or individuals is prohibited, without the written consent of Investor Group A.

As consideration for the investment of time, effort, and expense that Investor Group A will incur in order to proceed, Sponsor and the Company agree to the following, effective for 45 days beginning on the date of the execution of this Proposal Letter:

> (i) The Company will not, and will not cause or permit any of its affiliates or representatives (including the Sponsor) to, directly or indirectly solicit or accept or encourage any other proposal for or provide any information to a third party regarding (a) the direct or indirect sale of a significant portion of assets of the Company, excluding ordinary course sales; (b) the direct or indirect sale of any capital stock or debt or equity securities of the Company; (c) the merger of the Company with another company; or (d) any debt financing for the Company or its affiliates other than the Permitted Senior Debt and the Note.

> (ii) The Sponsor and the Company will promptly disclose to Investor Group A the substance (including copies) of any unsolicited discussions or proposals covered by Section (i) of this provision.

The obligations of the Sponsor and the Company under this Confidentiality and No-Shop provision shall automatically extend for 45 days from the date that Investor Group A delivers to the Company drafts of the definitive legal documents required to close this transaction. The Sponsor and the Company acknowledges that this Confidentiality and No- Shop provision is a material inducement to Investor Group A to move forward with its due diligence review of the Company. The Company and the Sponsor agree that Investor Group A may specifically enforce the Confidentiality and No-Shop provision.

Expiration:	This Proposal Letter will expire if not accepted by the Sponsor in the manner provided below prior to 5:00 pm Eastern Time on February 6, 2015.

Exhibit A-3a (continued)

If the terms and conditions set forth herein are acceptable to the Company, please evidence the Company's acceptance of this Proposal Letter by executing this Proposal Letter where indicated and returning a fully executed counterpart of this Proposal Letter to Investor Group A.

Sincerely,

Investor Group A

By: _____

Its: _____

Accepted and approved this _____ day of _____, 2015

_____

By: _____

Its: _____

Source: Company documents.

Exhibit A-3b   Investor Group B

Proposal Letter
February 1, 2015

Borrower(s):	Eastern Circle Industries, Inc. ("**Eastern Circle**") including any and all current and future subsidiaries (whether or not wholly owned) as joint and several borrowers.
Holding Company:	The ultimate holding company of Eastern Circle.
Guarantor(s):	All current and future subsidiaries of Holding Company not included as a Borrower under the terms and conditions of this transaction shall provide a guarantee on a senior basis.
Sponsor:	Fenton Avenue Capital, LLC.
Lender(s):	Investor Group B
Agent:	Investor Group B shall act as administrative and collateral agent.
Use of Proceeds:	Funded Amount and Capital Contribution shall be utilized as follows: (i) fund acquisition of 100% of the stock of Eastern Circle, (ii) costs, expenses, and all other payment amounts contemplated herein, (iii) transaction expenses (including those incurred by the Sponsor), and (iv) general working capital purposes.
Seller Note:	$2,200,000 to be fully subordinated with agreed upon payment blockage provisions.
Closing Date:	Anticipated to be on or about March 31, 2015.

Exhibit A-3b (continued)

Term Notes

Type:	Senior Secured Term Notes (the "**Notes**").
Facility Amount:	$10,000,000.
Funded Amount:	$7,500,000.
Future Draw(s):	Upon thirty (30) days written notice by Borrower to Lender, Borrower shall issue Notes to Lender in an amount not to exceed the Facility Amount less the then outstanding Senior Obligations (the "Future Draw(s)"). Any Future Draw shall be provided, subject to covenant compliance by Borrower, at the sole discretion of Lender.
Cash Interest:	11.0% per annum. The Cash Interest shall be payable monthly in cash in arrears.
PIK Interest:	2.0% per annum. The PIK Interest shall capitalize to principal monthly and be payable upon Maturity.
Closing Payment:	2.0% of the Funded Amount, which shall be fully earned and payable in cash on the Closing Date.
Term:	The Notes shall become due and payable five (5) years after the Closing Date (the "**Maturity**"). Any and all then outstanding principal amount of the Notes (the "**Notes Principal**") plus any unpaid accrued Interest plus any other amounts due under the Notes shall be repaid in full in cash at Maturity.
Amortization:	The Borrower will repay the Notes Principal quarterly in an amount equal to $150,000 beginning three months after the Closing Date, with any remaining outstanding principal amount due at Maturity.
Cash Flow Sweep:	The Borrower will repay the Notes Principal in an amount equal to 50% multiplied by the Excess Cash Flow (the "**CF Sweep**"). The CF Sweep shall be paid annually within fifteen (15) days of Borrower finalizing fiscal year end audited financial statements. "**Excess Cash Flow**" shall be equal to EBITDA less total scheduled debt service (principal and interest) less unfinanced capital expenditures less cash taxes.

Exhibit A-3b (continued)

Participating Preferred Equity

Capital Contribution:	$2,000,000.
Preferred Return:	$8.0% PIK per annum.
Closing Payment:	2.0% of the Capital Contribution, which shall be fully earned and payable in cash on the Closing Date.
Additional Closing Payment:	10.0% of Additional Equity payable to Investor Group B upon issuance.
Preference:	The Preferred Equity will be senior to the Common Equity, and will be entitled to receive its unreturned Capital Contribution and unpaid Preferred Return prior to distributions being made to the Common Equity.
Participation:	The Preferred Equity will participate in all dividends alongside the Common Equity after the Preferred Equity has received its unreturned Capital Contribution and unpaid Preferred Return.
Redemption Right:	If the Preferred Equity remains outstanding after five (5) years following the Closing Date, Investor Group B will be entitled, but not obligated, to cause the Company to redeem the Preferred Equity for the fair market value of such equity as determined in accordance with an independent appraisal procedure.
Additional Equity:	Eastern Circle will have the right to issue and sell up to $1,000,000 of additional Preferred Equity at par to other investors within 60 days following the Closing Date.

Common Equity

Sponsor Ownership:	The Sponsor shall be allocated Common Equity ownership based on the schedule below.

Investor Group B Return on Equity Capital	Sponsor Equity Ownership Share	Preferred Equity Ownership Share
<=1.25x	10.0%	90.0%
>1.25x and <=1.50x	12.5%	87.5%
>1.50x and <=2.00x	15.0%	85.0%
>2.00x and <=2.50x	20.0%	80.0%
>2.50x and <=3.00x	25.0%	75.0%
>3.00x	30.0%	70.0%

Exhibit A-3b (continued)

Governing Terms

Collateral:

The Senior Obligations shall be secured by (i) a perfected first priority lien on any and all current and future assets of Borrower including, without limitation, cash and cash equivalents, accounts receivable (including any cash proceeds derived therefrom), inventory, customer lists, intellectual property, minerals, mineral rights, plant machinery and equipment, patents, trade secrets, personal property, real property, property and/or leasehold rights, and all other tangible and intangible assets, (ii) a first priority pledge of any and all capital stock and/or equity interests held directly or indirectly by or in accounts in similar form and substance of lockbox and/or control accounts in form and substance acceptable to the Lender.

Covenants:

The Senior Debt shall contain usual and customary affirmative and negative covenants for transactions of this nature including, without limitation, limitation on liens, limitation on current and future indebtedness (inclusive of payments thereon and thereto prior to Maturity), limitation on investments, restricted payments, sales of assets and/or capital stock, business combination transactions, negative pledges, affiliate transactions, key man provisions, and legal and regulatory compliance.

The Senior Debt shall contain certain quarterly financial and collateral covenants including, without limitation, the following:

Maximum Total Debt to EBITDA thresholds;

1. Minimum Total Interest Coverage;
2. Minimum Fixed Charge Coverage;
3. Maximum Capital Expenditures; and
4. Minimum Cash and/or Minimum Liquidity Ratios.

Default Interest:

Upon the occurrence of any Event(s) of Default (as defined below), the interest shall increase to the lesser of the (i) current Interest plus 3.0% and (ii) the highest lawful rate.

Event(s) of Default:

The Senior Debt shall contain usual and customary events of default for transactions of this nature including, without limitation, payment, bankruptcy, cross-default to other indebtedness, breach of covenant or representation, default on any other contract, material adverse change (including but not limited to litigation), and a Fundamental Change. **"Fundamental Change"** shall include without limitation any merger or other change of control transaction.

Exhibit A-3b (continued)

Future Offerings: So long as any Senior Obligation is outstanding and without the express written consent of Investor Group B, Borrower may not issue any debt or equity securities (including debt securities with an equity feature); provided however that Borrower may issue Common Equity and/or options to purchase Common Equity (which would dilute both Sponsor and Investor Group B on a prorata basis) pursuant to any current employee compensation plans.

Governance: Investor Group B shall have the right, but not the obligation to (i) appoint at least three (3) members to the Company's Board of Directors ("**Board**"), as desired. Sponsor shall have the right, but not the obligation, to appoint up to two (2) members of the Company's Board. The Board shall consist of no more than five (5) members. Investor Group B requires that the Board (i) conduct regularly scheduled meetings (at least quarterly), and (ii) invite members of the management team to participate in Board meetings as appropriate.

Interest: Shall mean Cash Interest, PIK Interest, Default Interest and any other Interest contemplated herein including, without limitation, any interest owed under the Senior Obligation or otherwise.

Prepayments(s): Borrower shall have the right (but not the obligation) to prepay the Senior Debt at any time prior to Maturity (in cash) with the following premiums(s) to the total amount of all outstanding Senior Debt (including accrued interest); provided however that no Event of Default either exists or is anticipated at the same time of such Prepayment.

Year 1: 105%
Year 2: 104% and
Year 3: 101%

For the avoidance of doubt, the Prepayment premium shall exclude Prepayments resulting from a CF Sweep. Upon any Event of Default, Borrower shall be required to prepay the Senior Obligations (in cash) in such amount that would provide Lender with full yield maintenance on the Senior Debt (as if Lenders were able to hold the Senior Debt to Maturity but accounting for the Amortization).

The Senior Debt shall contain usual and customary mandatory Prepayments for transactions of this nature.

Rank: The Senior Obligations shall be senior to any and all current and future indebtedness of Borrower and Guarantors.

Senior Debt: Shall be the Notes and all other debt securities of the Borrower in favor of Agent or Lenders.

Senior Obligation(s): The Notes, Interest, and all fees, expenses, obligations and other amounts owed by Borrower to Agent and Lenders as contemplated herein and in the Fee Letter.

Exhibit A-3b (continued)

Transaction Costs: Borrower shall reimburse the Agent and Lender for all costs incurred in connection with the transaction contemplated herein, including, without limitation, legal fees, advisor fees, consultant fees, costs and expenses, collateral valuations, appraisals, surveys, field examinations, third party diligence, lien searches, filing fees, and all other out-of-pocket costs and expenses in any way related to the transaction contemplated herein, and the enforcement and collection thereof.

Closing Conditions: This Proposal Letter is subject to, amongst other items, the following:

1. Representation by Borrower indicating that the transaction contemplated in this Proposal Letter (i) will be valid and enforceable, (ii) does not violate any existing Borrower contract and/or agreement whether written or verbal (as the case may be), and (iii) will not cause any existing Borrower securities and/or loans and/or facilities to be subject to any "price reset" or any other material change in terms;
2. Payment in cash by Borrower to Agent of all the amounts that have become due and owing as of the Closing Date, including, without limitation, the Closing Payments and all Transaction Costs;
3. Subordination of all other creditors (including the contemplated Seller Note), excluding trade creditors in the ordinary course of business, and execution of an inter-creditor agreement acceptable to Agent in its sole discretion, including, without limitation, any seller notes, earnout obligations, management fees and subordinated debt.
4. Review and acceptance in Investor Group B's sole discretion of the Sponsor's quality of earnings report;
5. Completion of comprehensive business, financial, environmental, insurance and legal due diligence satisfactory to Investor Group B in its sole discretion;
6. Execution of an employment agreement with Earl Gordon.

Exhibit A-3b (continued)

Miscellaneous

This Proposal Letter does not set forth all the terms and conditions of the Transaction. Rather this is only an outline, in summary format, of major points of understanding, which will form the basis of the definitive documentation. Investor Group B and its counsel will prepare the definitive loan documentation.

Except for the Borrower's obligations in the next paragraph hereof, this Proposal Letter is not, and shall not be deemed to be a binding agreement by Lender to consummate the Transaction. Such agreement will arise only upon the execution and delivery by Borrower of definitive documentation satisfactory in form and substance to Lender and the fulfillment, to the satisfaction of Lender, of the conditions precedent required by Lender and set forth herein and therein.

If the above is acceptable to you and Borrower, please sign and return the enclosed copy of this Proposal Letter to Investor Group B no later than the close of business on the day that is three (3) business days after the date of this Proposal Letter

[Signature Page Follows]

Acknowledged, Accepted, and Agreed to:

Sponsor: Fenton Avenue Capital, LLC

By:
Its:
Date:

Lender: Investor Group B

By:
Its:
Date:

Source: Company documents.

Earl Gordon Case Study Assignment Questions

1. Name two advantages and two disadvantages of becoming an entrepreneur via acquisition.
2. What qualifies Earl to be an entrepreneur?
3. Should Earl do a stock purchase or asset purchase?
4. At an $11 million purchase price, is Earl paying too much?
5. If Earl purchases Eastern Circle, would you invest? Why?
6. What is a search fund? How does it work?

Notes

1. Andersen, Duncan M., Warshaw, Michael, and Mulvihill, Mari-Alyssa. "The #1 Entrepreneur in America: Blockbuster Video's Wayne Huizenga," Success. March 1995. p. 36. Accessed March 29, 2021.
2. "Epiq Collective." www.epiqcollective.com/. Accessed March 29, 2021.
3. Toone, Stephanie. "Former Georgia State Roommates Broker Historic, $8.3 Million Hotel Deal with Hilton." *The Atlanta Journal-Constitution.* January 7, 2021. www.ajc.com/news/former-georgia-state-roommates-broker-historic-83-million-hotel-deal-with-hilton/2XJUMR5SDFDJXO Q6ZLI4OAVZYQ/
4. Givens, Dana. "These Former College Roommates Just Bought a Hilton Hotel for $8.3M." *Black Enterprise.* January 5, 2021. www.blackenterprise. com/these-college-roommates-turned-business-partners-close-deal-on-8-3-million-hotel/
5. "Two Black Former College Roommates Close Historic Deal on $8.3 Million Hotel." Black Business. January 3, 2021. www.blackbusiness .com/2021/01/davonne-reaves-jessica-myers-black-former-college-roommates-historic-deal-83-million-hotel.html
6. Daoust, Mark. "4 Models for Building Value Through Acquisitions." *Entrepreneur.* July, 30 2018. www.entrepreneur.com/article/316130/
7. Dennis, Josh and Laseca, Eric. "The Evolution of Entrepreneurship Through Acquisition." University of Chicago Booth School of Business. November 7, 2016. https://polsky.uchicago.edu/wp-content/uploads/2018/03/Booth-Research-Evolution-of-ETA_FA110716.pdf
8. Ibid.
9. Ibid.
10. Ibid.

11. Anderson, Michele. "A Black Man's Journey to the Forbes 400 List." SFGate. February 10, 1995. https://www.sfgate.com/entertainment/article/A-Black-Man-s-Journey-to-the-Forbes-400-List-3045896.php
12. "Reginald F. Lewis." www.reginaldflewis.com/. Accessed March 29, 2021.
13. Ibid.
14. Helm, Angela. "Billion-Dollar Legacy: Reginald F. Lewis' Incredible Life Story Comes to Film." *The Root*. February 16, 2018. www.theroot.com/billion-dollar-legacy-reginald-f-lewis-incredible-li-1823041385/
15. McKinney, Jeffrey. "How Reginald F. Lewis Influenced Generations of Black Entrepreneurs." *Black Enterprise*. October 5, 2020. www.blackenterprise.com/how-legendary-businessman-reginald-lewis-continues-to-influence-generations-of-black-entrepreneurs/
16. Meily, Rene. "Butch." "Inside the Wall Street Acquisition That Transformed Black Business." *Black Enterprise*. May 1, 2020. www.blackenterprise.com/inside-reginald-lewis-wall-street-billion-dollar-acquisition-beatrice-international/
17. Ibid.
18. Ibid.
19. Ibid.
20. McKinney, Jeffrey. "How Reginald F. Lewis Influenced Generations of Black Entrepreneurs." *Black Enterprise*. October 5, 2020. www.blackenterprise.com/how-legendary-businessman-reginald-lewis-continues-to-influence-generations-of-black-entrepreneurs/

5

Entrepreneurship Through Franchising

AN EVER-INCREASING NUMBER of Blacks are finding entrepreneurial success via franchising. One of the first Black entrepreneurs to avail himself of this model was Homer B. Roberts. In 1923, he became a franchisee of Hupmobile automobiles.[1]

Born in a small rural community outside of Springfield, Missouri, in 1885, Roberts received a degree from the Kansas State Agricultural College and later studied at the Tuskegee Institute, an HBCU. He served a tour in France during World War I, where he was the first Black man to attain the rank of Lieutenant in the U.S. Army Signal Corps. At the end of the war, Roberts returned to Kansas City and, in 1919, began selling used cars in the Black community, placing ads in local African American newspapers, including the *Kansas City Sun*. By the end of his first year in business he had sold 60 cars.[2] As his business grew, White car dealers recruited him to serve as their sales agent in Black communities, believing that an African American would be better at selling cars to Blacks than a White salesperson.[3]

In 1923, needing larger facilities to accommodate his expanding business, Roberts built the Roberts Motor Mart, a 9,400 square foot building, to house his car operations as well as provide retail space for other Black-owned businesses. This facility was one of the first retail shopping centers in the country and housed his offices, automotive operations, a restaurant, dress shop, barber shop, and other retail businesses, along with six professional offices, including medical and dental offices. An amazing aspect of the facility was its 1,800-square-foot showroom, service areas, and space to store and display 60 vehicles.[4]

Seeing his phenomenal success, several niche car manufacturers awarded him distribution franchises, including his first with Hupmobile in 1923 and Rickenbacker in 1925. He also had a franchise arrangement with a local Oldsmobile dealer from 1924 through 1927. At the height of his franchise business, he was brokering vehicles from 15 other dealers/distributors in the Kansas City and Chicago markets, employing over 50 African American workers.[5]

Today, there are over 700,000 different businesses in the franchise industry and they employ over 8 million people. Table 5.1 shows the plethora of industries that offer franchising opportunities.

Table 5.1 Franchise Industry 2019 (estimates)[6]

Business Line	Establishments	Employment	Output (Billions)
Business Services	106,936	650,489	$106.0
Commercial & Residential Services	67,226	252,803	$45.8
Lodging	29,706	662,382	$78.0
Personal Services	118,825	547,094	$39.3
Quick Service Restaurants	196,794	3,880,612	$267.9
Real Estate	65,307	262,130	$55.3
Retail, Food, Product, & Services	155,649	1,061,686	$118.3
Table/Full-Service Restaurants	33,160	1,116,894	$76.5
Totals	773,603	8,434,090	$787.5

The chance to become an entrepreneur via franchising has become quite an attractive opportunity for Black entrepreneurs. Recent research shows that over a five-year period the number of Black-owned franchise businesses, as a percentage of all franchise businesses, increased from 3.1% to 8%.[7]

How Franchising Works

The International Franchise Association defines franchising as "a method of distributing products or services involving a franchisor, who establishes the brand's trademark or trade name and a business system, and a franchisee, who pays a royalty and often an initial fee for the right to do business under the franchisor's name and system."[8]

Franchisees own and operate the franchise unit and, typically, are responsible for selecting the locations, negotiating, renting or purchasing the real estate, and effecting any remodeling to satisfy franchisor specifications when required. Franchisees are also responsible for the costs associated with operating the franchise, including hiring, paying, and training staff, local marketing initiatives, purchase of inventory and supplies, payment of utilities, legal fees, insurance, payroll, and benefits.

The franchisor provides a detailed operating guideline, a document that provides information on how to set up the franchise unit, hiring and staffing policies, procedures on how to use the franchisor's system, marketing and sales plans, and design or appearance standards.[9] In addition, training and support is provided to franchisees to ensure adherence to franchisor's standardized operational guidelines. Some of the more common training and support services provided by franchisors include the following:

- Site development assistance
- Training for franchisee and management team
- Research and development of new products and services
- Headquarters and field support
- Financial assistance
- Initial and continuing national marketing and advertising[10]

The Franchisor

This contractual arrangement provides benefits and disadvantages to both the franchisor and franchisee. The benefits for a franchisor include the following:[11]

- The ability to expand business operations without incurring additional debt or giving up equity since the investment costs associated with setting up and operating a franchise unit are borne by the franchisee.
- Reduced liability exposure since the franchisee signs all leases relating to the facility, equipment and upgrades, and contracts to hire and retain staff. The franchisor is not liable for any litigation concerning employee issues, consumer complaints, or workplace-related claims.[12]
- Business expansion without incurring the costs and challenges of recruiting and retaining additional management, supervision, and operation staff, which would have been the case if a franchisor had expanded through new company-owned outlets instead of franchising.
- The ability to open new locations in markets that would not have been feasible or cost-effective for the franchisor. Franchising allows companies to expand and compete with much larger businesses and to saturate a market before competitors can respond.
- Enjoy the benefits of collective buying power where the franchisor can pass on savings to franchisees.
- Work with motivated partners (owner-franchisees) and workforce in franchises who may be more willing to work harder compared to company managers and employees.

Disadvantages for a franchisor include the following:

- Franchise recruitment, selection, and retention may be a time-consuming and costly process.
- Constant and timely communication with franchisees is required to ensure uniformity and adherence to corporate standards and procedures.
- A single franchisee's financial situation and reputation can have a deleterious impact on the entire franchise network.

The Franchisee

The drawbacks and benefits for going the entrepreneurial route for the franchisee include the following:

- Proven Concept   A franchise provides an entrepreneur the opportunity to go into a business that has a recognized brand with an established reputation, a proven track record, and systems in place to quickly launch and run a business without the costly mistakes startup entrepreneurs might make in daily operations. Statistics show that 25% of startup businesses fail within their first year, with 50% of the remaining failing within five years, and approximately 30% of the remaining last 10 years.[13]
- Franchisees benefit from the market research undertaken by franchisors, which shows that there is a demand for the product or service. This market research also provides a good overview of the competition which allows the franchisees to develop ways to differentiate themselves from the field. Also, being part of a wider franchise network can give a business owner the ability to compete against bigger businesses, much more so than when operating as a small independent business.
- Turnkey Operation   Franchisees are provided everything they need—a tested product or service to sell, proven national marketing strategies, materials, supplies, and equipment necessary for a facility, supply networks and negotiated prices, and proven operational procedures with necessary training—to quickly start and run a business. In addition, a franchisee benefits from national marketing initiatives and business development strategies that the franchisor already has in place.
- Franchisees also receive ongoing support from the franchisor and the existing franchise network, benefiting from the ability to share ideas and the opportunities to collaborate (including but not limited to joint marketing and advertising campaigns).
- Training   Most franchisees are provided an operational manual that contains detailed information on the development of the new franchise unit, relevant laws and regulations, and specific guidelines on how the location is to be operated, along with reporting and compliance requirements.

- Training programs, held at either headquarters or onsite, provide instructions on a wide range of topics, from corporate history and philosophy to daily operation guidelines and reporting procedures and requirements.
- Some franchisors provide ongoing certification and core competency training for franchisees and staff to ensure maintenance of franchisor standards, in addition to new product training when necessary.
- Collective Buying Power   A franchisee benefits from the collective buying power of the parent company, which can result in savings on inventory and supply costs for the franchisee. Franchisees benefit from the resulting economies of scale in buying materials, supplies, and services, as well as in negotiating for locations and leases.
- Success   The success rate for those who become entrepreneurs via franchising is significantly higher than the success rate of entrepreneurship via start-ups. Less than 10% of franchisees fail.

Disadvantages for a Franchisee:

Cost   Buying and operating a franchise can be an expensive endeavor. The following list details some of the costs incurred by new franchisees:[14]

- The initial franchise fee (which may not be refundable), and the costs for initial inventory, signs, equipment leases, or rentals.
- Continuing royalty payments that franchisees incur based on a percentage of their weekly or monthly gross revenue. In many cases, royalties must be paid even if the outlet is not generating significant revenue. In case of voluntary termination, some franchisors require royalty payments for the remainder of the franchise term.
- Advertising costs include payments for both local ad campaigns as well as contributions to an advertising fund, which may be used for national advertising or to attract new franchise owners to the franchise network.

- Grand opening or other initial business promotion costs.
- Business or operating licenses fees.
- Product or service supply costs.
- Real estate and leasehold improvements costs.
- Discretionary equipment, such as a computer or security system.
- Training costs.
- Professional services costs include legal, financial, and accounting services.
- Insurance costs include operations related and employee health coverage.
- Compliance costs for local ordinances, such as zoning, waste removal, fire, and other safety codes.
- Employee salaries and benefits.
- Initial franchise fees range from $10,000 for home-based or mobile franchises to upward of $5 million, depending on the industry and the brand within the industry; most franchises see such costs range between $75,000 and $200,000. Specifically, at the low end, fees for a home-based or mobile concept can come in for $10,000 or less. At the high end are hotels, which can cost more than $5 million, including the land. Full-service restaurants will see fees from $750,000 to $3 million, or more. Fast-food restaurant can range from $250,000 to $1 million, or more, depending on the chain. Auto repair and maintenance facilities range between $200,000 and $300,000.[15]

No Flexibility   A franchisee must conform to the rules and regulations set by the franchisor, which are detailed in the franchise agreement. These restrictions dictate the terms under which a franchisee can operate an outlet and limit a franchisee's ability to exercise its own business judgment in operating that outlet. Some of these restrictions are the following:

- Preapproval of site locations for franchise outlets.
- Imposition of design or appearance standards to ensure a uniform look among various outlets. While some franchisors even require

periodic renovations or seasonal design changes at the expense of the franchisee.

- Restrictions on goods and services that a franchisee sells.
- Restrictions on operations include dictating hours of operation, preapproving signs, employee uniforms, and advertisements, or demanding that a franchisee use a particular accounting or book-keeping procedure or system. In some cases, franchisors may require that a franchisee sell goods or services at specific prices restricting the ability of the franchisee to offer discounts or require the purchase of supplies only from approved suppliers, even if similar products or services could be purchased cheaper elsewhere.
- Restrictions on sales areas, thus limiting a franchisee's business to a specific territory.
- Restrictions on the use of the internet to market and sell goods or services to customers in or out of the franchisee's territory.
- Answering to a Boss   The franchisee must adhere to strict rules and guidelines set out by the franchisor and cannot exercise independent decision-making.
- The franchise monitoring process may be intrusive, but the franchisee is contractually obligated to meet all requirements as stipulated in the franchise agreement.
- Franchise contracts are for a specified period, and the right to renew is not guaranteed. A franchisee can lose the right to the franchise if he/she breaches the franchise contract. Renewals are not automatic and may not have the original terms and conditions. The franchisor may choose to raise the royalty payment, impose new design standards and sales restrictions, or reduce the scope of the territory.
- A franchisor can terminate a franchise agreement for a variety of reasons including but not limited to failure to pay royalties or abide by performance standards and sales restrictions. In most cases, if a franchise agreement is terminated, there are termination clauses with financial penalties to the franchisee.
- Most franchise agreements will have restraints of trade conditions on the sale or termination of a franchise.

Negatives for Blacks   A unique challenge that Black franchisees face is the anti-Black racism of franchisors. Recently, 77 Black former franchise-owners of McDonald's filed a class action suit against the corporation alleging racial discrimination. Their contention was that the franchisor treated them differently than White franchise-owners. These differences in treatment have led to Black-owned stores earning, on average, $68,000 less per month than White-owned stores with similar revenue levels.[16] Much of this difference in treatment had to do with offering Black entrepreneurs franchises in poorer neighborhoods with higher security, renovation, and maintenance costs.

Almost four decades earlier, in 1984, a Black franchisee, Charles Griffis, sued McDonald's for similar elements of racial discrimination in their treatment of Black franchise owners. McDonald's settled the suit for a payout of $4.7 million to Griffis.[17] But these charges of racism by Black franchisees have not been limited to McDonald's. Similar racial problems existed with 7-Eleven, Burger King, and Wendy's.

Black Franchisees

One Black franchisee who experienced anti-Black discrimination but did not sue the franchisor was Zirl A. Palmer. He was the first Black owner of a drugstore franchise, Rexall Drugs.[18]

Zirl Palmer was born in Bluefield, Virginia, in 1919. Graduating from the HBCU of Bluefield State College with a BS in chemistry, he applied to a pharmacy school in neighboring West Virginia. Palmer was denied admission because of a prohibition against African Americans attending state public professional schools, so he relocated to New Orleans and earned an MS from Xavier University of Louisiana College of Pharmacy.[19]

Palmer returned from World War II a decorated veteran and, along with his wife, moved to Lexington, Kentucky, in 1952. In 1959, he purchased an office building in the East End, an economically diverse, predominantly Black neighborhood that was the hub of the African American community, with thriving Black-owned businesses. In 1961, he established "Palmer's Pharmacy, Luncheonette, and Doctor's Office," a franchise of Rexall Drugs. The pharmacy was the only Black-owned drugstore in Lexington and represented Rexall's first drugstore to be owned by an African American.[20] It served not only as a pharmacy where people could get their medications but also a gathering place where they could meet and socialize with friends and family. The second floor of the office building housed doctors' offices that provided an essential service to the Black community.

Palmer was an activist involved with numerous civic organizations including the local branch of National Association for the Advancement of Colored People (NAACP), United Negro College Fund, Chamber of Commerce, Kentucky Human Rights Commission, and Planned Parenthood, among others. He was the first African American member of the Optimist Club and Big Brothers, and the first African American to be appointed to the University of Kentucky's Board of Trustees, serving from 1972–1979.[21]

In 1966, Palmer opened a second pharmacy in the West End Plaza, a newly developed commercial shopping center in Lexington. On September 4, 1968, a bomb exploded at the shopping mall, destroying his new pharmacy, as well as several other stores, and wounding several bystanders including Palmer, his wife, and their four-year-old daughter. Although Palmer and his family survived the attack, he never reopened his pharmacies and chose to retire for the safety of his family. He believed that the bomb attack was in retaliation for his civil rights activities, and he was proven right in 1970 when an all-White jury convicted former Ku Klux Klan grand dragon Phillip J. Campbell for the crime.[22]

Like Zirl Palmer, Kia Patterson is a Black franchisee who is a great asset to the Black community. She grew up in Lynwood, California, a city less than five miles from Compton, where residents have few stores in their neighborhood where they can buy fresh fruits and vegetables. With 17 years of experience with the Smart & Final grocery chain, Patterson gained a depth of knowledge that supported her dream of one day owning her own grocery store in her neighborhood that would provide healthier food options to its customers.

In 2016, executives for the Grocery Outlet, a competing grocery chain, recruited Patterson to help them expand their franchise in the Los Angeles area. Three years earlier, the USDA had officially labeled

Compton a food desert, a low-income area where a substantial number or share of its residents have limited access to a supermarket or large grocery store. With the closing of several grocery outlets in and around Compton, area residents had few nearby places they could go to buy fresh and healthy foods. After completing her franchisee training with the company, she took ownership of the Compton Grocery Outlet store in April 2017.[23]

Owning her own grocery store gave Patterson a sense of freedom and empowerment. She notes, "I made the decision to own a Grocery Outlet so that I could have the freedom to be able to do what I want to do and not be pigeon-holed to anything. Now I have the ability to set my own destiny."[24]

Patterson recognized that in addition to achieving a personal goal, operating her grocery store served a greater purpose for the City of Compton by offering much needed, healthier, and less-expensive food options to its low-income residents. The organic products and other fresh food items sold were discounted up to 60% when compared to brand-name items found in other grocery chains.[25] Significantly, the store also created jobs for local residents. Patterson notes, "It's not only about providing good quality food. What I've always been about is giving back. Like, I have a school drive at the end of August. It's about playing that role, helping with fundraising with schools and being there not just to say, Hey, come get your groceries from me, but also helping out the community."[26]

Black Franchisor

Another Black Californian in the franchise industry is Lovie Yancey. Unlike the Black franchisee owners discussed earlier in the chapter, Yancey was one of the few Black franchisors in the country.[27]

Lovie Yancey was born in Bashrop, Texas, in 1912. After working as a restaurateur in Tucson, Arizona, Yancey moved to Los Angeles in the mid-1940s hoping to start a new food business. After considering different cuisines she decided to launch a burger restaurant because hamburgers were the fastest-selling sandwich in America. In 1947, she partnered with Charles Simpson, a construction company employee.

Using scrap materials to build a three-stool hamburger stand, they started Mr. Fatburger in South Los Angeles. She called the stand "Mr. Fatburger" because she wanted the name to project the idea that the hamburger had everything on it and was a meal in itself.

In 1952, Yancey bought out her partner, retaining sole proprietorship of the Mr. Fatburger brand, then she took off the "Mr.," reestablishing her hamburger store as Fatburger. The store was initially operating with normal business hours, but the popularity of its large, cook-to-order hamburgers led to demands from its customers that Yancey keep the stand open all night. She remarked, "As word got out how good the food was, we started getting requests from night shift and early morning workers—bus drivers, mailmen, street sweepers—to stay open longer."[28]

Fatburger also became a favorite of many celebrities in the Los Angeles area and, in 1973, Yancey opened a Beverly Hills store. In the 1990s, the chain was further popularized when rappers Ice Cube and The Notorious B.I.G. mentioned it in their songs.[29]

Under the tagline The Last Hamburger Stand, Yancey began offering franchises in 1981 and by 1985 there were four company locations and 15 franchise outlets in California. The company continued its franchise expansion, mainly in the California region, throughout the 1980s and into the early 1990s. In fact, in the years 1985–1987, Fatburger was named in *Entrepreneur* magazine's annual Franchise 500 list. In 1990, Yancey sold Fatburger to an investment group, but retained control of the original store on Western Avenue in South Los Angeles. Today, Fatburger is owned by FAT Brands Inc., a global franchising company that owns eight other restaurant brands including Johnnie Rockets, Elevation Burger, and Buffalo's Café.[30] Fatburger employs over 4,000 workers and operates over 175 locations across the United States and in 15 countries worldwide, including in Canada, China, Pakistan, and Qatar.

The genesis of all of this success from Fatburger was a Black woman—a Black woman who did not rest on the laurels of her entrepreneurial success. In 1986, Lovie Yancey donated $1.7 million to the City of Hope National Medical Center for research into sickle-cell anemia, a disease that primarily affects Black people. The donation was made in honor of her grandson, Duran Farrell, who died from the disease in 1983.[31]

Another Black woman who had success as a franchisor was Annie Turbo Malone, mentioned in Chapter 3 about Black start-up entrepreneurs. As was noted, she created a franchise model, targeting Black women as franchisees, that was later adopted by blue chip cosmetic companies such as Avon and Mary Kay.

This phenomenon of Black franchisors creating entrepreneurship opportunities for Black businessmen and women, continued from Malone's work in the early 1900s to the 1930s when Victor Hugo Green created the *Green Book* directory, also mentioned in Chapter 3. This guide to Black-owned businesses that served Black patrons was published for 30 years from 1936 to 1966. Green was able to sell over 15,000 books annually throughout the country by providing franchising opportunities to Black entrepreneurs, who were one of his distribution channels.

An interesting thing about this entrepreneurial venture was the founder's prediction of the demise of the company. In 1948, he published the following, "There will be a day sometime in the near future when this guide will not have to be published. That is when we as a race will have equal opportunities and privileges in the United States. It will be a great day for us to suspend this publication for then we can go wherever we please, and without embarrassment."[32]

Introduction to the Case Study

The following case study is an introduction to franchising through the work of Valerie Daniels-Carter, who owns restaurant franchises across the country. The case looks at the history of franchising, franchise options, and how to do a financial analysis of franchise opportunities.

HARVARD | BUSINESS | SCHOOL

9-317-030
FEBRUARY 3, 2017

STEVEN ROGERS

ALYSSA HAYWOODE

Valerie Daniels-Carter: High Growth Entrepreneurship via Franchising

To be a Franchisee or a Franchisor

Valerie Daniels-Carter had been traveling across the states, visiting some of the 120 restaurants she owns through her Milwaukee-based company, V&J Holdings. After more than 30 years of owning franchises, she was considering a new direction. Instead of buying another franchise – she already owned well-known franchise stores, including Burger Kings and Pizza Huts – she was thinking about becoming a franchisor. It would take several years to develop and test ideas, but she knew she could create a restaurant business and sell it to other entrepreneurs.

Daniels-Carter wanted to create opportunities that had not existed when she was a young African-American businesswoman breaking into franchising. She wanted to create an opportunity for new entrepreneurs that they could learn quickly. She already owned two businesses that she could franchise: MyYoMy, a frozen yogurt store, and the restaurant Nino's Southern Sides.

But Daniels-Carter also had another project in mind. She wanted to expand the breadth of her franchises, and she was interested in seafood restaurants. Demand for seafood was rising, and many communities lacked local restaurants. Several national seafood chains had franchise opportunities, and Daniels-Carter wanted to expand in downtown areas and inner city communities.

She would have to figure out which project to focus on – or whether she could do both. And if she did both, she would have to do two things:

- develop a plan for becoming a franchisor of a restaurant, and

- pick a national seafood chain that she could invest in.

She wanted to create new entrepreneurial opportunities in new places. She just needed to figure out the best way to do it.

HBS Senior Lecturer Steven Rogers and independent researcher Alyssa Haywoode prepared this case. It was reviewed and approved before publication by a company designate. Funding for the development of this case was provided by Harvard Business School and not by the company. HBS cases are developed solely as the basis for class discussion. Cases are not intended to serve as endorsements, sources of primary data, or illustrations of effective or ineffective management.

The Evolution of an African-American Businesswoman

It was 1982. Ronald Reagan was the president. Michael Jackson's album, *Thriller,* was selling millions of copies. And the United States economy was in a recession.

Valerie Daniels-Carter was looking for a business opportunity that would be a long-term success. As a child, she had run small businesses: a lemonade stand and a service walking small children home from school. After college she had a great job at a bank but her plan had always been to own her own business. She had been saving the money to do it for years.

Daniels-Carter had her eye on a major fast food chicken chain when her brother, John Daniels, a lawyer, told her that Operation PUSH, the national nonprofit founded by the Rev. Jesse Jackson, had reached an agreement with Burger King to increase the participation of African Americans in all areas of the hamburger chain's business. Burger King was one of a number of corporations that Rev. Jackson confronted, pressing them to hire more African Americans, and advertise with African-American advertising agencies. Rev. Jackson estimated that the Burger King agreement could have a $500 million economic impact.

To capitalize on this opportunity, Daniels-Carter and her brother merged the initials of their first names to form V&J Foods. In 1984, using her savings and an investment from her brother, Daniels-Carter opened her first Burger King restaurant in her hometown of Milwaukee. She worked behind the counter. She took time to learn the lessons that managing a restaurant teaches. Then she began to grow, adding more and more restaurants.

In 2014, Daniels-Carter and four other African-American entrepreneurs formed Partners for Community Impact and became part owners of the Milwaukee Bucks, the city's franchise in the National Basketball Association. In October 2014, Daniels-Carter told the *Milwaukee Business Journal* that she and her partners wanted to help rebuild the team to help make Milwaukee a more appealing place to live.

"Part of attracting individuals to Wisconsin is what does the city have to offer? Is it a forward-thinking city?" she told the newspaper.

By 2016, V&J Holdings had grown into a multi-state franchising business (in Wisconsin, Michigan, Minnesota, New York, and Massachusetts) with more than 120 restaurants, 4,000 employees, and approximately $90 million in annual revenues. The franchises included:

- Burger King

- Auntie Anne's - a pretzel store

- Pizza Hut

- Häagen-Dazs ice cream

- Coffee Beanery

It was all run from Daniel-Carter's headquarters on Milwaukee's Brown Deer Road, where 30 employees worked and generous amounts of laughter and hard work filled the offices.

Why not declare victory and go on a permanent vacation?

"I'm not going where success has been," Daniels-Carter said. "I'm going where it's going."

Philanthropy and Faith: Reinvesting in Local and Global Communities

A tenet of Daniels-Carter's faith was that everyone has a God-driven purpose.

"It's not just about financial success, it's about the totality of life," she explained. "And if you can't put the pieces to life together – family, personal, work and spiritual – if you can't pull all that together and have a whole life, then you're missing part of who you are."

Daniels-Carter had invested a great deal of her time, energy, and money into Milwaukee. Working with government and nonprofit partners, including another brother, Bishop Sedgwick Daniels, pastor of the city's Holy Redeemer Church, she donated money to build an educational and social services complex.

Her favorite part of the complex was the Mother Kathryn Daniels Conference Center for Community Empowerment and Reunification, which opened in 2004 in an African-American neighborhood. Named after Daniels-Carter's mother, the center housed a Boys and Girls Club, a credit union, and a clinic that provided affordable health care. The center's gym was named after Daniels-Carter's husband, Jeffrey Alan Carter Sr. He died in 1999, and Kathryn Daniels passed away a year later – two losses that compelled Daniels-Carter to become stronger.

The complex also offered educational programs, housing services, and social services. Nearby, an empty factory building was being turned into a business incubator for start-up companies. Another building was to become an arts center.

A member of the Church of God in Christ (COGIC), Daniels-Carter served as the jurisdictional supervisor for COGIC's Kenya East Africa Jurisdiction Department of Women. This initiative includes a "self-sustainability project," essentially a microloan program that helped women and orphanage directors start poultry farms.

To launch the poultry farms, 18 farmers received chicks, food and other supplies. A facility was built where the chicks were raised. Once the chicks had grown into chickens, the farmers sold them. Participants were also required to help other women establish businesses, encouraging both generosity and community networking. More women were being recruited and the program was being expanded so that the farmers could also raise fish and pigs.

Daniels-Carter was also involved in funding the renovation of a local orphanage – rebuilding walls and installing a water tank and windows – and building a clinic with 10 exam rooms.

Why give away so much money?

"I enjoy seeing people be successful," she said. "That motivates me."

What is Franchising?

Franchise businesses cover America. The list of familiar ones includes McDonald's, Starbucks, Dunkin' Donuts, H. & R. Block, Planet Fitness, Ace Hardware, Midas, 7-Eleven, and the UPS Store. Embassy Suites and Days Inn are both franchises. Consumers rent cars and trucks from Hertz and U-Haul franchises. Toddlers play and sing at Gymboree franchises.

At the core of these businesses is a simple concept: a company sells an entrepreneur the right to offer a product or service using the company's brand name and business model. In this transaction, the company is the franchisor, and the entrepreneur is the franchisee.

Selling franchises helps companies generate cash that can finance future growth. And entrepreneurs who buy franchises can invest in a proven business model that typically has a strong brand name.

Franchising terms vary widely. It can take millions of dollars to buy a fast food franchise or a couple of thousand dollars to buy an office cleaning franchise. An individual can buy the rights to operate one store or run multiple stores across a region.

The history of franchising has several versions. Some point to the Middle Ages when feudal lords allowed other people to run markets. Others point to Germany in the 1840s when brewers sold rights to sell ale to taverns.

But in the United States, it was Isaac Singer who planted a fertile franchising seed in the 1800s with his sewing machine. Singer sold licenses that let buyers sell the machines and teach people how to use them. The license fees gave him the money he needed to manufacture more machines.

In 1968, Herman Petty became the first African American owner of a McDonald's franchise in Chicago. It was the first of his nine stores. And in 1972, Petty cofounded the National Black McDonald's Operators Association. In 1970, Brady Keys, a former player for the National Football League's Pittsburgh Steelers, became the first African-American owner of a Burger King, in Detroit.

By 2016, there were "more than 800,000 franchise establishments representing 300 lines of business. More than 9 million people work at locally owned franchises in neighborhoods across the country," according to the website, @OurFranchise.org, which was launched by the International Franchising Association to showcase "the positive attributes of the franchise industry by telling the stories of local franchise owners, employees and their communities."

The news for African American-owned franchises was not as good. A 2011 report from the International Franchise Association looked at data from 2007 and found that African-Americans -- who comprised 12 percent of the population of the United States -- owned 4.9 percent of franchised businesses. In addition, 2.9 percent of all businesses owned by African-Americans were operated as franchises.

More recent estimates appeared in a *USA Today* article on Daniels-Carter in 2016 that noted: "African-American owners make up just 3% of franchise owners, according to Eric Stites, CEO and Managing Director of the Franchise Business Review, an independent franchise market research firm, based on a survey of 27,000 franchises over the last 18 months."

Miriam Brewer, senior director of education and diversity for the International Franchise Association, who was quoted in the article said that African-Americans face several barriers in the franchising industry, including lack of knowledge about franchising and less access to capital.

However, there are a number of African-American franchisees, among them:

- Homer Roberts, who owned an Oldsmobile car dealership in 1923

- William Harvey, the first African-American owner of a Pepsi bottling franchise, who went on to become the president of Hampton University

- Nicole Enearu who owned two McDonald's restaurants in the greater Los Angeles area and ran the operations for 13 other McDonald's that were owned by her mother, Patricia Williams

- Magic Johnson, former NBA star, and the owner of movie theater and restaurant franchises

- Maurice Welton, an Edible Arrangements franchisee

- Clayton Turnbull, CEO of the Waldwin Group, a Dunkin' Donuts franchisee

- Venus Williams, tennis star and juice franchise owner

- Omar Simmons, a graduate of Harvard Business School, who owned more than 50 franchised Planet Fitness health clubs

Choosing a Franchise – and Financing It

Given the hundreds of choices of franchises, entrepreneurs have to decide: Which one is best for me?

To come up with an answer, entrepreneurs have to consider their personal preferences, assess their professional strengths, and crunch a lot of numbers.

To increase their chances of success, entrepreneurs should have relevant business and management experience as well as passion for the industry they are choosing and enough humility to do the grunt work that their franchise may require.

Companies will publish the criteria they expect franchisees to meet.

For example, the minimal financial requirements to open a Burger King in 2015 were:

- a net worth of at least $1.5 million

- $500,000 liquid capital

- paying a monthly royalty fee of 4.5% of gross sales

- paying a 20-year franchise fee of $50,000

- an advertising rate contribution of 4% of gross sales

Franchisees also have to enroll in a training program that can be as long as two years.

Full details were outlined in Burger King's 2015 Franchise Disclosure Document. It was posted online at http://gwdocs.whopper.com/FDD/FDD_USA.pdf.

Often referred to as FDDs, franchise disclosure documents can be quite long, and they provide exact franchising details as well as information about earnings. They should be carefully reviewed by entrepreneurs, their lawyers, and accountants.

Is there room to negotiate? Sometimes.

Burger King's 2015 disclosure document offers discounted royalty rates to military veterans who served in Iraq or Afghanistan as well as to police officers and fire fighters. Franchisees also get reduced royalty rates if they open a Burger King in a big box store. The location of a restaurant – whether in the mall, at the airport, on a college campus, or co-branded in a movie theater lobby with, say, an ice cream company – will also affect the development costs that a franchisee has to pay.

Entrepreneurs should also consider other financial and business information such as:

- average unit volume = sales / the total number of a franchisor's units or stores

- sales per square foot

- expected return on investment

- location, location, location, and

- exit strategies: the resale potential when the franchisee is ready to move

Once an entrepreneur chooses a franchise, she has to pay for it. Sometimes franchisors will offer financing assistance. If not, then franchisees have to find their own financing.

The options include:

- cash on hand

- commercial loans

- web-based lending portals

- personal loans

- loans approved by the Small Business Administration

Becoming a Franchisor

There are considerable financial and marketing challenges to becoming a franchisor. The Small Business Administration warns:

> You will need to pay attorneys to handle your legal documents and to register your franchise. Additional costs will include paying accountants, creating marketing materials and running advertising to promote the franchise to prospective franchisees. Don't forget about training the employees and developing manuals and other systems you'll need to run the franchise. All in all, you might be looking at $250,000 or more (in addition to the normal costs of running your business in the meantime) to create a sustainable franchise system.

An article in *Entrepreneur* magazine adds, "Just because you qualify to sell franchises doesn't mean you will find buyers. Data from the International Franchise Association shows that of the 105 companies that started selling franchises in 2008, more than 40 had not reported the sale of their first unit by the end of 2009."

Moving Forward: Franchisee, Franchisor, or Both

Option 1 – Invest in a Seafood Franchise in Urban and Inner City Markets

Daniels-Carter was also interested in opening seafood restaurants. The demand for seafood was high and had room to grow.

"Over the past two decades, per capita consumption of seafood products in the U.S. has ranged from a low of 14.6 pounds per person in 1997 to a record high of 16.6 pounds in 2004. Since 2004, U.S. annual consumption of fish and shellfish has gradually decreased to 14.6 pounds per person in 2014," according to SeafoodHealthFacts.org, a joint project of Oregon State University; Cornell University; the universities of Delaware, Rhode Island, Florida, and California; and the Community Seafood Initiative.

Often consumers who wanted fish had to cook it at home or leave their local market areas to get it. And as more people moved back to downtown areas, Daniels-Carter expected to see growing demand there. There was also potential in inner city communities among African-American residents. Daniels-Cater was looking at opening restaurants in Milwaukee and Detroit.

"We feel there is a huge opportunity to grow in these markets," Daniels-Carter said.

Optimism was running high in the seafood restaurant industry as more consumers sought to eat healthier food that also tastes good. Fish offers weight-conscious Americans a low-fat, low-carb meal with valuable omega-3 fatty acids. In a retail environment saturated with hamburgers, pizza, and chicken, seafood stood out as a different choice. While fried seafood might not be healthier, grilled seafood offered a more nutritiously sound option.

Daniels-Carter looked at all the national franchises in this arena. Two franchises -- Susannah's Seafood Emporium and the Coney Island Cookery -- laid out the opportunities and challenges in the seafood restaurant industry.

Both franchises are excited about the ready availability of Alaska pollock, a mild flavored white fish. NOAA, the National Oceanographic and Atmospheric Administration, reported that "During 2014, pollock made up 64% of the total groundfish catch off Alaska. The pollock catch for 2014 was 1,442,840 metric tons (t), up approximately 0.05% from 2013."

In 2012, NOAA had also warned, however, that warmer ocean conditions were "less favorable" for the large zooplankton that pollock like to eat. Warmer water is also more favorable for arrowtooth flounder, predators that eat young pollocks.

Other kinds of fish were also readily available, according to SeafoodHealthFacts.org, which explained the output of commercial fisheries and aquaculture:

Commercial Fisheries

"About 9.5 billion pounds of edible seafood products with a dockside value of $5.4 billion," in 2014. Most of this catch (over 84%) "is finfish and the rest is shellfish." The leading species "landed by U.S. commercial fishermen in 2014 in descending order includes: Alaska pollock, menhaden, flatfish, cod, salmon, hakes, sea herring, shrimp, crabs, and squid. Alaska led all states in volume of landings in 2014 with 60% of the total catch; followed by Louisiana at 9%, Washington at 6%, Virginia at 4.3%, and California at 3.6%."

Aquaculture Production

In 2013 some 662 million pounds of farm raised fish and shellfish were produced in 2013. "In the United States, the amount of fish and shellfish harvested from the wild annually is about 7 times greater than the amount produced by domestic aquaculture farms. Pond raised catfish represents a little over half of the total farm raised seafood products produced annually in the U.S. Other important domestically produced aquaculture products in order of the quantity produced include: crawfish, trout, oysters, salmon, tilapia, striped bass, shrimp, clams, and mussels."

Some analysts pointed out that seafood restaurants might also face competition from companies such as Blue Apron that deliver raw meal-in-a-box ingredients to consumers' homes. Fish was a popular choice, and some consumers might enjoy experimenting with new recipes in the comfort of their own kitchens.

One national seafood franchise reported its 2014 average profits per store by tiers:

Top-third franchise restaurants = gross sales of $1,386,419

Middle-third restaurants = gross sales of $938,420

Bottom-third restaurants = gross sales of $694,048

Coney Island Cookery

Founded in 1962 in Brooklyn, the Coney Island Cookery (CIC) offered "classic" fried seafood. With a vintage 1950s decor, CIC restaurants harked back to a time when consumers could eat what they wanted without feeling guilty.

Investment: $700,000 to $800,000

Required liquid assets: $360,000

Net worth required: $900,000

Franchise fee: $20,000

Royalty: 6% of sales

Advertising fee: $5,000

Susannah's Seafood Emporium

Founded in 1970 in Scarsdale, New York, Susannah's was a reliable, suburban favorite. It offered fried food in a low-key setting. In 2011, the chain updated its look and its menu.

Investment: $950,000

Required liquid assets: $400,000

Net worth required: $850,000

Franchise fee: $35,000

Royalty: 4.5% of sales

Advertising fee: 1.1% of sales

See **Exhibit 3** for more information.

Option 2 – Yogurt and Southern Food - A Franchisor Experiment

Daniels-Carter could franchise her MyYoMy frozen yogurt and Nino's Southern Cooking restaurants.

She wanted to demystify the business to create an opportunity "for individuals that have entrepreneurial spirits where the cost of entry would not preclude them from being able to realize their dream."

"I'm doing it from the perspective of: 'When I went into business, I didn't have that.' And that's what MyYoMy and Ninos are really all about."

When she entered "the franchising world it was very limited. Zero to almost no women and minorities."

Thirty years later, she wanted to lay out a welcome mat, or as she said, an opportunity map, for other entrepreneurs. "If I don't do it, who will?"

Frozen Yogurt

There were two MyYoMy stores. One was a stand-alone store in Milwaukee that opened in 2012. The other one was in a strip mall in the nearby suburb of Foxpoint. It opened in 2015. To bulk up softer sales in winter, when fewer people buy frozen yogurt, the MyYoMy stores sell Goody Gourmet's popcorn, a product made by Jacqueline Chesser, another local African-American entrepreneur.

"Nowadays, customers aren't just coming in for the frozen yogurt, but also for these franchises' 'chill' store settings. Trending away from the outdated ice-cream parlor environment, modern froyo [frozen yogurt] stores include high-end furniture, Wi-Fi, flat-screen televisions, and live musical performances," according to the International Franchise Association's FranchiseHelp.com website.

Frozen yogurt sales were strong in the 1980s when franchises like TCBY and I Can't Believe It's Yogurt were popular, according to the website FranchiseHelp.com. But in time, sales bottomed out.

"According to the Agricultural Marketing Resource Center, retail sales of frozen yogurt fell between 1998 and 2003, while ice cream sales grew by 24%," FranchiseHelp.com says, adding:

"However, with new frozen yogurt franchises like MY Culture, 16 Handles, Farr's Fresh, The Fuzzy Peach, Yogurtini, Pinkberry, and Yogurtland blending innovative varieties of flavors and toppings, the frozen yogurt industry is now back on track and more popular than ever before."

Guidant Financial reports that Bob Visse, managing partner of Peaks Frozen Yogurt Bars in Washington state, thinks "the frozen yogurt industry is quickly approaching 'maturation.' With so many stores launching over the past five years, existing stores have experienced increased competition and growth is expected to slow in the next five years as a result. IBISWorld estimates that the industry will grow at a tempered annual rate of 3.4 percent to reach $2.1 billion in revenue by 2019."

But frozen yogurt's saturation does vary by region. There is a great deal of competition in California and New York, but less competition in colder states and the Plains states.

Southern Cuisine

Nino's Southern Cooking was meant to be a takeout restaurant, but because of its popularity, Daniels-Carter added more seating. There were two locations, one in the Milwaukee suburb of

Shorewood, which opened in 2014, and the other in Milwaukee proper, which opened in 2015. The restaurants menus included collard greens, green beans, pinto beans, fried corn yams, okra, and macaroni and cheese. Customers could also order chicken, pork chops, and fried catfish.

"Despite the name, the restaurant sells more than soul food side dishes," the *Milwaukee Journal Sentinel* reported in a restaurant review. "Three pieces of fried chicken were at the center of one weekday dinner. Breast, thigh and wing; hot, crisp and juicy. It was deep-fried perfection."

Locally, Nino's faced competition from Daddy's Soul Food and Grille, Maxie's, and other restaurants. But Nino's was carving out its own niche with its take-out option and moderate prices.

Other southern food franchises were also pursuing opportunities for growth. Among them was Huddle House, which serves breakfast, lunch, and dinner at any time of day. With 400 restaurants in place or in development, the company was "in the midst of a plan to significantly accelerate unit growth over the next three to five years." Part of its strategy was to focus on small towns where competitors such as the International House of Pancakes (IHOP) had no stores.

This kind of comfort food also received a plug from Nestle Professional, "If there's one thing you can count on in this competitive, rapidly changing, trend-driven food service environment, it's consumer demand for comfort food. Classic favorites like barbecue, roast chicken, meat loaf, and macaroni and cheese continue to attract fans, even in venues like cutting-edge college dining halls where there may be dozens of other options on offer, from sushi to salad bars."

According to the 2014 Restaurant Industry Report released by Mazzone and Associates:

"For large players such as McDonalds, profit margins at company-operated restaurants can be as high as 15.0-20.0% due to the large economies of scale the organization has access to. However, the profit margin of a small enterprise that operates only one restaurant will be much lower. In 2014, the average QSR [quick service restaurant] obtained a profit margin of 5.0% of revenue, up from a low of 3.6% during the recession of 2009. This explains the high turn-over rate of businesses and the highly competitive nature of the industry. Typically, an operator's major costs are food and beverages purchased for sale and wages paid, and if these are not managed skillfully an operator's profit margin will take a hit."

See **Exhibit 4** for more information.

Next Steps

Daniels-Carter wanted to act quickly to keep ahead of competitors and keep up with industry growth. Markets conditions could change, and she wanted to make a decision and act on it.

Exhibit 1   Valerie Daniels-Carter's Resume

V&J Holdings

Valerie Daniels-Carter, president
John Daniels, chairman of the board
Est. 1982
First restaurant: Burger King, 1984

Headquarters: Milwaukee, Wisc.
Regional Office: Rochester, N.Y.

Restaurants:

Burger King
Pizza Hut
Auntie Anne's (partnership with former NBA player Shaquille O'Neal)
Häagen-Dazs
Coffee Beanery
MyYoMy Frozen Yogurt
Nino's Southern Foods

120 restaurants
4,000 employees

Education:
Lincoln University (MO.), BS, Business Administration
Cardinal Stritch University, M.S. Management, 1983; Honorary Doctor of Humane Letters, 2006

Career:
First Wisconsin National Bank - retail and commercial lender

MGIC Investment Corporation (mortgage insurance company) - auditor in the financial underwriting division

V&J Foods / V&J Holdings - president

Select Community Work and Awards:

Trustee of Green Bay Packers Foundation Trustee
Vice Chair of AAA's National Board
Essence magazine's Top 10 Black Female Entrepreneurs
Black Enterprise magazine's Women of the B.E. 100

Source: V&J Holding Companies website, http://www.vjfoods.com/about, http://www.vjfoods.com/our-president, accessed February 11, 2016; "Black female franchise owner battled 'cement ceiling' in quest for success," *USA Today*, http://www.usatoday.com/story/news/nation-now/2016/01/30/blacks-franchising-burger-king/78382550/, accessed February 11, 2016.

Exhibit 2   Select News Coverage

"Black female franchise owner battled 'cement ceiling' in quest for success," *USA Today*, February 11, 2016

"When Valerie Daniels-Carter tried to franchise her first Burger King in the early 1980s, there weren't many other African-American women in the sector – and she didn't exactly find a 'welcome mat,' she said.

"At times, she recalled, it felt less like she was up against a 'glass ceiling' than a 'cement ceiling.'"

"Hard Work and Charity," by Valerie Daniels-Carter, *The New York Times*, August 25, 2012

"My parents instilled a strong work ethic in my siblings and me.

"In first grade, I walked four kindergartners to and from school and made $1.25 a week. I was only a year older than them, but I was tall and looked older than I was. Their parents thought I offered some measure of protection. A couple of years ago, I became reacquainted with one of those girls.

"As a preteen, I started arranging my two younger brothers' work assignments. They cut lawns and shoveled snow. I'd price the jobs and distribute a schedule to their clients. In my teens, I worked for the parks system and managed a restaurant for a food vendor at Summerfest, a music festival. Later, I served on and was president of the board of the parent organization, the Milwaukee World Festival.

"My father died in my senior year in high school. While attending Lincoln University in Jefferson City, Mo., I worked several jobs to help my mother pay my way. I was a disc jockey, a supermarket cashier and an assistant to a professor in a chemistry lab."

"Mega Franchise Owner Valerie R. Daniels Carter Named a Women of Power Legacy Award Winner," *Black Enterprise magazine*, January 21, 2014

"Black Enterprise has brought together thousands of women who are serious about making power moves at the annual Women of Power Summit, now in its ninth year. Executives, entrepreneurs and innovators network, bond and share ideas that help them move their businesses, their careers and their personal lives forward. They also honor the leaders among them, those outstanding women who receive the coveted Legacy Award.

"Joining the group of this year's esteemed honorees is Valerie R. Daniels-Carter, president and CEO of V&J Holding Cos. Inc., ranked No. 33 on the Black Enterprise Industrial/Service 100 list with $88 million in revenues. V&J is one of the largest women-owned and African-American-owned food service franchise operators in the U.S. with 114 franchise units that employ 4,000 people."

Source: "Black female franchise owner battled 'cement ceiling' in quest for success," *USA Today*, http://www.usatoday.com/story/news/nation-now/2016/01/30/blacks-franchising-burger-king/78382550/, accessed February 11, 2016; "Hard Work and Charity," Valerie Daniels-Carter, *The New York Times*, August 25, 2012, http://www.nytimes.com/2012/08/26/jobs/valerie-daniels-carter-of-vj-holding-on-her-career.html?_r=0), accessed February 11, 2016; "Mega Franchise Owner Valerie R. Daniels Carter Named a Women of Power Legacy Award Winner," *Black Enterprise magazine*, January 21, 2014, http://www.blackenterprise.com/small-business/mega-franchise-owner-valerie-r-daniels-carter-named-a-women-of-power-legacy-award-winner/, accessed February 11, 2016.

Exhibit 3   Corporate Information for the Coney Island Cookery and Susannah's Seafood Emporium

Coney Island Cookery Corporation - 2015

Revenues	$550 million
Cost of goods sold	$350 million
Selling, General, and Administrative Expenses (SGA)	$150 million
Depreciation and Amortization	$10 million
Taxes	$15 million
Interest	$1 million

Investment: $700,000 to $800,000
Required liquid assets: $360,000
Net worth required: $900,000
Franchise fee: $20,000
Royalty: 6% of sales
Advertising fee: $5,000
Restaurants
    2013   890 in 40 states, 20 of these are company-owned
    2014   850 in 40 states, 15 of these are company-owned
    2015   815 in 40 states, 10 of these are company-owned
Total sales from all restaurants:
    2013 $710 million
    2014 $650 million
    2015 $550 million
Standalone restaurant size: 2,500 square feet
Required parking spots: 30

Susannah's Seafood Emporium Corporation

Revenues	$510 million
Cost of goods sold	$305 million
Selling, General, and Administrative Expenses (SGA)	$145 million
Depreciation and Amortization	$10 million
Taxes	$10 million
Interest	$1 million

Investment: $950,000
Required liquid assets: $400,000
Net worth required: $850,000
Franchise fee: $35,000
Royalty: 4.5% of sales
Advertising fee: 1.1% of sales
Restaurants
    2013   500 restaurants in 30 states, 270 of these are company-owned
    2014   490 restaurants in 30 states, 265 of these are company-owned
    2015   495 restaurants in 30 states, 265 of these are company-owned
Total sales from all restaurants:
    2013 $460 million
    2014 $470 million
    2015 $500 million
Stand alone restaurant size: 3,000 square feet
Required parking spots: 34-38

Source: Casewriter estimates.

Exhibit 4   Options for Becoming a Franchisor

The franchise options that Daniels-Carter is considering.

1. Projected MyYoMy Financials

Initial investment: $240,000 - $400,000
Net-worth requirement: $350,000 - $400,000
Liquid cash requirement: $40,000
Initial franchise fee: $30,000
Ongoing royalty fee: 4% of gross revenue
Ad royalty fee: 3% of gross revenue

	Year 1	Year 2	Year 3
Revenues:	$300,000	$340,000	$400,000
Cost of Goods Sold	$100,000	$110,000	$130,000
Operating expenses	$100,000	$105,000	$110,000
Depreciation & Amortization	$10,000	$10,000	$10,000
Taxes	$15,000	$20,000	$25,000
Interest	$20,000	$20,000	$20,000

2. Projected Nino's Financials

Initial investment: $190,000 - $680,000
Net worth requirement: $400,000
Liquid cash requirement: $200,000
Initial franchise fee: $30,000
Ongoing royalty fee: 6% of gross revenue
Ad royalty fee: 2% of gross revenue

	Year 1	Year 2	Year 3
Revenues	$500,000	$520,000	$550,000
Cost of Goods Sold	$180,000	$190,000	$200,000
Operating expenses	$140,000	$145,000	$150,000
Depreciation & Amortization	$20,000	$20,000	$20,000
Taxes	$20,000	$28,000	$35,000
Interest	$18,000	$18,000	$18,000

Source: Casewriter estimates.

Exhibit 5   Southern Food in the News

"Southern fast-food chains are taking over the rest of America," Business Insider, February 20, 2016

"For years, Southern transplants in New York City complained about the lack of Chick-fil-A.

"Then, in 2015, their prayers for chicken sandwiches were answered, with the opening of the first stand-alone Manhattan Chick-fil-A restaurant. On Tuesday, the company announced plans to open its second Manhattan location.

"Chick-fil-A isn't the only Southern chain gearing up for a Northern expansion.

"Winston-Salem, North Carolina-based Krispy Kreme announced on Monday that it signed a development deal to open seven locations in New Hampshire and Maine in the coming years."

"Bojangles' executive on expanding beyond the Southeast," CNBC, May 16, 2014

"Already proliferating, Bojangles' chicken chain may add "hundreds" of new locations in the Southeast and could move into other regions it had abandoned after a previous expansion, a top executive said."

"For now, the company plans to concentrate this expansion in its existing U.S. base. But moving forward, the company's fried chicken and biscuits could be soon outside its traditional markets."

"'We'll open 55 to 60 restaurants this year,' Eric Newman, Bojangles executive vice president, said in an interview with CNBC. 'Depending on how you look at that, it's one every six days.'"

"'I think we could go up and down the East Coast, further west, and maybe the Midwest,' Newman said. 'We are entertaining franchise conversations in the various states that are new to us.'"

"Carla Hall is renewing the business of soul food," Urban News Service, The Philadelphia Sun, July 9, 2016

"Partly by design, partly by accident, TV chef Carla Hall is becoming the new face of soul food.

"Hall launched her first Southern Kitchen in Brooklyn last month. This new venture features the chef's version of her hometown signature dish, 'Nashville hot chicken.'"

"She is uniquely positioned to introduce soul food as a fast-casual concept for broad appeal, while deferring to that same food culture's traditions in a venue where millions will experience 'authentic' black history. Expectations are high on both sides.

"A Kickstarter campaign to fund Hall's restaurant further confirmed new popular interest in soul cooking. Some 1,500 fans donated more than $250,000 in initial capital."

Source: "Southern fast-food chains are taking over the rest of America," *Business Insider*, February 20, 2016, http://www.businessinsider.com/southern-fast-food-is-taking-over-2016-2, accessed June 24, 2016; "Bojangles' executive on expanding beyond the Southeast," *CNBC*, May 16, 2014, http://www.cnbc.com/2014/05/16/bojangles-executive-on-expanding-beyond-the-southeast.html, accessed July 18, 2016; "Carla Hall is renewing the business of soul food," *The Philadelphia Sun*, July 9, 2016, http://www.philasun.com/food-and-beverage/carla-hall-renewing-business-soul-food/, accessed July 18, 2016.

Exhibit 6   Becoming a Franchisor

Franchisors' responsibilities include:

- refining the business model

- developing a schedule of franchise fees

- developing a Franchise Disclosure Document

- marketing the franchise opportunity

- screening potential Franchisees

- training franchisees

- providing ongoing support

"Franchise Your Business in 7 Steps," Entrepreneur Magazine

"The first question to ask is whether your business is suited to being franchised. Beyond having a track record of sales and profitability at the existing business, there's several factors to weigh here, says Mark Siebert, CEO of the national franchise-consulting firm iFranchise Group... Most good franchise concepts, he says, offer something familiar, but with some unique twist to it. A good example is Florida-based Pizza Fusion which offers a familiar product--pizza--but with all-organic ingredients, delivered in hybrid-electric cars."

"Most successful franchises take a business that's already profitable and try to replicate that success in other locales. Cleveland-based franchise consultant Joel Libava says he likes to see companies with at least a couple of profitable units beyond the first one already in operation before a company tries franchising."

"Selling franchises is difficult because of the high risk involved for franchisees, notes Siebert. Your salespeople should know your business well and be able to tell a compelling story about why you're a worth the investment of their time and money."

"Want To Franchise Your Small Business? 8 Tips To Get Started," Forbes Magazine, November 14, 2012

"**Be picky.** Just like dating, you should be extremely selective when it comes to choosing franchisees. It's easy to find people with capital, but are they the right people? Do they have the right background in order to run a business? This is someone who will be representing you, so it needs to be a good fit. After all, you are in this to protect *and grow* your brand. Set up an interviewing process and know what your deal-breakers are."

"**Choose the right locations.** What locations make the most sense for your business? Where do you have brand recognition already? Consider keeping your first few locations close to home, but far enough away that it doesn't hurt sales at your initial location. That way, you can manage logistics easily. Keep in mind you'll want to visit these locations in person from time to time, so choose locations with easy access to an airport."

A Survival Kit for the Female Franchisor, International Franchising Association

"One reason it's difficult to obtain an accurate figure representing females at the top of their system has to do with franchise documents. Usually a husband's name will appear on documentation even though he may or may not be involved in the business.

"And his name will probably make a difference at the bank. Even though lenders maintain there are no discriminatory practices against women today, it still isn't Easy Street for a woman who wants to finance her business model. It would be far easier to secure funds to become a franchisee. After all, established franchises have proven track records and clearly spell out the amount of capital outlay necessary. That makes it a neat package for a lender to evaluate.

"A woman looking to become a franchisor, on the other hand, must prove she's a good risk. And that could be a classic Catch 22—in order to borrow the money she needs to start, she'd have to prove she had plenty of it in the first place."

Source: "Franchise Your Business in 7 Steps," *Entrepreneur Magazine*, https://www.entrepreneur.com/article/204998, accessed July 18, 2016; "Want To Franchise Your Small Business? 8 Tips To Get Started," *Forbes Magazine*, November 14, 2012, http://www.forbes.com/sites/theyec/2012/11/14/want-to-franchise-your-small-business-8-tips-to-get-started/#17fb36b03759, accessed July 22, 2016; "A Survival Kit for the Female Franchisor," *International Franchising Association*, http://www.franchise.org/a-survival-kit-for-the-female-franchisor, accessed July 22, 2016.

Valerie Daniels-Carter Case Study Assignment Questions

1. What are Valerie's entrepreneurship traits?
2. Should Valerie become a franchisor? Give reasons for yes and no.
3. Why should Valerie reject seafood restaurant expansion?
4. What are the benefits of going the entrepreneurial route via franchising?
5. Using financial comparisons, which is the better investment? Coney Island Cookery or Susannah's Seafood Emporium?

Notes

1. Jezek-Ford, Susan. "Homer B. Roberts." The Kansas City Public Library. Accessed March 16, 2020. https://pendergastkc.org/article/biography/homer-b-roberts
2. Sheldon, Andrew. "The Black Pioneers of the Automotive Industry." *Your AAA Daily*. February 8, 2021. https://magazine.northeast.aaa.com/daily/life/cars-trucks/black-pioneers-automotive-industry/
3. "A History of African-American New Car Dealers, The Pioneers – Introduction." AA Car Dealers. Accessed March 16, 2021. http://www.aacardealers.com/intro.html
4. Restuccia, Rusty. "First Black Dealer: Homer Roberts in 1923." *Automotive News*, November 20, 2000. www.autonews.com/article/20001120/ANA/11200751/first-Black-dealer-homer-roberts-in-1923
5. Ibid.

6. "Franchise Business Economic Outlook 2020." International Franchise Association. February 6, 2020. www.franchise.org/franchise-information/franchise-business-outlook/franchise-business-economic-outlook-2020

7. The Survey of Business Owners ("SBO"), conducted every five years by the U.S. Census Bureau, provides comprehensive data on the economic and demographic characteristics of more than 27 million U.S. businesses and their owners. Included are all businesses that filed 2012 tax forms as sole proprietorships, partnerships, or corporations and had annual business receipts greater than $1,000. The SBO covers both firms with paid employees and firms with no paid employees.

8. "What Is a Franchise?" International Franchise Association. Accessed March 16, 2021. www.franchise.org/faqs/basics/what-is-a-franchise/

9. Wagner, Nancy. "How Does a Franchise Work?" Bizfluent. February 11 2019. www.bizfluent.com/how-does-4911632-a-franchise-work.html

10. Ibid.

11. Siebert, Mark. "The 9 Advantages of Franchising." *Entrepreneur*. December 4, 2015. www.entrepreneur.com/article/252591

12. Ibid.

13. Cubukcu, Ceren. "Franchise vs. Start-up: Which One Works for You?" *Entrepreneur*. November 12, 2016. www.entrepreneur.com/article/285035

14. "Consumer Guide to Buying a Franchise." International Finance Association. April 15, 2019. www.franchise.org/franchise-information/finance/consumer-guide-to-buying-a-franchise

15. Goldberg, Eddy. "The Costs Involved in Opening A Franchise." Franchising.com. Accessed March 16, 2021. www.franchising.com/guides/the_cost_of_opening_a_franchise.html

16. Frank, Annalise. "Black Former Franchisees in Metro Detroit File Discrimination Lawsuit Against McDonald's." Crain's Detroit. September 2, 2020. https://www.crainsdetroit.com/entrepreneurship/Black-former-franchisees-metro-detroit-file-discrimination-lawsuit-against

17. Jou, Chin. "The Long History Behind Allegations of Racial Discrimination Against McDonald's." *The Washington Post*. September 15, 2020. https://www.washingtonpost.com/outlook/2020/09/15/long-history-behind-allegations-racial-discrimination-against-mcdonalds/

18. "Dr. Zirl Palmer and Preserving Palmer Pharmacy." The Blue Grass Trust for Historic Preservation. Accessed March 16, 2021. www.bluegrasstrust.org/dr-zirl-palmer-and-preserving-palmer-place

19. Ibid.

20. Ibid.

21. Ibid.
22. Ibid.
23. Felton, Kesi. "Kia Patterson Opens First Black-Owned Grocery Store in Compton, CA." Walker's Legacy. September 18, 2017. www.walkerslegacy.com/kia-patterson-opens-first-Black-owned-grocery-store-in-incompton-ca/
24. Atwell, Ashleigh Lakieva. "Kia Patterson Opens Compton's First Black-Owned Grocery Store." *Blavity News & Politics*. October 30 2018. https://blavity.com/kia-patterson-opens-comptons-first-black-owned-grocery-store?category1=business-entrepreneurship&category2=news
25. "First Black Owned Grocery Store Franchise Opens in Compton." SHOPPE BLACK. May 28, 2017. www.shoppeBlack.us/2017/05/Black-owned-grocery-store-compton/
26. Perkins, Tom. "Why Are There So Few Black-Owned Grocery Stores?" *Civil Eats*. January 8, 2018. https://civileats.com/2018/01/08/why-are-there-so-few-black-owned-grocery-stores/
27. Robinson, Jade. "Lovie Yancey: The Black Woman Who Created The World-Renowned Fatburger." *Travel Noire*. February 8, 2021. https://travelnoire.com/lovie-yancey-black-woman-who-founded-fatburger
28. "Fatburger." West Adams Heritage Association, pg. 6. January–February 2009. https://www.westadamsheritage.org/sites/default/files/newsletters/2009-02_waha_news.pdf
29. Pomerantz, Dorothy. "A Juicy Tale." *Forbes*. September 28, 2007. https://www.forbes.com/forbes/2007/1015/046.html?sh=15c0485536bc
30. "The FAT Family." FAT Brands. Accessed March 16, 2021. https://www.fatbrands.com/#:~:text=The%20Company%20currently%20owns%20nine.franchises%20over%20700%20units%20worldwide
31. "Founder of Fatburger has died." ABC7 News. February 2, 2008. https://abc7.com/archive/5931464/
32. Andrews, Evan. "The Green Book: The Black Travelers' Guide to Jim Crow America." History.com. March 13, 2019. https://www.history.com/news/the-green-book-the-Black-travelers-guide-to-jim-crow-america

6

Access to Capital for Black Entrepreneurs

ONE OF THE major differences between Black and White entrepreneurs is access to capital. Whether the capital is for start-ups, acquisitions, or growth, there is a major inequity that favors White entrepreneurs. Voluminous empirical research from scholars at renowned universities as diverse as Duke University, Stanford University, Brigham Young University, Rutgers University, and Utah State University show that the primary reason for this disparity is anti-Black racism. The narrative surrounding the inability of Black entrepreneurs to procure only a fraction of the capital available to White entrepreneurs applies to equity and/or debt capital.

In a thumbnail, money given to an entrepreneur in the form of a loan is debt capital. The dollars lent is the principal, and the interest charges against that principal is the cost of the capital. Financial institutions like banks typically want to see that the business has a minimal monthly cash flow to debt obligation ratio of 1.25 to 1. This is called the *debt coverage ratio*. Simply speaking, they want the business to generate at least $1.25 in net profit for every dollar of debt (principal and interest) due each month. For example, if a loan was requested that had a payment of $7,000 per month, the lender expects minimum

157

profit of $8,750 per month, in order for the entrepreneur to qualify for the loan. The ratio looks as follows:

$8,750 / $7,000 = 1.25 coverage ratio.

While a valid component of the underwriting process for loan approval includes the scrutiny of variables such as credit history and debt obligations, the race of the entrepreneur should not be a factor weighted against the entrepreneur. With all elements being equal, a White entrepreneur should not have easier or greater access to debt financing than a Black entrepreneur if race is the only objective factor distinguishing them. Unfortunately, the aforementioned research conducted at the various universities referenced earlier (along with the research reflected in the Harvard Business School note that follows) found anti-Black bias and favoritism toward Whites at the base of this disparity in access to capital.

The phenomena of preferential treatment was best depicted in a comedic skit on an episode of *Saturday Night Live* televised on December 15, 1984. The skit was titled "White Like Me" and showed the Black comedian Eddie Murphy experiencing life as a White man.[1] Disguised as a White man, Murphy goes into a bank seeking a $50,000 loan. The Black loan officer correctly informs "White" Murphy that he does not qualify for a loan because he has no credit, personal identification, or collateral. A White loan officer intervenes and takes over the handling of the application from the Black loan officer. After the Black loan officer leaves, the White loan officer tears up the loan application papers and says, "We don't have to bother with these formalities, do we, Mr. White?" They both laugh as Eddie Murphy leans closer to the loan officer and says, "What a silly Negro!" All of this is followed by the loan officer giving stacks of dollar bills to Eddie Murphy with the closing statement, "Pay us back anytime. Or don't! We don't care!" Of course, this is a comedy sketch and exaggerates the nature of such encounters, but there is an enduring profoundness in this skit created over three decades ago. Most Black entrepreneurs believe that a bias in access to capital exists today—a gulf separating the level of difficulty that exists for Black as opposed to White entrepreneurs acquiring capital.

Unfortunately, the same disparity in treatment is true for Black entrepreneurs trying to procure equity capital. In such situations, the money is not a loan. Rather, it is money provided in exchange for a percentage ownership of the company. Equity financing is invested in the entrepreneurial venture and the investor gets a percentage of the company. To determine the percentage, the company's pre-money valuation must be agreed to by the investor and the entrepreneur. The pre-money valuation plus the dollars invested equals the post-money valuation. The ownership percentage is calculated off of the post-money valuation. The formula is simple and straightforward. The post-money valuation divided by the equity investment equals the percentage ownership that goes to the investor.

The following table best illustrates this information:

Equity Invest-ment Needed	Pre-Money Valuation	Post-Money Valuation	Equity Percentage Received by Investor
$100,000	$900,000	$1,000,000	10%

In this example, the investment ($100,000) plus the pre-money ($900,000) equals the post-money ($1,000,000). The equity percentage of 10% is determined by dividing the investment ($100,000) by the post-money ($1,000,000). While the formula is easy, the same cannot be said about the availability of equity capital for Black entrepreneurs. Less than 1% of all private equity capital has gone to Black entrepreneurs.[2] One of the major factors contributing to this dearth of equity capital flowing to Black entrepreneurs is the dearth of Blacks employed in an industry where it is commonly stated that investors give money to people that they are comfortable with, people who look like them. Therefore, with most equity investors being White, industry practice results in virtually no Black entrepreneurs receiving equity capital.

The experience of one Black entrepreneur confirms this dynamic of non-negative responses from White investors. In an article from *Barron's* magazine titled "The Hazards of Raising Venture Capital While Black," a Black entrepreneur shared his 18-month challenge seeking to raise venture capital. He said he made pitches to 150 investors. Ultimately, he received five term sheets offering equity capital. Those term sheets came from the group of 30 firms that had Black investors. He received no term sheets from the 120 firms with only White investors.[3]

In response to this history of denying capital to Black entrepreneurs, Blacks have developed tools and avenues of self-financing to pursue their entrepreneurial dreams. A study by the Small Business Administration showed that 70% of Blacks use their own financial savings to fund their start-up.[4]

The availability of growth capital for non-start-ups is also abysmal. Banks deny only 25% of loan applications from White entrepreneurs compared to 53% from Black entrepreneurs.[5] One such Black entrepreneur denied growth capital was a couple, Freddie Lee and Deborah James. Their company made gourmet sauces for food that were sold in over a thousand stores. Equally significant was the fact that their company generated over $200,000 in annual profits year after year, but they could not get a bank loan. An exasperated Freddie Lee said, "We have 750–760 credit score, we pay all our debts. We don't have no problems with that. But they were saying that the sauce business is not generating enough capital to their standards."[6]

Sadly, their story is all too common for Black entrepreneurs. The Federal Reserve reported that Black firms rank last among all racial and ethnic groups in terms of getting approval for all of their financing needs. In contrast, unsurprisingly, the most successful racial group in getting approval for all of their financing needs was White firms. Almost 50% of them got approval compared to 31% for Black firms.[7]

An entrepreneur who decided to be an agent for change is Arlan Hamilton, a Black woman, who is the founder of Backstage Capital. Born on October 30, 1980, in Jackson, Mississippi, Hamilton and her brother were raised by their mother in Dallas, Texas.

Wanting to see a band she liked that was going on tour, Hamilton reached out to them and offered to arrange and manage their tour. They agreed, and at the age of 21, she started her career as a music tour manager; a job that she continues to this day. She managed tours for several well-known performers, including Toni Braxton, CeeLo Green, and Kirk Franklin. While working in the music industry, she noticed that more and more celebrities were investing in the tech industry, and she became interested in learning more about the people who started tech companies and those who invested in them. She read books by investors and tech executives, in addition to watching instructive YouTube and Vimeo videos. She cold-called the founders of and investors in tech companies to offer them her services. She sought an internship doing anything they needed so that she could learn as much as possible about the industry. And, as time passed, the more she learned, the more she realized that there were few people that looked like her in the industry—that is, who were female, Black, and gay. Therefore, she decided that she needed to make a difference. She noted:

> . . . the more I learned about Silicon Valley and startups in general, I really felt a kinship to the founders. I then decided to—as a hobby—help different founders all across the country of all backgrounds on small little projects. It was a lot of fun, and I learned a lot. I started understanding that there was less capital that was being invested in people that weren't the traditional Mark Zuckerbergs . . . I decided then that I wanted to try to get more funding to underrepresented founders that I had been talking to, that I thought had a lot of potential. That led to me raising money for a very interesting group of people.[8]

In February 2015, Hamilton was invited to Y Combinator's Female Founders Conference in San Francisco, where she met with key founders and investors. When she got accepted into "500 Start-Ups," a two-week seminar for new investors a few months later, she purchased a one-way ticket to California with no expectation of ever returning to Texas. The pilot program held at Stanford University brought together 34 investors-in-training, including wealthy individuals who had extensive experience in the tech industry who were trying their hands at investing. One such investor-trainee was Susan Kimberlin, an 18-year tech industry veteran who had worked at Salesforce and PayPal and was focused on becoming an angel investor. Hamilton and Kimberlin would come to realize that they had a lot in common in terms of their visions for the venture capital industry.

During the seminar, one of the assignments was to write an essay for *Medium*, an online publishing platform and blog host. Hamilton wrote a piece titled "Dear White Venture Capitalists: If you're reading this, it's (almost!) too late," in which she criticized the venture-capital industry. In her blog, she wrote:

> Your goal is to make money as a VC or accelerator who is investing other people's money because you have a fiduciary duty to do everything in your power to bring your LPs returns. Therefore, if you *haven't* hired a team of people who are of color, female, and/or LGBT to actively turn over every stone, to scope out every nook and cranny, to pop out of every bush, to find every qualified underrepresented founder in this country, you're going to miss out on a LOT OF MONEY when the rest of the investment world gets it.[9]

The post went viral and Hamilton received many invitations for meetings from investors who encouraged her. She continued to write her blogs for *Medium*, sharing her personal experiences and thoughts on the gender and racial disparities in the tech industry.

Finally, after over a year of meetings and pitches, Hamilton received a call from an angel investor, Susan Kimberlin, who told her that she was willing to bet on her and her idea for a fund. She wrote Hamilton a check for $25,000, becoming Backstage Capital's founding limited partner. Kimberlin notes, "I got to the point where I understood what a difference it would make, what kind of possibilities it would unlock for somebody to write her that first check and let her form the fund. It was an opportunity for me to put my money where my mouth was."[10]

Soon after that initial investment, Hamilton was able to secure investments from Steward Butterfield, co-founder and CEO of Slack, and Aaron Levie, CEO of Box. Hamilton continued to build her roster of investors, many of whom are venture capitalist themselves. Backstage Capital's investors include prominent venture capitalists like Lowercase Capital founder Marc Sacca, Marc Andreessen, Crystal English, Rose Tech Ventures managing partner David Rose, Box co-founder and CEO Aaron Levie, and Swati Mylavarapu of Kleiner Perkins Caufield Byers. These investors invested in Backstage Capital because they believe that Hamilton presents them with opportunities to invest in entrepreneurs they would not have found on their own, choosing to work with her because they believe in what she is trying to do to increase diversity in the industry.

With funding in hand, Hamilton began to reach out to the many entrepreneurs she had been cultivating over the past several months and began making investments in founders she believed deserved her support. One of the first companies she partnered with was Blendoor, a company that sells an app designed to eliminate bias in hiring practices through software that eliminates the gender and race profiles of job candidate data while analyzing talent pipelines. Stephanie Lampkin, an African American woman who holds an engineering degree from Stanford and an MBA from MIT, came up with the idea for the app when she could not get a job at Google because the hiring manager did not think she was "technical enough." The app is currently used by several Fortune 500 companies, including Google and Salesforce.

Hamilton also was an early investor in CurlMix, a company founded by another African American woman, Kim Lewis. CurlMix manufactures natural hair care products and generated over $6 million in revenue last year. In 2019, Lewis and her husband, Tim, presented their company on the television show *Shark Tank* but rejected an offer of $400,000 for a 20% share of the company.

In 2018, Hamilton announced the launch of a $36 million fund set exclusively for Black female founders. Hamilton named her initiative "It's About Damn Time fund" in recognition of the fact that Black women entrepreneurs across the country are practically invisible in the realm of venture funding.[11] Only three dozen Black women entrepreneurs, nationwide, had raised more than $1 million in venture funding up to this point.[12]

By 2020, Backstage Capital had invested more than $7 million in 130 companies, typically investing between $25,000 and $100,000 into each start-up. So far, Hamilton has invested in roughly 3% of the companies that have pitched to Backstage, a percentage that is on par with many venture firms. The portfolio of companies into which Backstage has invested covers a wide range of industries, from personal care products to business analytics. Backstage Capital has sought to fill the gap in access to capital that Black women entrepreneurs have encountered historically.

Hamilton's successful investing in Black entrepreneurs has resulted in her inclusion in the directory that follows. This is one of the most comprehensive listings of funders who have done more than talk about racial inclusion. They have "walked the talk" by investing in Black entrepreneurs.

Introduction to the Case Study: Sources of Capital for Black Entrepreneurs

This publication is referred to by Harvard Business Publishing as a Note instead of a case study. Notes are written to give detailed information about an industry, country, or other topic. In contrast, a case study typically tells a story through the lens of a protagonist, with the objective of teaching the reader how to solve problems. Notes typically accompany case studies as homework assignments. Uncharacteristically, while it is not a case study, this Note was written to stand on its own and solve a major problem that has plagued Black entrepreneurs for centuries. One way to address this problem is by identifying funders who actually made investments in Black entrepreneurs. This Note encourages Black entrepreneurs to go to these people, organizations, and companies, to procure debt and/or equity capital. They have an affinity for helping Black entrepreneurs.

HARVARD | BUSINESS | SCHOOL

319-117
MAY 23, 2019

STEVEN ROGERS

STANLEY ONUOHA

KAYIN BARCLAY

Sources of Capital for Black Entrepreneurs

In 2017, a perplexed Harvard Business School professor asked a colleague why there was a need for a new course focusing on African-American business leaders and entrepreneurs. With all sincerity, he asked, "What is the difference between a white entrepreneur and a black entrepreneur?" In response, the professor who created the course (and is also the first author of this note) cited two major differences.

First, black entrepreneurs, specifically those who pursue non-black customers often practice "racial concealment." They preemptively hide the fact that their company is black-owned because of the concern that whites would not patronize their business. For example, Robert F. Smith, whose net worth is estimated at $5 billion, is a wonderful philanthropist with donations of $20 million to the African-American Museum of History and Culture, and $40 million to the 2019 graduates of Morehouse College to pay off their student loans.[1] Smith does not have his photo on the website of the company that he founded, Vista Equity Partners. This is an investment firm with over $46 billion of assets under management. He excluded the photo because he feared he "might lose out on opportunities if investors and executives knew he was African-American."[2]

The second major difference between black and white entrepreneurs is their access to capital. Throughout U.S. history, it has been almost impossible for black entrepreneurs to raise debt or equity capital.

This note was written primarily for black entrepreneurs, to help them raise capital. The second objective was to recognize the capital providers who are part of the solution to the problem. The note reviews the evidence that black entrepreneurs have less access to capital than do white entrepreneurs, examines the reasons for that disparity, reflects on the societal impact, and — uniquely — compiles a directory of entities that have funded black entrepreneurs.

---

[1] Kaur, H., "What to know about Robert F. Smith, the man paying off Morehouse grads' student loans," *CNN.com*, May 20, 2019, https://www.cnn.com/2019/05/19/business/robert-smith-billionaire-morehouse-gift-trnd/index.html

[2] Alexander, K., "Who is Robert Smith?: A quiet billionaire makes some noise with $20 million gift to the African American museum," *The Washington Post*, September 24, 2016, https://www.washingtonpost.com/national/who-is-this-robert-smith-a-quiet-billionaire-makes-some-noise-with-20-million-gift-to-the-african-american-museum/2016/09/23/547da3a8-6fd0-11e6-8365-b19e428a975e_story.html?utm_term=.238460b24978

HBS Senior Lecturer Steven Rogers; Stanley Onuoha (Founder & Managing Partner at Fruition Consulting, Harvard University Ed.M.); and Kayin Barclay (MBA Class of 2019) prepared this note as the basis for class discussion with the assistance of Darlene Le.

Unequal Access to Capital

Racial disparities in access to capital are sharp. For instance, in 2018 blacks received less than 2% of all capital deployed by equity investors and only 1.7% of debt capital guaranteed by the Small Business Administration. These percentages are paltry for a black community that makes up 13% of the U.S. population and over 7% (2.5 million) of the country's entrepreneurs. As one black entrepreneur stated, "It's just white folks giving money to white folks. We might as well buy lottery tickets to fund our ideas."[3]

Denied access to outside capital, most black entrepreneurs resort to self-funding their ventures. Unfortunately, this source of capital is woefully insufficient. The typical black family in America has a miniscule portion of the wealth of a white family. In 2016, white families had a median net worth of $171,000, compared with $17,600 for blacks.[4] In the city of Boston, the disparity is even worse, with white families at $247,500 compared to $8 for blacks.[5] Four centuries of ugly history account for such differences. For 246 years (1619-1865), most blacks were enslaved, worked for no compensation, and could not accumulate wealth. For the next 98 years (1865-1963), legal and ultimately unconstitutional, anti-black discrimination by the government (i.e. redlining) and every private industry in the country, including banking, impoverished the typical black family. The most recent 56 years (1963-2019) have seen systemic racial biases in education, housing, criminal justice, healthcare, and other institutions work against the economics of black households. The results? While whites were able to accumulate and transfer wealth from generation to generation, this vehicle for prosperity never existed for the vast majority of blacks. Therefore, it is virtually impossible for most black entrepreneurs to self-fund a venture through the seven stages of entrepreneurship.

Table 1   Seven Stages of Entrepreneurship

1.	Ideation
2.	Start-up
3.	Survival
4.	Pivot
5.	Stability
6.	Growth
7.	Exit

Source: Entrepreneurial Finance, 4th Edition.

---

[3] Friess, S., "In Chicago, black entrepreneurs seeking venture capital face excessive scrutiny and discrimination," *Belt Magazine*, February 6, 2018, https://beltmag.com/black-entrepreneurs-discrimination/

[4] Jan, T., "White families have nearly 10 times the net worth of black families. And the gap is growing." *The Washington Post*, September 28, 2017, https://www.washingtonpost.com/news/wonk/wp/2017/09/28/black-and-hispanic-families-are-making-more-money-but-they-still-lag-far-behind-whites/?utm_term=.cb80e1d36c78

[5] Johnson, A. "That was no typo: The median net worth of black Bostonians really is $8," *Boston Globe*, December 11, 2017, https://www.bostonglobe.com/metro/2017/12/11/that-was-typo-the-median-net-worth-black-bostonians-really/ze5kxC1jJelx24M3pugFFN/story.html

Table 2   Stage Definition

Stages of Entrepreneurship	Financial Status
1. Ideation	Pre-revenue, no product/service
2. Start-up	Pre-revenue, demonstrated demand
3. Survival	Revenue, unprofitable
4. Pivot (Strategy change)	Revenue, unprofitable
5. Stability	Revenue, breakeven
6. Growth a. Organic b. Acquisitions	Revenue, profitable

Source: <u>Entrepreneurial Finance</u>, 4th Edition.

While stories of successful entrepreneurs self-funding with meager amounts of capital are plentiful and make for inspiring anecdotes, the reality is that they are the exception, not the rule. That was the case with John H. Johnson, the founder of *Ebony* magazine. He began his company with $500 (approximately $7,519 in today's dollars) from his mother. In contrast, the Duke University study highlighted in Table 3, shows that most successful entrepreneurial ventures were similar to Jeff Bezos's story, who received $245,573 from his family to finance Amazon.[6]

While the overall black community has suffered from the lack of capital, black women have borne an even bigger share of the brunt of this travesty. For example, less than 0.2% of private equity capital has gone to black women, and as of June 2018, only 34 black women have ever raised more than $1 million in venture capital since the industry began in 1957.

Why the Disparity?

It has been stated many times that the only color investors see is green – the color of money. If black and white entrepreneurs brought investors equally attractive investment opportunities—one might argue—they would get equal funding. Unfortunately, that is not true! Research done by the following universities, organizations, and scholars show that investors have a definite bias against blacks.

---

[6] Mejia, Z. "Jeff Bezos got his parents to invest nearly $250,000 in Amazon in 1995 — they might be worth $30 billion today," CNBC, August 2, 2018, https://www.cnbc.com/2018/08/02/how-jeff-bezos-got-his-parents-to-invest-in-amazon--turning-them-into.html

Table 3   Research on Bias against Blacks by Investors

	Research Title	University	Organization	Scholars	Year Published
1.	"The Tapestry of Black Business Ownership in America"	N/A	Association of Enterprise Opportunity	N/A	2016 [7]
2.	"Black and White: Access to Capital among Minority-Owned Startups"	Stanford University	Stanford Institute for Economic Research	Fairlie, R., Robb, A., & Robinson, D.	2016 [8]
3.	The Color of Money	University of Georgia	N/A	Baradaran, M.	2017 [9]
4.	"What We Get Wrong About Closing the Racial Wealth Gap"	Duke University	Samuel DuBois Cook Center on Social Equity	Darity Jr, W., Hamilton, D., Paul, M., Aja, A., Price, A., Moore, A., & Chiopris, C.	2018 [10]
5.	"Policy Watch: Shaping Small Business Lending Policy Through Matched-Pair Mystery Shopping"	Utah State University Brigham Young University Rutgers University	Lubin Research National Community Reinvestment Coalition (NCRC)	Bone, S., Christensen, G., Williams, J., Adams, S., Lederer, A., & Lubin, P.	2019 [11]

The study by scholars at Utah State University gives the most compelling evidence of the anti-black bias by financial institutions. These researchers hired black and white actors to pose as entrepreneurs seeking capital to grow their company. Both groups had the exact same personal, business, and education profile. The black and white actors were almost identical in height, weight, and clothing. The only difference was their race. They were sent to the same banks to apply for a commercial loan. The

[7] Gorman, I., "The Tapestry of Black Business Ownership in America: Untapped Opportunities for Business Success," Association of Enterprise Opportunity, 2017, from
https://aeoworks.org/images/uploads/fact_sheets/AEO_Black_Owned_Business_Report_02_16_17_FOR_WEB.pdf

[8] Fairlie, R., Robb, A. & Robinson, D. "Black and White: Access to Capital among Minority-Owned Startups." Stanford Institute for Economic Policy Research, 2016, from https://siepr.stanford.edu/sites/default/files/publications/17-003.pdf

[9] Baradaran, M. The color of money: Black banks and the racial wealth gap. Harvard University Press, 2017.

[10] Darity Jr, W. et al. "What We Get Wrong About Closing the Racial Wealth Gap." Samuel DuBois Cook Center on Social Equity, 2018, from
https://socialequity.duke.edu/sites/socialequity.duke.edu/files/site-images/FINAL%20COMPLETE%20REPORT_.pdf

[11] Bone, S., et al. "Policy Watch: Shaping Small Business Lending Policy Through Matched-Pair Mystery Shopping." Journal of Public Policy & Marketing, 2019, from, https://journals.sagepub.com/doi/pdf/10.1177/0743915618820561

following results, where Blacks were asked to provide more information about their business and personal financials, demonstrates the hurdles blacks must jump to procure outside financing.

Table 4   Match-Pair Test Results

Item		Black	White
1.	Inquired about size of accounts receivable	11.5%	0%
2.	Asked about spousal employment	11.5%	0%
3.	Asked for personal W-2 forms	30.8%	0%
4.	Asked about marital status	23.1%	3.8%
5.	Requested business financial statements	73%	50%

Source: Bone, S., et al. "Policy Watch: Shaping Small Business Lending Policy Through Matched-Pair Mystery Shopping." *Journal of Public Policy & Marketing*, 2019, p. 6.

Impact on Society

This glaring disparity in the treatment of black entrepreneurs is harmful to America and to the black community. First and foremost, the country is missing out on the talent, great ideas, and innovations of black entrepreneurs. Second, it has stunted the ability of black entrepreneurs to grow their companies. The result? Fewer taxes paid to the government on company profits and employees' wages. It also hurts the black community because research shows that successful high-growth black entrepreneurs create jobs for other blacks, who have the highest unemployment rate in the country at 6.2% compared to 3% for whites. Dr. Timothy Bates's research showed the following for black employment.

Table 5   Black Employment

	Company Ownership and Location	Percentage of Black Employees
1.	White-owned, white community	15%
2.	White-owned, black community	32%
3.	Black-owned, white community	75%
4.	Black-owned, black community	85%

Source: Bates, T., and Joint Center for Political Economic Studies, Banking on Black Enterprise: The Potential of Emerging Firms for Revitalizing Urban Economies. *Joint Center for Political and Economic Studies*, 1993.

These results show that it is in America's best interest to help black entrepreneurs receive more outside capital.

Solution

Now that the problem has been identified and verified, the balance of this note aims to help black entrepreneurs raise capital. One of the solutions to the problem is for black entrepreneurs to approach people and organizations who have demonstrated their willingness to invest in black entrepreneurs. Therefore, this note identifies people, companies, and organizations that have invested in black entrepreneurs in the past two years. It does not include those who claim an interest in investing, or an intent to invest, in black entrepreneurs. This note identifies those who have *actually done it* and have a track record.

Capital providers usually invest debt or equity in entrepreneurs. There are some who provide both. Debt capital is money invested as a loan. It is ideal for profitable companies.

Equity capital is money invested in exchange for ownership in the company. It is ideal for unprofitable companies with prospects for fast growth.

The tables that follow describe where equity and/or debt capital can be procured.

Table 6   Debt

1.   Angel investors – wealthy individuals*, who could be family and friends
2.   Banks – government regulated financial institutions
3.   Foundations – social impact investing
4.   Government – capital access programs (CAP) and small business administration (SBA)
5.   Non-banks – factoring companies for working capital, supplier financing, purchase order financing
6.   Community Development Financial Institutions – community impact investing

Source: Entrepreneurial Finance, 4th Edition.
          * Also equity investors

Table 7   Equity

1.   Accelerators – organization that houses start-ups and provides capital
2.   Corporate venture capitalists – Fortune 500 companies that invests in start-ups with industry related products/services
3.   Growth capital fund – stable and growing
4.   Mezzanine fund – subordinated debt and equity
5.   Buyout fund – acquisitions
6.   Search fund – pre-acquisition stage
7.   Seed fund – earliest stage
8.   Turn-around capital fund – underperforming companies
9.   Venture capital fund – early stage

Source: Entrepreneurial Finance, 4th Edition.

Entrepreneurs in need of capital should first identify where their company is in the stages of entrepreneurship and match it to the sources of capital in Table 6 and 7.

Table 8   Stage Identification

	Stages of Entrepreneurship	Financial Status	Ideal Sources of Capital
1.	Ideation	Pre-revenue	Seed, angel, personal, family and friends
2.	Start-up	Pre-revenue	Venture capital, personal, family, friends, angel
3.	Survival	Revenue, unprofitable	Venture capital
4.	Pivot (Strategy change)	Revenue, unprofitable	Venture capital
5.	Stability	Revenue, breakeven	Mezzanine, growth, debt
6.	Growth a. Organic b. Acquisitions	Revenue, profitable	Mezzanine, growth, debt Private equity

Source: Entrepreneurial Finance, 4th Edition.

While the table above lists the debt and equity providers in broad categories, one of the unique aspects of this note is the identification, by name, of those who have provided capital to black entrepreneurs in the past two years.

The authors recognize that the Directory is not a complete list of every investor in black entrepreneurs. Given the methodology **(Appendix A)** used, this was the outcome.

Directory

The following Tables 9-20 identify the people and companies that have invested in black entrepreneurs.

Table 9   Accelerators

	Name	Historical Industries	Capital Type	Tier	Website
1.	500 Startups	Technology, consumer, and others	Equity	1	www.500.co
2.	Black Girl Ventures	Consumer, technology and others	Equity	1	www.blackgirlventures.org
3.	Camelback Ventures	Consumer, technology, and others	Equity	1	www.camelbackventures.org
4.	Founder Gym	Technology, consumer, and others	Equity	1	www.foundergym.com
5.	Invest Detroit	Technology, consumer, and others	Equity	1	www.investdetroit.com
6.	Techstars	Technology, consumer, and others	Equity	1	www.techstars.com
7.	1863 Ventures	Technology, consumer and others	Equity	1	www.1863ventures.net/
8.	Advanced Technology Development Center	Technology, consumer, and others	Equity	2	www.atdc.org
9.	American Underground	Technology, consumer, and others	Equity	2	www.americanunderground.com
10.	Barclays Accelerator	Technology, consumer, and others	Equity	2	www.barclaysaccelerator.com
11.	Boomtown Accelerators	Technology, consumer, and others	Equity	2	www.boomtownaccelerators.com
12.	CanopyBoulder	Agriculture, technology, and others	Equity	2	www.canopyboulder.com
13.	Expa Labs	Technology, business products/services, and others	Equity	2	www.expa.com
14.	Higher Ground Labs	Technology, business products/services, and others	Equity	2	www.highergroundlabs.com
15.	MTGx	Technology, consumer, and others	Equity	2	www.mtg.com
16.	Plug and Play Tech Center	Technology, consumer, and others	Equity	2	www.plugandplaytechcenter.com
17.	StartOut	Consumer, technology, and others	Equity	2	www.startout.org
18.	Y Combinator	Technology, consumer, and others	Equity	2	www.ycombinator.com

Sources: Pitchbook, Capital IQ, Company Websites, and TechCrunch.

Table 10 Angels

	Name	Historical Industries	Capital Type	Tier
1.	Adebayo Ogunlesi	Consumer	Equity	2
2.	Aiysha Holiday	Business products / services	Equity	2
3.	Alexander Bogusky	Technology, financial services, and others	Equity	2
4.	Anthony Saleh	Technology, consumer, and others	Equity	2
5.	April Underwood	Technology, healthcare, and others	Equity	2
6.	Baron Davis	Technology, consumer, and others	Equity	2
7.	Bart Partners	Business products / services	Equity	2
8.	Charles Phillips	Consumer	Equity	2
9.	David Chang	Technology, consumer, and others	Equity	2
10.	David Drummond	Technology, consumer, and others	Equity	2
11.	Dwight Smith	Business products / services	Equity	2
12.	Ellen Pao	Technology, consumer, and others	Equity	2
13.	Golden Seeds	Technology, consumer, and others	Equity	2
14.	James Cash	Technology	Equity	2
15.	Jewel Burks	Business products / services	Equity	2
16.	Johnny Hou	Technology	Equity	2
17.	Jonathan Weiner	Technology	Equity	2
18.	Joshua Schachter	Technology, consumer, and others	Equity	2
19.	Kal Vepuri	Technology, consumer, and others	Equity	2
20.	Kelvin Beachum	Technology, business products / services	Equity	2
21.	Kenneth Chenault	Technology, consumer, and others	Equity	2
22.	Kevin Lin	Technology, healthcare, and others	Equity	2
23.	Michael Dubin	Technology, consumer, and others	Equity	2
24.	Monique Woodard	Consumer	Equity	2
25.	Nasir Dara Jones	Consumer, technology, and others	Equity	2
26.	Nathaniel Turner	Technology, healthcare, and others	Equity	2
27.	New Media Ventures	Technology, consumer, and others	Equity	2
28.	Niija Kuykendall	Consumer	Equity	2
29.	Paul Judge	Technology, business products / services, and others	Equity	2
30.	Rahul Mehta	Technology, consumer, and others	Equity	2
31.	Richelieu Dennis	Technology	Equity	2
32.	Russell Okung	Technology, healthcare, and others	Equity	2
33.	Sean Combs	Technology	Equity	2
34.	Tony Catalfano	Technology, business products / services, and others	Equity	2
35.	William Lewis	Consumer	Equity	2

Sources: Pitchbook, Capital IQ, Company Websites, and TechCrunch.

Table 11   Banks

	Name	Historical Industries	Capital Type	Tier	Website
1.	Bank of America	Industrials, technology, and others	Debt	2	www.bankofamerica.com
2.	BNY Mellon	Financial services, technology, and others	Debt	2	www.bnymellon.com
3.	BMO Harris Bank	Consumer, business products / services, and others	Debt	2	www.bmoharris.com
4.	Capital One Financial	Industrials, energy, and others	Debt	2	www.capitalone.com
5.	CitiBank	Industrials, business products / services, and others	Debt	2	www.online.citi.com
6.	First National Bank	Industrials, business products / services, and others	Debt	2	www.fnb-online.com
7.	Guggenheim Securities	Industrials, consumer and others	Debt	2	https://www.guggenheimpartners.com/
8.	JPMorgan Chase	Business products / services, financial services, and others	Debt	2	www.jpmorganchase.com
9.	M&T Bank	Financial services, technology, and others	Debt	2	www.mtb.com
10.	Middlesex Savings Bank	Business products / services, financial services, and others	Debt	2	www.middlesexbank.com
11.	PNC	Business products / services, healthcare, and others	Debt	2	www.pnc.com
12.	Synovus Bank	Industrials, financial services, and others	Debt	2	www.synovus.com
13.	Wells Fargo	Technology, industrials, and others	Debt	2	www.wellsfargo.com

Sources: Pitchbook, Capital IQ, Company Websites, and TechCrunch.

Table 12 Black-Owned Banks

	Name	Website
1.	Alamerica Bank	www.alamericabank.com
2.	Broadway Federal Bank	www.broadwayfederalbank.com
3.	Capital City Bank Group	www.ccbg.com
4.	Carver Federal Savings Bank	www.carverbank.com
5.	Carver State Bank	www.carverstatebank.com
6.	Citizens Savings Bank and Trust	www.bankcbn.com
7.	Citizens Trust Bank	www.ctbconnect.com
8.	City National Bank of New Jersey	www.citynatbank.com
9.	Columbia Savings & Loan Association	www.columbiasavingsandloans.com
10.	Commonwealth National Bank	www.ecommonwealthbank.com
11.	Credit Union of Atlanta	www.cuatlanta.org
12.	FAMU Federal Credit Union	www.famufcu.com
13.	First Independence Bank	www.firstindependence.com
14.	First Security Bank and Trust Company	www.fsbokc.com
15.	First State Bank	www.keysbank.com
16.	GN Bank	www.gnbank.net
17.	Harbor Bank of Maryland	www.theharborbank.com
18.	Hill District Credit Union	www.hilldistrictfcu.org
19.	Industrial Bank	www.industrial-bank.com
20.	Liberty Bank & Trust	www.libertybank.net
21.	Mechanics & Farmers Bank	www.mfbonline.com
22.	Metro Bank	www.metrobankky.com
23.	Omega Psi Phi Fraternity Federal Credit Union	www.oppffcu.com
24.	One United Bank	www.oneunited.com
25.	Phi Beta Sigma Federal Credit Union	www.pbsfcu.org
26.	Optus Bank	www.optus.bank
27.	Toledo Urban Credit Union	www.toledourban.net
28.	Tri-State Bank of Memphis	www.tristatebank.com
29.	United Bank of Philadelphia	www.ubphila.com
30.	Unity National Bank of Houston	www.unitybanktexas.com
31.	Urban Partnership Bank	www.upbnk.com

Sources: Company websites, FDIC, and Watch the Yard.

Table 13 Community Development Investment Funds (CDIFs)

	Name	Historical Industries	Capital Type	Tier	Website
1.	Main Street Launch	Consumer, technology, and others	Debt	2	www.mainstreetlaunch.org
2.	Ascent Funding	Business services, consumer, and others	Debt	2	www.mainstreetlaunch.org
3.	Carolina Small Business Development Fund	Consumer, business services and others	Debt	2	www.carolinasmallbusiness.org
4.	Hoper Enterprise Corporation	Consumer, business services and others	Debt	2	www.hopecu.org/about/hope-enterprise-corporation
5.	Baltimore Community Lending	Consumer, business services and others	Debt	2	www.bclending.org/
6.	Opportunity Finance Network (List of 1200 CDIFs)	Various	Debt	Various	www.ofn.org/

Sources: Company websites.

Table 14 Corporate Venture Capital

	Name	Historical Industries	Capital Type	Tier	Website
1.	Adidas	Consumer, healthcare, and others	Equity	2	www.hydra-ventures.com
2.	Baron Davis Enterprises	Technology, consumer, and others	Equity	2	www.barondavisenterprises.com
3.	Comcast	Technology, consumer, and others	Equity	2	www.comcastventures.com
4.	GV	Technology, consumer, and others	Equity	2	www.gv.com
5.	Hyde Park	Technology	Equity	2	http://hydeparkvp.com/
6.	Magic Johnson Enterprises	Technology, consumer, and others	Equity	2	www.magicjohnson.com
7.	Roc Nation	Financial services, technology, and others	Equity	2	www.rocnation.com
8.	Unilever	Consumer, technology, and others	Equity	2	www.unileverventures.com

Sources: Pitchbook, Capital IQ, Company Websites, and TechCrunch.

Table 15   Fund-of-Funds

	Name	Historical Industries	Capital Type	Tier	Website
1.	Fairview Capital Partners	Private equity, venture capital, and others	Equity	1	www.fairviewcapital.com
2.	GCM Grosvenor	Private equity, venture capital, and others	Equity	1	www.gcmgrosvenor.com
3.	Muller & Monroe Asset Management	Private equity, venture capital, and others	Equity	1	www.m2am.com
4.	Neuberger Berman	Private equity, venture capital, and others	Equity	1	www.nb.com

Sources: Pitchbook, Capital IQ, Company Websites, and TechCrunch

Table 16   Non-Bank Lenders

	Name	Historical Industries	Capital Type	Tier	Website
1.	Brightwood Capital Advisors	Business products / services, consumer, and others	Debt	2	www.brightwoodlp.com
2.	CION Investments	Business products / services, financial services, and others	Debt	2	www.cioninvestments.com
3.	ExWorks Capital	Industrials, consumer, and others	Debt	2	www.exworkscapital.com
4.	Graycliff Partners	Business products / services, consumer, and others	Debt	2	www.graycliffpartners.com
5.	Good Tree Capital	Cannabis	Debt	2	www.invest.goodtree.capital
6.	Guggenheim Partners	Industrials, consumer, and others	Debt	2	www.guggenheimpartners.com
7.	Hines Securities	Industrials, consumer, and others	Debt	2	www.hinessecurities.com
8.	Main Street Capital	Business products / services, technology, and others	Debt	2	www.mainstcapital.com
9.	Montage Capital	Technology, healthcare, and others	Debt	2	www.montagecapital.com

Sources: Pitchbook, Capital IQ, Company Websites, and TechCrunch

Table 17   Not-For-Profit Venture Capital

	Name	Historical Industries	Capital Type	Tier	Website
1.	John S. and James L. Knight Foundation	Technology, consumer, and others	Equity	2	www.knightfoundation.org
2.	Minneapolis MBDA Business Center	Consumer, healthcare, and others	Equity	2	www.meda.net
3.	NIC Fund	Energy	Equity	2	www.novainvestmentclub.com/the-nic-fund/
4.	StartX	Technology, healthcare, and others	Equity	2	www.startx.com

Sources: Pitchbook, Capital IQ, Company Websites, and TechCrunch.

Table 18   Private Equity / Buyouts

	Name	Historical Industries	Capital Type	Tier	Website
1.	ABO Capital	Technology, consumer, and others	Equity	2	https://www.abocapital.net/
2.	Blue Consumer Capital	Consumer	Equity	2	www.blueconsumercapital.com
3.	GenNx 360 Capital Partners	Business products / services, consumer, and others	Equity	2	www.gennx360.com
4.	RLJ Equity Partners	Business products / services, consumer, and others	Equity	2	www.rljequitypartners.com

Sources: Pitchbook, Capital IQ, Company Websites, and TechCrunch.

Table 19   Search Funds

	Name	Historical Industries	Capital Type	Tier	Website
1.	Anacapa Partners	Technology, business products / services, and others	Equity	2	www.anacapapartners.com
2.	Aspect Investors	Business products / services, healthcare, and others	Equity	2	www.aspectinvestors.com/
3.	Broadtree Partners	Technology, business products / services, and others	Equity	2	www.broadtreepartners.com/
4.	Endurance Search Partners	Technology, business products / services, and others	Equity	2	www.endurancesearchpartners. com
5.	Futalefu Partners	Technology, business products / services, and others	Equity	2	www.futaleufu-partners.com/
6.	Housatonic Partners	Business products / services, technology, and others	Equity	2	www.housatonicpartners.com
7.	Relay Investments	Business products / services, healthcare, and others	Equity	2	www.relayinvestments.com
8.	Search Fund Accelerator	Business products / services	Equity	2	www.searchfundaccelerator.com
9.	The Cambria Group	Business products / services, technology, and others	Equity	2	www.cambriagroup.com
10.	The Operand Group	Healthcare, business products / services, and others	Equity	2	www.theoperandgroup.com
11.	Trilogy Search Partners	Business products / services, technology, and others	Equity	2	www.trilogy-search.com
12.	TTCER	Technology and healthcare	Equity	2	https://www.pivotcapitalfund.com /investor-group
13.	WSC & Co.	Business products / services, consumer, and others	Equity	2	www.wscandcompany.com

Sources: Pitchbook, Capital IQ, Company Websites, and TechCrunch.

Table 20   Venture Capital

	Name	Historical Industries	Capital Type	Tier	Website
1.	Authentic Ventures	Technology, consumer, and others	Equity	1	www.authentic-ventures.com
2.	Backstage Capital	Technology, consumer, and others	Equity	1	www.backstagecapital.com
3.	Black Angel Tech Fund	Technology	Equity	1	www.blackangeltechfund.com
4.	Bumble Fund	Consumer, healthcare, and others	Equity	1	https://bumble.com/the-buzz/bumble-fund/
5.	Essence Ventures	Consumer	Equity	1	Currently no website available at this time
6.	First Round Capital	Technology, consumer, and others	Equity	1	www.firstround.com
7.	Harlem Capital Partners	Consumer, business products / services, and others	Equity	1	www.harlem.capital
8.	Kapor Capital	Technology, consumer, and others	Equity	1	www.kaporcapital.com
9.	LDR Ventures	Consumer and technology	Equity	1	www.ldrventures.com
10.	Macro Ventures	Technology, consumer, and others	Equity	1	www.staymacro.com
11.	New Age Capital	Technology, business products / services, and others	Equity	1	www.newage.vc
12.	Plexo Capital	Technology, consumer, and others	Equity	1	https://www.ciscoinvestments.com/portfolio/plexo-capital/
13.	Precursor Ventures	Technology, consumer, and others	Equity	1	www.precursorvc.com
14.	Reinventure Capital	Financial services, consumer, and others	Equity	1	www.reinventurecapital.com
15.	Ulu Ventures	Technology, consumer, and others	Equity	1	www.uluventures.com
16.	11-11 Ventures	Technology, consumer, and others	Equity	2	www.11-11ventures.com
17.	645 Ventures	Technology, consumer, and others	Equity	2	www.645ventures.com
18.	8VC	Technology, healthcare, and others	Equity	2	www.8vc.com
19.	Acequia Capital	Technology, consumer, and others	Equity	2	www.acecap.com
20.	Adelfos	Business products / services	Equity	2	http://visionfirst.dev1844.com/
21.	Atlanta Seed Company	Business products / services, technology, and others	Equity	2	www.atlantaseedcompany.com
22.	Base Ventures	Technology, consumer, and others	Equity	2	www.base.ventures

	Name	Historical Industries	Capital Type	Tier	Website
23.	BBG Ventures	Technology, consumer, and others	Equity	2	www.bbgventures.com
24.	Bull Creek Capital	Technology and consumer	Equity	2	www.bullcreekcapital.com
25.	Connectivity Capital Partners	Healthcare, technology, and others	Equity	2	www.connectivitycapitalpartners.com
26.	Cross Culture Ventures	Consumer, technology, and others	Equity	2	www.crossculturevc.com
27.	Crosscut Ventures	Technology, consumer, and others	Equity	2	www.crosscut.vc
28.	Deep Space Ventures	Technology, business products / services, and others	Equity	2	www.deepspacevc.com
29.	Elysian Park Ventures	Technology, consumer, and others	Equity	2	www.elysianpark.ventures
30.	Engage Ventures	Technology, business products / services, and others	Equity	2	www.engage.vc
31.	Equipo Ventures	Consumer	Equity	2	www.equipoventures.com
32.	Excell Partners	Healthcare, business products / services, and others	Equity	2	www.excellny.com
33.	Future Positive Capital	Healthcare, technology, and others	Equity	2	www.futurepositivecapital.com
34.	GingerBread Capital	Technology, consumer, and others	Equity	2	www.gingerbreadcap.com
35.	Hudson River Ventures	Consumer, energy, and others	Equity	2	www.hudsonriverventures.com
36.	IA Ventures	Technology, business products / services, and others	Equity	2	www.iaventures.com
37.	Impact America Fund	Technology, consumer, and others	Equity	2	www.impactamericafund.com
38.	JumpStart	Healthcare, technology, and others	Equity	2	www.jumpstartinc.org
39.	LaunchCapital	Technology, consumer, and others	Equity	2	www.launchcapital.com
40.	Lerer Hippeau Ventures	Technology, consumer, and others	Equity	2	www.lererhippeau.com
41.	Lightspeed Venture Partners	Technology, consumer, and others	Equity	2	www.lsvp.com
42	Lingo Ventures	Energy	Equity	2	www.lingoventures.us/
43.	Liquid 2 Ventures	Technology, consumer, and others	Equity	2	www.liquid2.vc
44.	Loki Equity Ventures	Consumer, business products / services, and others	Equity	2	www.lokiequity.com
45.	LOUD Capital	Technology, business products / services, and others	Equity	2	www.loud.vc

	Name	Historical Industries	Capital Type	Tier	Website
46.	Morgan Creek Digital Assets	Technology and financial services	Equity	2	https://www.digitalassetindexfund.com/
47.	Naples Technology Ventures	Technology, business products / services, and others	Equity	2	www.naplestechnologyventures.com
48.	NCT Ventures	Technology, business products / services, and others	Equity	2	www.nctventures.com
49.	New Enterprise Associates	Technology, healthcare, and others	Equity	2	www.nea.com
50.	NFX	Technology, consumer, and others	Equity	2	www.nfx.com
51	Rev1 Ventures	Technology, healthcare, and others	Equity	2	www.rev1ventures.com
52.	Right Side Capital Management	Technology, consumer, and others	Equity	2	www.rightsidecapital.com
53	Samsung NEXT Ventures	Technology, business products / services, and others	Equity	2	www.samsungnext.com
54.	Science	Technology, consumer, and others	Equity	2	www.science-inc.com
55.	Slow Ventures	Technology, consumer, and others	Equity	2	www.slow.co
56.	Social Capital	Technology, consumer, and others	Equity	2	www.socialcapital.com
57.	SV Angel	Technology, consumer, and others	Equity	2	www.svangel.com
58.	Tech Square Venture Partners	Technology, business products / services, and others	Equity	2	www.techsquareventures.com
59.	Third Kind Venture Capital	Technology, consumer, and others	Equity	2	www.3kvc.com
60.	Transition Level Investments	Technology, consumer, and others	Equity	2	www.transitionlevel.com
61.	UpHonest Capital	Technology, consumer, and others	Equity	2	www.uphonestcapital.com
62.	Venture University	Business products / services, consumer, and others	Equity	2	www.venture.university
63.	Village Global	Technology, business products / services, and others	Equity	2	www.villageglobal.vc
64.	Wakestream Ventures	Technology, consumer, and others	Equity	2	www.wakestreamventures.com
65.	WndrCo	Technology, consumer, and others	Equity	2	www.wndrco.com
66.	XFactor Ventures	Consumer, technology, and others	Equity	2	www.xfactor.ventures
67.	Zelkova Ventures	Technology, consumer, and others	Equity	2	www.zelkovavc.com

Sources: Pitchbook, Capital IQ, Company Websites, and TechCrunch.

Appendix A: Methodology

1. Identified and verified a set of black-owned and/or black-led businesses.

    a. Discovered black business by referring to publicly available black- and diverse business-focused publications and reports such as *Black Enterprise* magazine and Harlem Capital's 2018 Diversity report.

    b. Verified the identities of the entrepreneurs through LinkedIn, press releases, periodicals, and other forms of publicly available information.

2. After identifying businesses and verified their leadership, the team identified transactions with debt and equity capital providers, using Pitchbook and Capital IQ as a system of record.

3. Tiered the debt and equity capital providers based on their mission and/or focus on black-owned and/or black-led businesses, verifying the capital provider missions through their respective websites.

    a. Tier 1 capital providers have provided capital to black entrepreneurs and provided verifiable evidence of a mission to provide capital to black entrepreneurs

    b. Tier 2 capital providers have provided capital to black entrepreneurs

4. Reviewed portfolios of Tier 1 and Tier 2 capital providers to identify additional transactions with black-owned and/or black-led businesses.

HARVARD | BUSINESS | SCHOOL

9-319-050

OCTOBER 26, 2018

STEVEN ROGERS

DERRICK COLLINS

Fairview Capital

"Pretty good growth, don't you think?" JoAnn asked her business partner. Larry chuckled to himself as his fork separated another sliver of key lime pie on his dessert plate and replied, "You know it was exactly ten years ago, in this very same restaurant, that we were trying to map out the future of Fairview and the issue at that time was also growth." In February 2014, the co-founders and Managing Partners of Fairview Capital, JoAnn Price and Laurence Morse, both graduates of Howard University, were discussing the news they received earlier that day regarding Fairview Capital's latest victory— the mandate to create and manage Lincoln Fund I, a private equity fund of funds, which will invest exclusively in private equity funds owned by Black, and other minority, as well as women fund managers. This dinner was a mini celebration of the official letter they received from the State University Retirement System of Illinois (SURS), the sponsor of Lincoln Fund I.

"Yes, I remember that conversation—do you recall my reply?" queried JoAnn, as she peered over the top of her reading glasses in classic schoolteacher fashion. Larry pushed back in his seat, removed his spectacles and began to use them like a symphony conductor's baton to punctuate the words as he spoke:

> How could I forget? You looked me dead in the eye and said, "It's also a question of mission—it's always a question of mission." At the time, I felt a bit like Robert Johnson[1] at the crossroads. It was 2003, and by then Fairview was the "go-to" fund of funds to deploy institutional capital into minority and women private equity and venture capital firms, but it was unclear if we could sustain the same pace of investment. The Fairview platform was poised with talent, experience, and infrastructure, but the growth of minority and women funds, at that time, was modest at best. So, yes, I remember your response quite well, because it helped bring clarity.

It was impossible for the other restaurant patrons to have known that these two people in business casual attire, informally talking over crème brûlée and key lime pie, were leaders of an investment organization that was currently managing over $3 billion in capital. It was even less likely that any casual observer could have known these two were also responsible for at least ten times that amount

---

[1] Robert Johnson was an African-American blues musician from Mississippi that achieved fame in the 1930s. Legend has it that Johnson met the Devil at a mystical intersection of two local highways, or "crossroads", whereupon he traded his soul for his prodigious musical talent.

HBS Senior Lecturer Steven Rogers and independent researcher Derrick Collins prepared this case. It was reviewed and approved before publication by a company designate. Funding for the development of this case was provided by Harvard Business School and not by the company. HBS cases are developed solely as the basis for class discussion. Cases are not intended to serve as endorsements, sources of primary data, or illustrations of effective or ineffective management.

flowing from other sources into African-American and other minority businesses in the United States since the founding of their firm, Fairview Capital, in 1994.

Now, eleven years since that defining meeting, they were not only celebrating their previous success, but again were asking the same questions: Where do we go from here? Do we keep doing what we have been doing or do we implement a new strategy? Are we beholden to the strategy that is responsible for our success? Don't we owe it to Black, and other minority-controlled, funds to keep providing them with capital because other funds of funds are less likely to be limited partners to funds that target Black and other minority entrepreneurs?

The Pioneer Status of Fairview Capital

Twenty years earlier, JoAnn and Larry, established themselves as pioneers in the private equity/venture capital (PEVC) industry as the first institutional fund of funds to focus its deployment of capital into funds that invest primarily in African-American and other minority-controlled companies and/or companies that operate in minority markets – referred to by Fairview and their contemporaries as *Emerging Domestic Markets* (EDM). Before Fairview, the only institutional capital deployed into EDM-related investment funds consisted of: i) a portion of the private capital invested in government-backed Minority Enterprise Small Business Investment Companies[2] (MESBIC), many of which were owned by Fortune 500 companies, such as Amoco Venture Capital Corporation (Amoco Corporation) and EquiCo Capital Corporation (Equitable Life Assurance Society); and ii) two private venture capital partnerships with a combined total capitalization of less than $40 million. The total amount of institutional capital deployed among these efforts was less than $250 million, or about 0.8% of the total $30 billion in private equity capital under management in 1993.

Now it's 2014, and over $3.5 billion and 21 funds later, Fairview has established a clear and solid reputation for being the leading expert in identifying African-American, and other minority and women, talent in the arena of private equity and venture capital investing. The PEVC industry is an exclusive one, where only the most talented and accomplished business professionals are entrusted with millions—sometimes billions—of dollars to buy and sell interests in privately-held companies with the objective of generating profits for their investors.

The Private Equity Market

Private equity is money invested in companies in exchange for partial ownership. It consists of equity and equity-like instruments invested directly in privately held enterprises, or in publicly-held companies for the purpose of taking the companies private. Private equity and venture capital are closely related entities. Venture capital falls under the private equity umbrella and denotes the investment of equity in early stage and growth stage companies (see **Exhibit 1**). When using the term "private equity" one must be aware of whether the reference is the technical description of the industry that invests in privately-held companies—which includes venture capital—or the more colloquial use of the term which refers to investing in later stage buyout transactions.

---

[2] MESBICs were part of a program created by the U.S. Small Business Administration (SBA) which sponsored the creation of PEVC companies by providing matching funds to private capital raised for the purpose of capitalizing investment funds that would invest in minority businesses. Later the name of the program was changed to Specialized Small Business Investment Companies (SSBIC).

Structure of Private Equity Funds

Private equity and venture capital funds are typically structured as a limited partnership (LP) or a limited liability company (LLC). Investors in the fund are Limited Partners (LPs) and the managers of the fund, who perform all of the investment-related activities, serve as the General Partner (GP) of the fund. The GP receives a management fee—typically 2% to 2.5% of the investment fund's committed[3] capital—that is used to cover the operating costs of the fund. These entities and their structure enable the investors (LPs) to shield themselves from liability emanating from the various companies in which the PEVC fund will invest. It should be noted that the LPs are forbidden from making any investment of management decisions regarding the portfolio companies. This limited authority is a key characteristic of the Limited Partner and serves as the basis for their limited liability protection.

The PEVC fund typically has a finite life of 10 years. As such, the first 3–5 years are dedicated to sourcing and investing in companies, followed by intense activity to assist the portfolio companies' growth and development. The ultimate goal is to exit these deals by selling the fund's equity positions—hopefully at a higher valuation than what they paid—in order to produce investment returns. Exits take the form of selling the investment fund's equity interest to strategic buyers, financial buyers, or to participants in the public equity markets via an initial public offering (IPO). Once the equity interest is sold, the proceeds are shared between the fund's LPs and GP: with typically 80% of the gains allocated to the LPs and 20% retained by the GP as the "carried interest" or "carry". The carried interest is the primary economic incentive for the PEVC fund management team—the larger the investment return, the larger this personal benefit.

The capital required to establish a PEVC fund ranges from $25–$50 million for smaller funds to over $1 billion for the largest investment platforms, with most firms capitalized in the range of $100–$500 million. The large capital requirements dictate that institutional investors are the primary sources for this type of capital: pension funds, insurance companies, banks, foundations and endowments—institutions with large cash reserves that are invested in various asset classes as part of their regular course of business.

Role of Funds of Funds

Funds of funds are an important component of the PEVC industry ecosystem. They serve as intermediaries between the sources of capital—such as pension funds, insurance companies, foundations and endowments—and the PEVC funds that ultimately invest this capital into entrepreneurial enterprises (see **Exhibit 2**). For most institutions that serve as capital sources, the PEVC industry is viewed as one of several asset classes to choose from in constructing their investment portfolio, alongside stocks, bonds, real estate, etc. For the purpose of portfolio asset allocation, the PEVC industry is referred to as the *alternative investment* asset class. Given the high-risk/high return profile of alternative investments, they typically represent a small percentage of most institutions' investment portfolios. The successful operation of a fund of funds is a specialized and complicated undertaking. One must: a) establish an alternative investment program strategy that is appealing to LP investors with various objectives; b) market the fund and cultivate relationships that provide access to the best private equity investment talent; c) identify, screen and select the appropriate PEVC funds in which to invest; and d) monitor and manage this portfolio of investment funds. Many institutions

---

[3] PEVC funds raise capital via "committed capital". The money is committed by LP investors, but cash is only invested into the fund of funds as needed: for investments into private equity funds, and/or for management fees to the funds' managers. Thus, capital is requested from investors, or "called" only when it can be put to work; if it is idle, then investment returns would be depressed by the impact of time.

choose to outsource this process to a fund of funds, rather than build an in-house organization to manage — what is typically — a single digit percentage of their aggregate investment portfolio.

One of the advantages of investing in the PEVC market via a fund of funds is that a modest institutional investor can achieve much better diversification in this manner, than they can by investing directly in PEVC partnerships on their own. An effective fund of funds can reasonably invest $100 million among 20 PEVC partnerships and achieve an underlying investment portfolio diversified by industry sector, as well as by stage or type of investment (i.e., venture capital, buyout, mezzanine, etc.) as those 20 funds will, in turn, invest in approximately 300 entrepreneurial companies. A small institutional investor could not reasonably invest $10 million by itself and achieve this same level of diversification. Moreover, if the small institutional investor desired to invest on its own, it would have to build a specialized staff to source, screen and manage such investments. The tradeoff is the fee that is charged by a fund of funds, which is typically in the range of 0.75%–1.25% of committed capital. Thus, the investor that wishes to place $10 million in the alternative asset class has the choice of paying annual fees of approximately $100k, or employing a team of two to five individuals that would likely cost more than this amount, per person.

Specialized expertise in particular areas, such as technical industry sectors, or international markets, is another way that some funds of funds distinguish themselves. JoAnn and Larry leveraged their specialized knowledge of the African-American and minority investment manager in establishing Fairview Capital. Their years of experience in the Emerging Domestic Marketplace informed their assessment of investment managers and their strategies, and became one of the key selling points for Fairview Capital.

In addition to the advantages of diversification and economic efficiency, the better funds of funds are able to gain access to the best performing PEVC funds because of their industry knowledge and networks. The competition is intense in accessing PEVC funds that provide investment returns that achieve top quartile performance, and this is almost impossible for the small institutional investor. Moreover, the difference in fund performance is significant. In the period between 1969 and 1999, the top quartile private equity funds (venture capital and buyouts) provided a rate of return of 27.9%, whereas the median return was 11.5%, and the bottom quartile firms posted a meager return of 1.5% (see **Exhibit 3**). The better funds of funds are able to not only gain access to the better performing PEVC funds, but are also typically able to negotiate better terms and conditions, given the leverage inherent in their larger investment placements.

PEVC Market Activity During Fairview's Early Years

The period from the mid-1990s through early 2000 ushered in an exponential growth of PEVC investing, driven largely by the explosion of technology and Internet-related enterprises. As an illustration of this phenomenal growth, consider the following: during the seven-year period of 1994–2000, approximately $219 billion was invested in venture capital transactions, which was 5.7x the $39 billion invested in the prior 24-year timeframe from 1970–1993! These investments were fueled by the parallel growth of investment fund assets where U.S. PEVC fund assets under management grew from $29 billion in 1993 to $257 billion in 2003 (see **Exhibit 4**).

As the PEVC market grew rapidly during the late 1990s, so did the fund of funds market. New commitments to funds of funds grew at a pedestrian level from $600 million in 1992 to $690 million in 1994, but then exploded from $2 billion in 1995 to $18 billion in 1999 (see **Exhibit 5**). The number of funds of funds, similarly grew from 6 in 1992 to 66 by 1999 (see **Exhibit 6**). This growth was bolstered by the institutional and high net worth investors attracted to the PEVC marketplace. To satisfy this demand, a number of new funds of funds were established by commercial and investment banks in response to the demands of their high net worth clientele. In fact, approximately half of the capital raised by funds of funds in 1998–99 were raised by *new* funds of funds (see **Exhibit 7**).

However, this Internet era explosion ultimately led to a crash in the year 2000 as the public stock markets' initial public offerings—which fueled the extraordinary returns—abruptly dried up. Valuations of venture-backed companies plummeted and venture financings followed suit. The year 2002 ended with $22 billion invested in 3,218 venture capital deals, which was a far cry from the zenith of the year 2000 where $105 billion was invested in 8,044 deals (see **Exhibit 8**). In spite of the precipitous decline of investment activity in the PEVC market, the 2002 performance actually represented a reasonable increase over the investment activity just five years earlier in 1997, where $15 billion was invested in 3,232 deals.

Emerging Domestic Markets: The Core of Fairview's Mission

Emerging Domestic Markets (EDM) represent areas of economic activity defined by the presence of ethnic minorities: (a) in the ownership of business enterprises; or (b) as customers or employees of the subject enterprises. Demographers and researchers began to track the dynamics of these markets and their potential for growth. Educational attainment, spending power, and business performance were oft-cited variables that forecasted business opportunity and growth in the EDM. A study sponsored by the Council of Urban Investors Institute[4] described the dynamics associated with Emerging Domestic Markets. A key portion of the study cited environmental factors that inferred the potential for successful investment opportunities, including:

- MBA degrees earned by minorities grew from 5,846 to 12,679 between 1985 and 1995—a 117% increase; this attainment also represented a 305% increase since 1977 when 3,130 degrees were awarded to minorities.

- Minority disposable income in the U.S. was projected to be $2 - $3 trillion for the period between 2000–2045.

- Total aggregate revenue of minority-owned firms posted a compound annual growth rate of 15.7% for the 10-year period 1987–1997, outpacing the 8.9% CAGR for all U.S. firms.

More specifically related to private equity investing, a study sponsored by the Kauffman Foundation[5] analyzed the investments made by 24 minority-focused funds in the period of 1989–1995. This analysis documented internal rates of return (IRR) produced by these funds between -32% and 79%, with a mean IRR of 23.9%, and median IRR of 19.5%. These results were comparable to the broader PEVC market, wherein Venture Economics[6] and the National Venture Capital Association calculated, as of early 2001, the 10-year trailing average annual return for their Private Equity Performance Index was 20.2%.

The data emanating from the study of Emerging Domestic Markets appeared promising and compelling—especially when compared to the disparity in the PEVC market at that time, where it was

---

[4] Fairchild, Gregory B. In Your Own Backyard: Investment Opportunities in Emerging Domestic Markets. Council of Urban Investors Institute.

[5] Bates, Timothy and Bradford, William. Minorities and Venture Capital: A New Wave in American Business. Kauffman Foundation, 2000.

[6] Venture Economics tracked the performance of over 1,400 U.S. venture capital and buyout funds on a quarterly basis.

estimated, by Fairview and others in the private equity marketplace, that less than 1% of PEVC was invested in minority enterprises.

The Fairview Founders: JoAnn Price & Larry Morse

JoAnn Price and Larry Morse entered the private equity market from different perspectives, but eventually teamed up to create the first institutional fund of funds that specifically targeted minority and women investment funds. Both JoAnn and Larry were graduates of Howard University in Washington, DC, but took different paths after their undergraduate experience at the historically Black institution, before their professional careers ultimately intersected in the relatively small community of minority-managed private equity funds. (See biographies of JoAnn and Larry in **Exhibits 9** and **10**.)

Howard University: An Early Influence

Howard University had a tremendous influence on JoAnn and Larry's early professional trajectories and their individual and collective thought processes regarding the advancement and development of the African-American community. This is not surprising, given the history of the institution.

Howard University was chartered in Washington, DC in 1867 for the purpose of providing educational opportunities to African-Americans. The founding of the school was part of a larger trend that took place during the post-Civil War era in which a number of colleges were established — mostly in the southern states — to educate African-Americans emerging from the institution of slavery. The schools established during this time period are now referred to as historically black colleges and universities or HBCUs.

Howard is one of the preeminent HBCUs and has historically served as one of the most prolific founts of African-American achievement. Its graduates have had a significant impact and influence in every major sector of American society including medicine, law, business, social work, and the arts. The following is a partial listing of some notable Howard University alumni:

- Patricia Booth, M.D: first African-American woman doctor to receive a patent for a medical invention

- Carter G. Woodson: historian, author, and founder of *Negro History Week* (now *Black History Month*)

- Thurgood Marshall: first African-American Supreme Court Justice

- Edward Brooke: second African-American elected to the U.S. Senate

- Kamala Harris: second African-American woman elected to the U.S. Senate and former Attorney General of California

- Andrew Young: first African-American United Nations Ambassador and former Mayor of Atlanta, Georgia

- Nnamdi Azikiwe: first President of Nigeria

- Ralph Bunche: first African-American to be awarded Nobel Peace Prize and former Harvard University professor

- Benjamin O. Davis: first African-American Brigadier General in the U.S. Army

- Doris Evans McGinty: first African-American woman to receive doctorate in musicology from Oxford University

- Toni Morrison: author, awarded Pulitzer Prize and Nobel Prize for literature

- Cathy Hughes: founder of TV One and Radio One

- Chadwick Boseman: actor, *Black Panther, Marshall, Get On Up, Jackie Robinson*

- H. Naylor Fitzhugh: one of the first African-American graduates of Harvard Business School and credited with creating the concept of target marketing

The scholarship and history of Howard University inspires a deep culture of self-determination among its students. Larry Morse was so moved by his tenure at Howard, he wrote about the African-American college experience in his novel, *Sundial*.

JoAnn Price and the Role of NAIC

Before forming Fairview, JoAnn Price served as President of the National Association of Investment Companies (NAIC), which is the trade association for private equity and venture capital firms either managed by minorities and women and/or firms that seek to invest in minority and women enterprises. The NAIC membership, in 1993, was comprised of less than 50 firms nationwide totaling approximately 300 employees.

NAIC was founded in 1970 as the American Association of MESBICs (AAMESBIC) by way of then-President Richard Nixon's Black Capitalism program, which sought to improve access to capital for minority-owned businesses. JoAnn originally served as the Deputy Director of the association for several years before ascending to the Presidential post. During the early years of the organization, there were relatively few realistic options for minorities to access equity and other forms of growth capital. Given this reality, many of the MESBICs would collaborate and co-invest in deals as a means to execute transactions that they could not finance alone. This collaborative deal making helped to foster a sense of community among these minority investment professionals and the American Association of MESBICs functioned as an extended business family. The extended family metaphor is an apt one as JoAnn Price functioned, not only as President, but also as den mother, conflict mediator, and chief motivator, among some of the brightest minds in the minority entrepreneurial business arena.

The organization that JoAnn led was significantly important to the development of the deal making among African-American and other minority investors. As an illustration of the impact and influence of AAMESBIC, it was during this time in the 1970s, Reginald Lewis, served as general counsel to the association. His law firm specialized in venture capital transactions for small- and medium-sized businesses, and helped in the formation and financing of a number of MESBICs, while also gaining the critical experience in structuring deals that would later define his approach to deal making. Years later, Lewis would become the first African-American to build a billion-dollar company, Beatrice Foods, via acquisition. He later described his experience in the best-selling book, *Why Should White Guys Have All The Fun?* Lewis was also a devoted alum of Harvard Law School, to which he donated $3 million in 1993 which, at the time, was the largest individual donation in the 175-year history of the school. He also donated $1 million to Howard University, and the Reginald F. Lewis Foundation donated $1.5 million to his undergraduate alma mater, Virginia State University.[7]

JoAnn continued to lead AAMESBIC as it searched for different ways to build larger pools of capital. During the mid-1980s through the early 1990s, many members began to move away from the SBA and the MESBIC program to build independent private equity firms. It was during this time, the organization changed its name to the National Association of Investment Companies to reflect a broader community of minority investors. It was also during this time that many of the senior board members of NAIC began to incubate an idea that would later become a true game-changing strategy for the minority private equity community.

Led by NAIC board chairman, Herbert Wilkins—Harvard Business School grad and Senior Partner of the well-respected Syncom venture capital fund—the senior leadership of NAIC developed a strategy to sponsor a fund of funds vehicle that would focus on their unique EDM marketplace. Many in the NAIC membership had developed strong investment skills that were reflected in impressive deal flow and investment returns, but felt that the traditional institutional investment community did not fully value their performance potential. They felt that a consolidated initiative that would provide an attractive view of the minority PEVC investment space, as well as the portfolio diversification and risk mitigation desired by institutional investors, would be an effective strategy to develop a pool of capital that would complement their individual firms' efforts. So, when Herb Wilkins called JoAnn to discuss their idea of her leading this pioneering fund of funds effort, she—without hesitation—replied, "Herb, I'm really busy and don't have time for this foolishness! Bye!", and—believing this to be a joke—hung up on one of the most respected members in the NAIC membership. After calling back and explaining that he was serious, Herb was able to convince JoAnn to consider leading the effort to establish an EDM-focused fund of funds.

JoAnn was a natural fit for this role, as she was intimately knowledgeable of the industry, its dynamics and participants. The NAIC board members—and JoAnn—also felt that she should partner with someone with strong direct private equity investing experience. Larry Morse was a universally well-respected member of the NAIC community and was considering a career move at the time. After a dinner, followed by several meetings, and many months of discussions and due diligence, JoAnn Price and Larry Morse founded Fairview Capital. The duo then began the process of educating the institutional investment community about the opportunities to deploy capital in Emerging Domestic Markets.

Laurence Morse

Larry spent his formative years inhaling the aroma of business and entrepreneurship as he was greatly influenced by his father's relationship with black entrepreneurs. He fondly remembered his parents moving from Birmingham, Alabama to Jacksonville, Florida so that his father could take a job with the Afro-American Life Insurance Company, co-founded by Abraham Lincoln Lewis, one of America's most successful African-American entrepreneurs. He later went on to found American Beach, which in 1935, was the only beach resort area in Florida established by blacks to cater to black people. This resort was 200 acres of beachfront property filled with black-owned homes, hotels, restaurants, nightclubs, and other businesses. Larry was raised hearing stories from his father about great African-American insurance titans including the aforementioned A. L. Lewis, A. G. Gaston

---

[7] Martha Minow, "Reginald F. Lewis Foundation Gifts $1.5 Million to Harvard Law School." *Harvard Law Today.* June 17, 2011. https://today.law.harvard.edu/reginald-f-lewis-foundation-gifts-1-5-million-to-harvard-law-school/, accessed October 2018.

(Birmingham Life); and Asa Spaulding (North Carolina Mutual). Self-determination and black business success became a part of Larry's DNA.

The cerebral nature of the young Laurence Morse loved that he could see the business concepts he learned from his father, and other black businesspeople, validated in economic theory. As a lover of the dismal science, Larry graduated from Howard University (where he later donated $1 million) with a baccalaureate degree in economics, which included spending his junior year at The London School of Economics and Political Science as a Luard Scholar. Morse subsequently earned Masters and PhD degrees in Economics from Princeton University and has been a postdoctoral fellow at Harvard University.

During the time JoAnn led the trade association, Larry honed his skills as a private equity investor as a Principal at minority-led venture capital firm, UNC Partners in Boston, Massachusetts. Larry later co-founded the private equity firm, TSG Ventures in Stamford, Connecticut. TSG was a firm that focused on buyouts, and where the senior team was comprised of three African-American and one Indian investment professionals. It was this experience—as a direct private equity investor—during which Larry learned the craft of private equity investing as well as established himself firmly in the EDM ecosystem and investor networks.

The Evolution of Fairview Capital

Fairview Capital sought to leverage the opportunity that was becoming more apparent via research focused on Emerging Domestic Markets, and overlooked by the broader equity investment community. As a nascent organization, Fairview partnered with an established fund of funds, Bigler Investment Management Company, located in Farmington, Connecticut. This was the first such partnership between an African-American firm and an established private equity player. Two of the Bigler partners, Peter Seigel and Claire Leonardi, joined JoAnn and Larry in the Fairview General Partner, to demonstrate the firm's commitment to the Fairview effort. At this time, there were fewer than ten funds of funds in the entire U.S. and the Bigler firm had a solid reputation for investing in top-tier venture capital funds, and had approximately $1 billion in assets under management. This partnership with Bigler, provided Fairview an imprimatur of marketplace legitimacy as well as provided organizational infrastructure in terms of administrative and fund management personnel (see **Exhibit 11**).

Fairview made history when it raised its first pool of institutional capital in 1994, totaling $92 million, as it was the first institutional fund of funds whose objective was the development of a portfolio of PEVC funds that would focus their investments into minority-controlled enterprises. This was followed by an additional six investment funds over the next eight years with varying objectives and strategies (see **Exhibit 12**).

The first three funds, Fairview Capital, L.P., Fairview Capital II, L.P., and New York CRF Investment Fund, L.P., focused on the firm's original thesis of investing in PEVC funds that address the Emerging Domestic Market. In 1999, Fairview leveraged the experience, insight and relationships it had gained in its partnership with Bigler Investment Management Company to establish an investment vehicle, Fairview Ventures Fund, L.P., which focused on investing in established venture capital partnerships that had demonstrated success in one or more prior funds. Fairview Capital III, L.P. was established in 2001 and focused on its traditional EDM as well as non-EDM emerging managers, given the increasing opportunity to back investment professionals that were leaving older, established funds, to strike out on their own in the growing PEVC industry. Institutional LPs were increasingly seeking these emerging managers in an effort to identify new investment talent as the growth of the industry made it harder to gain access to many of the traditional top-tier funds. Emerging managers were expected to represent 10% - 20% of the PEVC market for the foreseeable future. In 2002, Fairview established Fairview Ventures Fund II, L.P. and Fairview Ventures Fund II-NY, L.P.; both funds focused on investing in established venture capital partnerships with the latter vehicle customized for the New York Common Retirement Fund. By 2003, Fairview had a deep knowledge and comprehensive view of all the PEVC firms that operated in the EDM marketplace, as well as direct insight into the business practices, internal disciplines and cultures that characterized the top performing venture capital firms in the country. A survey of this market, documented by Fairview, is represented in **Exhibit 13**.

Back to the Future of Fairview Capital

While the Fairview partners continued their discussion over coffee and copies of documents emblazoned with "DRAFT" at the top, Larry glanced at his small dessert plate and noticed how clean it was. If it weren't for the tiny crumbs of graham cracker crust that he couldn't lift with his fork, there would be no indication that a full slice of key lime pie had ever occupied the space just a few minutes ago. With no crust left to conquer, Larry opined:

> This new commitment we've received for Lincoln Fund I makes this the eighth minority-focused fund of funds since our strategy shift in 2004. This now places Fairview at approximately $3.5 billion in assets under management. Yes—this is pretty good growth.

What type of shift in strategy, ten years earlier, could have been responsible for such impressive growth of minority-focused funds of funds within the Fairview Capital portfolio, while remaining true to their mission of providing capital to funds in the Emerging Domestic Market?

Exhibit 1   Private Equity Stages of Investment

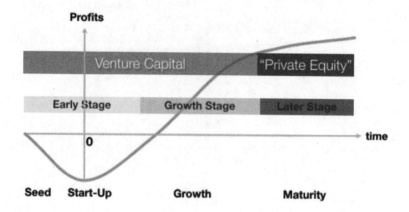

Source: Casewriter.

Exhibit 2   Investment Structure of a Private Equity Fund of Funds

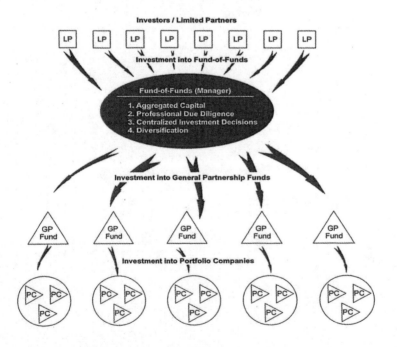

Source: Pease, Robert. *Private Equity Funds-Of-Funds: State of the Market.* Wellesley, MA: AssetAlternatives Inc, 2000.

Exhibit 3 Private Equity Fund Performance Comparison by Quartile For Period, 1969–1999

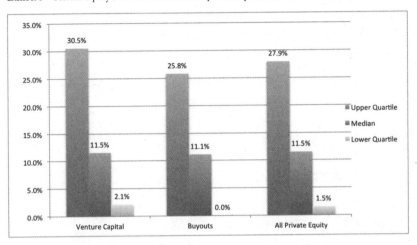

Source: "Private Equity Fund of Funds" AltAssets, August 1, 2003, Venture Economics, 2000.

Exhibit 4 Capital Under Management—U.S. Venture Funds, 1985–2003

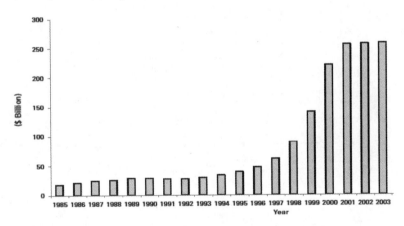

Source: National Venture Capital Association Yearbook prepared by Thomson Reuters.

Exhibit 5 Growth in Commitments to Funds of Funds

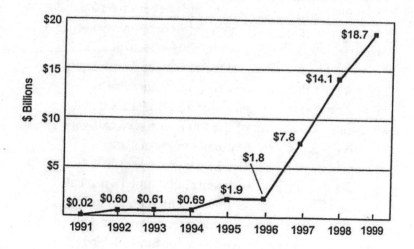

Source: Pease, Robert. *Private Equity Funds-Of-Funds: State of the Market.* Wellesley, MA: AssetAlternatives Inc, 2000.

Exhibit 6 Growth in Number of Funds of Funds

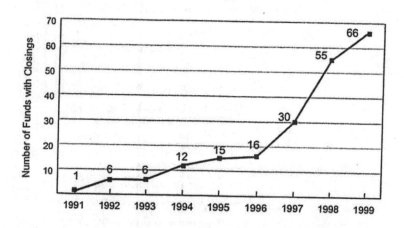

Source: Pease, Robert. *Private Equity Funds-Of-Funds: State of the Market.* Wellesley, MA: AssetAlternatives Inc, 2000.

Exhibit 7   Commitments to New vs. Established Fund of Funds Providers

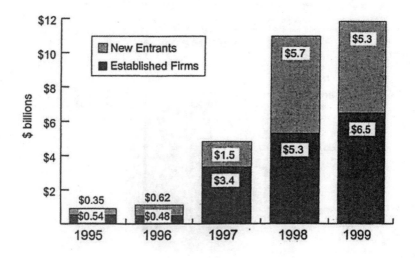

Source: Pease, Robert. *Private Equity Funds-Of-Funds: State of the Market*. Wellesley, MA: AssetAlternatives Inc, 2000.

Exhibit 8   Annual Venture Capital Investments, 1995–2002

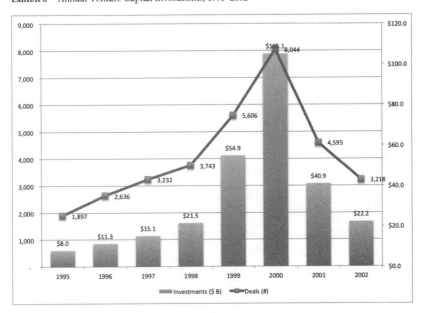

Source: Adapted by casewriter from PricewaterhouseCoopers/National Venture Capital Association MoneyTree Report, based on data from Thomson Reuters.

Exhibit 9   JoAnn Price

Ms. Price is a member of Fairview's investment committee and a manager of all Fairview-sponsored funds. Prior to co-founding Fairview, Ms. Price served as president of the National Association of Investment Companies headquartered in Washington, D.C. Ms. Price serves on a number of national advisory committees and private equity advisory boards. She is currently on the Howard University Board of Visitors and the YMCA of Greater Hartford Board of Directors. Ms. Price is on the board of the Apollo Theater Foundation in New York City and is the former Chairperson of the Amistad Center for Art & Culture in Hartford, Connecticut.

Ms. Price also serves as Chairperson of the Hartford Foundation for Public Giving and is on the Board of Regents for Higher Education, a position appointed by the Governor and legislative leaders. Ms. Price is a graduate of Howard University.

Source: Casewriter.

Exhibit 10   Larry Morse

Laurence C. Morse is Chief Executive Officer of Fairview Capital Partners, Inc., which creates and manages customized private equity fund investment vehicles for public and corporate pension funds, and other institutional investors. Prior to co-founding Fairview, Dr. Morse was a Principal at TSG Ventures. He began his career in venture capital and private equity at UNC Ventures in Boston.

Dr. Morse is a past Chairman of the Board of Directors of the National Association of Investment Companies. He is a member of the boards of Webster Financial Corporation (NYSE:WBS), Harris Associates Investment Trust (The Oakmark Mutual Funds), the Institute of International Education, Howard University, a former Trustee of Princeton University, and a former Trustee of the Princeton University Investment Company (PRINCO). He serves on the advisory boards Battery Ventures, GenNx360 Capital Partners, ICV Capital Partners, Trinity Ventures and U.S. Venture Partners (USVP).

Dr. Morse graduated summa cum laude and Phi Beta Kappa from Howard University with a BA in Economics, having spent his junior year at The London School of Economics and Political Science as a Luard Scholar. He earned MA and PhD degrees in Economics at Princeton University and has been a postdoctoral fellow at Harvard University.

Source: Casewriter.

Exhibit 11   Fairview Capital Structure, 1994

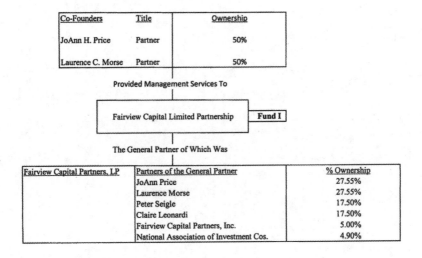

Fairview Capital Partners, Inc.

Co-Founders	Title	Ownership
JoAnn H. Price	Partner	50%
Laurence C. Morse	Partner	50%

Provided Management Services To

Fairview Capital Limited Partnership	Fund I

The General Partner of Which Was

Fairview Capital Partners, LP	Partners of the General Partner	% Ownership
	JoAnn Price	27.55%
	Laurence Morse	27.55%
	Peter Seigle	17.50%
	Claire Leonardi	17.50%
	Fairview Capital Partners, Inc.	5.00%
	National Association of Investment Cos.	4.90%

Source: Fairview Capital.

Exhibit 12   Fairview Capital Partners Investment Fund Portfolio Summary, December 31, 2004

Investment Fund	Inception Date	Committed Capital ($MM)	Capital Invested	
			($MM)	%
Fairview Capital, L.P. Invest in PEVC funds and emerging managers that provide capital to the emerging domestic market.	September 1994	92.10	85.48	93%
Fairview Capital II, L.P. Invest in PEVC funds and emerging managers that provide capital to the emerging domestic market.	December 1997	124.15	102.59	83%
New York CRF Investment Fund, L.P. Invest in PEVC funds and emerging managers that provide capital to the emerging domestic market.	July 1998	50.05	41.73	83%
Fairview Ventures Fund I, L.P. Invest in established venture capital funds with demonstrable success in one or more prior funds.	October 1999	301.50	165.97	55%
Fairview Capital III, L.P. Invest in PEVC funds and emerging managers that provide capital to the emerging domestic market, as well as non-EDM emerging managers.	November 2001	54.50	7.93	15%
Fairview Ventures Fund II-NY, L.P. Invest in established venture capital funds with demonstrable success in one or more prior funds.	August 2002	150.75	1.50	1%
Fairview Ventures Fund II-NY, L.P. Invest in established venture capital funds with demonstrable success in one or more prior funds.	November 2002	120.60	3.13	3%

Source: Fairview Capital.

Exhibit 13 Emerging Domestic Market—Summary of Investment Companies by Market Segment, June 2003

EDM Market Segment	Current	In Formation
I. Firms that invest in companies located in, or serving urban and/or underserved communities.	20	4
II. Firms owned/led by minorities and women.	28	4
III. Firms that invest in companies owned/led by minorities and women.	17	3

Source: Fairview Capital.

Note: Some firms are represented in multiple categories.
Total firms represented = 38, which include 6 in formation.

Fairview Capital Note Assignment Questions

1. What is a Fund of Funds? Is Fairview unique?
2. How many of the 38 EDM funds received investments from Fairview?
3. Should Fairview invest in all 38 EDM funds?

Notes

1. "White Like Me." *Saturday Night Live*, Season 10, 1984. https://www.youtube.com/watch?v=l_LeJfn_qW0
2. Norman, James. "A VC's Guide to Investing in Black Founders." *Harvard Business Review*. June 19, 2020. https://hbr.org/2020/06/a-vcs-guide-to-investing-in-Black-founders
3. Heller, Joseph. "The Hazards of Raising Venture Capital While Black." *Barron's*. June 25, 2020. https://www.barrons.com/articles/the-hazards-of-raising-venture-capital-while-Black-51593103012
4. Robb, Alicia. "Financing Patterns and Credit Market Experiences: A Comparison ay Race and Ethnicity for U.S. Employer Firms." Small Business Administration Office of Advocacy. February 2018. https://advocacy.sba.gov/2018/02/01/financing-patterns-and-credit-market-experiences-a-comparison-by-race-and-ethnicity-for-u-s-employer-firms/

5. Onley, Dawn. "Report: Black Business Owners Are Denied Bank Loans Twice as Often as White Business Owners." *The Grio*. January 15, 2020. https://thegrio.com/2020/01/15/report-Black-business-owners-are-denied-bank-loans-twice-as-often-as-White-business-owners/

6. Lewis-Thompson, Marissanne. "Black Business Owners Face An Uphill Battle Securing Bank Loans." St. Louis Public Radio. January 6, 2020. https://news.stlpublicradio.org/economy-business/2020-01-06/Black-business-owners-face-an-uphill-battle-securing-bank-loans

7. Steinberg, Julie. "Banks Give Black-Owned Businesses Advantage on Supply-Chain Finance Terms." *The Wall Street Journal*. November 22, 2020. https://www.wsj.com/articles/banks-give-Black-owned-businesses-advantage-on-supply-chain-finance-terms-11606060801

8. Hutchenson, Susannah. "How I Became a Venture Capitalist: Arlan Hamilton of Backstage Capital." *USA Today*. April 13, 2017. https://www.usatoday.com/story/college/2017/04/13/how-i-became-a-venture-capitalist-arlan-hamilton-of-backstage-capital/37429259/

9. Hamilton, Arlan. "Dear White Venture Capitalists: If You're Reading This, It's (Almost) Too Late." *Medium*. June 13, 2015. https://medium.com/female-founders/dear-White-venture-capitalists-if-you-re-not-actively-searching-for-and-seeding-qualified-4f382f6fd4a7#:~:text=Dr.,BILLION%20in%20976%20SEED%20deals.

10. Rodriguez, Salvador. "How This Woman Went From Homelessness to Running a Multimillion-Dollar Venture Fund." *Inc*. August 12, 2016. https://www.inc.com/salvador-rodriguez/arlan-hamilton-backstage-capital.html

11. Wagner, Kurt. "The 'IT'S ABOUT DAMN TIME fund' Wants $36 Million to Invest in Black Female Founders." Vox. May 6, 2018. https://www.vox.com/2018/5/6/17324506/backstage-capital-fund-invest-Black-women-founders

12. Hinchliffe, Emma. "The Number of Black Female Founders Who Have Raised More Than $1 million Has Nearly Tripled Since 2018." *Fortune*. December 2, 2020. https://fortune.com/2020/12/02/Black-women-female-founders-venture-capital-funding-vc-2020-project-diane/

7

Black Turnaround Entrepreneurs

"Early on in my business career . . . had to very quickly assess what the situation was, what the key issues were and what the key levers were that you could pull that would change the performance of a particular business. . ."[1]
— Ken Chenault, American Express

FOR SOME PEOPLE it might be hard to fathom the idea that there is a segment of entrepreneurs who are only interested in working with under-performing companies. These individuals are called *turnaround entrepreneurs*. They usually buy poorly run companies that may or may not be profitable. Expressed another way, the profit of such companies is either miniscule or significantly below the industry average. Accordingly, these entrepreneurs are driven to improve the company's performance and, in turn, it's value. To achieve such an end, they seek to increase the company's revenue, decrease its expenses, or a combination of both.

Don Cornwall is one such Black entrepreneur. In his business plan he outlined explicitly that his start-up, Granite Broadcasting, had the objective of creating a media conglomerate by buying and combining underperforming television stations.[2] In 1992, he took Granite Broadcasting public and the stock was traded on the NASDAQ. Three years later, *Black Enterprise* magazine named it Company of the Year to recognize and celebrate the fact that this Black-owned company was the top performing media company in the U.S.[3]

While Cornwall intentionally sought to be an entrepreneur engaged in turnaround activities, as a result of the coronavirus in 2020 and 2021, many Black entrepreneurs are now involuntarily doing the same. A study by H&R Block found that 53% of Black business owners saw revenues fall by 50% or more since COVID-19 became a widespread pandemic.[4] Due to lost revenues, it is estimated that over 40% of Black-owned businesses closed permanently.[5] A large percentage of those companies that remained solvent and in operation are engaged in the turnaround process.

The following is advice that I gave to over 1,000 entrepreneurs in the summer of 2020, most of whom were Black. I pointed out that the keys to a successful turnaround are to reduce expenses, create multiple lines of revenue, and load up on cash. Unfortunately, the advice about loading up on cash is easier said than done. Some of the lowest cost of capital that should have been available to almost all of the over 2 million Black entrepreneurs was funding from the federal government's Payroll Protection Program (PPP). The low-cost aspect of this funding was that it operated much like a forgivable loan. At a mere cost of 2%, the debt could easily be converted to a grant, with no interest or principal due to the government. The path to procurement of this low- or no-cost capital was extraordinarily simple to follow. The application did not require any financial statements, collateral, tax returns, or credit checks. Despite these seemingly low hurdles, only 2% of Black-owned businesses received PPP loans, when almost 5 million loans were issued, totaling more than $521 billion.[6] Before the pandemic, there were about 8%, or 2 million Black-owned businesses in the U.S.,[7] yet only 2% received any of this historic funding. On paper, the hurdles anyone needed to jump over to access the money seemed low, but those hurdles almost immediately became nearly insurmountable for Black entrepreneurs. The government's decision to distribute the money through large corporate banks was disastrous for Black business.

On May 28, 2020, the government announced that $10 billion would be set aside as funding to be disbursed by Community Development Financial Institutions, which primarily work as lenders for businesses in underserved and rural communities. A new law was also enacted that made it easier for businesses to turn these loans into grants. Previously, businesses had to spend the funds within eight weeks of receiving the loan, while 75% had to be spent on payroll. Under the reformed measures, businesses were granted an extension of up to 24 weeks to spend the money and only required to spend 60% of it on payroll expenses.

In response to criticism that Black- and other minority-owned firms did not get sufficient funding during the first two rounds of PPP, the third round of PPP funding had greater focus on smaller businesses and lenders.[8] This improved the chances for Black-owned businesses to access this extraordinary, attractive funding. Furthermore, the SBA is increasing its efforts and offering guidance to help make sure there is greater access to PPP loans for minority, underserved, veteran, and women-owned businesses.

The main features of the third round of PPP funding are the following:

- Businesses that received a PPP loan during the first round were eligible to receive an additional PPP loan if:
  o They employ 300 or fewer employees;
  o The business used all the funds it received from the first PPP loan or have plans to use any remaining funds;
  o Gross receipts during one of the first three quarters of 2020 were at least 25% that of the same quarter in 2019;
- Businesses applying for the first time to the PPP did not have these limitations;
- For businesses applying for another PPP loan, the loan was capped at $2 million; first-time PPP loan applicants were capped at $10 million;
- Businesses in the hospitality industry could multiply their payroll by 3.5 instead of 2.5 if they were applying for another PPP loan, but were subject to the $2 million cap;
- Businesses could choose the covered period between 8 and 24 weeks;
- The list of allowable expenses was expanded to include property damage costs, operations expenditures, supplier costs, and workers protection expenditures;

- Simplified PPP Loan Forgiveness Applications for loans under $150,000;
- Section 501(c)(6) not-for-profit organizations became eligible to apply for PPP loans; and
- Businesses in bankruptcy became eligible to apply for PPP loans.

On February 22, 2021, the Biden administration announced five changes to the PPP Program.[9] These changes were designed to make PPP funds available to very small businesses and those who had not been able to access funding from the program in previous rounds. The changes were the following:

- For a two-week period, from February 24, 2021, through March 9, 2021, only businesses with fewer than 20 employees would be allowed to apply for PPP funding;
- The formula used to calculate PPP loans was revised to provide more funding for sole proprietors, independent contractors, and self-employed individuals, while an additional $1 billion would be allocated for these individuals in low- and moderate-income (LMI) areas;
- Eligibility for PPP funding was extended to small business owners, with non-fraud related felonies, as long as the applicant was not incarcerated at the time of the application;
- Business owners with delinquent federal student loans were made eligible for a PPP loan; and
- U.S residents who are non-citizens were made eligible and allowed to use their Individual Taxpayer Identification Numbers (ITINs) to apply.

To ensure more equitable access to funding for minority-owned firms, community financial institutions, including Community Development Financial Institutions (CDFIs), were given priority and exclusive opportunity to begin making first-draw PPP loans on January 11, 2021, and second-draw loans on January 13, 2021. Small lenders with less than $1 billion in assets were scheduled to begin making both first- and second-draw loans on January 15, 2021, and all approved PPP lenders were able to begin lending on January 19, 2021.

As of this writing, it is unclear what impact all of the changes to the PPP loans have had on Black entrepreneurs. Hopefully, these changes will allow them to begin to "load up on cash" so they can experience successful turnarounds. In addition to cash, entrepreneurs who are turning around their company need to reduce expenses. There should be a three-step mindset to cut costs properly:

1. Reduce costs so that all fixed costs can be covered by revenue; this may not eliminate financial losses, but represents the first move toward profitability.
2. Eliminate the financial losses that allow the company to reach breakeven status. This position represents the point when the company is still not profitable because its total costs (fixed and variable) equals its total revenues. The mathematical formula is as follows:

$$\text{Fixed costs} \div (\text{Selling price per unit} - \text{Variable costs per unit})$$
$$= \text{Breakeven}$$

3. Cut costs so that revenues are greater than expenses. The result is the generation of profit.

There is a truism in the world of turnarounds, and that is the fact that a truly successful one can never be accomplished by reduction of expenses only, but requires some action to increase revenues.

Black Corporate Turnaround Specialists

Ken Chenault, once called the "Dean of Black CEOs," attributes part of his ascension as CEO of American Express to his understanding of how increasing revenue represents the central element for a turnaround to be deemed successful.

Chenault was born in Mineola, New York, a predominantly Black neighborhood on Long Island, the third of four children.[10] His father was a dentist and his mother worked as a dental hygienist. He attended the alternative Waldorf School where he served as senior class president. He received a BA in history from Bowdoin College in 1973 and a JD from Harvard Law School in 1976.

He began his professional career as an associate at the law firm of Rogers & Wells in New York City, where he worked from 1977–1979. Then, he was a consultant at Bain & Company from 1979–1981. He joined American Express in 1981 in its Strategic Planning Group and worked in various positions throughout the company, including its merchandising department, until he became the company's president and chief operating officer in 1997. He was appointed CEO of American Express in 2001, becoming the third Black CEO of a Fortune 500 company. He retired from the company in 2018.

One of his first assignments at American Express was to turn around the operations of the company's Merchandise Services division, which sold merchandise through the mail but was losing money. He overhauled the operations of the division and replaced the existing product lines with superior offerings, adding a line of personal accessories. Through his initiatives, sales increased from $100 million to $700 million. He notes, "In the early 1980s, American Express had a business that sold merchandise through the mail. I had the chance to run all aspects of the business—systems, operations, marketing, customer service. And also, we had to develop a strategy to sell a range of products to specific customer segments. I also had to learn how to motivate an organization that had been low performing to become a high-performing team."[11] He later notes, "The only problem was, they were losing money. And I really was able to put together a team and figure out how to motivate people to do things that they didn't think were possible. And we went from generating $100 million in sales and losing money, to over $700 million in sales. And it was one of the most formative experiences of my career."[12]

While most of Chenault's career and impact was at one company, another Black CEO of a Fortune 500 company, Marvin Ellison, is heralded as a turnaround specialist who successfully improved two Fortune 500 companies.

Ellison grew up in Brownsville, Tennessee, a rural town outside of Memphis.[13] He was the fourth of seven children. When he was born, his parents worked as sharecroppers picking cotton, and they both continued to work various jobs throughout his childhood to support the family. After completing high school, Ellison attended the University of Memphis, where he attained a business administration degree in marketing, then he acquired an MBA from Emory University. While his family provided financial support for him to attend college, Ellison worked multiple jobs to help cover his tuition and school expenses. His jobs as a janitor at a women's department store, a driver for a plumbing supply distributor, a warehouse operator, the graveyard shift at a convenience store, and as a part-time security guard at Target provided him with valuable lessons that he would apply later in his corporate career.

Ellison got the job at Target through his college's employment office. It paid $4.35 an hour and he worked in this position until he graduated with a marketing degree. Target hired him as a member of its store management team. Ellison worked there for 15 years, spending most of his tenure in the loss prevention department, and rose to senior vice president. Ellison left Target in 2002 to take a position at The Home Depot, where he worked for 12 years in various executive positions. He was executive vice president of Target's 2,000 U.S. stores from 2008 to 2014, responsible for sales, profit, and operations, while overseeing a workforce of more than 275,000 workers with $65 billion in annual sales.

In 2007, Home Depot was facing lagging e-commerce revenue, dissatisfaction of both customers and employees, and the consequences of several failed strategic initiatives. As head of U.S. sales, Ellison began to implement several initiatives aimed at reversing the decline in revenue and customer dissatisfaction, emphasizing excellence in customer service, strengthening the company's online presence to boost online sales, and refurbishing store locations. He began broadcasting a weekly video feature on internal store TVs across the country that showcased exceptional customer-service experiences. He instituted a policy that required employees to spend more of their time (60%) attending to customers and began the "Power Hour," a set time each day when workers must help customers instead of doing administrative tasks. By the time he left the company, sales had rebounded and the stock price had almost tripled.

After his success at Home Depot, Ellison joined JCPenney in November 2014 to serve as Interim CEO and president before he assumed the role of permanent CEO in August 2015, a position he held until his resignation in May 2018. When Ellison took over the reins at JCPenney, the company had experienced substantial reductions in sales and profits, its stock price had dropped substantially, and the company had not only lost the loyalty of its customers but the confidence of its investors. The series of initiatives implemented by the departing CEO, Ron Johnson, in 2011, had included a branding campaign that featured changing the company's logo and store design, a change in its product pricing, a move away from existing brands to new ones, and the elimination of coupon sales that had not worked. Within a year, the company's sales had declined by $4.3 billion, a 25% reduction from the previous year.[14]

Johnson was forced to resign in mid-2013 and the company brought in a former CEO, Myron Ullman, to deal with the crisis. Ullman reversed several of Johnson's initiatives, reinstating coupons and returning to former brands. Although Ullman's efforts were successful in stabilizing sales and stopping the stock price from dropping further, management recognized that drastic changes needed to be made to ensure that the company survived in the competitive retail market.

Ellison was recruited from Home Depot to lead JCPenney's turnaround. He inherited a company that was struggling to recover—sales had fallen by 35%, the stock price had plummeted, and the company had laid off 40,000 employees. Ellison focused on three strategic goals that he believed were key to the success of the company's transformation: revenue per customer (through better customer service), omnichannel (use of traditional as well as e-commerce), and refocus on private brands and reconfiguration of product placement within stores (updated merchandise, including new clothing brands, handbags, and jewelry, with higher gross profit margins).[15] He invested in inventory tracking technology, installing a team to introduce "demand-based logic" inventory technology. He also brought back the sales of appliances, hoping to take advantage of the collapse of Sears and to attract younger, first-time homebuyers. Within 18 months, the company was able to get back the 20 million shoppers it had lost between 2011 and 2013, while its sales per square foot was $165 in fiscal 2015, an increase of 12% from two years prior. Share prices also increased by 47%.[16] Ellison also implemented strategies to reduce the company's debt. By the time he left, the company had retired $1.4 billion in debt. In 2018, Ellison was appointed the CEO of Lowe's.

Black Entrepreneurs

Ellison's success can be attributed partially to his attention to customers. Customer dissatisfaction is why Kwame Spearman became majority owner of Tattered Cover Book Store in Denver, Colorado. While he is happy to lead the largest Black-owned bookstore in the country, he is also tasked with turning around the company. Revenues declined significantly because long-time customers were unhappy over statements of the bookstore owners related to the Black Lives Matter movement during the summer of 2020. The following excerpts from the letter sent to their customers on June 6, 2020, 12 days after the murder of George Floyd,[17] reflect how the controversy developed:

> Dear Tattered Cover Customers,
>
> Tattered Cover has been largely quiet in the wake of the events that have unfolded over the last ten days. We want to make a statement of support and take a moment to explain why we've been quiet.
>
> Black Lives Matter.
>
> We agree with, embrace, and believe that black lives matter. So why have we been quiet?
>
> First, we think this is a time for voices other than ours to be heard. As a white-owned business, with a predominantly white staff, we feel this is a time for us to take a step back, to allow others to command more and greater attention.
>
> More significant, though, is our nearly 50-year policy of not engaging in public debate. For Tattered Cover to shout this from the rooftops, to drape our spaces with banners proclaiming these simple and unalterable truths, would be anathema to a different principle that we also hold dear, and one that is central, we believe, to the role of an independent bookstore.
>
> *(continued)*

(*continued*)

Our value to the community is to provide a place where access to ideas, and the free exchange of ideas, can happen in an uninhibited way. It's not for us to determine which ideas in the pages on our shelves are valid and which are not. We leave that to you, our readers.

Consider Tattered Cover's history:

Whom a person chooses to love is as plain and simple a concept as equity and justice for all Americans. Yet, Tattered Cover did not take a stand when the Defense of Marriage Act (DOMA) was being debated in Congress and was ultimately passed by Congress. This was in spite of the many members of the LGBTQ community on our staff who were appalled at the law. Nor did we publicly cheer when the Supreme Court struck down DOMA as being unconstitutional.

Ted Nugent, a controversial and outspoken advocate of gun rights, was scheduled to appear at Tattered Cover not long after the Columbine High School shooting – the first school shooting in what would be a horrifically sad trend of school shootings in the two decades to follow. Mr. Nugent's comments about Columbine were both insensitive and abhorrent. Yet, despite staff opposition and the threat of violence, Tattered Cover went forward with the event.

Tattered Cover did not take a stand on Denver's Urban Camping Ban, which according to some, criminalized homelessness. This in spite of Occupy Denver protesting outside our downtown store most Friday nights for three and a half years. They threatened and cajoled staff and customers, they defaced the building, and they disrupted business. The easy thing to do would have been to write the letter to city hall decrying the camping ban that Occupy Denver demanded. We did not.

Why? Why go through this heartache?

Because this is a slippery slope.

If Tattered Cover puts its name and weight either behind, or in opposition to, one idea, members of our community will have an expectation that we must do the same for all ideas. Engaging in public debate is not, we believe, how Tattered Cover has been and can be of greatest value to our community.

We provide access to knowledge, information, and ideas, and we create a safe space for those ideas to be discussed. We provide access to books filled with a multitude of life experiences. Books that heal, educate, challenge or bring any range of emotions to the reader. The unprecedented number of orders we received over the last week, and are still receiving, for books about anti-racism, is evidence of how we can serve you best -- by being a conduit to information and stories that matter to our community.

Some people may also think we take these positions for financial gain, or to protect sales. We don't, and the reality is usually the opposite. In many cases where we refuse to proactively engage in debate, it costs Tattered Cover business and customers. We do it for the principle.

We have tried to do all these things in our five years of stewardship of this business, but we acknowledge we have fallen short. Our priority is to make Tattered Cover a more equitable space for customers and staff alike, and we will take steps to do that. We expect you to hold us accountable.

All we can offer is our conscience and industry to do what we think is right for Tattered Cover, its customers, and the larger community, and to continue to transparently communicate our goals and intentions to you.

Thanks as always for your support.

Len & Kristen

Co-Owners of Tattered Cover Book Store

This letter infuriated many of the bookstore's customers, and staff, resulting in the decline in revenues. Excerpts from a letter written and signed by customers and staff filled 25 pages, illustrating some of the backlash[18]:

To Len and Kristen, owners of Tattered Cover,

After your recent letters of June 6, we the undersigned, write to insist that the concerns raised in response to your initial letter, concerns which reverberate from past events, be met with more than a written apology. We write to insist that Tattered Cover take immediate actions necessary to its responsible participation in our community.

As you acknowledge, neutrality with regard to the murders of innumerable members of the Black community owing to nothing other than the color of their skin does not arise from a neutral political stance. It is not a political matter that humanity demands that an individual not be shot, choked, or beaten to their death simply for being born into their existence. It is not a political matter that members of the Black community should not be made to bear over and over again the loss of sons, sisters, mothers, uncles, fathers, daughters, neighbors, community leaders, stolen by unconscionable brutality. We ask further: where is the safe space you aim to provide for all members of the community when, for its Black members, the most basic right to breathe is one you do not feel you can insist upon?

An independent bookstore is meant to be a trusted partner, a uniting space. Every indie bookstore has its own DNA, personality, voice. We do not expect Tattered Cover to have the same central mission, the same look as its sister indies near or far. But we do expect Tattered Cover to reflect the community of which it aims to be a part. An indie bookstore that is disconnected from its heart cannot remain relevant to the larger body it serves.

Championing the free exchange of ideas is a laudable central goal, but turns quickly dangerous without clarity of the principles you seek to steward. Free expression is curbed when voices are muted by state-sanctioned genocide. Additionally, holding your business in line with the silencing of systemic marginalization of communities of color does nothing but deny your readers the knowledge of these groups.

We insist on clear articulation of Tattered Cover's plans within 30 days of this letter. Until that response is received, the undersigned individuals and organizations will not pursue purchases or partnerships with Tattered Cover.

In closing, we share a statement from a former employee who recently resigned to protest the handling of this matter. "This is voluntary evil; white America is choosing to do this. America is a rootless land. This country did not just end up this way. It was built this way. And the spectacle of a black person terrorized by a white person, struggling to breathe and stay alive while other folks looked on, is not new; in fact, it's foundational to America's becoming. This violent America was built on king cotton on stolen grounds. To be black in America and survive is to be of dual wakefulness on how to survive a country bent on your not becoming, all the while clasping for dear life onto a dream, to fantasize that it will one day include you."

It is this customer revolt that was a major reason why Tattered Cover Book Store required a business turnaround. Spearman and his group of investors purchased the four-store book company six months after the previous owner's "mishap."

In an interview following the closing of the purchase on December 9, 2020, Spearman described the initial plans for the turnaround. Unsurprisingly, its focus was on customers as he stated, "The first thing we want to do is to go out and start listening to people. We've actually already had a virtual town hall with our staff and we have a call with our customers (on December 16). That will be one of many calls."[19]

Cathy Hughes

The most successful Black turnaround entrepreneur in history is Cathy Hughes—broadcast visionary, radio personality, social activist, philanthropist, and chairwoman of Urban One, a media conglomerate targeting African Americans. Hughes was born in Omaha, Nebraska. Her father, William Alfred Woods, was the first African American to earn an accounting degree from Creighton University. Her mother, Helen Jones Woods, was trained as a nurse and taught music at the Piney Woods School, a private boarding school that Hughes's maternal grandfather, Laurence Jones, established in 1909. She also played the trombone in the school's all-female swing band, the International Sweethearts of Rhythm.

Hughes's early childhood was a time of financial difficulties for her family, who had to live in housing projects for several years where "they'd turn the heat off at 11 p.m. and we often had to sleep in our coats."[20] Sponsored by a White priest who paid her tuition, Hughes attended the Duchesne Academy of the Sacred Heart, a Catholic all-girl school, as the first Black student admitted to the school.[21]

A transistor radio Hughes received as a Christmas present when she was 8 years old began a lifelong passion. By age 10, Hughes had decided that her goal in life was to be the first African American to own a radio show. Equipped with a toothbrush mic, Hughes began "broadcasting" her "radio show" in the bathroom of her childhood home every morning, refusing to come out until she had completed her news and entertainment segments.

Getting pregnant unexpectedly at 16 was an inflection point in her life. The birth of her son became an impetus to achieve, not just imagine, success. She was determined that her child would have an opportunity for a better life, noting, "It was the reason I took my life seriously for the first time as a teenager and made a promise to myself, my son and God that he would not become a Black statistic."[22] Hughes believed that being a mother gave her the motivation to become an entrepreneur. She notes, "I became an entrepreneur because of him. One day, he had a fever and my employer said, 'if you walk out that door, don't come back.' That's when I decided I needed to be in control of my professional environment so I could be there for my child."[23]

Hughes had begun working from a young age. By 10 she was maintaining the journal ledgers in her father's accounting firm and by 12 she was proficient in typing and shorthand. After completing high school, with her son in tow, Hughes attended the University of Nebraska and Creighton University taking business administration courses; but, she did not complete her studies. However, while attending college, Hughes worked at KOWH (AM), a station owned by a group of African American professionals in Omaha. In 1971, her reputation at the radio station led Tony Brown, assistant dean of the newly established School of Communications at Howard University, to offer her a job as a lecturer at Howard and as his administrative assistant. Hughes moved to Washington, D.C., and, in 1973, she was offered the position of general sales manager at WHUR-FM, the University's radio station. She took on management of the struggling station and, during her tenure, increased the station's revenue from $250,000 to $3 million.[24] In 1975, Hughes was promoted to vice president and general manager of the station, becoming the first woman to hold those positions in the nation's capital. Against the station's management advice, Hughes created a format known as the "Quiet Storm," a genre of contemporary R&B, performed in a romantic, jazz-influenced style, which revolutionized urban radio. Hughes explains her rationale for pushing this new music format:

> Quiet storm was the simple recognition of the fact that the city (DC) had a sizable population of single unattached human beings who still wanted to feel good about a Friday night or Saturday night. All they were missing was the entertainment, so I structured a format. . . . that basically was a 5-hour presentation of entertaining yourself by yourself. First the gay community and then African Americans. It grew by word of mouth.[25]

After working in the radio industry for several years, Hughes decided to fulfill her lifelong dream of owning a radio station. Research led her to WOL-AM, an R&B station in Washington, D.C., which was going through a distress sale arising from an FCC investigation of its owners and disc jockeys, looking into their alleged violation of laws prohibiting payola (paying an illegal bribe to someone to do a favor). Federal regulators mandated that the station be sold at a discounted price to a minority buyer.[26] At $995,000, the price tag was steep for Ms. Hughes, but she moved forward with her plan, determined to find financing. With her husband and business partner, Dewey Hughes, she began approaching banks. After being denied by 32 lenders, she finally secured $1 million in seed capital from a minority enterprise investment group and a $500,000 loan from Chemical Bank (actually getting approved by a sympathetic Puerto Rican female loan officer who had just started her job at the bank). Hughes purchased the station, beating out several well-known competitors, including Muhammed Ali, Reggie Jackson, and *Essence* magazine. At that moment, she founded her company, Radio One.[27] Hughes had to come up with a down payment of $100,000 (10% of the sale price) and was required by the FCC to have one year of working capital, approximately $600,000. She raised $100,000 from 10 investors who provided $10,000 each and borrowed the rest.[28]

The first few years were a struggle, and despite working 24/7 to build WOL's audience, Hughes suffered several financial and personal setbacks. Servicing the debt she had accrued to buy the company put a strain on her personal finances and marriage. Following her divorce and the loss of her home and car, she moved into the radio station with her infant son and continued the work to build her radio audience. Hughes sold a family heirloom, her great-grandmother's pocket watch, which had been made by slaves, using the $50,000 she got for it to survive.[29]

Despite the concerns of lenders who wanted a music format for her show, Hughes insisted on hosting a show that provided information targeting the African American community. A compromise was reached with the agreement to program a morning talk show that was followed by music throughout the day. Consequently, Hughes pioneered a new format, the 24-hour talk show from a Black perspective. With the theme, "Information is Power," she served as the station's morning show host for 11 years. Hughes secured advertisers by going door-to-door to retail stores and small produce vendors convincing them that advertising on her radio station, at 10 cents a minute, was worth their investment.[30] She kept her creditors at bay by always maintaining communications with them and never missing a payment. WOL finally achieved profits in year seven of operations. Hughes recounts, "The radio station was a financial disaster for seven years. But I stayed focused on not losing my company, and that's why I moved into the station and did whatever it took. I was willing to let everything go except my son and my business, in that order."[31]

Hughes then decided to acquire more radio stations, focusing on struggling and underperforming stations that operated in major urban areas, turning them around with the same strategies she used at WOL—changing the program format to better meet the targeted needs of the African American listening audience, while employing aggressive advertising and marketing campaigns to secure advertisers and listeners. Hughes summed up her strategy by saying, "We were forced to become a fix-it company because we didn't have the money to buy $50 million stations."[32]

Hughes bought her second radio station, WMMJ, Magic 102.3, in 1987. Her financiers insisted that financial viability for the radio station would only be achieved if its programs catered to a White suburban audience, but Hughes, once again, refused to be dictated to and developed an "urban adult" music genre that made the station popular. She then purchased WKYS in 1995 for $34 million. In the next several years, Radio One continued to purchase stations in major markets throughout the country and, today, owns 57 radio stations in 15 major markets across the U.S.

In 1999, to raise capital to buy stations in the Richmond, VA, and Boston, MA, markets, Hughes took Radio One public, becoming the first African American woman to chair a publicly held corporation. The Radio One IPO was one of the most successful public offerings for a Black-owned company—raising $172 million, while its offering price increased from $24 to $96.50; Radio One's market value increased to $1.8 billion in seven months.[33]

Hughes was successful in securing investment financing, including $4 million investment from a minority venture capital fund and $5 million in financing from the former DC National Bank in 1987, investment funds from AT&T Corporation in 1992, Greyhound Lines Inc. in 1993, along with NationsBank and several other traditional investors in 1995. A high-yield bond offering in 1997 raised $75 million.[34] She was also able to secure a $57 million line of credit from Bank of America.

Radio One launched a television network, TV One, in 2004 and entered the digital space with Interactive One, now iOne Digital, in 2007. In 2017, Radio One's name was changed to Urban One, to reflect the target market it served and the diversified portfolio of products and services it offered. Urban One, Inc. is the parent corporation of several subsidiaries: TV One, the largest African-American owned cable television network in the country; Reach Media, which presents well-known syndicated radio programs like the *Rickey Smiley Morning Show* and the *Tom Joyner Morning Show*; iOne Digital, a collection of over 30 websites that focus on news, sports, and entertainment; and One Solution, a marketing firm that allows advertisers to take advantage of all of the assets under the Urban One brand. In 2017, Urban One purchased a 7% stake in the $1.4 billion MGM casino, hotel, and resort in Maryland.[35]

Urban One reaches 82% of Black households through its different media platforms. The company boasts of reaching 59 million households, 22 million listeners, 40 million video streams, and 20 million unique Web visitors; it owns 57 broadcast stations in 15 urban markets, two cable networks, and some 80 websites.[36] Hughes is among the wealthiest African American women in the country.

Hughes has earned numerous awards and recognitions, which are highlighted on her website: the naming of Cathy Hughes Boulevard in her hometown of Omaha, Nebraska; the 2018 Lowry Mays Excellence in Broadcasting Award; the naming of the Cathy Hughes School of Communications at Howard University in 2016; the ADColor Lifetime Achievement Award; the Congressional Black Caucus Foundation Chair's Phoenix Award; the NAACP Chairman's Award; the Giant of Broadcasting Award; the Uncommon Height of Excellence Award; the Essence Women Shaping the World Award; the Ida B. Wells Living Legacy Award; induction into the American Advertising Federation Hall of Fame; an honorary doctorate from Sojourner Douglass College in Baltimore in 1995; inducted as a member of the Maryland Chamber of Commerce's Business Hall of Fame; awarded the First Annual Black History Hall of Fame Award; and recipient of the National Action Network's "Keepers of the Dream" award.[37] She is a supporter of The Piney Woods School in Piney Woods, Mississippi, which her grandfather founded in 1909—the largest of the only four African-American boarding schools in the country.

Introduction to the Case Study

The following case study is about a bold woman, Rev. Morgan-Thomas, who has minimal business experiences. She buys her first company that has not been profitable for years. This case focuses on the key actions that she needs to implement to make the company profitable and make her a successful "turnaround" entrepreneur.

HARVARD | BUSINESS | SCHOOL

9-319-009
REV: MAY 6, 2019

STEVEN ROGERS

ARIEL ROGERS

Rev. Georgiette Morgan-Thomas & The American Hat Factory

On a sunny Monday morning, Rev. Morgan-Thomas walked into her newly acquired hat factory thinking, "What have I gotten myself into? Things are worse than I imagined. Can I ever turn this company around given all of the known and unknown problems? Can I make it profitable?"

Over the previous weeks, Rev. Morgan-Thomas had been in conversation with the former owner, who after a 15-month attempt at reviving the hat manufacturing company, decided to sell the business. She remembered his final statement, "It just doesn't make money." After several weeks of due diligence and discoveries, Rev. Morgan-Thomas realized the uphill battle she was facing. She was not a factory manager. She was a pastor of a Christian church in Harlem, New York who grew up loving women's hats! Having now completed an asset purchase instead of a stock purchase, she acquired all of the factory assets including several pieces of antiquated equipment, a shrinking customer list, and a staff of 8 milliners who had depended on the factory for their livelihood for the past three decades.

While Rev. Morgan-Thomas was a woman of faith, she knew that faith without work was not enough. She was aware of several high profile businesses that were not able to be turned around including Compaq, Blockbuster Video, Kodak & Lehman Brothers. Rev. Morgan-Thomas was also aware of turn around success stories including IBM, Apple, General Motors and Starbucks (**Exhibit 1**). What could she learn from both groups?

As Rev. Morgan-Thomas entered her new business, her final thoughts were, "We are on the brink of closing, but closing is just not an option. There are too many people counting on their jobs and it is just not an option. So let's see what we can do here!" She began her mission by making a list of the top three things that she needed to do to turn the company into a profitable enterprise.

The Milliner Industry

The producers of hats for women are called milliners. The name comes from the merchants who resided in the Italian city of Milan during the early 16th century. These merchants were known as "mileners" and they traveled throughout Europe selling their handmade hats and other fine garments. Up until the 1960's, throughout the world, it was customary for women to wear hats. The first evidence

HBS Senior Lecturer Steven Rogers and independent researcher Ariel Rogers prepared this case. It was reviewed and approved before publication by a company designate. Funding for the development of this case was provided by Harvard Business School and not by the company. HBS cases are developed solely as the basis for class discussion. Cases are not intended to serve as endorsements, sources of primary data, or illustrations of effective or ineffective management.

of the waning popularity of women's hats occurred in the 1960's which was also referred to as the "bare-headed era," which was all about women showing their hair. While the first hairspray was created in the 1940's, it became extremely popular during the 60's, resulting in women covering their hair with product that would hold the style in place instead of a hat. This was the beginning of the women's hat industry becoming fad-driven.

The women's hat industry rebounded in the 1980's and its phoenix was partially due to the young Princess Diana who regularly wore stylish hats. The industry got another wonderful jolt when Aretha Franklin, the Queen of Soul, wore a big beautiful grey crown adorned with a large, bejeweled bow during her 2009 performance at the Presidential Inauguration[1]. The hat reportedly cost $500, and was so popular that it attracted 90,000 fans to a Facebook page dedicated to it and over 10,000 tweets. The hat was even displayed at the Smithsonian along with other Inauguration items.[2]

Today, Princess Diana's daughter-in-laws, Kate Middleton and Meghan Markle adorn their heads with beautiful hats. That same cloche costs as much as $3,000.00. But the reality is that the hat industry has never truly recovered from its heyday of the 1950's and 60's. Now hats are typically worn on special days such as weddings and horse races including the Kentucky Derby and the Preakness.

Most millinery companies are small 1-2 person operations, where the hat producer also has a boutique retail store or does customized hats for individual customers. One such milliner is Harriet Rosebud. She designs and makes up to 4,000 hats annually in her studio in Harlem. Like many milliners today, she is a skilled craftswoman with formal training. Rosebud is also the creator of the Great American Hat Show, which is an annual Fashion Show for hats, held in Harlem, telling the history of hats worn by African American women and using black runway models (Exhibit 2). Rosebud completed 2 years of training at The Fashion Institute of Technology in New York and is a member of the Milliners Guild of New York and the National Millinery Institute of America.

In attendance, at every one of the Great American Hat Shows, was Rev. Morgan-Thomas. Rosebud was a member of her congregation and the personal hat designer of over 2 dozen of Rev. Morgan-Thomas's wide hat collection (Exhibit 3). When Rev. Morgan-Thomas attended the 2009 Presidential Inauguration, she wore a hat made by Rosebud. It was a beautiful white wool hat with a big shiny buckle and fox trim. The proud Rev. Morgan-Thomas declared, "My hat was better than Aretha's. She should have had a Harriet Rosebud creation."[3]

Rev. Morgan-Thomas' son was recently married. To be respectful to the bride, she planned not to wear one of her hats, so as not to draw attention away from her future daughter-in-law on her special day. However, her daughter-in-law would have none of it and insisted that her mother-in-law wear one of her signature custom-made hats. For this particular occasion, she had a hat made with pearls around the trim (Exhibit 4). Rev. Morgan-Thomas stated with a big laugh, "It was me: soft, feminine and yet outstanding."[4]

---

[1] "Aretha Franklin Was Already Famous, But Her Hat-Maker Wasn't" by Karen Grigsby Bates, NPR, January 21, 2013, https://www.npr.org/2013/01/21/169731646/aretha-franklin-was-already-famous-but-her-hat-maker-wasnt, accessed May 24, 2018.

[2] Joanne Stern, ABC News, January 18, 2013.

[3] Jeff Mays, BNAinfo, New York, NY, Jan 15, 2014.

[4] Ibid.

Black Milliners

In addition to Rev. Morgan-Thomas and Mrs. Rosebud there were many other blacks in the millinery industry. One of the first was Mildred Blount who was born in 1907. She had an enormously successful career, which included making all of the hats worn by the female actors in the 1939 movie, "Gone with the Wind."

Two other notable veteran milliners were Vanilla Beane and Mae Reeves. At 90 years old in 2010, Mrs. Beane was still making hats and operating her Washington D.C. hat shop called "The Beane." That same year, Mae Reeves from Philadelphia was inducted in the Smithsonian National Museum of African-American History and Culture.

The Weakening Millinery Business

In 1937 there were over 800 U.S. Millineries employing about 22,000 people and grossing over $91 million in annual sales — an industry value of $1.58 billion dollars in 2018.[5] In the late 1950's there were 400 millineries. The recent U.S. census Bureau reported there are 152 millineries today.

One successful owner said, "When we started out, there were a handful of domestic manufacturers. But we realized to be price competitive we had to manufacture overseas."[6] Another owner explained her success with the following: "We were a wholesale company founded in 1982, but two years ago, we started selling online. We are profitable and do a lot of business in Japan, where American products are quite popular."[7]

Successful Turnarounds

It has been reported that as many as 9 out of 10 business turnarounds will fail.[8] Some of the most exciting and interesting stories in business are about successful turnarounds and the people behind them.

Ken Chenault, the longest tenured African-American CEO of a Fortune 500 company, successfully turned around the Merchandising Department of American Express before he became its CEO. The department was not growing satisfactorily and was about to be closed. Ken Chenault volunteered to take over the operation and in a few years grew its revenue over 200%, from $150 million to $500 million.[9]

Another story about African American involvement in a blue chip company includes the Cadillac Division of General Motors (GM). In 1932, during the Great Depression, this car division was about to be shut down due to declining revenue and unprofitability. During this same period, Cadillac had an unwritten "No Sale to Negroes" policy.

---

[5] Bertha Nienburg, "Conditions in the Millinery Industry in The United States: Women's Bureau Bulletin, No. 169," United States Department of Labor: P. 9.
https://fraser.stlouisfed.org/content/?filepath=/files/docs/publications/women/b0169_dolwb_1939.pdf&title_id=5442, accessed May 24, 2018.

[6] Bill Glovin, "No Cap on Growth for Headwear Makers," Crains, Jan 12, 2014.

[7] Ibid.

[8] The CEO TV SHOW, Forbes, August 22, 2011.

[9] "Kenneth I. Chenault," Reference for Business, https://www.referenceforbusiness.com/biography/A-E/Chenault-Kenneth-I-1951.html

The head of Cadillac's service department noticed that Black people were regularly bringing cars in to be repaired. Given the company's policy forbidding blacks from buying Cadillacs, which represented white success, the assumption was that these black people were chauffeurs for the white owners. When this assumption was tested by interviews, it was discovered that the black people were actually the car owners and they had paid white middlemen a service fee to buy the car for them. Even the legendary world heavy weight boxing champion, Joe Louis, owned a Cadillac using this humiliating purchase model.

Once the GM Chairman, Alfred P. Sloan, was informed of this discovery, he assigned an executive to develop the "Negro" market. The plan was successfully executed resulting in the turnaround of the Cadillac division. By 1934, sales had increased 70% and the division was breakeven.[10]

In addition to GM there have been hundreds of other Fortune 500 companies that have successful turnaround stories. At the top of all such lists is Apple and Steve Jobs. When he returned as the CEO of Apple in 1997 the company was close to bankruptcy. Steve reduced the number of marketing departments from 22 to 3. He raised $150 million from Microsoft. He also decreased the number of projects being developed from 350 to 50, which was later reduced to 10. New products including the iMac, iPod, iTunes and iPhone were commercialized. During his leadership, the stock price increased over 9000%. Today Apple is the most valuable company in the world.[11]

The model for successful business turnarounds can also be applied to other industries. In 2015, the parishioners of St. Mary of the Lake Church in Gary, Indiana were told by the Catholic Bishop that the church would be closed due to increasing debt and declining membership. The parishioners were not happy about the decision. They complained and were given a "year of opportunity" to turn the church around.

The new pastor assigned to the church did not take a salary and lived in his own house. The congregation held fundraisers including spaghetti dinners, concerts and fish fry's. They used social media to inform former church members about the closing mandate resulting in new donations from people who had fond memories of the church. They opened a food pantry that gives free food to almost 100 families. They purchased a big freezer and refrigerator so that the food pantry could provide meats and produce. They knocked on over 3,000 doors in the community, inviting people to attend a church service or partake of the food pantry.

Within 12 months, they paid off the $121,000 debt to the diocese and added 40 new families. They repaved the church's parking lot and now have plans to convert an old unused football field into a community garden. The Bishop who told them 12 months earlier that the church would close, announced that the church is financially stable and will remain open.[12]

From these examples and other successful turnarounds, Rev. Morgan-Thomas was confident that she could create a template, weaving together the key elements of each aforementioned anecdote that contributed to turnaround success. Some of these elements included setting realistic expectations, taking responsibility, and being open to new ideas. She would use that template to guide her from the beginning to the end of her journey.

---

[10] Raynard Jackson, Mid-SouthGospelTribune.com, accessed May 24, 2018.

[11] Entrepreneur Magazine, https://www.entrepreneur.com

[12] Carole Carlson, "The comeback church: Keeping the faith saved Gary's St. Mary of the Lake," Post-Tribune, March 31, 2018.

Previous American Hat Factory Performance

The process of making a hat consists of 7-10 steps (**Exhibit 5**). It requires as many as three days between construction and setting time. The production costs range between $33 and $57 per hat (material and labor), depending on the hat style and size (**Exhibit 6**) as well as the amount of adorning material (rhinestones, ribbon, bows, metallic embellishments, etc.).

Since its 1939 opening, The American Hat Factory of Philadelphia, Pennsylvania was and still is one of the few hat factories in America specializing in women's headwear. During its peak years of production in the 60's, the factory manufactured and shipped 80 hats daily to female customers around the world. Its average monthly revenue was $200,000. Now sales are $40,000 per month.

The company was producing 80-100 hats per week, but only selling 60-90 per week. The production floor was equipped with all the necessary equipment to make women's hats from scratch with over 600 "blocks" ("blocks" are the wooden molds that a hat is constructed around) and an entire assembly line including: 14 sewing stations, 4 trim stations, 1 cutting station (needed for felt hats only), 5 steam huts for blocking (where each hat's shape is set and dried around the wooden block), 2 ovens, 12 stampers and 9 work stations (for the decoration and adornment of each hat with items such as colorful silks and rhinestones).

The primary material for creating a hat is called Crinoline, which is the preferred material rather than felt due to its porous property, allowing better airflow to the wearer, an overall lighter weight, and the ability to maintain its shape once steamed and dried. A bundle of Crinoline, equaling 144 years of material, can make up to five hats at a cost of $25.00 per bundle. The cost to decorate a hat varies depending on the size of the hat and amount of decoration applied. For rhinestones, a 5-yard blanket of clear stones costs $240; and each hat (on average) will use $4.48 worth of that "rhinestone blanket." Hats like these sell for about $169. A "cluster" of stones cost TAHF about $1.25/hat and these hats sell for as little as $89 and as much as $189. Loose stones cost $10.06 a gross for 30 stone size (ss) and $4.58 a gross for 20ss; a "gross" of stones can be used for 6-60 hats depending on the amount of loose stones used but on average, one gross can make 20 cloches, a bell shaped women's hat, which sells for $109 each.

The factory space has capacity for 34 employees but at the time of acquisition, there were 8 on the payroll. These employees were paid $10-18/hr. for five 8-hour days per week.

The American Hat Factory Acquisition

Harry Saft founded the company in 1923. His sons, Mike and Alvin, inherited it at Harry's death in 2013. Due to disagreements, Mike bought out Alvin and became the sole owner in 2014. In June of the same year, the factory was seized and sold by the IRS for back taxes owed to the government. Sid Meyers, the son of another hat factory owner, purchased the business, but unfortunately could not turn a profit and after 15 months, he decided to sell it. Harriet Rosebud was a designer for Sid Meyers at the time and a member of Rev. Morgan-Thomas' church. When she heard that Sid Meyers wanted to close the factory, she informed Rev. Morgan-Thomas that the hat factory was up for sale. With her savings, she acquired TAHF in 2017 via an asset purchase. She paid $47,000, which was the same price that Sid Meyers paid the I.R.S. The price was determined by the value of the raw and finished inventory. The equipment was so old that it had been completely depreciated and had no value (**Exhibit 7**). Rev. Morgan-Thomas pays Pepper Environmental $1500/month to lease their workshop space where the factory constructs its hats and houses its small boutique showroom.

Reverend Georgiette Morgan-Thomas

Rev. Morgan-Thomas was raised in segregated Alabama by her grandmother - a woman who was a member of the National Council of Negro Women (NCNW). This was an organization devoted to improving the civil rights of black women in American. One of the organization's common practices was to publicly fight against racial and gender inequalities by protest marches. This experience had a profound impact on Rev. Morgan-Thomas. "It was very common for women to put on a hat when hitting the streets in civil protest...I was always around women wearing a hat...so I grew up wearing a hat...wearing a hat is not just about style, it means taking care of business. It makes you stand up straight, and makes your outfit pop, in addition to making you look pretty...I grew up thinking a hat was a part of being dressed."

Rev. Morgan-Thomas' career would closely follow that of her late grandmothers as a servant of the community. She is the Pastor of Mustard Seed Faith Ministry, established in 2002 in Harlem, New York. For more than 10 summers, she sponsored a PAL Play Street for young pre-teens to gain life skills at summer camp. This organization also created more than 20 jobs annually for the community. She is also a member of the United Muslim Alliance, which serves to strengthen Christian/Muslim relationships within the Harlem community. She is the Chair of Community Board 9, an organization that acts as a liaison and monitor of civilian needs that are addressed to the city: issues pertaining to arts & culture, economic development, health & environment, landmarks preservation/parks, housing land use & zoning, uniformed services & transportation, senior issues, strategic planning (ad-hoc), and youth education and libraries. Rev. Morgan-Thomas is also the Director of Harlem Services for Goddard Riverside Community Center, one of the city's largest not-for-profit organizations. The organization's objective was to reduce homelessness by purchasing and rehabbing homes for the elderly and mentally ill. This decrease in homelessness and increase in quality housing resulted in an overall increase in community beautification. In turn, the community improvement attracted businesses to open in the area, which provided local jobs.

Rev. Morgan-Thomas also serves on the Board of Managers of the Harlem YMCA, and is the former President of the local section of the National Council of Negro Women. She has received numerous awards and recognition from many organizations including the "Robin Hood Hero of 2005," Harlem YMCA Volunteer of the Year 2009, Outstanding Leader in Human Rights in 2010, the NAACP Community Dedication award, and the Virtuous Woman award in 2012.

It is from these experiences as well as her experience running a household as a single mother that allowed her to see an opportunity and have the confidence to run TAHF. Additionally, her son Robert James Morgan III was now out of law school so she was no longer paying tuition bills. She had the capital available to invest in the purchase of the factory to fulfill her vision of creating jobs and keeping manufacturing on American soil.

The American Hat Factory Operations under Rev. Morgan-Thomas

On December 6, 2015, her first day of ownership, there were several customers that Rev. Morgan-Thomas worked to retain and grow. Two of those were companies that made women's suits, Tally Taylor, and Lily & Taylor. These customers accounted for 20% of the previous year's revenue. Their largest customer was a private label women's suits manufacturer who would purchase a small batch of hats from the TAHF at a price of $36/hat. (Each hat cost the Hat Factory $32 to make in materials alone). In addition to purchasing hats, this customer also gave TAHF repair business.

To Rev. Morgan-Thomas' disappointing surprise, she discovered that Tally Taylor terminated its buying relationship with the TAHF a week before she acquired the company. Other lost customers included JC Penny and Macy's, and despite her herculean efforts, she lost Lily and Taylor eight months later to a manufacturer in China.

In addition to unexpectedly losing key customers, Rev. Morgan-Thomas was shocked to discover that the company was losing money to theft. Unlike the previous owner, she worked seven days a week. One day she uncovered the fact that a key longtime employee had been stealing hats and selling them out of the factory back door on the weekends.

Competition

The Great American Hat Factory sold their hand made women's artisanal quality hats for as low as $36 each. The Chinese hat manufacturers sold their hats to department stores for $18 each. These hats were often made of lower quality material under an automated assembly line-style process. Hats would arrive to the department stores from the Chinese in need of repair. The department stores would contract TAHF to repair the hats that were falling apart; often times the glue used (instead of stitching) would not withstand the temperature fluctuations during shipping, nor the weight of the body of the hat itself (i.e., rhinestones, ribbons, stacking hats on top of one another, etc.) The department stores only had one company willing to do this repair work - TAHF. Rev. Morgan-Thomas decided to repair these hats for the breakeven cost of labor and parts in order to develop a positive relationship with the client. She saw this as an investment and was hopeful this good will would turn into orders for The American Hat Factory.

The American Hat Factory COO

One of the first hires by Rev. Morgan-Thomas was her son, a recent law school graduate with a concentration in Corporate Law. He is responsible for the company's financials, internet, customer interface, operations, and legal compliance of regulations.

Concluding Thoughts

Rev. Morgan-Thomas was an extremely confident woman, but as she sat and pondered her future, if she was honest, she had to confess to some trepidation about what she faced. At the same time, she knew that other men and women who had turned companies around endowed her with many of the traits and skills that were possessed. Therefore, it was time to go to work!

Exhibit 1   Successful Turnarounds

1.   Gordon Bethune | Continental Airlines
     * Losing $55 million per month
     * 12 months later, profit of $224 million
     * Eliminated unprofitable routes

2.   Richard Clark | Merck Pharmaceutical Co.
     * Closed 5 manufacturing plants
     * Introduced 8 new drugs
     * 3 years later stock price doubled

3.   Doug Canalt | Campbell Soup
     * First 3 months replaced 300 of top 350 executives
     * Wrote 10 year plan

4.   Isaac Permatter | Marvel Comics
     * Reduced headcount
     * Even digging paper clips out of the trash
     * Was bankrupt a few years earlier

5.   Lee Iacocca | Chrysler
     * Introduced the K-Car and minivan
     * Became profitable 3 years later

6.   Angela Ahrendts | Burberry
     * Used social media to reach a new generation of consumers
     * Sales assistants in retail stores have iPads
     * Mirrors turn into screens displaying catwalk images
     * Revenue & profits doubled in 5 years

Source: Stephanie Vozza, "Successful Turnarounds," February 22, 2013, https://www.entrepreneur.com/slideshow/225890, accessed May 15, 2018.

Exhibit 2   Runway Model

Source: Rev. Morgan-Thomas.

Exhibit 3   Reverend Morgan-Thomas's Collection of Hats

Source: Rev. Morgan-Thomas

Exhibit 4   Rev. Morgan-Thomas and Her Son at His Wedding, Wearing a Custom Hat

Source: Rev. Morgan-Thomas.

Exhibit 5   Manufacturing Flow Diagram

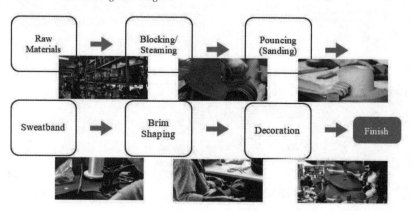

Source: Image 3, Adventurebilt Hat Company, 2015, http://www.adventurebiltdeluxe.com/hats.php, accessed June 6, 2018.
Rev. Morgan-Thomas, images 1, 2, 4-6.

Exhibit 6 Hats Prior to Decoration

Source: Rev. Morgan-Thomas.

Exhibit 7 Equipment in The American Hat Factory

Equipment	Value
1. 600 Blocks	$150 each
2. 14 Sewing Machines	$900 each
3. 4 Millineries	$1000 each
4. 5 Steam Huts	$300 each
5. 2 Ovens	$450 each
6. 12 Stampers	$700 each
7. Drying cabinets, scissors, pliers, wire cutters, pressing cushion , iron, ironing board, thimble, tailors chalk, pins, hat stands, brushes, dolly heads, drawing pins, millinery wire, plastic bags, threads, glues, tape measure, rulers	$5,500 total

Source: Rev. Morgan-Thomas.

Rev. Morgan-Thomas Case Study Assignment Questions

1. Did Reverend Morgan-Thomas pay too much for the company?
2. What are the top two things that Reverend Morgan-Thomas must do to turn this company around?
3. Why has this company been unprofitable?

Notes

1. Chenault, Kenneth. "An Interview with Kenneth Chenault, CEO at American Express." London Business School. May 6, 2014. https://www.london.edu/think/an-interview-with-kenneth-chenault-ceo-at-american-express
2. "Granite Broadcasting Corporation." Reference for Business. Accessed March 18, 2021. https://www.referenceforbusiness.com/history2/86/Granite-Broadcasting-Corporation.html
3. Lowery, Mark. "B.E. 100s Company of the Year: Solid as a Rock." pg. 122–132. June 1, 1995. Accessed March 18, 2021. https://books.google.com/books?id=_FwEAAAAMBAJ&pg=PA122#v=onepage&q&f=false
4. Brooks, Khristopher J. "Black-owned Small Businesses Hit Harder by Pandemic than White-owned Firms." CBS News. February 23, 2021. https://www.cbsnews.com/news/black-owned-businesses-revenue-drop-covid-pandemic/
5. Ibid.
6. Hale, Kori. "Here's What the New Round Of PPP Loans Means for Black-Owned Businesses." *Forbes*. January 5, 2021. https://www.forbes.com/sites/korihale/2021/01/05/heres-what-the-new-round-of-ppp-loans-means-for-black-owned-businesses/?sh=14f3723446ee
7. Marshall, Brian K. "Are We There Yet?—The State of Black Business and The Path to Wealth." Blended Media. February 13, 2019. http://blndedmedia.com/are-we-there-yet/
8. McKinney, Jeff. "Third Round of PPP Funding Starts with Greater Focus on Minority-Owned Small Businesses." *Black Enterprise*. January 13, 2021. https://www.blackenterprise.com/third-round-of-ppp-funding-starts-with-greater-focus-on-minority-owned-small-businesses/
9. "FACT SHEET: Biden-Harris Administration Increases Lending to Small Businesses in Need, Announces Changes to PPP to Further Promote Equitable Access to Relief." The White House Briefing Room. February 22, 2021. https://www.whitehouse.gov/briefing-room/statements-

releases/2021/02/22/fact-sheet-biden-harris-administration-increases-lending-to-small-businesses-in-need-announces-changes-to-ppp-to-further-promote-equitable-access-to-relief/

10. "Kevin Chenault Biography." Britannica. March 18, 2021. https://www.britannica.com/biography/Kenneth-Chenault

11. Chenault, Kenneth. "An Interview with Kenneth Chenault, CEO at American Express." London Business School. May 6, 2014. https://www.london.edu/think/an-interview-with-kenneth-chenault-ceo-at-american-express

12. Patrick, Alvin. "Ken Chenault on Leadership and Success at American Express." August 26, 2018. https://wdef.com/2018/08/26/ken-chenault-on-leadership-and-success-at-american-express/

13. Cain, Aine. "How Lowe's CEO Marvin Ellison Went from Making $4.35 an Hour as a Target Security Guard to Running the Second Biggest Home-Improvement Retailer in the US." *Business Insider*. February 23, 2019. https://www.businessinsider.com/lowes-ceo-marvin-ellison-life-career-2019-2

14. Meyersohn, Nathaniel. "How It All Went Wrong at JCPenney—CNN Business." CNN, Cable News Network. September 27, 2018. https://www.cnn.com/2018/09/27/business/jcpenney-history

15. Gumbs, Alisa. "Black Enterprise Corporate Executive of the Year Marvin Ellison." *Black Enterprise*. November 18, 2017. www.blackenterprise.com/corporate-executive-of-the-year-ellison/

16. Ibid.

17. "A Statement from Tattered Cover About Recent Events." Tattered Cover Book Store. June 6, 2020. https://www.tatteredcover.com/statement-tattered-cover-about-recent-events

18. "Community Letter to the Owners of Tattered Cover Bookstore." *The Word*. June 11, 2020. https://www.thewordfordiversity.org/communityletter

19. Van Divier, Casey. "Meet the New Owners of the Tattered Cover Book Store." *303 Magazine*. December 18, 2020. https://303magazine.com/2020/12/new-owners-tattered-cover-book-store/

20. "How I Built This with Guy Raz—Radio One: Cathy Hughes." NPR. August 14, 2017. https://www.npr.org/2017/09/29/542650845/radio-one-cathy-hughes

21. Kelly, Michael. "Omaha Native Cathy Hughes, the 2nd-Richest Black Woman in U.S., Is 'Thrilled' to Come Home." *Omaha World Herald*. May 16, 2018. https://omaha.com/archives/kelly-omaha-native-cathy-

hughes-the-2nd-richest-black-woman-in-u-s-is-thrilled/article_5c
6359bd-9ca1-529f-86a4-5b9dd74b9669.html

22. Chun, Janean. "From Teen Mom To Media Mogul." *HuffPost*. October 4,
2012 www.huffpost.com/entry/catherine-hughes-radio-one_n_1798129

23. Ibid.

24. "About Cathy Hughes." www.cathyhughes.com/. Accessed March 22,
2021.

25. "How I Built This with Guy Raz—Radio One: Cathy Hughes." NPR.
August 14, 2017. https://www.npr.org/2017/09/29/542650845/radio-one-
cathy-hughes

26. "The Comeback Queen." *Forbes*. June 6, 2013. www.forbes.com/forbes/
1999/0920/6407086a/?sh=35a0067f3dd9

27. Milloy, Courtland. "WOL." *The Washington Post*. December 2, 1979.
www.washingtonpost.com/archive/local/1979/12/02/wol/ab74dfdd-ca6c-
485b-9077-0c3e16f50267/. Accessed March 22, 2021.

28. Biga, Leo Adam. "Cathy Hughes." *Omaha Magazine*. November 21,
2018. www.omahamagazine.com/2018/11/21/301576/cathy-hughes

29. "The Comeback Queen." *Forbes*. June 6, 2013. www.forbes.com/forbes/
1999/0920/6407086a/?sh=35a0067f3dd9.

30. Ibid.

31. Ibid.

32. Ibid.

33. McKinney, Jeffrey. "45 Great Moments in Black Business—No. 20:
First Black Woman To Take Company Public On NASDAQ." *Black
Enterprise*. December 20, 2017. www.blackenterprise.com/45-great-
moments-in-black-business-no-20-radio-one-founder-cathy-hughes-
first-black-woman-to-take-company-public-on-nasdaq/

34. Noguchi, Yuki. "The Money of Color - Built on High-Wattage Black
Advocacy, Radio One Is Turning Its Dial to the Bottom Line." *The
Washington Post*. January 24, 2000. www.washingtonpost.com/wp-srv/
WPcap/2000-01/24/070r-012400-idx.html. Accessed March 22, 2021.

35. Alexander, Keith L. "EXCLUSIVE: 40 Years of Cathy Hughes' Leadership at Urban One." *The Washington Informer*. January 15, 2020.
www.washingtoninformer.com/exclusive-40-years-of-cathy-hughes-
leadership-at-urban-one/

36. Ibid.

37. "About Cathy Hughes." www.cathyhughes.com/. Accessed March 22,
2021.

8

Entrepreneurial Exits: Selling the Company

"Most entrepreneurs that receive investments, do not give any returns to those investors. So, to be able to see that we got there and had an exit, I was excited. I was proud."[1]

—Juanita Lott, founder of Bridgestream Inc.

WHILE ENTREPRENEURS CAN leave a company for many reasons, voluntary or involuntary, this chapter focuses on the former. When a Black entrepreneur willingly sells part or all of his company for the purpose of "cashing out," it is a definitive marker of entrepreneurial success. Almost all entrepreneurs want to monetize a portion, or all, of the value they have created in their entrepreneurial venture. Typically, cashing out is considered the final stage in the entrepreneurship process. That follows the stages of concept, start-up, survival, stability, and/or growth. One Black entrepreneur who reached the cashing out stage was Juanita Lott, the founder of Bridgestream Software.

With an academic background in liberal arts and no training or experience in technology and engineering, Lott was not the traditional candidate to start a technology company. However, she believes that her extensive experience in the nontechnical side of the software industry provided her with unconventional and valuable insights. She notes, "I had spent over 10 years at the C-Suite level as an executive in software, as the chief of HR (human resources) officer. So, I dealt

235

with all of the people issues. I dealt with all of the changes that needed to happen to take what was a startup, to over a billion-dollar software company at that time. My job was the people, but I understood the business. Because from my perspective you can't solve for one without understanding the other."[2]

At the time that Lott launched her company, in 2000, technological and legislative changes were taking place that would fundamentally change how businesses operate. Lott recognized and believed that these changes presented a business opportunity. Regarding the technological changes, she notes:

> I was sitting front and center as the technology that underpins enterprise software was about to go through another change in the way the architecture was structured. By sitting in that room, and kind of hearing and knowing that was happening I got an understanding of what it would enable that wasn't possible before. And so, I convinced myself that I didn't need to be an engineer. I needed to understand how to build it which is just kind of product management . . . that is probably what you would call me. I knew how it needed to work. I knew how the new technology was going to make it possible so I sat with a couple of very interesting engineers and I said, 'This is what I think we could do. It needs to work this way.' They were excited about the possibility and I couldn't think of a reason not to do it.[3]

One relevant legislative change was the passage of the Health Insurance Portability and Accountability Act (HIPAA), in 1996, which mandated national standards to protect patient health information from being disclosed without consent of the patient. The act placed restrictions on the sharing of health care information, specifically stipulating how health care and insurance companies should maintain personal, sensitive heath information to ensure against fraud and theft.

The second legislative change was the Sarbanes-Oxley Act of 2002, which was enacted in response to several corporate and accounting scandals that had occurred in the late 1990s and early 2000s. Also known as the Corporate and Auditing Accountability, Responsibility, and Transparency Act, it was enacted to put in place compliance regulations with the intent to ensure the integrity of corporate financial reporting and to better regulate the auditing and accounting of firms. While the focus of the act was on publicly held corporations, companies in all industries, including health care, began to implement compliance measures aimed at ensuring accuracy and transparency in their financial accounts and reports, as well as in their operations.

To meet these new compliances and reporting requirements, companies in all industries, particularly in health care, began to overhaul their information gathering and reporting systems. Initially, most businesses lacked the relevant capabilities to comply with these regulations and had to develop such capacity internally or seek solutions from other companies. Both options were complicated and costly.

Lott began to develop her idea for a software product that would allow companies to better manage and monitor access to sensitive customer and corporate information. While she had her detractors, many encouraged her pursuit of this idea, including those who introduced her to angel investors. One of the law firms she approached provided the pro bono services to incorporate her company, while one of the partners introduced her to a VP of software at Oracle—an African American who had started one of the first incubators for African American start-ups and had purchased an old bank building in downtown Oakland, CA, where Lott and her team worked rent-free, for their first three years.

The funds she secured through angel investors enabled her to develop the first prototype, which led to the "proof of concept" for her product. Soon after, the company realized its first major sale. At that point, Lott was able to secure her first venture capital investment, after months of unsuccessful pitches to venture firms. Lott believes that her racial and gender identities were factors delaying her acquisition of venture capital investment. She stated, "I would suggest that had I not been an African American woman, I think I would've gotten venture funding before I removed all of the risk."[4]

Bridgestream's Enterprise Role Management solutions enabled companies to provide and manage access to sensitive information. It provided the capability to analyze and monitor the use of this information. In 2007, Lott sold Bridgestream to Oracle. Although the terms of the sale were not disclosed, some sources report it to be worth upward of $30 million. In a press release following the announcement of the sale, the vice president of Oracle's Identity Management and Security Products division noted:

> With the acquisition of Bridgestream, Oracle can help organizations streamline compliance related tasks and automate role management. We believe that the combination of Bridgestream's Enterprise Role Management capabilities and Oracle Identity Management will enable the next generation of integration between security and business process controls by delivering a closed-loop solution that combines role discovery, modeling, enforcement, attestation and audit in a single integrated solution.[5]

Lott identified several factors that her team, board members, and investors considered when making the decision to sell the company. Those factors included the following: the viability of Bridgestream to remain an independent company, the demand for Bridgestream's products, the state of the financial markets, and the timing of the sale. She explains the reasons for considering the sale of the company as follows:

> We've been talking about defining what "exit" looked like. We've been having that conversation for a good year. And things we were considering were: are we a company that sells directly or are we selling in some other model, in this case a partnership? And the reason that was important for us is our product was a piece of a larger enterprise software puzzle. Was there a market for this technology that stood apart from being a partner with the guys who owned all the other pieces. . . .? So, our future, by definition, was tied to working very closely with those companies. And so, when we asked the question, 'Is it possible that we can be an independent software company?' the answer was probably maybe but more likely you're going to be a partner with the likes of the big players in the industry. . . .We were sitting at a time (2007). . .where the IPO market, what market? There was no real IPO opportunity.[6]

She recognized that the capability gap in the solutions provided by the larger software companies, such as Oracle, made Bridgestream a valuable acquisition target. She noted, "We need to take a really hard look at where we are, given that this is one of the ways we get into these big deals. It's why the Oracles and these other guys want to do business with us because they can't solve this piece of data security to help their customers check off 'yes I can cover myself' from a HIPAA standpoint."[7]

Another factor that was considered was funding. The investment funds raised up to that point were nearly depleted, and Lott knew that she would have to raise additional funds if the company were to continue operating. The decision to sell the company brought on a surge of mixed emotions. Lott recounts how she felt when she sold her company:

> A huge sense of validation. I think that's the word I would use. There were so many messages that said you didn't belong. Is your business truly a Silicon Valley opportunity? Why you? And so, at some point you begin to think, is it real? Am I really going to make this happen? So, the validation that comes from the fact that you were able to do what 90 percent of any of their portfolios were not able to do.
>
> The second thought was a sense of loss. I don't think you put in the kind of effort you have to put in to build a business from an idea where you are not giving 100 percent of yourself 24/7. And then at some point say here, let someone else take it forward from there. There is a part of you . . . it's like losing a child. I know it's the right thing to do. As a CEO and you look at all of the business reasons that tell you that that's the right decision to make. You still have this pit of the stomach feeling that this is going to be tough to let go. It has defined you.[8]

After the sale of Bridgestream, Lott began a career in investing and is currently an investment partner in the Portfolia Investment Fund for Women, a fund that supports and invests in women entrepreneurs. Lott is also a trustee alumna of Springboard Enterprises, a venture catalyst organization that provides support to women-led businesses and works as an advisor and mentor to women entrepreneurs.

Reasons Why an Entrepreneur May Want to "Exit" a Business

An entrepreneur sells a company for many reasons, including personal and strategic.

Personal reasons include:

- Desire to cash out to do something different or just to enjoy life;
- Desire to get out of the business because of exhaustion/frustration;
- Desire to retire;
- Health issues or family crisis;
- Family dispute, including divorce, where liquidation of the equity interests in a business may be part of a divorce settlement;
- Need to ensure continuity of business when the entrepreneur does not have a succession plan; and
- To reduce ownership in a company.

Business/strategic reasons include:

- Closing a nonprofitable business to limit losses;
- Raising capital to finance another business opportunity;
- Strong buyer interest;
- Gaining market share—the company buying the business may have complementary brand or distribution channels that can be leveraged;
- Financial expansion—acquiring company has the resources to finance the necessary equipment and/or fund the required strategies to expand product/service into new markets;
- Diversify product/service offered;
- Diversify customer base;
- Installing more productive management; and
- Closing a business in the event of a significant change in the macroeconomic environment (an economic recession) or due to external factors beyond management's control (9/11 or the COVID-19 pandemic).

As listed below, there are several types of exit strategies. There is no such thing as one being right or wrong. The decision belongs to the entrepreneurs.

1. *Management buyout*—Involves selling the company to managers within the company through a combination of private equity investment and debt, which is collateralized by the assets of the company.

2. *Strategic acquisition*—A strategic acquisition takes place when one company (acquiring company) purchases another company. The business rationales for an acquisition are similar to those for mergers; however, in a strategic acquisition, the combining of the two companies takes place when one company (usually the larger one) buys outright the other. The acquiring company may or may not choose to retain staff from the company being bought.

3. *Initial public offering (IPO)*—An initial public offering, or IPO, is the first sale of a company's stocks to the public, also known as "going public." In an IPO, an entrepreneur gives up a portion of the ownership of the company to investors and stockholders.

4. *Mergers*—In a merger, two businesses combine into one business entity. The idea behind a merger is that combining the two companies, which may have complementary skills or resources, will lead to cost savings or operational efficiency that will, in turn, yield higher value for all stakeholders, including investors. There are various types of mergers, including horizontal (businesses are in the same industry), vertical (businesses are part of the same supply chain), conglomerate (businesses do not have anything in common), market expansion (companies have similar products/services but operate in different markets), and product extension (companies' products complement one another).[9] In most mergers, the owner and management team of the company being bought will become part of the acquiring company's team and will help manage the newly merged company.

Special Purpose Acquisition Companies

The popularity of mergers today can be attributed to the recent introduction and phenomenal use of special purpose acquisition companies (SPAC). Mergers that emanated from SPACs and later went public as an initial public offering (IPO) increased from 59 in 2019 to 248 in

2020, which is a 320% increase. Cash fueled this exponential growth. In 2019, $13.6 billion was raised via mergers. That figure grew to $83 billion a year later, which was a 510% increase![10] One reason for this rapid increase in SPAC activity is the fact that going public in this manner is a relatively easier and faster way to get capital than going through a traditional IPO, given that the registration and regulatory requirements for a SPAC acquisition are less stringent than those for an IPO.

Most SPACs do not find operating companies to merge with via an acquisition. And those that do often end up with poorly performing operating companies. Their returns to investors underperform those from traditional IPOs. A report by Renaissance Capital found that of the 313 SPACs that had been created since 2015, 93 had taken a company public, delivering an average loss of –9.6% and a median return of –29.1%, compared to the average aftermarket return of 47.1% for traditional IPOs in the same time frame. Only 29 of these SPACs had positive returns (as of September 2020).[11]

To many, these negative results are not a surprise. Carson Block, founder of Muddy Waters Research, calls the SPAC trend the "Great 2020 Money Grab" and notes, "a business model that incentivizes promoters to do something—anything—with other people's money is bound to lead to significant value destruction on occasion."[12] While one motivation for SPAC sponsors is the 20% transaction fee, entrepreneurs have additional drivers to exit via SPAC. It provides an inexpensive way for the company to go public. And, as a publicly traded company, the entrepreneur can sell some stock in the public markets. The SPAC process also provides an exit opportunity for the company's employees and investors as venture capitalists.

SPACs and Black Entrepreneurs and Investors

Black entrepreneurs and investors have been involved in the SPAC space as sponsors, advisors, and acquisition targets. One such example occurred on March 2011, when Robert L. Johnson, chairman of The RLJ Companies and founder of Black Entertainment Television (BET), raised $143.75 million through his SPAC, RLJ Acquisition,

Inc. At that moment, he was the first African American to raise money through a SPAC (He was also a master of the IPO exit mechanism, and you'll learn more about him later in the chapter). The significance of this entrepreneurial event is reflected in the prestigious nature of the board members, which included Bill Cohen, former U.S. Secretary of Defense and chairman of the Cohen Group, and Mario Gabelli, chairman and CEO of GAMCO Investors Inc. In October 2012, RLJ Acquisitions purchased two entertainment companies, Image Entertainment, Inc. and Acorn Media Group, Inc., and created RLJ Entertainment, Inc.

In March 2021, Capital Partners Acquisition, a SPAC, was created by Grain Management, a Black-owned private equity firm, and General Catalyst Partners, a venture capital firm, to raise $400 million. In addition to its acquisition targets, the SPAC announced that it also seeks to empower Black entrepreneurs through the creation of Catalyst Partners Foundation, a nonprofit that would support initiatives fostering the economic empowerment and inclusion of underrepresented groups.[13] In the same month, the Apollo Strategic Growth Company, another SPAC, was engaged in talks with Vista Equity Partners, a Black-owned private equity firm, to acquire and merge three companies in its portfolio—Solera Holdings Inc., DealerSocket Inc., and Omnitracs.[14]

As of this writing, there are no known Black-owned operating companies that have actually merged with a SPAC. Unfortunately, history has shown that SPAC-like financial securities have had a negative impact on Blacks. In 1720, the stock market in England burst with trading activities. One of the catalysts for that extraordinarily high level of trading was the rapid appreciation of and collapse in the stock of a proposed slave-trading company. Similar to SPACs in today's world, this company and others like it were simply entities filled with cash, no operations, and unstated reasons for their existence. They did not want to publicize that they were investing in the bondage of Black people, so they clouded the actual intent of their conduct and stated that the money was needed "for carrying an undertaking of great advantage, but nobody to know what it is."[15]

Initial Public Offerings

The intentional obfuscation of a company's purpose is usually counter-productive for its success in the public market. However, the current popularity of SPACs proves that there is a place in today's markets for these financial securities that operate as an IPO exit mechanism for entrepreneurs.

An initial public offering takes place when a private company issues and offers shares to public investors for the first time. Companies wanting to go public must register with the Securities and Exchange Commission (SEC) and, once public, must meet various reporting and accounting requirements set by the SEC and the stock exchanges. Going public allows a company to raise capital and provides an exit strategy for its founders and initial investors, giving them the option to sell their stock to buyers in the public market.

A company starts the process by selecting underwriters, one or more investment companies, who will guide it through the process of going public. Underwriters take the lead for every aspect of the IPO to ensure that the company has met the legal, accounting, and financial reporting requirements of going public. This would include conducting due diligence, preparing filing documentation, prospectus and marketing collateral, marketing, pricing of the stock offering, and finalizing the date of the IPO.

The IPO process involves a substantial commitment of time and resources. On average, it takes six to nine months to prepare, plan, manage, and complete an offering. Costs associated with the IPO process include underwriter fees as well as legal, accounting, and tax expenses. Underwriting fees range from 3.5% to 7% of gross IPO proceeds.

Advantages of an IPO include:

- Access to a wider investor pool to raise capital for expansion and growth;
- Ability to raise additional funds through secondary offerings;
- Increased prestige and public exposure;

- Increased auditing and financial accounting procedures and systems and transparency required, as a public company may prompt financial institutions to have confidence in the company's financials leading to a lower cost of capital; and
- Increased ability to recruit and retain better-qualified employees through the incentive of stock options.

Disadvantages of IPOs include:

- Costs associated with preparing to operate as a public company, including but not limited to investments in organizational systems and human resources;
- Ongoing regulatory compliance costs associated with being a public company, including the disclosure of financial, accounting, tax, and other business information for public scrutiny;
- Ongoing additional accounting, marketing, and legal costs;
- New stakeholders and a new layer of leadership, including a board of directors, which reduces the control and decision-making powers of owners and managers;
- Stock price fluctuations, which affect market capitalization and therefore a company's value; and
- Potential increased liability.

In 2020, there were 1,415 IPOs globally raising a total of $331.3 billion, representing the increase from 1,040 IPOs and $199.2 billion raised in 2019. Of the total proceeds, 53% was raised in U.S. markets.[16] The growth in IPOs was due to the increasing number of deals in the technology, e-commerce, and health care sectors as well as an increase in SPAC IPOs.

Public Companies in the U.S.

According to the *Wall Street Journal*, the number of publicly traded companies in the U.S. has been declining steadily since reaching a peak in the late 1990s. In 1996, 7,322 companies were listed on U.S.

stock exchanges, a number that had declined to 3,671 by 2017,[17] but the trend reversed and rebounded to approximately 6,000 in 2020.

Black-Owned Public Companies

The first Black-owned company to go public was the Baltimore-based Parks Sausage Company, which completed a $1.5 million IPO in 1969. Its stocks were traded on the National Association of Securities Dealers Automated Quotation (NASDAQ) exchange until 1977, when H. G. Parks, the founder, sold the company to a group of White investors for $5 million. While the deal was lucrative for Parks personally, it was not a good business decision for the buyers, as the company experienced several years of poor performance. In 1981, a group of African American senior executives engineered a repurchase of the company.

Also, in 1969, the Chicago-based Johnson Products Company, a hair and beauty products company, went public by completing a $6.5 million initial offering of stock on the AMEX. This company was the initial sponsor of the television dance show *Soul Train*, which was extremely popular in the African American community.

Remarkably, it would be another 14 years before the next Black-owned business would go public. In August 1983, Ault Inc., a Minneapolis-based manufacturer of custom power supply units, raised $9 million in its IPO. That same year, PKS Communications Inc., a manufacturer of telecommunications equipment based in Connecticut, raised $2 million in its IPO and was listed on NASDAQ. In 1984, American Shared Hospital Services (ASHS), a California-based company that provides diagnostic imaging and radiotherapy services to hospitals, raised $4 million via an IPO. A partial listing of Black-owned firms that have gone public from 1993 until 2015 is presented in Table 8.1.

Table 8.1   Partial Listing of Black-Owned Firms That Have Gone Public from 1993 until 2015

Name of Company	Founder	Date of IPO	Listing	Funds Raised/ Offering Share Price
1. Envirotest Systems	Chester C. Davenport	4/1/93	NAS-DAQ	—
2. Caraco Pharmaceuticals Labs	Dr. C. Arnold Curry	2/10/94	OTCBB	$7.5 million
3. Carver Federal Savings	M. Moran Weston et. al.	10/26/94	NAS-DAQ	$24 million
4. Chapman Holdings	Nathan Chapman Jr.	2/27/98	NAS-DAQ	$7.7 million
5. Chapman Capital Management Holding	Nathan Chapman Jr.		NAS-DAQ	$8 million
6. United American Healthcare Corporation	Dr. Julius V. Combs & Ronald R. Dobbins	8/20/98	NYSE	$65 million
7. Radio One	Cathy Hughes	5/6/99	NAS-DAQ	$24/share
8. eChapman	Nathan Chapman Jr.	6/20/00	NAS-DAQ	$13/share
9. Worldspace Inc.	Noah Samara	8/4/05	NAS-DAQ	$21/share
10. Fluid Music Inc.	Justin Beckett	6/19/2008	TSX	$27 million
11. IntelliPharmaCeutics	Isa Odidi	10/22/09	TSX & NAS-DAQ	$7.5 million
12. RLJ Lodging Trust	Robert L. Johnson	5/12/11	NAS-DAQ	$495 million
13. Axsome Therapeutics	Herriot Tabateau	11/19/15	NAS-DAQ	$51million
14. PAVmed Inc.	Lishan Aklog	4/28/16	NAS-DAQ	$5 million

Robert and Sheila Johnson

Mastery of this entrepreneurial technique was demonstrated in the most successful such exit for Black entrepreneurs by Sheila and Robert Johnson, the founders of Black Entertainment Television (BET). They generated significant wealth when they took the company public on the NYSE in 1991. The stock was priced at $17 per share and the company raised $74.3 million. In 2001, they became billionaires when they sold the company to Viacom for approximately $3 billion.

Robert L. Johnson was born on April 8, 1946, in Hickory, Mississippi. He was the ninth of 10 children. He graduated from the University of Illinois and received a master's degree from Princeton, the only one of his siblings to graduate from college. After finishing school, he moved to Washington, D.C., where he worked as a lobbyist for the cable industry. He met John Malone, the CEO of Tele-Communications Inc. (TCI) at that time, and the two men began discussing Johnson's idea for a cable TV company targeting the Black community. Malone, whose company was trying to build TCI's business in Black neighborhoods, found the concept attractive.

In 1979, Robert and Sheila Johnson founded the Black Entertainment Television (BET) as "a special channel that will showcase the full creative range of black entertainment."[18] They borrowed $15,000 in seed money and received $500,000 from Tele-Communications Inc. (TCI) for a 35% stake of the company. John Malone served as an advisor and a member of the board of directors.

Starting with broadcasts of gospel music videos and low-budget old movies on the USA Network, the company moved its programming to its own satellite signal after receiving investment from Taft Broadcasting Company in 1982. Charging a subscriber fee, it expanded its offerings by producing original content, including popular gospel and soul music programs. By 1984, the network was reaching more than 7 million homes, but had yet to achieve profitability.

BET faced several challenges in its efforts to increase its viewership. Cable providers, who catered mainly to White audiences, were not willing to add BET programming to their channel lineup. In addition, cable services were not readily available in most large urban cities, the areas where the majority of BET's viewers lived. Despite these challenges, the Johnsons continued to expand BET's program services. In 1984, they established a Washington news bureau and reached an agreement with ABC to carry its national and international coverage. An entertainment magazine and a talk show were also added to its programming. In September 1984, BET struck a deal with Time Inc. to exchange 16% of BET stock for the use of one of ABC's satellite transponders allowing BET to begin 24-hour programming. By 1986, subscribers to the network reached 12 million, enabling the company to report profits for the first time. By 1989, subscribed viewership had increased to 22 million, while advertising revenue was increasing. Revenues for that year reached $23 million.

In 1991, one of BET's investors, Great American Broadcasting Inc. (formerly known as Taft Broadcasting), announced that it was considering selling its BET shares to pay down debt. The Johnsons decided to take the company public and completed an IPO on October 30, 1991, making BET the first Black-owned company to be listed on the New York Stock Exchange. The offering consisted of 4.25 million shares, which had initially been valued at $11 to $13 per share but were priced at $17 per share for the IPO. The offering was oversubscribed to 54 million shares and the stock price closed at $23.5 per share. The IPO raised $72.3 million, with the Johnsons personally making $6.4 million. The Johnsons retained 56% of the now public company's voting rights, with 37% of its Class A shares. Great American Broadcasting sold off its BET stocks, netting $40 million.[19]

At the time of its IPO, BET's revenues had grown to $51 million, with a net profit of $9.3 million. Its programming had expanded to include college sports and public affairs, and its brand recognition among Black families had reached 90%.[20] Cable operators were more willing to add BET to their channel offerings and advertising revenue increased as it became clear that BET was an effective way to reach Black households. Following the IPO, Johnson began a massive expansion strategy to reshape BET into "the preeminent black media brand in the world—in entertainment and leisure-time activities and merchandise."[21]

To reach a younger and more diverse audience, BET bought a controlling interest in *Emerge* magazine, a publication known within the African American community for providing insightful commentary on social issues, and it launched *Young Sisters and Brothers (YSB)*, a youth magazine. In 1993, BET launched BET Direct, a direct-marketing firm. In 1996, BET launched BET on Jazz, the first 24-hour program dedicated exclusively to jazz music. BET also formed three joint ventures with film production companies to produce movies. Other areas BET expanded into included restaurants, a nightclub, a soundstage at Disney World, a line of skin care products, a branded credit card, a publishing company, and an international subsidiary to bring BET programming to the Caribbean, South Africa, and the United Kingdom.[22]

Johnson's expansion efforts came at a cost. Although subscriber numbers increased as urban areas wired up for cable—from 1990 to 1998 BET added approximately 4 million subscribers a year—operating income declined in the four consecutive years from 1995 through 1998 due to losses from new ventures. Investors became skeptical of the feasibility of Johnson's plan and its stock price took a hit.

Facing increasing market skepticism of his plans and wanting to regain control of his company, Johnson offered to buy back BET's stock. In September 1997, Johnson made an offer at $48 a share, a 20% premium on the stock's average price over the previous month. On July 30, 1998, BET shareholders accepted his offer to buy all outstanding shares for $63 each, enabling Johnson to take BET back to private ownership. Three years later, it was sold and the Johnsons became one of the handful of Black billionaires in the country.

Though they later divorced, Sheila later went on to become an excellent philanthropist. One of her benefactors is the Harvard Kennedy School, where she endowed the Sheila C. Johnson Leadership Fellowship in 2013, which now has been renamed The Fellowship for Serving African American Communities, for graduate students "from any race or ethnicity working to reduce disparities in African American and other underserved communities in the U.S. through efforts in health care, education, economic development, public policy, criminal justice reform, social entrepreneurship, and a variety of other fields."[23]

Introduction to the Case Studies

The *Corey Thomas and the IPO* case study is about a CEO's decision-making process for determining if the time is right to do an IPO. Corey Thomas, the CEO, is concerned that the public markets may not respond favorably to the fact that his company has never made a profit. At the same time, he knows that the venture capital investors in the company would love to get a return on their investment via an IPO exit.

On the other hand, while taking a company public is considered by many to be the sexiest business exit, it is an anomaly. There are over 25 million companies in the United States, and less than 3,000 are publicly owned. Thus, this case study, *United Housing—Otis Gates*, is about the more common means of an entrepreneurial exit, which is selling the company.

HARVARD | BUSINESS | SCHOOL

9-317-082
REV: FEBRUARY 12, 2020

STEVEN ROGERS

DERRICK COLLINS

Corey Thomas and the IPO

As the first fiscal quarter was coming to a close in March of 2015, Rapid7 CEO, Corey Thomas, (HBS '02) was facing a decision. His board of directors and executive leadership team were in general agreement that now was the time to take the 15-year old startup public, as Rapid7 stood poised to capitalize on what appeared to be the next frontier for digital technology markets – cybersecurity.

The Threat Exposure Management (TEM) market is included within the broader Cybersecurity market; International Data Corporation (IDC) estimated that TEM was a $1.3B market, growing at a 15% - 18% annual clip (see **Exhibit 1**). Rapid7's core products, Nexpose and Metasploit, grew the company's market share from 1.6% of TEM in 2009 to almost 7% in 2013 (see **Exhibit 2**), supported – in large measure – by the heightened cyber threat environment of the time.

Rapid7 also competed in the Vulnerability Management subsector of TEM, which was a very fragmented market. By early 2015, competitors in the space included Qualys, a competitor similar to Rapid7 (which went public in 2012), and larger, established players like IBM and HP.

In spite of the positive trends, however, Thomas had some nagging concerns about an initial public offering (IPO). Firstly, he saw evidence that this was, a more risky time than recent history in the public markets. The U.S. Federal Government had been signaling an interest rate increase for a number of months, which had the potential for creating market turbulence during the time of this potential IPO. Secondly, Thomas wanted to ensure the success of their recent acquisition of AppSpider, which was expected to be a major product offering to drive future growth. If the company went public now, how would the public market's expectations influence their strategy decisions going forward – would it tolerate the inevitable early losses and not punish a publicly-traded Rapid7 stock price? Thirdly, given the current market uncertainty, should the company seek a private sale to a strategic buyer? Rapid7 had been funded principally with venture capital and these investors, by definition, seek a lucrative exit that an IPO can provide, but if the public markets decline after the IPO this becomes extremely difficult. The risk associated with the public markets is one of the downsides of a public offering and why many private equity investors actually *prefer* a private sale, or merger, to an IPO.

HBS Senior Lecturer Steven Rogers and independent researcher Derrick Collins prepared this case. It was reviewed and approved before publication by a company designate. Funding for the development of this case was provided by Harvard Business School and not by the company. HBS cases are developed solely as the basis for class discussion. Cases are not intended to serve as endorsements, sources of primary data, or illustrations of effective or ineffective management.

The Heightened Cyber Threat Environment

Vulnerability Management is the management of known "security holes." In software, security holes are natural, because code is written by humans and often contains millions of lines of software code. Certain holes that are present can go undetected for some period of time and replicate themselves via copies made into code written for other software systems. That code creates a weakness in the system that hackers can exploit and take control of computer systems, or create botnets (software robot machines) that can spread more malware throughout a network. The National Institute of Standards and Technology (NIST) defines an IT vulnerability as, *"a flaw or weakness in system security procedures, design, implementation, or internal controls that can be exercised (accidentally triggered or intentionally exploited) and result in a security breach or a violation of the system's security policy."*

In recent years, cyber-attacks and compromised information security systems were becoming more frequent, were happening on a larger scale, and with greater depth of impact. During the 2014 Thanksgiving holiday, Sony Corporation was famously hacked and embarrassed executives saw personal email and financial information completely exposed to willing buyers, and the public at large.

Rapid7 founders saw the need for a *proactive* security tool to supplement the existing strategies of antiviruses and firewall protection. In the words of Rapid7 founder, Alan Mathews:

> I started Rapid7 because I knew that a library of vulnerabilities and the tests for them would provide companies a way to protect themselves by knowing where their vulnerabilities lay. Nexpose leads professional organizations' approach to institutionalized security assessment while Metasploit's become the de facto standard in penetration testing.

The Rapid7 Evolution

Rapid7 was founded in 2000 and evolved over the years into a multi-product and single-platform product and services company providing monitoring, event management and proactive security maintenance of sensitive technology networks. The company described its differentiation and value proposition as follows:

> We understand the attacker better than anyone and build that insight into our security software and services to improve risk management and stop threats faster. Our IT security analytics solutions collect, contextualize, and analyze the security data you need to dramatically reduce threat exposure and detect compromise in real-time. Unlike traditional vulnerability assessment or incident management, Rapid7 provides insight into the security state of your assets and users, across virtual, mobile, private and public cloud networks.

> We offer advanced capabilities for vulnerability management, penetration testing, endpoint controls assessment, and incident detection and investigation. Our threat intelligence is informed by more than 200,000 members of the Metasploit community, the industry-leading Rapid7 Labs, and our experienced professional services team. Rapid7 solutions are the choice of 3,000 organizations across 78 countries, including more than 250 of the Fortune 1000.

By 2015, the company's anchor products were Nexpose and Metasploit. Nexpose served as one of the leading vulnerability assessment tools in the marketplace. Users were able to analyze vulnerabilities, test configurations, and understand the different controls across an IT environment. Vulnerabilities could be ranked by risk, thus allowing a security team to prioritize where needed. Nexpose could also be deployed across physical, virtual, mobile and cloud environments. Servicing compliance needs, allowing organizations to meet certain imposed requirements such as PCI DSS, were among other services Nexpose provided. Product features like interactive charting, risk tracking, and reporting and scan customization set the product apart in the market. Nexpose represented approximately two-thirds of Rapid7's product revenue, with Metasploit comprising the vast majority of the remainder.

Metasploit, acquired by Rapid7 in 2009, is a penetration-based testing solution that allows for attack simulation of vulnerabilities before they can be utilized by cybercriminals. It is perhaps easiest to think of Metasploit as a virtual sandbox (distinctly separate from the user's network) in which malware can be safely observed and executed. Files are then allowed to run, and the effects are monitored for undesirable outcomes, which would indicate the presence of malware. This stage also reduces "false positives", which is legitimate data traffic that is incorrectly quarantined. Metasploit acts as the secret sauce that helps prioritize and validate the vulnerabilities that Nexpose identifies. Given the synergies experienced when the products work together, they were often sold as a bundle (see **Exhibit 3**). By 2015, more than 45,000 active security researchers were on the Metasploit open source framework.

Funding History and Management Evolution

In 2008, Rapid7 initiated a relationship with the venture capital firm, Bain Capital, and raised $7 million in a Series A round of growth financing at a $21 million pre-money valuation. This was followed by a Series B round with Bain for $2 million in 2010, with no post-money valuation change from Series A. Bain Capital signaled its expectations for Rapid7 in a press release[1] following its investment:

> It is extremely rare to find a company that has doubled sales for each of the past four years despite the challenging economic environment. Rapid7's customers told us repeatedly that the company's Nexpose solution uniquely addresses their need for far-reaching security assessments that quickly identify and expose IT risks that can have severe business consequences. With its record of providing enormous value to more than 400 customers of all sizes and industries, we believe Rapid7 has the opportunity to continue to transform the market landscape and become the go-to technology provider for organizations seeking a superior security solution.

Also in 2008, Corey Thomas was hired as Executive Vice President of Sales, Marketing and Products, after being recruited from his role as Vice President at Parallels, Inc. He was one of the few African-Americans at the company. Thomas leveraged his prior executive experience to guide a newly formed, and entrepreneurial, sales force to achieve rapid scale.

To improve upon the company's performance was a challenge for Thomas as Rapid7 had, by 2008, already amassed 400 customers and enjoyed a 100 percent annual growth rate for the past four years, principally due to demand for its Nexpose product offering, which had established itself as the technology leader in vulnerability assessment, policy compliance, and risk management. Could he continue and exceed this impressive annual growth pattern?

---

[1] "BusinessWire", September 17, 2008.

Throughout his early time at Rapid7, Corey established himself as an astute sales and marketing executive with an intuitive leadership style that was respected throughout the company. In 2009, Corey was very involved in Rapid7's purchase of Metasploit and saw it as the future of the company's *UserInsight* technology. Thomas understood the potential data and algorithmic advances that Metasploit would provide and the value of the Metasploit open source user community, which utilizes the open source software and provides insight and improvements that would ultimately benefit the company's internal platforms and lead to the development of new products.

Rapid7's continued growth and market potential attracted the attention of venture capital investor, Technology Crossover Ventures (TCV), a leading provider of growth capital to later-stage private and public technology companies. In November 2011, Rapid7 announced the close of a $50 million Series C funding round from TCV at a significant increase in valuation to $210 million pre-money. The new capital would support Rapid7's growth strategy in three main areas: hiring critical talent to accelerate product innovation, strategic acquisitions and international expansion.

In 2012, Corey Thomas was appointed as CEO after serving in various senior executive sales, marketing and operational roles in the company. Simultaneously, the company hired an industry veteran as Chief Financial Officer and terminated a significant portion of the inside sales function in order to focus on rebuilding the sales team with individuals focused on more technical sales. Additionally, Thomas and his executive team brought in a new Senior VP of Sales, hired new international sales personnel and strengthened channel relationships. As CEO, Thomas held approximately 3% of Rapid7's fully-diluted equity.

Corey Thomas

Corey E. Thomas held several positions at Rapid7 – each with increasing responsibility – prior to becoming the Chief Executive Officer: he served as Executive VP of Sales, Marketing and Operations, VP of Marketing and Product Management, and VP of Marketing. Mr. Thomas focused on implementing strategies for product management, product marketing, and lead generation and management and was instrumental in broadening Rapid7's global presence in target markets and further driving demand for Nexpose. Prior to Rapid7, Thomas served as Vice President of Consumer and Business Marketing of Parallels, Inc. where he led product marketing, product management and business development. His experience in a number of leadership positions in the Microsoft Server and Tools division, where he led the product planning effort to define Microsoft's Data Platform and Storage strategy helped him to hone his management skills in a technology product company environment.

Thomas began his professional career as a management consultant for Deloitte Consulting, focusing on technology and operations at large multinational banks. He earned a B.E. in Electrical Engineering and Computer Science from Vanderbilt University and an MBA from Harvard Business School, where he was a member of the African-American Student Union (AASU) and graduated as a Baker Scholar – a distinction reserved for HBS graduates that achieve academic performance in the top 5% of their class.

Performance Under Thomas

In late 2012, Rapid7 acquired Mobilisafe, a cloud-based provider of mobile risk management solutions. This acquisition provided the company a security solution to handle the proliferation of mobile devices in the marketplace. More importantly, Rapid7's internally-developed, UserInsight product became available in late 2013. A significant development in the cyber security landscape,

UserInsight provided Rapid7 clients the ability to spot unusual activity by leveraging user-based and behavioral analytics driven by proprietary algorithms. Unlike Metasploit and Nexpose, UserInsight is offered in an SAAS (software-as-a-service) model and is priced based on the number of IPs (Internet Protocols) being tracked. Importantly, UserInsight does not require any additional hardware, therefore allowing an easy rollout for customers.

From 2013 to 2014, Rapid7 grew total revenues from $60 to $77 million ($39 and $47 million in products, respectively). During the same time period, the company posted gross profits of $48 and $59 million, respectively, and maintained a 77% gross profit margin. However, operating income slipped further into the red, from ($16) to ($26) million as a result of increases in operating expenses from $64 to $86 million (see **Exhibit 4b** for details).

By the end of 2014, Rapid7 completed a Series D funding round of $30 million from existing investors, Bain Capital ($5 million) and Technology Crossover Ventures ($25 million), which was completed at another big step-up in valuation to $400 million pre-money. With this Series D round of investment, Rapid7 began the development of a more robust field sales force, as well as the acceleration of product development and additional acquisitions for the company's product portfolio, including the acquisition of AppSpider in March 2015.

Venture Capital Investors Consideration

Rapid7 had two significant venture capital investors – Bain Capital and TCV – that had to be considered as part of any IPO decision. VC investors usually operate within an investment horizon of five to seven years, from initial investment to the monetization and exit of its investment in a target company. The primary option for the venture capital investor is the sale of the company – and thereby, its stockholdings – to a strategic or financial acquirer, such as a private equity investor seeking to grow an industry platform via merger or acquisition. These types of buyers typically will pay a premium for the complementary nature of a company's product or operations. This is an attractive option for many venture capital investors as it usually is a cash sale, thus allowing for a definitive investment return. In fact, the sale of a venture capital investment to a strategic (or another private equity) acquirer comprises more than 80% of total venture-backed exits (see **Exhibit 5**).

An IPO is an attractive option for a venture capital exit as it – if successful – will typically provide the highest valuation for the company's stock. However, the time, expense and uncertainty of the public market's acceptance (as manifest in the stock price) of the newly issued stock provides a fair amount of risk to the situation. Moreover, the stock held by VC investors is almost always subject to a 180-day "lock up period" after the IPO, thus preventing any disposal of these investors' holdings during this time. This is to allow for the company to establish a market equilibrium before relatively large stock positions are sold, which have the potential to adversely impact the pricing and volume of the company's stock.

The IPO Consideration

By 2015, Rapid7 was poised for an initial public offering (IPO). The company held a 7% market share of the large and growing vulnerability management marketplace, exceeded 3,600 customers, and expanded international sales to 12% of revenue. At the same time, the need for domestic, cybersecurity leadership was a reality understood at the household level. These factors and others led the Executive Team at Rapid7, the Board of Directors, and investors Bain and TCV, to urge Thomas and the Board of Directors to file for an IPO.

The IPO Process

At its core, the IPO is a financing event. The completion of the process results in the offering of shares of company stock to the investing public. A growing company needs cash, and the capital provided by the purchase of shares is, in turn, used to finance the company's growth strategy, which can take the form of acquiring machinery and equipment, hiring employees and/or providing capital to acquire other companies using cash and/or the newly issued stock as currency. Additionally, the process of going public provides an opportunity for the company's private equity investors to monetize their investment and achieve some liquidity.

The IPO process typically requires the guidance of an investment bank that serves as a consultant and underwriter to the company in the offering process, which lasts from six months to a year. The fee for these services is typically in the range of 3% - 7%, based on the size of the offering. Rapid7 estimates that it will cost approximately $7 million in fees and expenses to complete an IPO.

The IPO process begins with the company entering a "quiet period" wherein the company is to avoid self-promotion (as a means to promote the company's stock) and the publication of information about the company is restricted to a normal level of advertising. During this time, the company will have its financial statements prepared and audited for public review. Additionally, the Securities and Exchange Commission (SEC) registration forms are prepared so that potential IPO investors can evaluate the stock offering. This leads to the development of the offering prospectus which describes the business operations and financial performance, the type of securities offered, the planned use of proceeds from the offering, pro forma financial statements that illustrate the result of anticipated business operations, the risks associated with the company and its strategy, and information regarding the company's officers, directors, and principal shareholders.

The resulting preliminary registration statement and prospectus (also call a "red herring") is distributed to potential investors and the company begins its "road show" wherein the company's senior management team makes presentations to institutional investors, financial analysts and brokers in advance of the stock offering. Feedback from these constituents help the company and its underwriter determine the optimum offering price among the interested investors that will ultimately become the investment syndicate committed to purchasing the stock at the IPO.

Final adjustments are made to the company's registration statement, based on negotiations with the underwriter and input from the SEC, which includes the offering price, the underwriter's compensation, and net offering proceeds to the company which will occur three to five days later on the closing date, when the underwriter receives the securities from the company, receives payment for the issuance and proceeds to offer the company's securities for sale to the public.

Rapid7 Growth

Looking at the estimates for 2015, Corey felt confident of the value that Rapid7 had created and could create in the future.

As Cowen analysts forecasted at the time, Rapid7's cash flow was expected to recover quicker than operating income. Given that the company was investing for growth, operating losses were anticipated through 2017. However, cash flow was expected to break-even sooner than that, because of the company's practice of collecting billings upfront. Nexpose was primarily deployed as a perpetual license with maintenance and content subscription, and given the nature of the licensing arrangements, Rapid7 chose to recognize revenues on a future schedule that is booked upfront in billings; hence, billings are separate from revenues. As expected, Rapid7 experienced billings growth that was faster than revenue growth.

The overall marketplace context in 2015 seemed to provide an encouraging opportunity as Rapid7 stood a strong possibility of establishing a firm leadership position in the expanding threat exposure market (TEM).

The IPO Marketplace

The American IPO market in 2015 was experiencing its most robust activity level since the dot-com era as it set a 14-year record against a mostly low-volatility backdrop. With 244 IPOs, 2014 was the most active period of issuance since 445 companies went public in 2000 and represented a 23% increase over 2013, spurred by a doubling of biotech issuances. IPO proceeds totaled $74 billion (inflated by Alibaba's $22 billion offering) and were up 80% over 2013 (see **Exhibit 6**). While various global events, such as Russia's incursion into the Ukraine and conflicts in the Middle East, caused nervousness in global markets, they largely failed to disrupt the U.S. IPO applecart.

From a macroeconomic perspective, the beginning of 2015 was a continuation of a robust stock market as a stagnant interest rate rendered the stock market as one of the last resorts for return-seeking capital. However, it was still unclear if the public market would remain robust and thereby provide a valuation necessary to generate attractive returns on the equity investments made by Bain, TCV and others.

An illustration of this dynamic can be seen when comparing the trend of the S&P 500 market activity to the market activity among unprofitable IPOs (see **Exhibit 7**), which has historically been used to demonstrate an oncoming market bubble as investors seek returns from more established, less risky markets in a *"flight to quality."* This activity appeared to be a harbinger of a oncoming market correction. With forecasted operating losses into FY17, would there be reactionary market behavior that would depress a newly-public Rapid7 stock?

IPO or No?

As Corey sat in his downtown Boston office, and looked across to the banks of the Charles River where he studied at HBS, the timing of an IPO appeared right, but the aftermath was far from certain. Was an IPO worth the risk, given the signs of an overheating stock market? After all, an IPO is a *financing* event, and the company needed the capital to continue its development and growth. Investors had commitments to keep and needed to be able to provide significant returns to its stakeholders. And, the CEO would receive the blame if things did not go well, regardless of the reason.

Thomas was deep in thought as he wrestled with these questions. He chuckled to himself as he mused, "now I truly understand Henry IV when he said, *Uneasy lies the head that wears a crown.*"

Exhibit 1

Worldwide Vulnerability Assessment market estimated to be $1.3B in 2015, and growth continues through 2018

	2011	2012	2013	2014E	2015E	2016E	2017E	2018E	2013 - 18 CAGR (%)
Vulnerability Assessment - Device	522	570	628	696	779	897	1,019	1,141	13%
Vulnerability Assessment - Application	315	346	390	445	531	633	739	839	17%
Total Vulnerability Assessment	837	916	1,018	1,141	1,310	1,530	1,758	1,980	14%
y/y Change	11%	9%	11%	12%	15%	17%	15%	13%	-

Source: International Data Corporation (IDC)

Source: "IDC Market Analysis: Worldwide Security and Vulnerability Management 2014-2018 Forecast and 2013 Vendor Shares (Doc #250223)," International Data Corporation, August 2014, http://docplayer.net/14777321-Worldwide-security-and-vulnerability-management-2014-2018-forecast-and-2013-vendor-shares.html, accessed September 2016.

Exhibit 2

Source: "IDC Market Analysis: Worldwide Security and Vulnerability Management 2014-2018 Forecast and 2013 Vendor Shares (Doc #250223)," International Data Corporation, August 2014, http://docplayer.net/14777321-Worldwide-security-and-vulnerability-management-2014-2018-forecast-and-2013-vendor-shares.html, accessed September 2016.

Exhibit 3

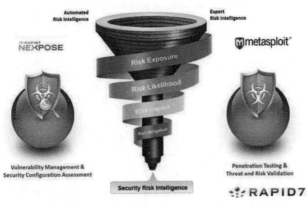

Source: Rapid7 Marketing Materials.

Exhibit 4a

RAPID7, INC.

Consolidated Balance Sheets

(in thousands, except share and per share data)

	December 31,		March 31, 2015 (Unaudited)
	2013	2014	2015
Assets			
Current assets:			
Cash	$20,612	$36,823	$33,343
Accounts receivable, net	19,475	25,412	21,027
Prepaid expenses and other current assets	2,023	4,209	4,995
Total current assets	42,110	66,444	59,365
Property and equipment, net	4,278	7,922	7,619
Goodwill	11,265	11,265	11,265
Intangible assets, net	2,025	1,156	953
Other assets	177	179	180
Total assets	$59,855	$86,966	$79,382
Liabilities Redeemable, Convertible Preffered Stock and Stockholders' Deficit			
Current liabilities			
Accounts payable	$ 2,969	$ 3,563	$ 2,892
Accrued expenses	9,062	11,907	7,956
Deferred revenue, current portion	40,761	58,164	60,539
Term loan payable, net of unamortized debt discount	—	—	1,703
Contingent consideration	1,416	—	—
Other current liabilities	457	642	887
Total current liabilities	54,665	74,249	73,977
Deferred revenue, non-current portion	19,094	26,892	28,104
Term loan payable, net of unamortized debt discount	16,318	16,871	15,306
Other long-term liabilities	2,355	4,218	3,958
Total liabilities	92,432	122,230	121,345
Redeemable convertible preferred stock:			
Series A redeemable convertible preferred stock	54,962	68,892	74,061
Series B redeemable convertible preferred stock	4,538	5,681	6,101
Series C redeemable convertible preferred stock	68,944	80,286	83,310
Series D redeemable convertible preferred stock	—	56,739	59,399
Stockholder's deficit:			
Common stock	128	126	127
Treasury stock	(161,149)	(243,462)	(261,435)
Accumulated deficit	—	(3,526)	(3,526)
Total stockholders' deficit	(161,021)	(246,862)	(264,834)
Total liabilities, redeemable convertible preferred stock and stockholders' deficit	$ 59,855	$ 86,966	$ 79,382

Source: SEC Form S-1 Filing.

Exhibit 4b

RAPID7, INC.

Consolidated Statements of Operations

(in thousands, except share and per share data)

	Year Ended December 31,			Three Months Ended March 31,	
	2012	2013	2014	2014	2015
				(Unaudited)	
Consolidated Statements of Operations Data:					
Revenue:					
Products	$ 29,414	$ 38,633	$ 47,030	$ 10,615	$ 13,645
Maintenance and support	9,727	14,017	19,016	4,145	5,799
Professional services	6,903	7,380	10,834	1,976	4,127
Total revenue	46,044	60,030	76,880	16,736	23,571
Cost of revenue:					
Products	1,691	4,048	4,557	1,239	1,546
Maintenance and support	2,069	3,388	4,495	988	1,210
Professional services	4,462	5,442	9,420	1,631	3,736
Total cost of revenue	8,222	12,878	18,472	3,858	6,492
Operating expenses:					
Research and development	17,820	21,411	25,570	6,120	6,414
Sales and marketing	23,278	31,779	49,007	11,004	13,230
General and administrative	9,436	12,586	12,972	3,482	4,053
Total operating expenses	50,534	65,776	87,549	20,606	23,697
Loss from operations	(12,712)	(18,624)	(29,141)	(7,728)	(6,618)
Interest income (expense), net	(71)	(122)	(2,802)	(695)	(685)
Other income (expense), net	(29)	43	(305)	41	(305)
Loss before income taxes	(12,812)	18,703	(32,248)	(8,382)	(7,608)
Provision for (benefit from) income taxes	(418)	170	379	96	74
Net loss	(12,394)	(18,873)	(32,627)	(8,478)	(7,682)
Accretion of preferred stock to redemption value	(25,606)	(33,553)	(52,336)	(12,178)	(11,273)
Net loss attributable to common stockholders, basic and diluted	$ (38,000)	$ (52,426)	$ (84,963)	$ (20,656)	$ (18,955)
Net loss per share attributable to common stockholders, basic and diluted	$ (3.09)	$ (4.18)	$ (6.65)	$ (1.62)	$ 1.50
Weighted-average common shares outstanding, basic and diluted	12,308,428	12,549,266	12,770,916	12,716,675	12,642,188

Source: SEC Form S-1 Filing.

Exhibit 4c

RAPID7, INC.

Consolidated Statements of Cash Flows

(in thousands, except share and per share data)

	Year Ended December 31,			Three Months Ended March 31,	
	2012	2013	2014	2014	2015
				(Unaudited)	
Cash flows from operating activities:					
Net loss	$ (12,394)	$ (18,873)	$ (32,627)	$ (8,478)	$ (7,682)
Adjustments to reconcile net loss to net cash used in operating activities:					
Depreciation and amortization	1,529	2,631	4,140	878	1,134
Amortization of debt discount	—	—	553	138	138
Stock-based compensation expense	1,720	2,047	2,159	528	575
Provision for doubtful accounts	431	460	581	172	165
Deferred income taxes	(433)	111	196	—	—
Loss on sale of property and equipment	25	—	—	—	—
Foreign currency re-measurement loss	—	—	—	—	241
Change in operating assets and liabilities:					
Accounts receivable	(6,621)	(4,012)	(7,127)	2,568	4,179
Prepaid expenses and other assets	(887)	28	(2,165)	(673)	(778)
Accounts payable	91	1,064	567	(902)	(688)
Accrued expenses	45	2,971	3,534	333	(3,928)
Deferred revenue	16,468	15,126	25,200	1,282	3,588
Contingent consideration	(1,058)	(3,081)	(560)	23	—
Other liabilities	393	915	2,193	1,992	44
Net cash used in operating activities	(691)	(613)	(3,356)	(2,139)	(3,012)
Cash flows from investing activities:					
Business acquisitions, net of cash required	(4805)	—	—	—	—
Purchases of property and equipment	(2133)	(2,778)	(7,082)	(5,014)	(573)
Proceeds from sale of property and equipment	14	—	—	—	—
Net cash used in investing activities	(6,924)	(2,778)	(7,082)	(5,014)	(573)
Cash flows from financing activities:					
Proceeds from issuance of Series D redeemable convertible preferred stock, net	—	—	30,818	—	—
Borrowings from term loan	—	18,000	—	—	—
Borrowings from line of credit	—	5,000	—	—	—
Repayments on line of credit	—	(5,000)	—	—	—
Payments of debt and equity issuance costs	(11)	(135)	—	—	—
Payments of capital lease obligations	(220)	(300)	(256)	(70)	(59)
Payments of contingent consideration related to business acquisitions	(2,622)	(1,500)	(856)	—	—
Repurchase of common and preferred stock	(3,260)	—	(3,526)	—	—
Proceeds from stock option exercises	140	257	489	39	408
Net cash (used in) provided by financing activities	(5,973)	16,322	26,669	(31)	349
Effects of exchange rate changes on cash	—	14	(20)	1	(244)
Net (decrease) increase in cash	(13,588)	12,945	16,211	(7,183)	(3,480)
Cash, beginning of period	21,255	7,667	20,612	20,612	36,823
Cash, end of period	$ 7,667.00	$ 20,612	$ 36,823	$ 13,429	$ 33,343
Supplemental cash information:					
Cash paid for income taxes	$ —	$ 34	$ 61	$ 29	$ 58
Cash paid for interest	$ 13	$ 96	$ 2,095	$ 402	$ 549

Source: SEC Form S-1 Filing.

Exhibit 7

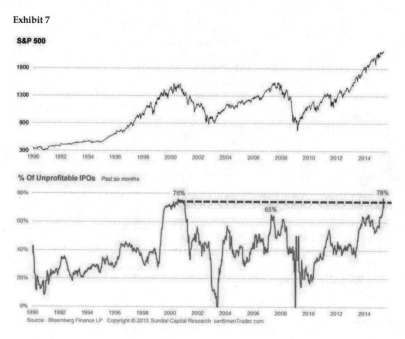

Source: Bloomberg Finance LP   Copyright © 2015 Sundial Capital Research sentimenTrader.com.

Corey Thomas Case Study Assignment Questions

1. Should Corey take Rapid7 public?
2. How should the company finance growth if it does not do an IPO?
3. Should Corey sell Rapid7 to a private buyer?
4. What is the value of Rapid7?

HARVARD | BUSINESS | SCHOOL

9-317-059
REV: MARCH 8, 2018

STEVEN ROGERS

MERCER COOK

United Housing — Otis Gates

Meet Otis Gates

Otis Gates, with his balding head, eyeglasses, and youthful skin, looked like someone's favorite grandfather. Indeed, he had four grandchildren and two great-grandchildren whom he adored visiting during his time away from work.

At 81 years old and 6' 5" tall, Gates had none of the bluster that one might expect from a wildly successful entrepreneur. Having started a new business at age 67, when most individuals think of retirement, Gates was now the co-owner and cofounder of a successful affordable housing management firm, United Housing. (See **Appendix A** for background on affordable housing.)

Now, almost 15 years after starting United Housing, Gates and his seven partners were considering retirement. Retirement would require sending out a *request for proposal* (RFP) to buyers in Boston interested in buying out Gates and his partners. As the de facto Chief Financial Officer (CFO), Gates was primarily responsible for putting the RFP together and evaluating the proposals that came in. Gates had to evaluate these proposals on two main criteria: personal economic benefit and the continued survival of United Housing. In terms of the former, Gates needed to evaluate whether or not he and his partners would get a good return on investment (ROI). In addition, he had to decide whether waiting a few years might yield a substantially higher ROI.

At the same time, Gates was committed to ensuring that United Housing was in a position to continue with its social mission intact. While excited about the prospect of moving to the next phase of his life, Gates found it critically important that United Housing remain a healthy, profitable, and socially involved company after he and his partners departed. Additionally, it was important to him to preserve United Housing's mission as a profitable organization that also served its community.

As he considered these questions while crafting the RFP, Gates was forced to evaluate the current state of his company, and its track record and reputation over the past 13 years.

About Otis Gates

Gates's humility could be traced back to his father. Gates grew up in Boston's Dorchester neighborhood, the son of a Pullman Porter. Pullman Porters were African Americans who worked on the

HBS Senior Lecturer Steven Rogers and independent researcher Mercer Cook prepared this case. It was reviewed and approved before publication by a company designate. Funding for the development of this case was provided by Harvard Business School and not by the company. Certain details have been disguised. HBS cases are developed solely as the basis for class discussion. Cases are not intended to serve as endorsements, sources of primary data, or illustrations of effective or ineffective management.

cross-country railroads, serving white passengers. When the porters unionized under the leadership of Asa Philip Randolph in 1937, it marked one of the most significant advances for African American labor rights.[1] Pullman Porters were widely admired in the African American community because they had relatively high pay compared with other African Americans and got to travel the country.[2]

Growing up, Gates never imagined that he would one day own the apartments in the housing complex he could then see from his bedroom window, along with hundreds of other residential buildings. Nor did he imagine he would graduate from both Harvard College and Harvard Business School.

But in 1952 Gates matriculated to Harvard College from the Boston Latin School. Although Harvard College had been integrated since the 1870s, in 1952 African American students made up less than 1% of the student body. Two years after Gates enrolled, the Supreme Court issued its landmark decision in *Brown vs. Board of Education*, which held that segregated schools were unconstitutional.[3,4] *Brown v. Board of Education* was a landmark moment, but integration did not happen overnight. When Gates graduated from Harvard, there were still only 12 African Americans in his graduating class of 1,200.

A member of the ROTC in college, Gates joined the Air Force in December after his graduation. His commanding officers offered Gates the options of serving from several military bases in the South. But Gates was reluctant to move anywhere in the region because of its Jim Crow laws. Jim Crow laws were a number of policies passed in the South that enforced discrimination against African Americans. These laws allowed for the creation of separate school districts for African Americans, required African Americans to sit at the back of buses and other forms of public transportation, prevented African Americans from building houses in white neighborhoods, required separate public facilities for whites and African Americans,[5] forbid interracial marriages, along with a host of other discriminatory policies. Gates, knowing that the South was the home of Jim Crow, requested a different posting. When

---

[1] Eric Arnesen, *Brotherhoods of Color: Black Railroad Workers and the Struggle for Equality* (Cambridge, MA: Harvard University Press, 2001).

[2] "Pullman Porters: From Servitude to Civil Rights," WTTW, http://www.wttw.com/main.taf?p=1,7,1,1,41, accessed May 30, 2016.

[3] The case consisted itself consisted of 13 African American plaintiffs from Topeka, Kansas, who were suing the Topeka schoolboard on behalf of their 20 children, who were forced to go to separate, segregated schools in their district. Oliver L. Brown, the named plaintiff in the case, had a daughter who was forced to walk six blocks to take a bus another mile to her segregated school, even though the white school was just seven blocks from her house, according to the complaint. At the urging of the Topeka branch of the NAACP, each of the plaintiffs tried to enroll their child in the nearest elementary school to their house. The Topeka Board of Education denied their requests, requiring all of them to enroll in the local African American elementary school.

The district court initially ruled in favor of the Topeka Board of Education, citing *Plessy v. Ferguson* decision. However, the NAACP lawyers appealed the case until it made it to the Supreme Court. The Supreme Court case *Brown v. Board of Education* actually included five separate cases rolled into one: the *Brown* case, *Briggs v. Elliott* (South Carolina), *Davis v. County School Board of Prince Edward County* (Virginia), *Gebhart v. Belton* (Delaware), and *Bolling v. Sharpe* (Washington, DC). Of the five cases, only the lower court in Delaware had found that the separate schools for different races was unconstitutional because the schools for African Americans were so clearly inferior to white schools.

Notably, *Brown v. Board of Education* did not simply decide that segregated schools were unequal because African American schools were of lesser quality. Rather, they found the even if the schools were of separate quality, segregation was unequal because it had negative psychological effects on African American children.

[4] The ruling overturned the decision in *Plessy vs. Ferguson*, which had been issued nearly 60 years before and declared that segregation in schools was legal under the theory that schools could be "separate but equal." In *Brown vs. Board*, the Supreme Court unanimously ruled that separate schools were inherently unequal, and that segregated schools therefore violated the Fourteenth Amendment of the U.S. Constitution, which guarantees all citizens "equal protection of the laws."

[5] Depending on the state, other races were sometimes included in Jim Crow or similarly discriminatory laws. For example, in California, an influx in Chinese immigrants led to several Jim Crow–like laws directed specifically at Chinese Americans.

his commanding officer told Gates he could move to Indiana, Gates was excited about the possibility of being stationed in a northern city that was within driving distance of major cities like Detroit and Chicago.

Gates was not aware that Indiana had one of the densest populations of members of the Ku Klux Klan, a white-supremacist organization best known for its lynching of African Americans. Gates spent the next three years at the Grissom Air Force Base in northern Indiana, afraid to walk outside the military base after dark. He spent most of his free weekends in Detroit and Chicago, fleeing the state at every opportunity.

After finishing his three-year service in the Air Force, Gates worked at the technology company Honeywell in its new computer department.[6] There, he wrote code and helped to manage the company's computer operations. After two years at Honeywell, Gates enrolled in Harvard Business School (HBS). He started at HBS in 1961, just months after a bus carrying 13 Freedom Riders (7 black, 6 white) was firebombed in Alabama, and the riders were beaten by Klan members.[7] He graduated from the business school in 1963, just a few months before Martin Luther King Jr. gave his famous "I Have a Dream Speech" at the March on Washington. Although he had entered business school with one other African American, Gates was the only African American to graduate in his class of more than 600 students. He reentered the workforce just as the Civil Rights Movement was building momentum and breaking down barriers for African Americans in all aspects of American life, including the workforce.

Gates had been interested in housing and architecture since his undergraduate years, and pursued this interest after earning his MBA. He was hired to work in the real estate division of Jones Kaufman and Ackerman, a real estate and law firm. After traveling the country as a trainee to get a better understanding of how Kaufman's business worked, Gates began working as a salesman for Kaufman in Michigan. In that job, Gates learned the ins and outs of selling both commercial and residential real estate.

Because of some racial tensions with his company, Gates transitioned to a job at Blue Shield in Michigan, working in the computer operations department of the nonprofit health insurer. At the same time, he and his college friend Melvin Miller pooled their savings of $12,500 to cofound a weekly newspaper, the *Bay State Banner*. Miller served as the publisher of the newspaper, while Gates ran the business side. Both founders maintained their full-time jobs, with Gates continuing at Blue Shield and Miller working as an assistant district attorney.

Months after the paper was founded in 1965, Gates decided he had to move to Boston for the good of the newspaper. So he got a job at Zayre, a discount retailer that was the predecessor to the T.J. Maxx

---

[6] Computers were only just starting to become common in workplace environments across America.

[7] The Freedom Riders were groups of individuals who protested the continued segregation of buses in the Jim Crow South. In 1960, the Supreme Court had ruled that segregated interstate bus terminals (and segregated restaurants within bus terminals) were illegal in the landmark *Boynton v. Virginia* case. That ruling followed up a similar ruling that had come almost 14 years before, in 1946 in the case of *Irene Morgan vs. Commonwealth of Virginia*, which found that Virginia's segregation laws were unconstitutional on interstate travel buses. While Rosa Parks is often given much-deserved credit for her refusal to give up her seat on a public bus in Montgomery, Alabama, Irene Morgan had refused to give up her seat on an interstate bus almost 15 years before Parks. Unfortunately, her name is less often remembered because the decision of the court was not enforced in the Southern states. Despite the court's ruling, segregation in interstate busing remained the norm. Similarly, while *Boynton v. Virginia* also ruled that segregated interstate busing (and segregated interstate bus terminals) were illegal, the law was not enforced in the South. It was this lack of enforcement that the Freedom Riders protested, by riding racially integrated buses throughout the South and challenging the segregation enforced there. The rides were sponsored by the Congress for Racial Equality and the Student Nonviolent Coordinating Committee, both civil rights groups. The firebombing made national news, even as the Freedom Riders continued to protest the enforcement of Jim Crow segregation throughout the South. It was into this politically charged climate that Gates entered Harvard Business School.

and HomeGoods stores. Gates worked in its computer operations department, but then decided to leave there as well.

Thanks to a recommendation from a friend, Gates transitioned into consulting for companies on information and operating systems at Andersen Consulting (which became Accenture), starting in 1968. Gates made partner in 1976, making him one of the first two African American partners at the company.

By 1985, Gates felt ready to transition away from Accenture. By this time, he had sold his interest in the newspaper and was ready to return to his roots in housing. Despite an impressive salary, Gates left Accenture and began privately developing commercial real estate with one partner. In 1987 they purchased a property for $395,000 and spent $3.9 million rehabbing it. Unfortunately, it did not succeed and foreclosure soon followed. But his work on that project led to Gates winning the role of project manager for a joint venture between the Minority Development and Education Association and the Quincy Geneva Community Development Corporation called the Brooks School Project, a 56-unit affordable housing development in Dorchester. That role required that Gates manage both the budget and operations of the development, while also working to make sure the development met all government regulations. Afterward, Gates was eager to continue working in the affordable housing market, and he joined Half Moon Management in 1988.

The History of United Housing

When the partners founded United Housing in 2003, they did not fit the most common profile of American entrepreneurs. Whereas almost 84% of entrepreneurs in 2016 were white and most likely under age 45,[8] Gates was a 67-year-old African American and already a grandfather when he and his diverse mix of seven partners cofounded United Housing.

All the partners had previously worked at Half Moon Management, an affordable housing management firm founded by three Haitian brothers in Boston in 1973. Gates served as a senior executive in the company, overseeing the company's finances. At the time of its founding, Half Moon Management was one of the few affordable housing management firms in the Boston area. Such firms specialized in managing affordable housing complexes. They were responsible for maintaining the properties, finding tenants, and responding to tenants' concerns, as well as dealing with any other property-related issues that arose.

In 2003, the three Haitian owners announced that they were ready to retire and wanted to sell the affordable housing division of Half Moon Management (the brothers also ran a commercial, market-rate business, in which Gates and his partners were not involved). Gates, who was 66 at the time, was not ready to retire, nor did he want to find another housing development firm to work for. So he, along with six other executives in the company and a lawyer who worked closely with Half Moon Management, decided to make an offer to the owners. Pulling together the deal in only a few months, Gates and his partners bought out the three Haitian brothers for $2.5 million. The owners were happy to pass the firm to Gates and his partners, knowing that they would continue their commitment to serving the community. At the time of the sale, Half Moon Management was still one of the only minority-owned affordable housing management firms in the Boston area.

---

[8] Jordan Weissman, "Entrepreneurship: The Ultimate White Privilege?," *The Atlantic*, August 16, 2013, http://www.theatlantic.com/business/archive/2013/08/entrepreneurship-the-ultimate-white-privilege/278727/, accessed July 5, 2016.

Instead of simply continuing as Half Moon Management, Gates and his partners decided to create a new company with an expanded scope. While they were proud of the work they had done for Half Moon, they did not want to be limited by its reputation for working with only small, residential complexes. Gates and his partners thus used the properties they had acquired from the previous owners of Half Moon Management to create United Housing. The partners divided responsibilities, with Gates serving as the CFO, though no official C-suite titles were ever given to any of the eight owners.

Initially, the company managed 720 units, and the owners made most of their income from their salaries at United Housing. The firm employed 31 employees who had worked at Half Moon and continued to work for Gates and his partners.

United Housing inherited more than just properties and employees from Half Moon. Despite the change in the company's name, Gates and his partners found that they were still widely viewed in the larger affordable housing sector of Boston as Half Moon. They had inherited their predecessors' reputation. Not only was this reputation a more limited view than Gates and his partners had imagined for their company, but it also meant that United Housing's new ownership inherited the mistakes made by the previous owners. Gates and his partners felt that these had been relatively small errors—a few quickly corrected code violations in one project.

Because of its inherited reputation, United Housing at first had trouble convincing private developers and Boston Housing Authority officials to use United Housing on their projects. Gates and his partners knew that the only way to create more opportunities for United Housing was to enhance their reputation.

Enhancing Reputation with a Big Project

One of the most significant and riskiest ways United Housing attempted to shift its reputation was by finding creative ways to generate value in housing projects that other firms considered "hopeless causes." One that United Housing considered taking on was an abandoned affordable housing complex in Dorchester called Quincy Heights. Gates and his partners thought the complex, with 129 units, had the potential to generate revenue for any firm that managed it. In addition, Gates and his partners believed that rehabilitating the abandoned complex would provide substantial benefits for the surrounding urban community. The neighborhood around Quincy Heights was a working-class neighborhood, with relatively high poverty levels. African Americans and foreign immigrants from the Caribbean and South America dominated the neighborhood, while there were relatively few Asian and Caucasian residents.[9]

There were several difficulties in developing and renovating these units. The reason that the complex had been abandoned in the first place was because of several problems with the basic design of the building. Many units inside were small and cramped, and did not meet state government regulations for the minimum size of a rental unit in an affordable housing complex. The paint was peeling, windows were broken, and the floors were rife with cracks. Moreover, the building had significant pest infestation. In short, the development would need to be almost completely redone, renovated from the ground up at a high cost. The previous owners of the complex had spent a measly $20,000 per unit on renovation. This amount was not sufficient to meet the project's deferred capital

---

[9] Mark Melnik and Lingshan Gao, "American Community Survey 2007–2011 Estimate: Dorchester," Boston Redevelopment Authority, retrieved April 4, 2016.

needs. Gates and his partners knew it would take more than $350,000 per unit in order to properly develop the Quincy Heights project.

For context, most affordable housing developments that Gates and his partners had taken on required spending around $20,000–$50,000 per unit on development. The large amount required for the Quincy Heights project made it obvious that private funding would not be enough to complete the project. United Housing would need government subsidies to help fund the Quincy Heights redevelopment. However, because United Housing was a for-profit company, it could not apply for federal or state government funds to help it defray the massive development costs for the Quincy Heights project the way a nonprofit might. The exceedingly high capital cost to develop the property had scared off all of the other for-profit firms that might have been interested. Given such a high price tag per unit, it would be years before the development became profitable, assuming that none of the previous problems returned and no future code violations occurred.

In addition to concerns about the capital required to renovate the complex, many affordable housing developers were also scared off by the surrounding neighborhood, which had a reputation for crime and decay.

Nonprofit firms that could have applied for government money to do the renovation were also afraid to get involved, for several reasons. First, most nonprofits dealing with affordable housing tended to work with smaller collections of units and on smaller projects in general. As a result, they lacked experience in managing such a large complex.

Second, the neighborhood was not particularly friendly to the entrance of any firm—for-profit or nonprofit—that wanted to rehabilitate the complex. Having already been burned once by the previous developer, who left the complex in its bad condition, the local community was skeptical about any firm that claimed to have an interest in renovating or developing the property. As a result, none of the nonprofits that worked in affordable housing in Boston had stepped up to take on the Quincy Heights project.

But despite these obstacles, Gates and his partners could not shake the feeling that they could create value in the properties, and that by doing so, they could both enhance the community and also improve the bottom line of United Housing. When he and his partners decided to take on the project, the shock sent ripples throughout the housing community in Boston. Many of the other for-profit affordable housing firms saw the decision as a huge mistake, one that could have severe negative economic consequences for United Housing.

United Housing's Social Mission: Good for Business?

In addition to evaluating its successes and failures, Gates also had to evaluate whether or not the company's core mission of serving the community was helping or hurting its bottom line. Because almost all affordable housing was in dense, urban areas with high minority populations, United Housing considered it vital to give back to those communities, both through creating additional programs and by hiring a diverse workforce that represented the communities they were serving.

Because affordable housing firms depended so heavily on government funding, all of them had to meet certain diversity requirements with regard to their workforce and certain requirements for giving back to local communities. (See **Appendix A** for more information on those specific requirements.) Gates and his partners were determined to exceed those requirements, in terms of both who they hired and how much they gave back to the communities in which they owned or managed developments.

As a result of this commitment, United Housing employed by far the most diverse workforce of any of its competitors in Boston. Whereas most affordable housing management and development firms in the Boston area had a workforce consisting of between 20% and 30% persons of color, United Housing boasted a workforce of 70% persons of color. Instead of hiring the "standard" labor forces, United Housing instead often hired contractors and employees from the local communities that it was serving, a significantly rarer practice in the affordable housing sector. Some people in the sector were skeptical of this practice, thinking that the quality of United Housing's product would suffer from using less experienced workers on its developments. But Gates and his partners believed that their diverse workforce actually added value to their firm because they engaged local community members in the development, thereby earning more community support and adding more value to the local community.

United Housing also exceeded the requirements for giving back to the community. Instead of settling for the standard practice of hiring security guards for its complexes (a practice that the company found to be largely ineffective at making neighborhoods more secure), United Housing redirected some of its funds toward creating a reading program for kids called Freedom School in the local community around one of its developments. The program was designed to keep kids off the streets, especially in the summer, while also enriching their educational experience. As a free program, the Freedom School generated no revenue for United Housing and actually cost it thousands of extra dollars to maintain every year. No other firm in Boston's affordable housing sector had taken on such a project, considering it to be a waste of money. Beyond simply serving the public good, Gates believed that these types of community projects actually added to the monetary value in the bottom line of United Housing.

Profile of United Housing's Business

By 2016, 13 years after its founding, United Housing had more than doubled its workforce and its portfolio. It supported 64 employees and more than 1,800 affordable housing units, primarily in the Roxbury and Dorchester neighborhoods of Boston. Dorchester and Roxbury were both dominated by low-income residents, predominately African Americans and immigrants. Over 75% of residents in both neighborhoods were people of color,[10] and over half of the residents of Dorchester were not American citizens. [11] Both neighborhoods also had extremely low rates of educational attainment. In Roxbury, a quarter of the population had not graduated from eighth grade.[12] United Housing's projects in these neighborhoods generated almost $3 million in gross revenue every year.

The management structure of United Housing was unique among corporations in that there was technically no C-suite overseeing the company, and no partner who overshadowed the others. Instead, the company was run by eight partners, each with an equal share of the company and equal say in all of United Housing's decisions but different areas of specialization. (See **Exhibit 1** for partners' biographies.)

Beneath the partners, United Housing divided its organization into separate divisions, each of which was concerned with maintaining a specific complex or set of complexes. Each discrete affordable housing complex that it managed—such as Roxbury Hills or Newton Antonio complex—had a separate team within the company. Overall, United Housing generated $659,000 in net profit each year. (For United Housing's balance sheet and income statement, see **Exhibit 2.**)

---

[10] "At a Glance," Boston Redevelopment Authority, Bostonredevelopmentauthority.org, retrieved March 25, 2015.

[11] Mark Melnik and Lingshan Gao, "American Community Survey 2007–2011 Estimate: Dorchester."

[12] Areavibes, "Roxbury, Boston, MA Public Schools, High Schools & Education Data," www.areavibes.com, retrieved April 15, 2016.

But Wait, There's More

While a respectable income, $659,000 dollars in net profit for United Housing actually represented a relatively small piece of the potential financial return for the co-owners. The bulk of their potential financial return would not come from Gates and his partners' sale of their shares of United Housing. Rather, it would come from the shares of the housing complexes that Gates and his partners owned outside of United Housing as limited partners (see **Appendix A** for more information on limited partners versus general partners) that generated a majority of their financial returns. To understand their business model, it is first necessary to understand how affordable housing firms generally created value for their owners.

Coming from Both Sides: The Affordable Housing Approach

As of 2017, when an affordable housing complex was developed, the government incentivized private investors to put money into the property by offering them a number of tax breaks and tax credits (see **Appendix A**). Investors in these affordable housing complexes were often big banks. Usually, the tax benefits of investing in affordable housing expired after 10 to 15 years. At that point, investors were usually ready—or even in a rush—to sell their ownership stake (known as a limited partnership) in the affordable housing complexes (for more on limited partnerships, see **Appendix A**).

Because affordable housing management companies were already the general partner in many of the complexes they managed, owners of the companies often had first access to buying out the limited partners. And because the limited partners were often using the housing developments for tax credits rather than for generating significant revenue, the investors were often willing to sell their ownership shares relatively cheaply. Sometimes, banks and other limited partners were so eager to sell that they were willing to be bought out for what they initially paid without interest, which was the case in several of Gates' and his partners' dealings.

But Gates and his partners did not buy out the limited partners through United Housing. Instead, Gates and his partners set up separate LLC corporations to buy an ownership stake in the housing development as limited partners. For example, in the case of Blue Mountain Housing Complex, they set up a separate LLC called Blue Mountain LLC, which then bought 99% of the property. One percent of the property remained for United Housing, the general partner. In other words, Gates and his partners owned the Blue Mountain Housing project through two different businesses. They were both the general partner (through United Housing) and the limited partner (through Blue Mountain LLC). This practice is common in the world of affordable housing.

Why did the owners buy through a separate corporation instead of through United Housing? When Gates and his partners bought through a separate company, that company became a limited partner. Limited partners in an affordable housing complex assume little personal financial risk. Were Gates and his partners to buy all their shares in Blue Mountain through United Housing, the general partner, then they would be open to much more financial risk if something went wrong with the properties (i.e., there was a code violation). But by investing in the properties through a separate entity, the owners of United Housing were able to be limited partners in a number of the properties that United Housing managed.

When considering his exit from the world of affordable housing, Gates knew that he and his partners would make a majority of their money from selling their limited partnership shares than from selling United Housing itself. Of the 16 properties that United Housing managed, Gates and his partners separately owned 6 of them as limited partners. Of these properties, only a few complexes were ready for relatively immediate sale: Blue Mountain (217 units), Newton Antonio (227 units), and Roxbury Hills (88 units).

The amounts they paid for the various properties included:

$1.75 million for 99% of Newton Antonio complex. (The same price Bank of America had paid for its ownership in the complex in the mid-1990s.)

$3 million for 99% of Blue Mountain complex.

$3.6 million for 100% of Roxbury Hills.

Making a Decision

While all the partners were involved in the decision to try to sell, much of the decision rested on Gates's shoulders. Looking at his diverse portfolio in the Boston area, including both their properties and their community engagement, Gates had to decide whether it was the right time to exit United Housing.

Gates had to consider a variety of factors in his decision.

One was the increasing demand for affordable housing in the Boston area, where home prices and rents were increasing more quickly than median wages or inflation.[13] As a result of these mismatched rates, an increasing number of families were struggling to make their rental payments. More than 40% of the lower-middle-class households in the greater Boston area were spending more on rent than they could afford to. As a result, the demand for affordable housing in the Boston area had skyrocketed.

This demand was only expected to increase because the number of working and lower-income families was expected to increase. Since the 1990s, the number of working families in Boston had increased by 40%, with nearly half of that increase attributed to an increase in low-income households.[14] As a result, the demand in particular for low-income-oriented affordable housing had gone up.

At the same time, the neighborhoods of Roxbury and Dorchester, where Gates and his partners owned and managed properties, had rapidly increased in value. Once viewed as undesirable areas and made up mostly of minority populations, those parts of Roxbury and Dorchester were seeing increasing numbers of white, well-educated young professionals and their families moving into the neighborhoods, particularly those that seemed safe and offered family-friendly options (see **Appendix B** on the Boston housing market).

At the same time, Gates had to balance profits against personal considerations. At 81 years old, he was still energetic, but he was also ready for a transition. With a newborn great-grandchild, Gates was thinking of spending more time with his family. While most of his partners were younger than Gates — ranging in age from 55 to 72 — they, too, were almost unanimously ready to move on. While Gates might be willing to wait a year or two to sell if the delay were to generate significantly more profit, waiting longer than a few years was undesirable for him and his partners.

If he did exit, how much should he expect to receive for his properties? And how could Gates and his partners exit in way that not only benefited them, but also left United Housing strong enough to continue thriving and giving back to the community?

---

[13] Evan Horowitz, "Boston Housing Market is Expensive But Could Be Worse," *Boston Globe,* May 31, 2016, https://www.bostonglobe.com/metro/2016/05/31/boston-housing-expensive-but-could-worse/fJw0ao3zBV21z5FbD9XC5J/story.html, accessed July 23, 2016.

[14] Alex E. Weaver, "Boston's Mid-Market Housing Crunch Will Ease as Middle Class Shrinks," *Boston Inno Magazine,* May 16, 2016, http://bostinno.streetwise.co/2016/05/16/affordable-homes-in-boston-report-finds-middle-class-demand-shrinking/, accessed July 11, 2016.

Exhibit 1   Partners of United Housing

United Housing was run by 8 equal partners, with equal ownership shares in the company and equal decision making power. The partners consisted of 2 women and 6 men, a majority of whom were African American.

Otis Gates: Served as the de-facto chief financial officer. He was responsible for managing United Housing's expenses and balancing its budget, as well as calculating the costs and potential benefits of new projects.

Shauna White: Served as the director of compliance. In this role, she was responsible for ensuring that all properties managed by United Housing met government regulations. She began her career in affordable housing in 1986 as a property manager at Half Moon Management, before rising to become director of operations.

Ryan Rudolph: Served as the general counsel. He started his career in affordable housing at the Boston Redevelopment Authority, where he worked as a lawyer.

Gabriel Hubbard: Served as the general manager, responsible for overseeing the company's management of its various properties. He worked in property management since graduating from the University of Massachusetts in 1979.

Michael Brown: Served as the comptroller, responsible for all of the company's accounting practices. His job included recording all rent. Prior to working at United Housing, Michael worked as the comptroller for McNeil & Associates, Inc., a consulting firm specializing in professional training and business strategy.

Alexandra Cobb: Served as the director of human resources. In her own words, she was a "one-woman HR department." An immigrant from Jamaica, Alexandra started out as an administrative assistant and then office manager before rising to head of the HR department.

Jerome Williams: Served as director of maintenance, responsible for maintenance-related tasks (like cleaning, etc.) and maintenance workers. Prior to joining Half Moon Management, Jerome managed the engineering division of the Guyana Rice Milling and Marketing Authority, where he oversaw all the civil, mechanical, mill, project, and electrical engineers. In 1990, he returned to the United States and became the director of property maintenance at Half Moon.

R. Evan Jones: Served as senior portfolio manager. Evan was responsible for managing the individual property managers of each of United Housing's properties. He first got involved in housing as a construction worker in high school. After graduating from college, he worked his way up through Half Moon Management, starting as a maintenance supervisor.

Source: Company documents.

Exhibit 2   The Finances of United Housing (balance sheet and income statement)

Balance Sheet for United Housing in 2014			
ASSETS			
		Cash	899,143
		Accounts receivable	485,880
		Holdback escrow	500,000
		Deposit	59,000
		Deferred costs, net of $1,630,975 of accumulated amortization	250,912
		Investments in LLC and partnership	15,845
	Total other assets		2,210,780
	Property and equipment, at cost		
		Land and land improvements	775,379
		Building and building improvements	2,816,931
		Furnishings and equipment	256,044
		Less accumulated depreciation and amortization	1,057,134
	Property and equipment, net		2,791,220
	Total assets		5,002,000
LIABILITIES			
		Accounts payable - operations	39,799
		Accrued wages	21,118
		Accrued vacation	18,514
		Deferred gain on sale of partnership interest	500,000
	Total liabilities		579,431
	Commitments and contingencies -		
		Members' capital	4,422,569
	Total liabilities and members' capital		5,002,000
Revenue and Costs for United Housing in 2014			
REVENUE			
	Sources of Revenue for UH in 2014		
		Annual Property Management Fees:	1,400,000
		Annual Development Fees:	400,000
		Annual Payroll and Cost Reimbursements*:	1,000,000
		Annual Accounting Fee Income*:	50,000
	Costs for UH in 2014 were:		
		Payroll and related:	1,000,000
		General and Administrative:	800,000
		Operating and Maintenance (managing their properties):	300,000
		Taxes and Insurance:	85,000
		Office expenses:	6,000
	Net Income in 2014		659,000

Source: Company documents.

Appendix A: Background on Affordable Housing

A. What Is Affordable Housing?

Affordable housing refers to units that middle- and low-income families can afford to rent. With regard to low-income residents, affordable housing is also sometimes known as Section 8 housing. "Section 8" refers to a specific section of the Housing Act of 1937 (see the section below about the history of affordable housing in the United States), which authorizes the government to subsidize rent payments for low-income families. Affordable housing also refers to housing built specifically for middle-class workers.

Affordable housing is a popular practice in the United States, Europe, and Australia that aims to give more of the population access to housing without breaking the household budget. Affordable housing units have different income requirements, depending on whether they are meant to cater to middle-income or low-income tenants. Usually, to qualify for middle-income affordable housing, a household must make between 66% and 200% of the median household income for that area. To qualify for low-income-oriented affordable housing, households usually need to make less than 60% of the median income in that county. To qualify for government subsidies, tenants usually can make no more than 50% of the median income for the area, though this can vary from city to city.[15] As of 2013, over 10 million households in the country lived in affordable housing units. This represented less than half of the nearly 20 million households that were eligible for affordable housing.[16]

There are two types of affordable housing units: those owned by the government, and those that are not owned by the government. In government-owned affordable housing properties, households are usually asked to pay somewhere between a quarter and a third of their income in rent to the government, regardless of what the unit's market value is. When the unit is not owned by the government, tenants usually pay between a quarter and third of their income in rent to the landlord. The government then pays the landlord the difference between the market value of the unit and rent paid by the tenants. The market value is determined by a thorough third-party investigation, which determines the value of the rent by comparing rents in similar buildings in the area along with evaluating the structure and space of the units themselves. Thus, in effect, the government is subsidizing affordable housing for the tenants of private landlords.

Table A-1 shows the relationship between affordable housing rents and income in Boston in 2016. (AMI stands for Area Median Income, which is simply the median income in a given area. In this instance, that area is the city of Boston in 2016.)

---

[15] "Common Questions about Affordable Housing," http://affordablehousingonline.com/housing-common-questions, accessed July 11, 2016.

[16] National Low Income Housing Coalition, "Affordable Housing is Nowhere to be Found for Millions," March 2015, http://nlihc.org/sites/default/files/Housing-Spotlight_Volume-5_Issue-1.pdf, accessed July 11, 2016.

Table A-1 Relationship between Affordable Housing Rents and Income in Boston, 2016

Bedrooms	50% AMI	60% AMI	65% AMI	70% AMI	75% AMI	80% AMI	90% AMI	100% AMI	110% AMI	120% AMI	150% AMI
Micro	$684	$821	$890	$958	$1,026	$1,094	$1,232	$1,368	$1,504	$1,642	$2,052
Studio	$760	$913	$989	$1,065	$1,140	$1,216	$1,369	$1,521	$1,672	$1,825	$2,281
1	$887	$1,065	$1,153	$1,242	$1,331	$1,419	$1,597	$1,774	$1,951	$2,129	$2,662
2	$1,013	$1,216	$1,318	$1,419	$1,521	$1,622	$1,825	$2,027	$2,230	$2,433	$3,041
3	$1,140	$1,369	$1,482	$1,597	$1,711	$1,825	$2,053	$2,281	$2,509	$2,737	$3,421
4	$1,267	$1,521	$1,648	$1,774	$1,901	$2,027	$2,281	$2,534	$2,788	$3,041	$3,801

Source: Table from the Boston Redevelopment Authority, http://www.bostonredevelopmentauthority.org/housing/income-price-limits, accessed July 1, 2016.

From this table, we can determine that a Boston resident making 50% or less of the AMI would pay no more than $684 per month in rent for a micro apartment. Some tenants might actually pay less than $684, depending on their income. If $684 per month is more than 30% of their monthly income, tenants would pay less than that amount in rent every month. In the same table, we can see that a family renting a four-bedroom apartment or house in Boston would pay no more than $2,534 per month.

It is important to note that, in affordable housing, median income is determined by household size. Larger households typically make more money than smaller households, and also need more income to provide for their members. As a result, most cities in the United States and Europe separate median income by household size. **Table A-2** is a sample chart of median incomes in the city of Boston in 2016.

Table A-2 Median Incomes in Boston, 2016

HH Size	50% AMI	60% AMI	65% AMI	70% AMI	75% AMI	80% AMI	90% AMI	100% AMI	110% AMI	120% AMI
1	$34,350	$41,250	$44,650	$48,100	$51,550	$54,950	$61,850	$68,700	$75,550	$82,450
2	$39,250	$47,100	$51,050	$54,950	$58,900	$62,800	$70,650	$78,500	$86,350	$94,200
3	$44,150	$53,000	$57,400	$61,850	$66,250	$70,650	$79,500	$88,300	$97,150	$105,950
4	$49,050	$58,900	$63,800	$68,700	$73,600	$78,500	$88,300	$98,100	$107,950	$117,750
5	$53,000	$63,600	$68,900	$74,200	$79,500	$84,800	$95,400	$105,950	$116,550	$127,150
6	$56,900	$68,300	$74,000	$79,700	$85,350	$91,050	$102,450	$113,800	$125,200	$136,600

Source: Table from the Boston Redevelopment Authority, http://www.bostonredevelopmentauthority.org/housing/income-price-limits, accessed July 1, 2016.

From this chart, we can see that the AMI for Boston in 2016 for a household with only one member was $61,850, but that the median for a household with six members was $113,800.

The government subsidizes affordable housing as a way to incentivize developers and owners to provide affordable housing, since otherwise they would have little economic incentive for offering reduced-rent units. Governments subsidize affordable housing because providing affordable housing has been inextricably linked to the health of a city and its working population.

B. History of Affordable Housing in the United States

While there had been a few attempts at creating affordable housing units in the early twentieth century, affordable housing became a widespread practice in American cities in the 1930s during President Franklin D. Roosevelt's administration.[17] At the time, low-income workers struggled to find affordable housing in the cities in which they worked, often enduring long commute times or living in decrepit, decaying projects. Increasingly, members of the Roosevelt administration felt that good housing was a right that should be enjoyed by every citizen regardless of income level.[18] In 1937, Congress passed the Housing Act of 1937, which stated that the government would provide funds to local governments in cities and towns across the nation if they built housing projects oriented toward low-income and middle-income families. The administration then created the United States Housing Authority to oversee loans and subsidies to local housing authorities creating affordable housing units.[19]

In 1940, the administration made another concentrated effort at providing affordable housing, this time primarily for middle-income Americans. As part of the string of New Deal policies aimed at strengthening the American middle class, FDR's administration created the Mutual Ownership Defense Housing Division (MODHD) of the Federal Works Administration.[20] The MODHD was particularly concerned with creating affordable housing for defense workers, who were flooding coastal regions because of increased military spending at the beginning of World War II. The MODHD spent over $17 million in creating housing for middle-income Americans, the equivalent of nearly $300 million in 2016.[21] While the MODHD only lasted for two years before closing, it had a significant impact on the national political discussion around affordable housing. Affordable housing for low-income and middle-income Americans came to be seen as vital to a city's health. [22]

After the New Deal and the end of World War II, affordable housing became a smaller part of the national conversation as incomes were on the rise. It was not until the 1980s that affordable housing surged again in both the United States and Europe, in response to what was seen as growing income inequality and a dearth of housing options, particularly for poor urban workers.[23] One of the results of the initiatives to create more affordable housing was the Low Income Housing Tax Credit (LIHTC)

---

[17] Charles L. Edson, "Affordable Housing: An Intimate History," Apps.americanbar.org. http://apps.americanbar.org/abastore/products/books/abstracts/5530024%20chapter%201_abs.pdf, accessed July 10, 2016.

[18] Charles L. Edson, "Affordable Housing: An Intimate History."

[19] Charles L. Edson, "Affordable Housing: An Intimate History."

[20] Kristin M. Szylvian, *The Mutual Housing Experiment: New Deal Communities for the Urban Middle Class* (Urban Life, Landscape, and Policy). (Philadelphia: Temple University Press, 2015), accessed July 11, 2016.

[21] Kristin M. Szylvian, *The Mutual Housing Experiment: New Deal Communities for the Urban Middle Class.*

[22] Kristin M. Szylvian, *The Mutual Housing Experiment: New Deal Communities for the Urban Middle Class.*

[23] Alain Bertaud, "10th Annual Demographia International Housing Affordability Survey: 2014," http://www.demographia.com/dhi2014.pdf, accessed July 12, 2016.

law, which was passed as part of the Tax Reform Act of 1986. This law gives owners a tax credit for developing (but not maintaining) affordable housing complexes.[24]

C. How Do Affordable Housing Complexes Get Funding?

Affordable housing is funded through both public and private investment. On the public side, the government funds, subsidizes, and encourages affordable housing in several ways:

1. **By investing in affordable housing projects.** Federal and local governments invest millions of dollars every year in buying and maintaining property that they offer as affordable housing. These properties are often those referred to as "the projects" in big cities around the country. Approximately 1.2 million households live in public housing in the United States.[25]

2. **By paying additional rent for affordable housing tenants.** As mentioned above, most affordable housing requires that tenants pay no more than a third of their income for rent. This limit almost always means that tenants in affordable housing are paying less than market rate for their units. As a result, most developers would have no incentive to develop affordable housing units, since they would get paid less than market value for those units. In order to incentivize developers, the government pays the difference between the tenant's rent and market rate for affordable housing units.

3. **By providing tax incentives for private investors who invest in affordable housing developments.** Most of these tax incentives are stipulated and regulated by the Community Reinvestment Act of 1977 (CRA). The CRA was passed in order to combat the discriminatory lending practices of banks, which were far more likely to make loans to high-income borrowers. The CRA encourages banking institutions to serve middle- and low-income members of their community by assessing banks for their community involvement and then considering those assessments when authorizing banks to open new branches. By investing in affordable housing complexes, banks meet their CRA requirements with limited risk.

D. Why Do Governments Subsidize Affordable Housing?

There are a number of reasons local and federal governments subsidize affordable housing for low-income and middle-income workers. A lack of affordable housing has been shown in numerous economic studies to put a severe strain on the economy.[26,27] When low- and middle-income Americans do not have access to affordable housing, they increase the strain on the public transportation system and often spend less on consumption and have less in savings.[28] This lowered consumption makes local and national economies vulnerable to minor dips and major crashes, especially in the long term.

---

[24] "Common Questions About Affordable Housing," http://affordablehousingonline.com/housing-common-questions, accessed July 11, 2016.

[25] Department of Housing and Urban Development (HUD), "Public Housing," http://portal.hud.gov/hudportal/HUD?src=/program_offices/public_indian_housing/programs/ph, accessed July 11, 2016.

[26] Michelle Gabriel, Keith Jacobs, Kathy Arthurson, Terry Burke, and Judith Yates, *Conceptualising and measuring the housing affordability problem,* National Research Venture 3: Housing Affordability for Lower Income Australians, Australian Housing and Urban Research Institute, May 2005.

[27] Trip Pollard, *Jobs, Transportation, and Affordable Housing: Connecting Home and Work* (Richmond: Southern Environmental Law Center and Housing Virginia, 2010), https://www.southernenvironment.org/uploads/publications/connecting_home_and_work.pdf, accessed July 11, 2016.

[28] Trip Pollard, *Jobs, Transportation, and Affordable Housing: Connecting Home and Work.*

The lack of affordable housing also leads to higher levels of homelessness and lower levels of education in the community, which put both an immediate strain on a local economy and limit the economy's ability to grow in the future. [29],[30]

E. Benefits to Large Corporations and Individuals of Investing in Affordable Housing

Because of government tax credits, many private enterprises, particularly banks, benefit from investing in affordable housing complexes. Corporations and individuals receive tax credits for 10 to 15 years, depending on the development and the ownership contract. After this point, the benefits to banks investing in these complexes tend to expire, motivating them to sell their stake.

F. Criticism of Affordable Housing in the United States

Critics argue that affordable housing provisions, in combination with government zoning and building regulations regarding housing, inhibit the free market and create skewed real estate markets that lean toward the rich. [31] These critics argue that if governments did not interfere in the housing market, the demand for housing for middle-class and lower-income tenants would be high enough that some businesses would fill that demand. [32]

G. Limited Partners versus General Partners

There are two types of owners in a privately owned affordable housing.

Limited partners: Limited partners typically consist of companies (particularly banks) and, occasionally, individuals who invest in the property. Typically, limited partners together own a majority of the complex, usually 99% or more (Otis Gates, Personal Communication, July 7, 2016). [33] While they own a majority of the complex, limited partners are not liable for the property at all. That means that if the property receives a code violation or something else goes wrong, limited partners are not personally vulnerable to any legal repercussions. As a result, investing in affordable housing is a relatively safe investment. [34],[35]

General partners: General partners are typically the management companies that are contracted to manage and maintain affordable housing complexes. Typically, general partners own around 0.01% (or, in rare cases, up to 1%) of a complex. [36] Yet despite their small ownership share, general partners bear most of risk in an affordable housing complex. They are responsible for any code violations or

---

[29] Michelle Gabriel et al., *Conceptualising and measuring the housing affordability problem.*

[30] Trip Pollard, *Jobs, Transportation, and Affordable Housing: Connecting Home and Work.*

[31] Cheryl Cort, "Why the Left Is Wrong About Affordable Housing," Greater Washington, March 4, 2015, http://greatergreaterwashington.org/post/25509/why-the-left-is-wrong-about-affordable-housing/. Accessed July 8, 2016.

[32] Cheryl Cort, "Why the Left Is Wrong About Affordable Housing."

[33] Mary Joe Sallins and Robert Fontenrose, "Housing Partnership Agreements," Internal Revenue Service, 2003, https://www.irs.gov/pub/irs-tege/eotopicg03.pdf, accessed July 11, 2016.

[34] Office of the Comptroller of Currency, "Investing in Low-Income Housing Tax Credits," Spring 2006, http://www.occ.gov/static/community-affairs/community-developments-investments/spring06/investinginlowincome.htm, accessed July 11, 2016.

[35] Mary Joe Sallins and Robert Fontenrose, "Housing Partnership Agreements."

[36] Office of the Comptroller of the Currency, "Low-Income Housing Tax Credits: Affordable Housing Investment Opportunities for Banks," March 2014, http://www.occ.gov/topics/community-affairs/publications/insights/insights-low-income-housing-tax-credits.pdf, accessed July 11, 2016.

other problems that occur. General partners usually receive a fee from the limited partners for maintaining and managing the property. These fees typically range between 4% and 12% of the rent.[37]

H. How Does Someone Obtain Affordable Housing?

Usually, residents can obtain an affordable housing unit either by placing their name on a list and waiting for their turn (section 8 housing and some privately owned complexes) or by entering a lottery with the landlord or property owner. In order to comply with government regulations, owners of affordable housing units are required to create a lottery system that does not discriminate based on race, ethnicity, or gender.[38] Almost all affordable housing lotteries, however, do show preferences for certain individuals or households.[39] Which preferences are legal or illegal depend on the local housing regulations.[40] Some groups that commonly receive preference in the lotteries include:

Veterans

Victims of domestic violence

People who were evicted through no-fault evictions (for example, someone whose home burned down in a fire or was flooded in a storm)

People who are or will imminently become homeless

People with disabilities

Working people (As contrasted with unemployed individuals. Although, in accordance with federal regulations, any preference for working people must also include people who are unable to work due to disability.)

Local residents of the community

In addition to these preferences, most affordable housing developments are required to set aside a certain number of units for extremely low-income households, usually defined as those making 30% of the AMI or less. Any federally run affordable housing program must set aside at least 40% of its units for extremely low-income households.

I. Benefits of Working in Affordable Housing

In some ways, working in affordable housing is low risk compared to other real estate ventures. Because the government is subsidizing the rents, and because affordable housing is only available to roughly a quarter of those who qualify for it financially (and an even smaller percentage in many concentrated urban areas), it is never difficult for affordable housing developments to find tenants (Otis Gates, Personal Communication, July 7, 2016). Because the government is subsidizing much of the rent, affordable housing landowners rarely have to deal with chasing down delinquent rent payments. Furthermore, if a tenant, for whatever reason, vacates a unit, there is always a long line waiting via the

---

[37] Jordan Muela, "Property Management Fees—Part 1," Managemyproperty.com, http://www.managemyproperty.com/articles/property-management-fees-part-i-10, accessed July 11, 2016.

[38] "Section 8 Questions," Affordable Housing Online, http://affordablehousingonline.com/housing-help/search/Section-8/, accessed July 12, 2016.

[39] "Section 8 Questions," Affordable Housing Online.

[40] "Section 8 Questions," Affordable Housing Online.

lottery system. As a result, affordable housing landlords have to do little work to find new tenants and are almost always operating at full capacity (Otis Gates, Personal Communication, July 7, 2016).

J. Risks of Working in Affordable Housing

Because of its reliance on government, state, and sometimes even city governments, affordable housing is a strictly regulated industry with hundreds if not thousands of pages filled with rules about what is permissible (Otis Gates, Personal Communication, July 7, 2016). Affordable housing laws regulate a variety of elements in the unit, including a minimum size and upkeep standards. Violating any of these regulations, even by accident, can lead to a suspension that prevents the landlord from renting out any of the properties in the complex, sometimes even after the original problem is fixed.

K. Major Players in the Affordable Housing Industry

There are three entities primarily involved in the affordable housing market.

Government

The federal and local governments are responsible for regulating affordable housing and providing the financial subsidies that incentivize developers. Governments also own some low-income housing, though they rarely own middle-class affordable housing.

Nonprofit Businesses

In the affordable housing market, there are a variety of nonprofit entities across the United States and in Boston that help build, develop, and maintain affordable housing developments. These nonprofits are usually oriented toward low-income housing developments or developments in impoverished neighborhoods. Such nonprofits are usually funded through a combination of government funds and grants and private financing from corporations and individuals. For example, a nonprofit like the Boston-based Mercy Housing might apply for government funds and raise private capital in order to refurbish an abandoned house or apartment to return the units to the livable standards. As a condition of receiving the funds, Mercy Housing would have to commit to refurbishing the units up to government standards for affordable housing.

For-profit Businesses

For-profit businesses, like United Housing, are ineligible to receive funds from local or federal governments. Instead, they generate income by either managing affordable housing complexes that are owned by the government or another private owner, or by developing new affordable housing projects. Often, a nonprofit developer will hire a for-profit business to manage its affordable housing property.

Appendix B: The Boston Housing Market, 2003–2016

As of 2014, Boston was considered one of the 10 hottest housing markets in the United States, with housing prices and property values continuing to climb.[41] Boston was also distinguished from other housing markets by its low downside. Economists speculated that even if another large recession were to hit the United States, housing prices in Boston might only drop somewhere between 2% and 6%, as opposed to 27% for the rest of the country.[42]

Boston's rental market was particularly strong in 2016 relative to the rest of the country. There were several factors that contributed to Boston's surging rental market:

1. **The large concentrations of schools and universities.** Boston had the highest concentration of colleges and universities of any urban area in the United States and, in 2016, was home to more than 150,000 college and university students,[43] meaning that students made up almost a quarter of Boston's population.[44] Students are by nature a transient population, usually far more interested in renting than buying.

2. **General population increase.** Boston's overall population had increased by more than 14% since 1990, but construction of new housing failed to keep pace with population growth.[45] Indeed, little housing was built between the 1950s and 2000 because the city's population was shrinking during most of that period. The relatively slow rate of construction had not accelerated quickly enough to keep up with the surging population. [46]

3. **High cost of living.** The cost of living in Boston was 39% higher than the average for the United States, but the median salary was roughly even with the rest of the country.[47] As a result, many residents simply could not afford to buy and were pushed into the rental market.

As a result of these factors, the values of properties in Boston surged after the turn of the twenty-first century. The average rental price of a one-bedroom apartment in Boston exceeded $2,000 per month in 2016, the third highest in the country.[48] And Boston's rental prices showed no signs of slowing

---

[41] Laura Entis, "The 10 Hottest Housing Markets for 2014," Entrepreneur.com, January 9, 2014, https://www.entrepreneur.com/slideshow/230732, accessed July 11, 2016.

[42] Tim Logan, "Think Boston Housing is Expensive Now? Wait Five Years," *Boston Globe*, January 7, 2016, https://www.bostonglobe.com/business/2016/01/07/think-boston-housing-expensive-now-wait-five-years/6qTjKdarDT2AdZkpqrJWaJ/story.html, accessed July 10, 2016.

[43] "Boston by the Numbers: Colleges and Universities," Boston Redevelopment Authority, Research Division, March 2011, http://www.bostonredevelopmentauthority.org/getattachment/3488e768-1dd4-4446-a557-3892bb0445c6/, accessed July 11, 2016.

[44] United States Census Bureau, "Boston city, Massachusetts QuickFacts," retrieved June 17, 2016.

[45] Raleigh Werner, "Average Rent in Boston, MA: Median Prices + Trends," Jumpshell.com, https://www.jumpshell.com/posts/average-rent-in-boston, accessed July 10, 2016.

[46] Rachel Slade, "Boston Is Getting Really Expensive," *Boston Magazine*, March 2016, http://www.bostonmagazine.com/property/article/2016/02/21/boston-expensive/, accessed July 10, 2016.

[47] Rachel Slade, "Boston Is Getting Really Expensive."

[48] Raleigh Werner, "Average Rent in Boston, MA: Median Prices + Trends."

down. The vacancy rate in Boston decreased by more than 50% between 2010 and 2015, remaining at a relatively low 2%. [49]

The neighborhoods in Boston experiencing the highest surges in property value were the traditionally working-class neighborhoods of Dorchester, Roxbury, and East Boston. Young professionals were increasingly pushed out of their traditional neighborhoods, like the South End, and increasingly sought housing in these low-income neighborhoods. As a result, property value assessments in the neighborhoods had skyrocketed. In Roxbury, Dorchester, and East Boston, new property assessments increased by between 19% and 20% between 2014 and 2015. [50] While the rental values of these properties used to be far lower than those of the greater Boston area, average monthly rents in Dorchester and Roxbury had increased to approximately $2,000 per month for one-bedroom apartments. [51] Rental rates are tied to overall property values. While there is no fixed rule about how rent is related to overall property value, a general rule of thumb is that monthly rents usually amount to somewhere between 0.8% and 1.1% of a property's total value. [52,53]

[49] Raleigh Werner, "Average Rent in Boston, MA: Median Prices + Trends."

[50] Raleigh Werner, "Average Rent in Boston, MA: Median Prices + Trends."

[51] Raleigh Werner, "Average Rent in Boston, MA: Median Prices + Trends."

[52] Amanda Dixon, "How to Figure out How Much You Should Charge for Rent," Smartasset.com, March 30, 2016, https://smartasset.com/mortgage/how-much-you-should-charge-for-rent, accessed July 11, 2016.

[53] Jennifer D. Melville, "How Much Should I Charge to Rent My House?," SFGate.com, http://homeguides.sfgate.com/much-should-charge-rent-house-8314.html, accessed July 11, 2016.

United Housing—Otis Gates Case Study
Assignment Questions

1. Is United Housing's social mission in the best interest of its shareholders, including investors and owners? Why? Why not?
2. Should Otis Gates sell United Housing?
3. What are two reasons he should not sell United Housing?
4. If he sells, what should be the asking price?
5. In addition to price, what else should Otis Gates require of the potential buyers?

Notes

1. "Juanita Lott: Timing Your Exit: Access and Opportunity Podcast." Morgan Stanley. October 31, 2019. www.morganstanley.com/ideas/carla-harris-juanita-lott-access-and-opportunity-podcast.
2. Ibid.
3. Ibid.
4. Ibid.
5. Blau, John. "Oracle Buys Bridgestream." PCWorld, IDG News Service, September 5, 2007. www.pcworld.com/article/136839/article.html. Accessed March 10, 2021.
6. "Juanita Lott: Timing Your Exit: Access and Opportunity Podcast." Morgan Stanley. October 31, 2019. www.morganstanley.com/ideas/carla-harris-juanita-lott-access-and-opportunity-podcast.
7. Ibid.
8. Ibid.
9. "Exit Strategies—Examples, List of Strategies to Exit an Investment." Corporate Finance Institute. September 30, 2020. www.corporate financeinstitute.com/resources/knowledge/strategy/exit-strategies-plans/
10. Cunningham-Cook, Matthew. "Speculative 'Blank Check' Companies Surround Tony Blinken, Biden Administration." *The Intercept.* January 10, 2021. https://theintercept.com/2021/01/10/spac-blank-check-companies-biden/
11. "Updated: SPAC Returns Fall Short of Traditional IPO Returns on Average." Renaissance Capital. October 1, 2020. www.renaissancecapi-tal.com/IPO-Center/News/71816/Updated-SPAC-returns-fall-short-of-traditional-IPO-returns-on-average.

12. Huddleston Jr., Tom. "What Is a SPAC? Explaining One of Wall Street's Hottest Trends." CNBC. February 24, 2021. www.cnbc.com/2021/01/30/what-is-a-spac.html.

13. "General Catalyst's SPAC Catalyst Partners Acquisition Files for a $400 Million IPO." Renaissance Capital. March 11, 2021. www.renaissancecapital.com/IPO-Center/News/79224/General-Catalysts-SPAC-Catalyst-Partners-Acquisition-files-for-a-$400-milli.

14. Sharkey, Grace. "Vista Eyes SPAC for Another Attempt at Omnitracs Exit." FreightWaves. March 11, 2021. www.freightwaves.com/news/vista-eyes-spac-for-another-attempt-at-omnitracs-exit.

15. Chancellor, Edward. "A 300-Year Bubble Worth Remembering." Reuters. December 12, 2019. https://www.reuters.com/article/us-england-finance-breakingviews/breakingviews-chancellor-a-300-year-bubble-worth-remembering-idUSKBN1YG2NH

16. PricewaterhouseCoopers. "Global IPO Watch—Q4 2020." PwC. www.pwc.com/gx/en/services/audit-assurance/ipo-centre/global-ipo-watch.html. Accessed March 16, 2021.

17. Thomas, Jason M. "Where Have All the Public Companies Gone?" *The Wall Street Journal*. November 17, 2017. www.wsj.com/articles/where-have-all-the-public-companies-gone-1510869125./

18. McKinney, Jeffrey. "45 GREAT MOMENTS IN BLACK BUSINESS—NO. 3: BET Holdings $72.3M in IPO." *Black Enterprise*. January 12, 2019. www.blackenterprise.com/45-great-moments-in-black-business-no-3-bet-holdings/.

19. Ibid.

20. Whitford, David. "Taking BET Back from the Street Seven Rocky Years after Black Entertainment Television's IPO, Founder Bob Johnson Asked Himself, 'Why Do I Need Shareholders Anyway?'" *Fortune*. November 9, 1998. www.archive.fortune.com/magazines/fortune/fortune_archive/1998/11/09/250838/index.htm. Accessed March 16, 2021.

21. Ibid.

22. "$15,000 Loan to $3 Billion Franchise." *Forbes*. June 6, 2013. www.forbes.com/forbes/2001/1008/042tab/?sh=1d1a7edf252d.

23. "Fellowship for Serving African American Communities." Harvard Kennedy School Center for Public Leadership. https://cpl.hks.harvard.edu/fellowship-african-american-communities#:~:text=The%20Fellowship%20for%20Serving%20African,%2C%20economic%20development%2C%20public%20policy%2C. Accessed March 25, 2021.

9

Black Intrapreneurs

"The Virgin Group could never have grown into the more than 200 companies it is now were it not for a steady stream of intrapreneurs who looked for and developed opportunities often leading efforts that went against the grain."[1]
— Richard Branson, founder of The Virgin Group

As NOTED IN my book *Entrepreneurial Finance: Finance and Business Strategies for the Serious Entrepreneur, Fourth Edition,* an intrapreneur is a person who succeeds by engaging in entrepreneurship in a corporate environment. The intrapreneur creates new products or services that are distinctively different from or the same as the company's core business, or the intrapreneur can target a completely new customer base with existing or new products or services. The intrapreneur who is not a member of the company's research and development or new product teams has the primary objective of increasing the corporation's revenues and profits.

One of the best examples of a successful intrapreneur is the brilliant Black business executive Linda Gooden. As a powerful force inside and outside of the company, she worked at Lockheed Martin for more than two decades.[2]

In the late 1980s, Lockheed's main source of revenue was from its contracting work with the U.S. Department of Defense. The company's projects were focused on delivering large and complex technology solutions to meet the DoD's needs. At the time, the company had only two standalone information technology (IT) contracts outside of the Defense Department, but the revenue from those contracts was relatively small. Linda Gooden was working as a lead on one of those two contracts with the Social Security Administration, and she wondered why the company did not pursue more IT contracts outside of the defense arena. She and her team researched the feasibility of such expansion and concluded that a new business model was emerging for the U.S. government in the IT sector. Looking at the market and policy trends, they concluded that the U.S. government's need for IT services would increase substantially over the impending years and that federal IT procurement policy would need to change to meet the demand. They anticipated the need to shift from in-house development to the increased use of outside contractors. She recognized that this shift would benefit companies that provided IT services.

On her own initiative, she set out to convince senior management that this strategic move was essential for Lockheed's long-term viability and growth. She was a convincing intrapreneur. To service this new market, Gooden persuaded the tech giant to create the Lockheed Martin Information Technology (LMIT) subsidiary, with herself as president, a condition in her proposal.

The federal contract proposal solicitation and submission process was complex, and Gooden had to learn, through trial and error, how to develop, prepare, and submit successful bids as well as keep abreast of changes in federal procurement policies. She recalled:

> We won our first two jobs with the Social Security Administration very easily. As soon as we felt we understood the market and knew how to execute a successful bid, the one thing we had not counted on occurred—the market changed. Instead of writing a proposal and waiting for the customer to answer, we were required to give oral proposals. I learned that you have to pay attention to the changes in legislation but also to changes in the market that you're working in. We won our second oral proposal. And we learned a hard lesson. Change is constant. In business the strategic advantage is usually fleeting and so you have to always adjust.[3]

As Gooden had predicted, the U.S. federal government's expenditure on IT services has increased substantially. In the federal government budget for 2021, the government has allocated $53.36 billion to civilian federal agency IT budget. This figure did not include the portion of the budget allocated to the Department of Defense or another classified IT spending.[4]

During her 10-year tenure as president of LMIT, Gooden grew the unit's revenue from $8 million to $2.5 billion with a staff of 11,000 working in over 50 locations and 16 foreign countries. LMIT enabled Lockheed Martin to not only become competitive in the market but to be a dominant player in the federal IT space. Gooden was then named executive vice president of Lockheed's Information Systems and Global Solutions (IS&GS) unit, a business unit established in 2007 to provide integrated IT solutions, systems, and support to civil, defense, intelligence, and other government customers. Today, the business unit generates $10 billion in revenue and employs a global team of 40,000 employees operating across the U.S. and 20 countries around the world.[5] In 2013, she retired from IS&GS after a 20-plus year career at Lockheed.

Gooden has received many awards and honors for her accomplishments over her nearly 40-year career in IT in the Aerospace and Defense industry. Among her accolades, she was recognized as one of the Top 50 Most Powerful Women in Business by *Fortune* for three consecutive years and in *The Washingtonian* magazine as one of Washington's Most Powerful Women. *Black Enterprise* magazine featured her as one of the 100 Most Powerful Executives in Corporate America for 2009. She has been inducted into the Maryland Business Hall of Fame and named to Corporate Board Member Magazine's Top 50 Women in Technology. She was selected as Executive of the Year by the Greater Washington Government Contractor Awards and as Black Engineer of the Year by U.S Black Engineer and IT magazine. And, in 2002, she won Federal Computer Week's Federal 100 Eagle Award and received Women in Technology's Corporate Leadership Award.

She holds a bachelor of science degree in business administration and master of business administration from the University of Maryland. She also received a degree in computer technology from Youngstown

State University. In 2005, Gooden was awarded an honorary doctor of public service from the University of Maryland College, in 2010 she was awarded an honorary doctorate in law from Morgan State University, an HBCU, and an honorary doctorate in engineering from Drexel University in 2012.[6]

Intrapreneur vs. Entrepreneur

Like entrepreneurs, most intrapreneurs are problem solvers and risk takers. But as Table 9.1 shows, there are some major differences between these businesspeople.

Table 9.1   Comparison of Entrepreneur and Intrapreneur

	Entrepreneur	Intrapreneur
Status	Self-employed, owner or co-owner of company	Employee of a company allowed to pursue entrepreneurial venture within the company
Bringing idea to market	Develop idea/product/service and start company to bring to market	Selected by company management to pursue venture and bring idea/product/service to market under the company
Ownership	Owns enterprise/initiative	Enterprise/initiative is owned by the company
Capital	Uses own funds or secures funding from investors	Company provides funding for initiative
Customers	Has to build own customer base	Has established customer base
Resources & support systems	Builds own organization, network, support and infra-structural systems	Works within an established corporate and organizational structure with existing resources and support system

	Entrepreneur	**Intrapreneur**
Recognition/ rewards	Reaps all the recognition and rewards	Most of the recognition & rewards go to the company but the intra-preneur can get career rewards— promotion, bonus, etc.
Risk	Bears all the risk – in case of failure, will face finan-cial, reputational risk	Risk is borne by the company – intrapreneur may keep job and salary, in case of failure
Standards of operation	Determine their own opera-tional strategy	Must adhere to corporate standards of operation
Stakehold-ers	Investors, employees, cus-tomers, board members	The first and most important stakeholder is corporate leadership without whose buy-in is required for the venture to go forward. Then similar stakeholders as an entrepreneur

Intrapreneur Categories

All intrapreneurs are not the same. They can be categorized as follows:

Developer

Gooden's success as an intrapreneur places her in the category of developers, meaning that she did not create a new product or service but generated more revenues and profits for the company through the development of a new customer base. Developers are intrapreneurs who sell existing products/services to an entirely different market of clients.

One of the greatest success stories of intrapreneurship is that of a White developer in the Black consumer market. During the Great Depression, from 1928 to 1934, the Cadillac division of General Motors was on the brink of being shut down due to low sales. At that time, Blacks were not permitted in Cadillac showrooms to make a purchase.

Nicholas Dreystadt was Cadillac's national service manager and head of its repair and service department. Sensing an opportunity for the company, Dreystadt made a pitch to Alfred P. Sloan, the chairman of General Motors Company (GM), and the person to whom the Business School is named after at the Massachusetts Institute of Technology (MIT). He told Sloan and GM's Board of Directors that the Cadillac division could be saved if they sold the car to a new customer base, "the Negro."[7] Blacks were barred from buying this automobile, a symbol of White affluence and success, because GM believed that Black ownership of Cadillacs would damage its brand. Furthermore, they assumed that Blacks could never afford the car.

Dreystadt pointed out several of the fallacies concerning the ability of Blacks to afford Cadillacs and the negative effect of such ownership on the viability of the brand when he informed them that many Blacks already owned Cadillacs. He knew this fact from the servicing and repair records of his division for cars owned by Blacks. Members of the board had assumed incorrectly that the Blacks were chauffeurs for White owners of the cars. Dreystadt argued that Blacks also wanted to drive in the symbol of success, the Cadillac. So, Blacks, including the universally popular heavyweight boxing champion Joe Lewis, paid Whites to purchase the car for them. Blacks paid a premium to own a Cadillac. The board was persuaded and approved Dreystadt's plan. They gave him 18 months to show success. By the end of 1934, Cadillac sales had already increased by 70%, reaching the break-even point for the division.[8] By 1940, the revenue for the division had risen tenfold compared to 1934.[9]

Innovator

Like an entrepreneur, an innovator identifies an unmet customer need or problem. Such a person then creates a new product or service in response to that customer need or problem. The new product or service can then be sold to either existing or new customers.

Karen Thomas's success as an intrapreneur is through her role as an innovator. A Black woman who has loved books her entire life, she had a long career in the book publishing industry. Starting in 1992 as an editorial assistant at Berkley Publishing, she worked at the company for over five years, eventually becoming an editor. Her experience at this publishing firm enabled her to gain a keen understanding of the editorial process as well as an exposure to a wide range of book genres. She recounts, "I learned everything from how to do a character count to line editing, writing revision letters, and dissecting a book. But most importantly, I learned to enjoy so many different types of books."[10]

She left Berkley Publishing for an editorial position at Kensington Publishing Company. Kensington, located in New York City, was founded in 1974 by Walter Zacharias and Roberta Bender Grossman. Initially specializing in paperback romance novels, the company later expanded into the science fiction, fantasy, thriller, true crime, and western genres. In 1994, Zacharias noted the lack of Black representation in romance books—both as authors and protagonists. He decided to launch an imprint, Arabesque, to promote Black female authors. Arabesque Books was successful in publishing several new women authors and did well within the African American book market. Zacharias began talks with Robert Johnson, CEO of Black Entertainment Television (BET), to start jointly a book club, using BET's television presence to gain members. Johnson counter offered with the idea to buy Arabesque. BET bought the imprint and retained Kensington as publisher for a five-year period. As part of the deal, Kensington was able to publish African American fiction but not romance novels for a period of five years.

By 2000, Thomas had become editorial director at Kensington. The publishing industry, which had been predominantly White, was changing and Thomas noticed the emergence of many talented African American authors, along with an increasing demand for books that spoke to and were about the African American experience. Although Kensington was publishing a variety of Black authors at the time, Thomas felt that the company was not well positioned to take advantage of the emerging market trends. She noted, "I wanted to develop a way to focus those titles toward the community and also to focus some of the publicity and attention those titles should receive. I didn't want those titles to get lost in the huge list of [Kensington] titles."[11]

She approached senior management and suggested that the company launch a spinoff that would focus exclusively on recruiting, cultivating, and marketing Black authors. The company agreed and the imprint, Dafina Books, was launched in 2000 with Thomas heading it as founding editor. Dafina, which is Swahili for "an unexpected treasure," was established to focus on publishing original hardcover and paperback fiction and nonfiction books aimed at the African American book-buying market. As Esi Sogah, executive director of Dafina, noted in February 2020, "When it was first established, Dafina's slogan was "Publishing books by and about African-Americans." At a time when African American was a genre by default, having an imprint that acquired, promoted, and published books categorized in this way was vital."[12]

Within five years, Thomas increased Dafina's gross revenue from $5 million to more than $12 million.[13] During her nine-year tenure at the company, Thomas was able to launch the careers of several African American authors including Mary B. Morrison and Wahida Clark. Today, Dafina Books prides itself as being the leading publisher of commercial fiction written by and about people of African descent. It publishes books in a diverse range of genres including historical fiction, women's fiction, street lit, suspense, romance, teen, and inspirational. It publishes over 50 books a year in hardcover, trade paperback, mass market, and eBook. Dafina currently publishes the works of many well-known African American authors including Mary Monroe, Kiki Swinson, De'nesha Diamond and Lutishia Lovely, Rochelle Alers, ReShonda Tate Billingsley, Tu-Shinda Whittaker and Rebekah Weatherspoon, Briana Cole, Nita Brooks, Sharina Harris, Porscha Sterling, and Leo Sullivan.[14]

Benefits and Risks of Intrapreneurship

The benefits of intrapreneurship for the *employee* include the following:

1. The autonomy and flexibility to bring to fruition an idea or concept without the personal exposure to the associated financial risk;
2. Monetary rewards in terms of increases in compensation or performance bonuses;
3. Boost to employee's career profile and prospects both within and outside the company;

4. An increased sense of purpose and value as a contributor to the company's success;
5. Involvement in work that is challenging, interesting, and meaningful;
6. Opportunities to develop new skills that can be helpful for career mobility; and
7. The financial and organizational support of the company.

The risks for an *employee* associated with an intrapreneurial venture include the following:

1. Mistakes or failures can be detrimental and result in demotion or loss of job.
2. As the intrapreneur is an employee of a company, he/she does not have ownership of the new product/service and therefore has no claims to it should management decide to give the development and/or execution of the project to another employee.

The benefits of intrapreneurship for the *company* include the following:

1. Allowing employees the autonomy to pursue work that interests them and that they are passionate about creates an engaged workforce that is motivated to use their talents and skills to contribute to the success of the company;
2. Fostering an environment that encourages innovation and departure from the status quo, while valuing the lessons learned from failures, will encourage more and more workers to step forward with new concepts thereby increasing the pool of innovative ideas for the company;
3. Encouraging employees to think creatively and come up with innovative solutions that help keep a company more nimble, adaptive, and responsive to market dynamics, potentially leading to longer-term viability and sustainability of the company;
4. Ensuring that employees are working for a company that encourages creativity and fosters an environment where employees are free to

pursue new ideas, with the necessary organizational support to bring those ideas to fruition, will attract individuals who have an entrepreneurial spirit. In general, employees, particularly millennials, would prefer to work for a company that values and rewards these efforts to be innovative over a company that does not. Employees with greater job satisfaction will have less incentive to look for employment elsewhere, thereby lowering staff turnover rates. Recruiting is easier for companies that foster intrapreneurship;

5. Empowering employees to develop cross-functional proficiency in management, technical, and leadership skills while working on their ventures, which provides the company with highly trained staff that can be utilized in various departments across the company; and

6. Creating value for the organization, if the venture is successful, by developing new products/services, new revenue streams, and its overall growth.

While there are several benefits to intrapreneurship within a company, there are a few downsides as well. First, after acquiring valuable skills at the company's expense, employees may choose to leave. Second, if change brought about by the new venture is not managed properly then it could create tension and disruption within the company.

Intrapreneurship Models

Successful intrapreneurship often occurs in companies through systematic processes and practices. Two such intentional approaches to developing new business are through either the Enabler or the Producer model. The latter model exists when a company establishes formal resources, procedures, or even a distinctive department unit that is tasked with generating new ideas. The Enabler model is relatively more haphazard, but does have a formal structure in place. Company employees are allowed and even encouraged to come up with new ideas, but they are instructed to use a specific process. In contrast to these two models, a third way is the Opportunist model, which operates with almost no guardrails, with companies being less structured with no established system or process.

Several organizations, particularly tech companies, use "10% or 20% Time" to give employees an allocated percentage of hours in their daily work schedule devoted to thinking up new ideas and projects that are not necessarily related to their jobs. This flows from the Enabler model. Alternatively, several tech companies hold hack-a-thons, all-night competitions for coders and engineers, to develop new ideas or prototypes. This is characteristic of the Producer model.

A great example of the Opportunist model occurred at Sony. Following the merger with Nintendo, Sony engineer Ken Kutaragi re-imagined the Nintendo game console as one imbued with more power and more user-friendly. He faced resistance from Sony senior management, who viewed the gaming industry as a passing trend and did not see the strategic value in further penetrating the market. Finally, a senior manager saw potential in Kutaragi's suggestions and supported the engineer's ideas. In 1991, Kutaragi developed the Sony PlayStation, which became the most popular game station in the world, generating approximately 40% of Sony's profits by the late 1990s.

Another successful example of the Enabler model occurred at DreamWorks. The animation studio unit encourages all of its employees to be a part of the creative filmmaking process, regardless of their position or the department in which they work. The studio provides employees with training in script writing and pitching stories, and supports them when they pitch story ideas and scripts to management. Several of the company's most popular movies, including *Shrek* and *Madagascar*, were envisioned and developed by staff not directly involved in filmmaking.

Another successful employer of the Enabler model is Google. The company allows employees to spend 20% of their time working on personal projects, with the hope that this will spur productive creativity. In fact, some of Google's most successful products have been developed through this process. Paul Buchheit, a computer engineer and developer, created the template for Gmail and came up with ideas like search functionality and extra storage facility, ideas that no other company in the industry was providing, which ultimately led to the success of Gmail. Other products that came out of intrapreneurial efforts include Google News (created by research scientist Krishna Bharat), Driverless Cars, and Google Glasses.

Finally, one of the best Producer models was an integral part of Apple. Steve Jobs, its co-founder, organized a small, independent team to develop the Macintosh computer. Jobs noted that the developers of the Mac was a team of intrapreneurs: "The Macintosh team was what is commonly known now as intrapreneurship . . . a group of people going in essence back to the garage, but in a large company."[15] That intrapreneurial spirit has led to many innovative products for Apple, including the iPod, the iPhone, iTunes, and iCloud.

Introduction to the Case Study

This case study is about Dr. William Carson and his successful intrapreneurial experiences. The case will let the reader observe and analyze all of the traits of an intrapreneur. Another fascinating aspect of this case study is that the intrapreneur is a Black psychiatrist who works for a company headquartered in Japan.

HARVARD | BUSINESS | SCHOOL

9-318-005
SEPTEMBER 14, 2017

STEVEN ROGERS
ALYSSA HAYWOODE

Dr. William Carson — Intrapreneurial Innovation in the Pharmaceutical Industry

Dr. William Carson didn't have an office when he joined a U.S. affiliate of Otsuka Pharmaceutical Company, Ltd. in 2002. What he did have was a thorough knowledge of aripiprazole, an antipsychotic drug that Otsuka had developed in Japan and was co-marketing in the United States with Bristol-Myers Squibb.

Working with a handful of colleagues, Carson set up shop in Princeton, New Jersey.

At the end of 2002, the Food and Drug Administration approved aripiprazole for the treatment of schizophrenia. Otsuka and Bristol-Myers Squibb marketed the new drug under the name Abilify.

Sales took off.

Table 1   U.S. Sales of Abilify[1]

2003	$364 million
2004	$747 million
2005	$1 billion

Source: Drugs.com.

Abilify won approval in Europe. And Otsuka officials wanted to win approval to sell Abilify in Japan to treat bipolar disorder. But that would require running clinical trials to test the drug on Japanese patients.

An Otsuka official came to Carson and asked if he could run those trials. He would have five years — a standard amount of time — and $100 million to get the work done. Coming in under budget would, of course, increase overall profits.

Clinical trials can fail. But the fact that Abilify had been successfully tested in the United States meant it had a strong chance of being approved in Japan.

Carson said he could run the trial. All he had to do was figure out how.

---

[1] Pharmaceutical Sales 2003, Drugs.com, https://www.drugs.com/top200_2003.html, accessed July 30, 2017.

HBS Senior Lecturer Steven Rogers and independent researcher Alyssa Haywoode prepared this case. It was reviewed and approved before publication by a company designate. Funding for the development of this case was provided by Harvard Business School and not by the company. The contract research organizations are fictional. HBS cases are developed solely as the basis for class discussion. Cases are not intended to serve as endorsements, sources of primary data, or illustrations of effective or ineffective management.

From the Segregated South to Harvard

William Carson was born in the 1950s to African-American parents. He and his family lived in a middle-class, black neighborhood in Columbia, South Carolina.

His mother and father were both teachers. He went to racially segregated schools until junior high school. As a kid, he read the encyclopedia for fun, starting with the letter "A" and moving through the volumes systematically.

He had pivotal role models and mentors. "My family doctor used to encourage me," Carson said. "His name was Dr. C.E. Morgan. And he always would say you're smart; you can do it; you like science. It was that kind of encouragement at a very young age that led me to think that I could do it."

Carson's older sister went to Duke University. And by the time Carson was in the sixth grade, he was telling people he was going to go to Harvard University. "People were like, 'oh yeah that crazy Carson kid, whatever.'"

Nonetheless, Carson bought a copy of the *Insider's Guide to Colleges.*

> I purchased that in ninth grade, and that was my encyclopedia at that time. I knew every school. I knew all of their average SAT scores. I knew all the requirements. And when people said, 'how did you get into Harvard?' I said it was completely contrived. I had planned it. I knew what courses I needed to take. I knew what scores I needed to have. It wasn't random.

Carson's high school guidance counselor was an African-American family friend. "He would tell anybody: 'That Bill Carson; he made me do my job that year, because everything had to be typewritten.'" Carson would drop off forms one day, then go back the very next day to ask if they had been mailed.

At Harvard, Carson majored in the History of Science, an interdisciplinary field. He took classes in art history and architecture. He went on to Case Western Reserve Medical School in Cleveland, impressed by the school's "organ systems approach" to medical education that focused on organs instead of disciplines. (See **Exhibit 1** for his full resume.)

"I became fascinated with psychiatry in medical school," Carson said. He had thought he would become a small-town physician in South Carolina, just like his mentor Dr. Morgan. But he found that, "I felt immediately comfortable on a locked psychiatric ward."

"I went into medicine to advocate for patients. Let me tell you, mental patients need advocates. They are the most poorly treated people in all of medicine."

"It pushed all of my advocacy buttons that these folks needed help, especially black folks."

Carson did his psychiatry residency at Tufts University School of Medicine in Boston. Then he became a psychiatry professor at the Medical University of South Carolina, teaching students and seeing a dozen patients a day. He found himself reading the newspapers, scanning the articles about adults acting erratically, to see what patients he would be treating the next day.

After 10 years in academic medicine, Carson followed an old friend into the pharmaceutical industry. He became the Group Director in the Princeton office of Bristol-Myers Squibb in 1998. The experience was "business school on steroids." Carson was determined to learn something new every day, and he planned to stay for five years, to see if he could be successful or not.

He began running drug trials on atypical antipsychotics, second generation drugs that are used to treat psychiatric disorders. Among the drugs that Carson was studying was aripiprazole.

Otsuka had discovered the drug and was working with Bristol-Myers Squibb to develop and market the drug. The work drew Carson into a close relationship with Taro Iwamoto from Otsuka. At the time, Iwamoto was Otsuka's Global Product Leader for aripiprazole.

The two would engage in "Appleby conversations," talking over dinner at what was in those days the nicest place to eat.

Eventually, Iwamoto asked if Carson would move from Bristol-Myers Squibb to Otsuka.

Otsuka and Bristol-Myers Squibb had an agreement: No Otsuka employees could leave and work for Bristol-Myers. But there was no reciprocal agreement, because it seemed highly unlikely that anyone at Bristol-Myers Squibb, a Fortune 500 company whose roots stretch back to 1858, would leave to join Otsuka, which, at the time the agreement was made, had only a small presence in the United States: a single research laboratory located in Maryland.

Months later, it was this loophole that left Carson free to make the unlikely move from Bristol-Myers Squibb to Otsuka.

Intrapreneurship

"Intrapreneurship is the spirit and act of entrepreneurship in a corporate setting," Steven Rogers writes in *Entrepreneurial Finance: Finance and Business Strategies for the Serious Entrepreneur*, his 2014 textbook published by McGraw-Hill Education.

Intrapreneurs function in corporate settings as if they were entrepreneurs. They spot new opportunities. They come up with new products and services. They develop new customers and markets. They help companies evolve.

"An intrapreneur brings the creativity and drive often associated with startups to larger, established companies," *Forbes* magazine notes.[2]

One classic example is Steve Jobs' work at Apple.

"When Steve Jobs and a group of 20 Apple employees separated themselves from the remaining organization in order to develop the world-famous Apple Macintosh computer, they operated with complete freedom, often neglecting organizational rules and structures for the sake of their vision. Jobs' and this team's intrapreneurial efforts resulted in radical product and service innovations, an outcome traditional R&D labs often fail to generate," according to a Deloitte Digital white paper[3] called "Five Insights into Intrapreneurship: A Guide to Accelerating Innovation Within Corporations."

---

[2] "Why Big Companies Should Act Small to Engage Millennials," Forbes, November 14, 2016, http://www.forbes.com/sites/wesgay/2016/11/14/why-big-companies-should-act-small-to-attract-millennials/#17093d5f4b08, accessed November 17, 2016.

[3] "Five Insights into Intrapreneurship: A Guide to Accelerating Innovation Within Corporations," Deloitte Digital, 2015, https://www2.deloitte.com/content/dam/Deloitte/de/Documents/technology/Intrapreneurship_Whitepaper_English.pdf , accessed December 1, 2016.

Without intrapreneurs, companies can stagnate.

"It has been well-documented that big companies typically struggle with innovation," *Entrepreneur* reported.[4] "Once companies get to a certain size, their investors become more conservative, their leaders less entrepreneurial, decisions are managed by consensus and their employees become less willing to stick their neck out with 'out-of-the-box' ideas, that may not work out and result in losing their jobs."

"Companies like Google, 3M and Intel are well known for their efforts in this regard," *Forbes* added. "But, they are surely the minority, and more big companies need to get on board here."[5]

Some companies build intrapreneurial cultures to engage millennials, as *Forbes* reported in November, 2016: "Employee engagement is one of the biggest challenges in the American workforce. Earlier this year a Gallup survey indicated only 29% of millennials are engaged at work, which is the lowest percentage among any generation."[6]

An intrapreneurial culture offers these workers a chance to engage in creative innovations.

One example of an African-American intrapreneur is Linda Gooden, an innovator who used an Opportunistic Model. While she was working at Martin Marietta, an aerospace and chemicals manufacturer, Gooden started an IT business inside the company.

"With four of her team members, Gooden mapped out a business plan to significantly increase Martin Marietta's government IT business," the *Washington Post*[7] reported in 2004. "She projected $11 million in revenue in the first year. She asked for $200,000 in seed money to cover the cost of preparing bids. Her boss gave her $600,000."

"After the Martin Marietta-Lockheed merger, Gooden was able to consolidate several of the company's IT departments into one unit and expanded that unit through acquisitions and internal moves." She became "a top executive at one of Lockheed's five divisions and one of the company's nine business-unit presidents."

Another example of an intrapreneur is Ken Kutaragi. He was working at Sony when he noticed his daughter playing with her Nintendo and decided he could improve the game's sound quality.

---

[4] "Big Companies That Embrace Intrapreneurship Will Thrive," *Entrepreneur*, March 19, 2015, https://www.entrepreneur.com/article/243884, accessed December 11, 2016.

[5] George Deeb, "Big Companies Must Embrace Intrapreneurship To Survive," Forbes, February 18, 2016, https://www.forbes.com/sites/georgedeeb/2016/02/18/big-companies-must-embrace-intrapreneurship-to-survive/#4f2fb18a48ab, accessed 1/29/2019.

[6] Wes Gay, "Why Big Companies Should Act Small To Engage Millennials," Forbes, November 14, 2016, https://www.forbes.com/sites/wesgay/2016/11/14/why-big-companies-should-act-small-to-attract-millennials/#7754f69b1628, accessed 1/29/2019.

[7] "Linda R. Gooden," *The Washington Post*, April 26, 2004, https://www.washingtonpost.com/archive/business/2004/04/26/linda-r-gooden/85801a24-beea-4d07-9360-f706cc140ca8/?utm_term=.6477cd6f3ed7, accessed November 17, 2016.

The Intrapreneurship Conference's website[8] explains: "Because the Sony Corporation was not involved in computer games, Ken Kutaragi negotiated to keep his job at Sony, while working as an outside consultant (entrepreneur) for Nintendo on their computer gaming devices."

"After Ken's success as a consultant to Nintendo the senior executives at Sony Corporation threatened to fire him. Fortunately for Ken, he had the strong support of Norio Ohga, the Chief Executive Officer of Sony Corporation. Chairman Ohga personally recognized the value of Ken's creativity, entrepreneurial spirit, and innovation, so he encouraged Kutaragi's efforts."

"Then with the Sony Corporation CEO's support (and begrudgingly the rest of Sony's senior management's blessing) Kutaragi continued to work as a part-time consultant to Nintendo. Ken successfully developed a CD-ROM-based system for Nintendo. Nintendo elected not to go forward with the CD-ROM system. Ken Kutaragi saw the market and business opportunity of computer gaming systems for Sony. With his Intrapreneurial spirit, Ken pressed hard to convince the Sony Corporation to enter the electronic gaming business.

"Ken was persistent and he went on to lead the effort to help Sony develop its own gaming system, which became the blockbuster product success 'PlayStation.'"

Otsuka Pharmaceutical

As of 2016, Otsuka's motto[9] was, "People creating new products for better health worldwide."

Otsuka's roots stretched back to 1921 in Japan when Busaburo Otsuka founded Otsuka Seiyaku Kogyo-bu, a factory where 10 employees worked manufacturing chemical raw materials. Over decades, Otsuka diversified its product line, adding intravenous solutions, over-the-counter medicines, and energy drinks.

In 1964, as part of the Otsuka group, Otsuka Pharmaceutical Company, Ltd. was founded. As it grew, the company added a drug development department. It launched a blood pressure medicine, a bronchodilator for asthma sufferers, and so-called "nutraceuticals," which are "functional beverages and foods that help maintain and promote day-to-day well-being."

Its website in 2016 described Otsuka as "an international network of over 150 companies and more than 40,000 employees across Asia-Pacific, America, Europe, and the Middle East."

Otsuka America Pharmaceutical, Inc. (OAPI) is part of an alliance that sponsors Connect 4 Mental Health (C4MH), "a nationwide initiative calling for communities to prioritize serious mental illness and advocate for new approaches that aim to help make a difference for individuals living with these conditions, their families and their communities," according to OAPI's website.

"The campaign encourages collaboration among the mental health community and other community-based organizations—such as emergency services, law enforcement and public housing—

---

[8] "The Sony PlayStation: An Intrapreneurship Story," by Anis Bedda, https://www.intrapreneurshipconference.com/the-sony-playstation-an-intrapreneurship-story/, accessed December 11, 2016.

[9] Otsuka company website, https://www.otsuka-us.com, accessed September 28, 2016.

to develop localized interventions that provide additional support for those with serious mental illness and also may help address larger community problems."

OAPI's website explained that the other alliance members were the National Alliance on Mental Illness (NAMI), the National Council for Behavioral Health (National Council), and Lundbeck, a Danish manufacturing company that began producing pharmaceuticals in the 1930s.

Clinical Trials

When did clinical trials start? Some historians point to the Bible's account of King Nebuchadnezzar of Babylon who "ordered his people to eat only meat and drink only wine, a diet he believed would keep them in sound physical condition," an article from *Perspectives in Clinical Research*[10] explains.

"But several young men of royal blood, who preferred to eat vegetables, objected. The king allowed these rebels to follow a diet of legumes and water—but only for 10 days. When Nebuchadnezzar's experiment ended, the vegetarians appeared better nourished than the meat-eaters, so the king permitted the legume lovers to continue their diet."

In 1937 in the United States, a drug company developed a so-called wonder drug, sulfanilamide, which was "used to fight streptococcal infections (i.e., strep throat). The product was not tested in animals or humans prior to marketing," the U.S. Food and Drug Administration (FDA) says on its website.[11] And tragically: "The solvent used to suspend the active drug, diethylene glycol, was a poison (chemically related to anti-freeze)."

More than 100 people who took the drug died. The following year, Congress enacted the 1938 Food, Drug, and Cosmetic Act, which required "drug sponsors to submit safety data to FDA officials for evaluation prior to marketing."

Over time the FDA's rules tightened and matured. Companies had to prove that drugs were both safe and effective by subjecting the drugs to clinical trials, a structured way of testing the drugs.

Often, pharmaceutical companies ran their own clinical trials. But as the industry grew so did the demand for clinical trials. To meet this need—and to streamline costs—pharmaceutical companies outsourced this work to contract research organizations or CROs.

"The CRO market grew from $1 billion in 1992 to more than $8 billion in 2002," according to Kalorama Information[12], a company that publishes market research.

By 2022, the CRO industry is expected to grow to $45.2 billion.[13]

---

[10] "Evolution of Clinical Research: A History Before and Beyond James Lind," by Dr. Arun Bhatt, Perspectives in Clinical Research, January-March, 2010, accessed January 31, 2017. https://www.ncbi.nlm.nih.gov/pmc/articles/PMC3149409/.

[11] "FDA and Clinical Drug Trials: A Short History," by Suzanne White Junod, http://www.fda.gov/AboutFDA/WhatWeDo/History/Overviews/ucm304485.htm, accessed January 31, 2017.

[12] "Outsourcing in Drug Development: The Contract Research Market from Preclinical to Phase III," Kalorama Information, January 1, 2004, https://www.kaloramainformation.com/Outsourcing-Drug-Development-910773/, accessed February 9, 2017.

[13] "Healthcare CRO Market to Reach $45.2 Billion by 2022," Grand View Research, January, 2016, http://www.grandviewresearch.com/press-release/global-healthcare-cro-market, accessed February 9, 2017.

The Association of Clinical Research Organizations represents many CROs, and it advocates "on a global basis for safe, ethical, high-quality medical research so patients can benefit from the development of new treatments and therapies. Our members are dedicated to helping their clients bring efficiency, innovation and value to the clinical research process."

To choose the right CRO[14], companies often rely on a handful of criteria including:

— Time — how long the project will take

— Cost

— Team chemistry — how well employees from the company and the CRO get along

— CRO's relevant experience

— CRO's geographic reach

Introducing Abilify in Japan

"Can you really do this?"

That was the question an Otsuka colleague asked Carson about running trials for Abilify in Japan. The budget was $100 million. The timeline was five years.

And principles were at stake. Otsuka was a company where "Medical Care is deeply connected to culture." If Carson took on the job, he would have to blend scientific excellence and cultural sensitivity. Doing business in Japan was a matter of building relationships.

To gain access to patients for the clinical trial, Carson, met with clinicians and patients in Japan.

"The hardest part for me was not being able to ask questions ad lib," Carson recalled. Questions were sent to doctors beforehand. They read their answers instead of speaking spontaneously. "This is the formal culture of Japan. I needed to be responsible for not embarrassing the doctors. If I asked additional questions that a doctor might not be able to answer, the doctor would lose face and I would need to take responsibility for embarrassing him."

"Throughout the process, I never got any sense that race mattered. Japan is much more clear about being Japanese or being non-Japanese. Clearly, I was non-Japanese."

In addition, Japan was streamlining its regulatory process, but challenges remained: "Traditionally, the pharmaceutical industry does not receive a lot of trust from the public in Japan, following a number of scandals in past, and recent years," according to an article in *Dialogues in Clinical Neuroscience*.[15] "Western medicines are seen as potentially dangerous, and the Japanese authorities have always put the emphasis on safety and quality issues, rather than efficacy. Incentives for patients taking part, in

---

[14] "Key Factors in CRO Selection: A recent survey uncovers key criteria that influence a sponsor's decision when selecting a CRO," by Harold E. Glass and Daniel P. Beaudry, Applied Clinical Trials, April 1, 2008, http://www.appliedclinicaltrialsonline.com/key-factors-cro-selection-0?id=&sk=&date=&%0A%09%09%09&pageID=4, accessed on February 19, 2017.

[15] "Japanese pharmaceutical and regulatory environment," Ryoichi Nagata and Jean-David Raflzadeh-Kabe, Dialogues in Clinical Neuroscience, December, 2002, https://www.ncbi.nlm.nih.gov/pmc/articles/PMC3181698/, accessed February 19, 2017.

clinical trials were already low, because of the comprehensive coverage of medical costs that Japan offers, and the very strict rules for compensation."

Carson reviewed his options.

- **Option 1:** Hire staff to run the clinical trials. This would give him close oversight of the work. Although once the trial was done he might have to lay off staff, and layoffs were frowned upon in Japan. Carson estimated that he could run the trial in-house for $90 million and finish in four years. He would have to hire roughly 175 employees.

- **Option 2:** Outsource the trials to a CRO, a contract research organization that specializes in one-time research assignments from pharmaceutical and biotechnology companies. Otsuka could put out a Request for Proposal (an RFP) asking the CROs to develop a pitch for how they would handle the Abilify trials in Japan. Carson would have less control, but there would be no need for layoffs, since employees would work for the CRO.

- **Option 3:** Carson thought he could develop a CRO selection questionnaire, a list of questions about how a CRO would handle the project. The questionnaire would be scored, and high-scoring CROs would move to the next phase of evaluation.

The core of Carson's CRO questionnaire was:

- Describe the key factors that your company has determined are drivers of competitive success.

- How do your senior leaders communicate and promote values that encourage ethical, consumer-focused behavior?

- What would the ideal planning and feedback system look like?

- How do you assess risk to projects and programs?

- How do you assure the integrity, validity, and timeliness of your data?

- Describe your project management process and approach?

- What are your organization's key customer satisfaction results?

Now Carson had to decide what to do. He could:

- hire researchers and find jobs for them later,

- stick with the traditional RFP process, or

- proceed with his questionnaire approach.

Exhibit 1   William Carson's Resume

Harvard University
   A.B. History and Science

Case Western Reserve University School of Medicine
   MD

Tufts University School of Medicine
   Psychiatry Residency

2010–present
   President and CEO
   Otsuka Pharmaceutical Development & Commercialization, Inc.

2008–2010
   SVP Global Clinical Development
   Otsuka Pharmaceutical Development & Commercialization, Inc.

2007–2010
   VP Global Clinical Development
   Otsuka Pharmaceutical Development & Commercialization, Inc.

2002–2007
   Vice President CNS/Aripiprazole
   Otsuka America Pharmaceutical, Inc.

1998–2002
   Group Director
   Bristol-Myers Squibb

1988–1998
   Professor of Psychiatry
   Medical University of South Carolina

Philanthropy:

   Chair of the Sphinx Organization's Board of Directors

   "The Sphinx Organization is the Detroit-based national organization dedicated to transforming lives through the power of diversity in the arts. Led by Afa S. Dworkin, its President and Artistic Director, Sphinx programs reach over 100,000 students, as well as live and broadcast audiences of over two million annually."

   "The organization's founding and mission were informed by the life experiences of Aaron Dworkin, who, as a young Black violinist, was acutely aware of the lack of diversity both on stage and in the audience in concert halls. He founded Sphinx while an undergraduate student at the University of Michigan, to address the stark under-representation of people of color in classical music. President Obama's first appointment to the National Council on the Arts, Aaron P. Dworkin currently serves as dean of the University of Michigan's School of Music, Theatre & Dance."

Source: Sphinx website, http://www.sphinxmusic.org/about/, accessed on December 1, 2016.

Exhibit 3   Responses to the Contract Research Organization Questionnaire

Poltec Analytics, 5234 Johnson Way, Coralville Iowa

No response. But according to industry news reports, the company had run a similar clinical trial in Asia for $85 million. A portion of the work was done in Eastern Europe where labor and programmatic costs were lower. The clinical trial took four years to complete.

NuViewMatics, 322 San Antonio Blvd, San Francisco, California

Questionnaire Answers:

> We respectfully suggest that Otsuka opt to issue a standard Request for Proposal, which would clarify this project's key objectives, needs, and challenges. We've found that this is the most effective way to develop a comprehensive approach to managing today's research challenges.

> We believe that Otsuka would be extremely well-served by our Culture View unit, which has successfully run drug trials among a number of ethnic groups, including Chinese, Filipino, and Mexican people. We have facilities located in Japan. Our commitment to diversity in scientific research is unparalleled, and we look forward to responding to any future RFPs from Otsuka.

> Our ballpark estimate is that this project would cost $97 million and take 5.33 years to complete.

North Star Dynamics, 15663 Avondale Road, Laneville, New Jersey

Questionnaire Answers:

Describe the key factors that your company has determined are drivers of competitive success.

> Competitive success requires vigilant collaboration at every phase of a project. We build the relationships required for planning, execution, problem-solving, and reflecting on the many lessons learned from meeting all our clients' needs.

How do your senior leaders communicate and promote values that encourage ethical, consumer-focused behavior? And how do you foster an organizational culture that is conducive to high performance and a motivated workforce?

> We articulate our values daily in our spoken and written communication. We also lead by example. Our executives, our research team, and our administrative staff all "walk the talk."

> Our employee recognition program has two tracks: we reward innovation, and we reward responsibility. Our employees know that they are each a unique and important point of contact for the company. So, whether they're chatting in the grocery store or making a presentation at a high-stakes sales meeting, they know that they have the power to showcase the company at its best.

What would the ideal planning and feedback system look like?

> We set up operations and governance committees that oversee our work with clients to ensure a good fit on every level, including information technology as well as values and goal.

How do you assess risk to projects and programs?

We continually assess the quality of our "inputs" — trial subjects, data, and operating assumptions — in order to protect against faulty outcomes.

Our compliance team focuses on local and global regulations and laws about intellectual property, corruption, and health and privacy safeguards for patients.

How do you assure the integrity, validity and timeliness of your data?

We hire world-class professionals, and we double check their work.

Describe your project management process and approach?

- *We start by sitting down with clients and developing a plan. This is also the phase where we start building the high-quality relationships that contribute to a project's success.*

- *We're sticklers for timeline, budget, and data management*

- *We're experts at bioethics and protecting human subjects*

- *We provide clients with extensive status updates*

- *Our analytical expertise is world class*

- *We stick with a project for the life of a product*

What are your organization's key customer satisfaction results?

We pay close attention to the time it takes products to get to market. Speed is important, but at North Star we place a higher value on safety and accuracy.

We always ask customers the same question: How did we do?

Customers can respond in a variety ways that include surveys, wrap-up interviews, and follow-up calls to assess long-term outcomes.

We estimate that this trial would cost $100 million and take four and a half years.

Source: Casewriter.

Note: The three contract research organizations are all fictional companies, and their responses are fictional.

Exhibit 4   Examples of Support for Intrapreneurs

The *Harvard Business Review*[a] says, "**Barclays and Disney** run Social Intrapreneur Challenges—internal venture teams—across the world. Employees are invited to propose ideas for new products and services that have a business case and promise to make a positive impact on society. Hundreds of employees (the majority of them millennials) have applied in the two companies."

The *Review* adds: "In each case, a subset is selected to join an intrapreneurial version of a start-up accelerator. Participants work full-time on their day-jobs, but over a 6-month period they attend workshops and get expert coaching on how to develop their proposition. Time and money are limited so participants learn to enlist peers and even bosses as volunteers. They use the internet and social networks to unearth best practices, often in other industries and sectors. They pitch back to senior leadership, who then decide if the idea should be 'taken off the side of desk' of the intrapreneur and awarded funding and resources to progress."

"The **U.S. Forest Service Eastern Region** changed its innovation suggestion process from a 4-page form to telling its employees, 'If you have an idea, tell your supervisor or send an e-mail. If you do not get a response in 2 weeks, as long as the idea is not illegal, go ahead and implement it.' Before the change, the 2,500 employees submitted, on average, 60 ideas annually. A year after the new procedures were implemented, 6,000 new ideas were submitted!" Harvard Business School Professor Steven Rogers writes in *Entrepreneurial Finance*.[b]

Intuit, a software company, frees employees to work on side projects. But as the *Harvard Business Review*[c] explains, that's often not enough "to coax people away from their everyday work. According to Intuit's Jeff Zias, Unstructured Time and Grassroots Innovation Leader, the company needed to go further and "inject some structure into that unstructured time."

"One way it achieves this is through periodic multiday hackathons[d] where teams of developers present pet projects and compete to tackle specific challenges aligned with the company's broader strategy (e.g., easy, fast tax return completion) in exchange for prizes and recognition. Adding this measure of structure not only cultivates a powerful ecosystem by bringing intrapreneurs together in one place, allowing for cross-functional interaction, but also allows the organization to keep innovation aimed at themes that Intuit wants to investigate."

McKinsey & Company[e] describes hackathons as events that pool "eager entrepreneurs and software developers into a confined space for a day or two and challenges them to create a cool killer app. Yet hackathons aren't just for the start-up tech crowd. Businesses are employing the same principles to break through organizational inertia and instill more innovation-driven cultures. That's because they offer a baptism by fire: a short, intense plunge that assaults the senses and allows employees to experience creative disruption in a visceral way."

---

[a] "Your Leadership Development Program Needs an Overhaul," by Milan Samani and Robert J. Thomas, *Harvard Business Review*, December 5, 2016, https://hbr.org/2016/12/your-leadership-development-program-needs-an-overhaul, accessed December 12, 2016.

[b] Rogers, Steven; Makonnen, Roza (2014-04-18). *Entrepreneurial Finance, Third Edition: Finance and Business Strategies for the Serious Entrepreneur* (Kindle Locations 4419-4422). McGraw-Hill Education. Kindle Edition.

[c] "How Intuit Built a Better Support System for Intrapreneurs," by Simone Ahoja, *Harvard Business Review*, April 5, 2016, https://hbr.org/2016/04/how-intuit-built-a-better-support-system-for-intrapreneurs, accessed December 6, 2016.

[d] "Highlights from the QuickBooks Connect 2015 Hackathon," YouTube video, https://www.youtube.com/watch?v=fGUZCPWLc2c&feature=youtu.be, accessed July 30, 2017.

[e] "Demystifying the hackathon," by Ferry Grijpink, Alan Lau, and Javier Vara, http://www.mckinsey.com/business-functions/digital-mckinsey/our-insights/demystifying-the-hackathon, accessed on December 11, 2016.

Dr. William Carson Case Study Assignment Questions

1. Which of the three options for working with a contract research organization should he pick?
2. What makes Carson an intrapreneur?
3. What intrapreneurial model did he find himself in?
4. Should he handle the project as a caretaker, a developer, or an innovator?
5. What personal traits would help or hinder his efforts?
6. Is Otsuka a fertile environment for intrapreneurs?

Notes

1. Branson, Richard. "Richard Branson on Intrapreneurs." NBC News. January 31, 2011. https://www.nbcnews.com/id/wbna41359235
2. "Linda R. Gooden, Retired Executive Vice President Lockheed Martin." University of Maryland. Accessed March 17, 2021. https://www.usmf. org/directory/linda-r-gooden/#:~:text=President%20Lockheed%20 Martin-,Linda%20R.,the%20Aerospace%20and%20Defense%20 industry
3. Richardson, Nicole Marie. "What It Takes To Be A Successful Intrapreneur." *Black Enterprise*. December 1, 2005. https://www.blackenterprise. com/what-it-takes-to-be-a-successful-intrapreneur/5/
4. "U.S. Federal Government IT Budget 2021." *Statista*. January 22, 2021. www.statista.com/statistics/605501/united-states-federal-it-budget/
5. "Linda Gooden." AFCEA International. November 20, 2015. www .afcea.org/site/gooden
6. Ibid.
7. Koscs, Jim. "How Nicholas Dreystadt Ended Racism at Cadillac in the 1930s—or Tried To." Hagerty Media. October 22, 2019. https://www .hagerty.com/media/automotive-history/nicholas-dreystadt-ended-racism-at-cadillac-in-the-1930s/
8. "African Americans Saved Cadillac." *The Charleston Chronicle*. August 5, 2019. https://www.charlestonchronicle.net/2019/08/05/african-americans-saved-cadillac/
9. "Cadillac." *Automotive Database*. Accessed March 17, 2021. https://www .autocarbase.com/2012/12/cadillac.html

10. Pride, Felicia. "Karen Thomas." PublishersWeekly.com. March 31, 2008. https://www.publishersweekly.com/pw/by-topic/authors/interviews/article/7927-karen-thomas.html

11. Richardson, Nicole Marie. "What It Takes To Be A Successful Intrapreneur." *Black Enterprise*. December 1, 2005. https://www.blackenterprise.com/what-it-takes-to-be-a-successful-intrapreneur/3/

12. "About Dafina." Kensington Publishing Corp., April 23, 2020. www.kensingtonbooks.com/pages/dafina/about-dafina/

13. Pride, Felicia. "Karen Thomas." PublishersWeekly.com. March 31, 2008. https://www.publishersweekly.com/pw/by-topic/authors/interviews/article/7927-karen-thomas.html

14. "About Dafina." Kensington Publishing Corp., April 23, 2020. www.kensingtonbooks.com/pages/dafina/about-dafina/

15. Lubenow, Gerald, et al. "Jobs Talks About His Rise and Fall." *Newsweek*. September 29, 1985. Accessed March 17, 2021. www.newsweek.com/jobs-talks-about-his-rise-and-fall-207016/

Epilogue

Robert Blackwell Jr. is a Black man described by the *Los Angeles Times* as "a savvy and successful entrepreneur."[1] He owns a technology consulting firm, and in 2000, after then–Illinois State Senator Barack Obama lost his bid to become a congressperson, Blackwell hired him. Blackwell's company, EKI-Digital, paid Obama $8,000 per month.

Blackwell has always sought to use his entrepreneurial success to help the Black community. He recently proposed that the federal government should create more jobs for Blacks by supporting Black-owned technology firms. In his presentation, he says, "Try this experiment: name two well-known Black entrepreneurs with no connection to entertainment. If you can't, Black kids trapped in poverty can't, either."

Fortunately, this book has armed the reader with the ability to pass Blackwell's experiment. There are more than 10 successful Black entrepreneurs included in this book who are not athletes or entertainers.

Another wonderful fact is that these entrepreneurs are in almost every industry imaginable, including technology, finance, real estate, cosmetics, manufacturing, accommodations, and franchising.

---

[1] Neubauer, Chuck and Hamburger, Tom, "Obama Contributor Received State Grant." *Los Angeles Times*. April 27, 2008. https://www.latimes.com/archives/la-xpm-2008-apr-27-na-killerspin27-story.html

They have also gone the entrepreneurial route via every process in the entrepreneurship spectrum. Black entrepreneurs have gained wealth and experienced success by purchasing independent businesses, becoming franchisees and franchisors, and starting companies from nothing.

The contributions that these men and women make to the Black community by creating jobs, providing products/services, and making philanthropic donations personifies business at its best. This occurs when the objective of successful entrepreneurship becomes measured by more than monetary gains.

As my Williams College classmate Gary Hutchinson said, "It's like a fusion reactor. The result is a sum greater than the parts, but a new creation. America becomes a greater version of itself."

That is exactly what happens to our country when Black people become successful entrepreneurs and make the aforementioned contributions. Anything that benefits and positively impacts the Black community also positively impacts America.

APPENDIX

Course Description

Aise African American business leaders successfully have contributed to the growth of the American economy for centuries. This course is not only for Black students, but for every student interested in learning about great business leaders who might be a Black entrepreneur, intrapreneur (entrepreneur in a corporate setting), union leader, or social entrepreneur.

Topics include the entrepreneurship spectrum, leadership, start-up and underserved markets, financial statement analysis, financing for Black entrepreneurs, acquisitions, selling a company, franchising, intrapreneurship, and private equity.

Most of the case studies concentrate on protagonists who are HBS alums, including Otis Gates 1963, the oldest living Black HBS alum who sold his real estate company for over $100 million; Earl Gordon 2008, who purchased a company a few years after graduation; and Amanda Johnson and Kristen Jones Miller 2014, who founded a cosmetics company after graduating. There are also case studies highlighting non-alums; Larry Morse and JoAnn Price, the founders of Fairview Capital, a private equity fund with over $5 billion of assets under management; and John Rogers Jr., the founder of Ariel Investments, the largest Black-owned asset management firm in America.

The course examines the great business opportunities that have emerged from identifying underserved markets of Black consumers, and the unique interplay between, and intersection of, race and successful entrepreneurial ventures.

Syllabus

The course will be taught once a week during a 3-hour period. It is a three-credit course with a final project. Two-thirds of the course will be devoted to classroom work and the balance to a team project outside the classroom. Fifty percent of the final grade will be derived from class participation and the remainder from the final project.

The classes will be organized in two parts. The beginning of every class will be devoted to the analysis of a traditional case study, with the protagonist possibly serving as a guest speaker in person or via video call. The second portion of the class will be the practicum on entrepreneurship. Students will work in teams and apply the FIELD 3 model of identifying, testing, and creating an entrepreneurial firm that specifically targets underserved markets in poor, middle class, and affluent Black communities throughout the United States. Final grades will be based on class participation, peer reviews, and presentations of final projects.

Course Reading Materials

1. HBS Case Studies
2. *Entrepreneurial Finance*, 3rd edition by Steven Rogers

Sample Course Schedule

Week	Date	Case Study	Topic	Guest Speaker	Chapter
1	September 5	Lecture	Entrepreneur Spectrum		
2	September 12	John Rogers and Ariel Investments	Leadership	John Rogers Jr.	

Week	Date	Case Study	Topic	Guest Speaker	Chapter
3	September 19	Amanda and Kristen: Mented Cosmetics	Start-up and Underserved Markets	Amanda Johnson & Kristen Jones Miller	
4	September 26	The Stories Behind the Numbers	Financial Statement Analysis		2 & 3
5	October 3	*Policy Watch* Article AND *Belt Magazine* Article	Financing for Black Entrepreneurs		
6	October 10	Rev. Georgiette Morgan-Thomas & The American Hat Factory	Acquisitions	Rev. Morgan-Thomas	5
7	October 17	United Housing—Otis Gates	Selling a Company	Otis Gates	
8	October 24	Team work outside of class	NO CLASS		
9	October 31	Valerie Daniels-Carter: High Growth Entrepreneurship via Franchising	Franchising	Valerie Daniels-Carter (Zoom Conference Call)	
10	November 7	Career & Professional Development Events	NO CLASS		

(Continued)

Week	Date	Case Study	Topic	Guest Speaker	Chapter
11	November 14	Dr. William Carson—Intrapreneurial Innovation in the Pharmaceutical Industry	Intrapreneurship	Dr. William Carson	8
12	November 21	Thanksgiving Break	NO CLASS		
13	November 28	Fairview Capital	Private Equity	Larry Morse and JoAnn Price	
14	December 5	Team Presentations	LAST DAY OF CLASS		

Acknowledgments

ONE OF THE most enjoyable experiences that I had as a professor at Harvard Business School (HBS) was my relationship with Professor Henry McGee. I referred to him as my good brother from the G.I. (Gary, Indiana)! Our strong bond emanated from the fact that we were both African American faculty members who were former businessmen and loyal alums. We were also committed to making our alma mater the best business school in the country for Black students.

As the volunteer faculty sponsors of the African American Student Union (AASU), at the beginning of every school year, Henry and I gave welcoming speeches at the first AASU meeting. The objectives of our speeches were to inform students that they belonged at HBS, they could excel, and there were Black faculty members who cared about their happiness and success.

It was this same spirit of caring by Henry that led to the publication of this book. After I wrote several case studies for my new course "Black Business Leaders and Entrepreneurship," he repeatedly encouraged me to write a book on the topic, comprised primarily of my case studies. Additionally, he gave me the names of other HBS professors who had successfully done the same. It is for these reasons that I give a heartfelt statement of acknowledgment and gratitude to Professor Henry McGee.

I would also like to recognize and thank the following people from HBS, including Professor Paul Gompers, who shared his experiences with me about publishing his book made up of case studies about private equity; and my outstanding former assistant, Darlene Le. Darlene worked tirelessly with me on this book, my podcasts, website, case studies, and other book. *A Letter to My White Friends and Colleagues: What You Can Do Right Now to Help the Black Community.*

The help provided to me from Harvard also included Carol Sweet and Van Morrill from Harvard Business Publishing. Their support was invaluable, and I thank them.

We all know that it takes a team to write and publish a book. I was fortunate to have on my team Roza Makonnen, my former student, who was the primary researcher; Gary Hutchinson, Dawn Kilgore, and Adaobi Obi Tulton, who were the editors; and Sally Baker, Chloe Miller-Bess, and Jeanenne Ray from Wiley. I am forever grateful to all of these brilliant, hardworking people.

I would like to give a special statement of thanks to Jeanenne, both my editor and my friend. A few weeks after George Floyd was murdered in 2020, she reached out to me with an offer to write a book about any topic of my choosing. She told me that the Black Lives Matter movement was the catalyst for her to use her senior editor position at Wiley to do something that could positively impact the Black–White issues in the country. While I knew that I wanted to write a book about successful Black entrepreneurs, I also knew that the time was perfect for a book that focused on providing solutions to the country's racial problems. Therefore, Jeanenne and I agreed that my first book would be *A Letter to My White Friends and Colleagues: What You Can Do Right Now to Help the Black Community.* Before completing this book, I submitted the proposal to Jeanenne for *Successful Black Entrepreneurs.* Her immediate response was, "YES!"

Other friends that I would like to thank at this time are Dawn, a brilliant writer who will win a Pulitzer Prize one day, and Gil. He and I have been friends for 51 years. The phrase "brothers from other mothers" applies to us.

I would also like to give thanks to my brother, Johnnie, from the same biological mother. He has always been one of my biggest supporters. The same can be said about my 99-year-old Uncle Ray. I dearly love both of these men.

My final thank you goes to my wonderful, brilliant, and kind daughters, Akilah Naeem Rogers and Ariel Naillah Rogers. They love Black entrepreneurship as much as I do. When the COVID pandemic was killing Black-owned businesses, they separately interviewed me on podcasts, targeting Black entrepreneurs. The topic was how to help Black-owned businesses access emergency government cash from the Payroll Protection Program (PPP). I thank them for supporting Black entrepreneurs and for being my marvelous daughters.

About the Author

Steven S. Rogers retired from Harvard Business School in 2019, where he was the "MBA Class of 1957 Senior Lecturer" in General Management. He taught Entrepreneurial Finance and a new course that he created, titled "Black Business Leaders and Entrepreneurship."

A 1985 graduate of the school, Professor Rogers holds a Bachelor of Arts degree from Williams College. Prior to HBS, Professor Rogers taught in the MBA and PhD programs at the Kellogg School of Management, Northwestern University. He received the Outstanding Professor Award for the Executive MBA Program 26 times and daytime program twice. Both are records.

He joined the Steans Family Foundation as an advisor in 2020 to develop an economic plan for a poverty-stricken Black community in Chicago. The same year, he joined the University of Miami Business School as an Executive-in-Residence, where he teaches Entrepreneurial Finance in the Master of Science Finance Program.

In 2019, he toured 10 Historically Black Colleges and Universities (HBCUs) where he taught a workshop in Entrepreneurial Finance.

Poets & Quants magazine selected him as one of "Our Favorite MBA Professors of 2017."

In 2016, he was a volunteer professor at the United States Military Academy at West Point Army, where he received the West Point cadets' sword for "Expert Teaching and Professionalism." He has taught in Africa, Australia, Canada, Germany, Hong Kong, India, Mexico, Philippines, and Vienna.

Before becoming a professor, he owned and operated two manufacturing firms and one retail operation. Prior to becoming an entrepreneur, Professor Rogers worked at Bain + Company consulting firm, Cummins Engine Company, and UNC Ventures, a venture capital firm.

He also owned a real estate investment company that invested in residential properties on the South Side of Chicago.

He received the "Bicentennial Medal for Distinguished Achievement" by an alum from Williams College, and the "Bert King Award for Service" from the African American Student Union at HBS. *Ebony* magazine named him one of the top 150 influential people in America.

In 2017, he received the "Black Brilliance in Service" award from Harvard Law School's BLSA. In 2020, he published the fourth edition of his book *The Entrepreneur's Guide to Finance and Business*. Professor Rogers originally published the book in 2002. In 2021, he published his second book, *A Letter to My White Friends and Colleagues: What You Can Do Right Now to Help the Black Community*. He has also authored 24 HBS case studies, and recorded six podcasts, three of which were uploaded to *Black Enterprise* magazine.

In 2021, he became a founding partner of Nubian Square Ascends, a $150 million real estate development project in Boston's Roxbury community. Professor Rogers's governance experiences span over two decades. He has served as a trustee for Williams College, and the Visiting Committee for HBS. His corporate board experiences include SuperValu (chairman, Governance Committee), Duquesne Light (chairman, Finance Committee), Oakmark Mutual Funds (chairman, Audit Committee and Investment Review Committee), W. S. Darley (lead director), and S. C. Johnson Wax.

He has completed five triathlons and is part owner of the 2021 World Champion, Chicago Sky in the WNBA.

Index

A

Abbott, Robert, 1

Abilify
  clinical trials, 302–303
  introduction (Japan), 303–304
  U.S. sales, 297t

Accelerators, list, 172t

Acquisition entrepreneurship
  advantages, 76–77
  disadvantages, 77

Acquisition prospects
  deal negotiation/closure, 80
  identification, 79–80

Advocacy advertising, 27

Affordable housing
  background, 274–280
  complexes, funding process, 277
  corporation/individual
      investments, benefits, 278
  criticism, 278
  defining, 274–276
  government subsidization,
      reasons, 277–278

history, 276–277

industry, entities
    (involvement), 280

median incomes (Boston), 275t

obtaining, process, 279

private investments, tax
    incentives, 277

projects, investments, 277

rents/income, relationship
    (Boston), 275t

tenants, rent (payments), 277

United Housing approach,
    270–272

work
  benefits, 279–280
  risks, 280

African-American businesswomen,
    evolution, 139

Agon, Jean-Paul, 60

Ahrendts, Angela, 228

Air Atlanta, founding, 50–52

Airbnb, entrepreneurial
    venture, 49

Alternative investment asset
    class, 186
American Association of MESBICs
    (AAMESBIC), 190
American Hat Factory. *See* The
    American Hat Factory
American Shared Hospital Services
    (ASHS) IPO, 246
Andreessen, Marc, 162
Andrews, Tom, 31
Angel investors, 173t
    funds, 237
Annual venture capital
    investments, 197e
Anti-Black bias, 158
Anti-Black racism, impact, 133, 157
Arabesque Books, 291
Argenti, Paul, 30
Ariel Capital Management, 17
Ariel Community Academy (ACA),
    support, 9–10, 12
Ariel Fund, launch, 11
Ariel Investments Co., 6
    money management, 6–7
    performance, 8
Atis, Balanda, 61
Ault Inc. IPO, 246
Azikiwe, Nnamdi, 189

B
Backstage Capital, 160–163
Bain Capital, impact, 255, 256
Ball, Ryan, 23
Banking on Black Enterprise
    (Bates), 38
Banks
    black-owned banks, 175t
    investor directory, 174t

Barclays, Social Intrapreneur
    Challenge, 308e
Bare-headed era, 222
Bates, Timothy, 38, 169
Beane, Vanilla, 223
Beatric International Foods,
    purchase, 80–81
Beatric Lynum v. Illinois, 25
Beauty industry
    analysis/demographic
        shifts, 58–59
    competitive landscape, 68e
    consumers
        behavior, 58–59
        voices, impact, 60
    data, 65e
    diversity, business, 59–61
    nude, redefining, 59
Benioff, Marc, 28, 30
Berry, Chuck, 54
Bethune, Gordon, 228
Bharat, Krishna, 295
Bhatti, Saqib, 15
Biss, Daniel, 20
Black business models,
    48–55
Black community, success, 4–5
Black Corporate Directors'
    Conference, launch, 9
Black corporate turnaround
    specialists, 207–211
Black Entertainment Television
    (BET), 1, 242,
        248–251, 291
    challenges, 249
    expansion, cost, 250
    investors, 249
    Johnson buyback, 250

Black entrepreneurs
  capital
    access, 157–164
    sources, 164, 165–171
  equity capital, procurement
    (treatment disparity),
    158–159
  examples, 211–220
  investor
    directory, 172t–182t
  investor bias, 167–169
    solution, 170–171
  PPP loans, impact, 207
  private equity capital access,
    percentage, 159
  SPACs, relationship, 242–243
  White entrepreneurs,
    differences, 157
  White investor non-negative
    response, 159–160
Black entrepreneurship
  history, 1
  importance, 37
Black franchisees, 133–135
  negatives, 133
Black franchisors, 135–137
Black Holocaust in America, 3, 9
Black intrapreneurs, 285
Black Lives Matter, 4, 30, 211
Black males/White males, violent
    crimes (contrast), 37–38
Black milliners, examples, 223
Black-owned banks, 175t
Black-owned businesses, COVID
    (impact), 4
Black-owned firms, public
    listing, 247t
Black-owned newspapers, impact, 39

Black-owned public companies, 246
Blacks, investor bias, 167–169
  research, 168t
Black start-up entrepreneurs, 43
Black turnaround entrepreneurs, 203
Black Wall Street, whitewashing, 4
Blackwell, Jr., Robert, 311
Black women
  cosmetic brand launches, 66e
  spending (dollars), 59–60
Blankfein, Lloyd, 27
Blockbuster, industry differentiation,
    45–47
Block, Carson, 242
Blue Mountain LLC, 270
Bond, Julian, 51
Boone, Sarah, 39
Booth, Patricia, 189
Boseman, Chadwick, 190
Boston
  affordable housing rents/income,
    relationship, 275t
  housing market, 281–282
  median incomes, 275t
Braga, Leda, 17
Branson, Richard, 285
Brewer, Miriam, 141
Bridgestream Software, 235–239
  Enterprise Role Management
    Solutions, 237
  launch, 236
  sale, 237–238
Brooks School Project, 266
Brown, Michael, 272
Brown, Tony, 217
Brown vs. Board of Education, 264
Bruce, Willa/Charles, 55
Buchheit, Paul, 295

Bunche, Ralph, 189
Burridge, Lee, 40
Business, acquisition process, 77–80
  crowdfunded search, 79–80
  deal negotiation/closure, 80
  entrepreneur financing
        options, 80
  search phase, financing, 77–78
  self-financed search, 78
  sponsored search fund, 79
  traditional search fund, 78–79
Business exits
  reasons, 240–241
  strategies, 241
Business Leadership Council, 12–13
Business PPP loans, 204–207
Butterfield, Steward, 162

C
Cadillac, "No Sale to Negroes"
        policy, 223
Canalt, Doug, 228
Capital
  capital under management
        (U.S. venture funds), 195e
  corporate venture capital,
        source, 176t
  sources, 170–171
  venture capital, 180t–182t
Capital, access
  disparity, 157
  inequality, 166–167
Capital Partners Acquisition, money
        (raising), 243
Carson, William, 296, 297–308
  CRO questionnaire, 304
  intrapreneurship, 299–301
  Iwamoto, relationship, 299
  philanthropy, 305
  résumé, 305e

Carter, Jimmy, 51
Caruso, Phil, 13
Cement ceiling, battle, 149
Chatterji, Aaron, 29
Chenault, Kenneth, 83, 203,
        207, 223
Chicago, money makers
        (ranking), 14e
Chick-fil-A sales, increase, 29
Civil Rights Era, 4
Clark, Richard, 228
Clarkson, Charles, 83
Cobb, Alexandra, 272
Cohen, Bill, 243
Community Development Financial
        Institutions (CDFIs),
        PPP priority, 206
Community Development
        Investment Funds
        (CDIFs), 176t
  funding disbursement, 204–205
Community Reinvestment Act of
        1977 (CRA), 277
Companies
  entrepreneur purchase, financing
        options, 80
  intrapreneurship benefits, 293–294
  pre-money valuation, 159
  sale, 235
    appearance, 238
    exit strategies, 241
    owner validation, 239
Coney Island Cookery (franchise),
        144–145
  corporate information, 150e
Contract research organizations
        (CROs), 302–304
  questionnaire, responses,
        306e–307e
Cook, Tim, 30

Cornwall, Don, 203–204
Corporate activism, 27–29
Corporate and Auditing
        Accountability,
        Responsibility,
        and Transparency
        Act, 236–237
Corporate venture capital, 176t
Cosmetics brand launches, 66e
Cosmetics industry
    competitive landscape, 68e
    data, 65e
Costs, cutting (mindset), 207
Cyber threat environment, 253

D
Dafina Books, launch, 292
Daniels-Carter, Valerie, 137,
        138–154
    evolution, 139
    franchises, investment
            examples, 144–147
    news coverage, 149e
    résumé, 148e
Davis, Benjamin O., 189
"Dear White Venture Capitalists"
        (Hamilton), 161–162
Debt capital, sources, 170t
Debt coverage ratio, 157–158
Developer (intrapreneur category),
        289–290
Dickerson, Earl, 26
Discrimination, perpetuation, 27
Disney, Social Intrapreneur
        Challenge, 308e
Disparity, anti-Black racism
        (impact), 157
Diversity
    absence (consulting firms), 15
    business, 59–61

formula, success, 61
Illinois pension managers,
        diversity (increase), 23–24
Illinois State Board of Investment
        (ISBI) diversity policy,
        18–19
    promotion, investment
            consultants (impact), 15e
Downing, Philip, 41
DreamWorks, changes, 295
Drew, Charles, 41
Drexel Burham Lambert, 83
Dreystadt, Nicholas, 290
Duncan, Arne, 26

E
Eastern Circle
    acquisition, 93
    base case projections/returns, 99t
    business description, 94–95
    case study, 85
    competitors, 94, 94t
    customers, identification, 94
    downside case, 100
    exit strategies, 100
    financial models, 101e–109e
    financial results/projections,
            discussion, 97
    financial review, 95–97
    financial summary, 95
    funding, search, 88
    growth initiatives, 98
    historical/forecasted financial
            performance, 96, 96t
    information technology, 95
    investment analysis, 98–100
    investment memorandum, 92–101
    litigation, 95
    management/employees, 95
    operating results, adjustments, 97

Eastern Circle (*Continued*)
  opportunity, 88
  preliminary information request
      list, 90e–91e
  products, 93
  proposal letter, 116e–122e
  revenue/EBITDA, 96f
  sales/marketing, 94
  scenario analysis/base case, 98
  upside case, 99, 100
  valuation creation
      opportunities, 97
  working capital, 97
EKI-Digital, 311
Ellison, Marvin, 208–211
Emancipation Proclamation, 2
Emerging Domestic Market
      (EDM), 185, 187
  importance, 188–189
  investment company
      summary, 201e
Emerging/minority investment
      managers, utilization
      (goals), 18–19
Employees, ideas/projects
      (creation), 295
Enabler model, 294–295
Enearu, Nicole, 142
English, Crystal, 162
Entrepreneurial Finance (Rogers), 285
Entrepreneurs, exits, 235
  reasons, 240
Entrepreneurship. *See* Black
      entrepreneurship
  franchising, usage, 125
  stages, 166t
    definition, 167t
    identification, 171t
Entrepreneurship via
      acquisition (EVA), 75

advantages/disadvantages, 76–77
  process, 77–80
Entrepreneurs, intrapreneurs
      (contrast), 288, 288t–289t
Equity
  financing, 159
  private equity market, 185–188
Equity capital
  procurement, treatment
      disparity, 158–159
  sources, 170t

F
Fairview Capital, 184–201
  EDM, importance, 188–189
  evolution, 192–193
  founders, 189–192
  future, 193
  partners investment fund
      portfolio summary, 200e
  pioneer status, 185
  private equity market,
      185–188
  structure, 199e
Fatburger, popularity, 136–137
Fenton Avenue Capital, 92
  deal criteria, 89e
  establishment, 87
  Gordon résumé, 110e
  investor group,
      proposal, 111e–116e
Financial Services Pipeline
      Initiative, launch, 12
Fine, Sam, 61
First Annual Convention of the
      People of Color, 50
Fitzhugh, H. Naylor, 190
Floyd, George (murder), 211
Food, Drug, and Cosmetic Act
      (1938), 302

For-profit businesses
(affordable housing
involvement), 280
Franchisee
benefits, 129–130
Black franchisees
negatives, 133
disadvantages, 130–131
ownership/operation, 127
selection, 138
Franchises
cost, 130–131
flexibility, absence, 131–132
industry, 126t
investment, examples, 144–147
negotiation, 142
selection/financing, 142–143
Franchising
defining, 140–143
history, 141
International Franchise
Association
definition, 127
process, 127–133
usage, 125
Franchisor
anti-Black racism, 133
becoming, 143, 153e–154e
options, 151e
benefits, 128
disadvantages, 128
female franchisor,
survival kit, 154
responsibilities, 153e
SBA warnings, 143
selection, 138
services/operating guideline, 127
Freedom Riders, 265
Funded search funds, 87
Fund-of-funds, 177t

Fund of funds
investment structure, 194e
providers, commitments, 197e
Funds of funds
commitments, growth, 196e
number, growth, 196e
role, 186–187

G
Gabelli, Mario, 243
Gaines-Ross, Leslie, 31
Gammel, Joseph, 40–41
Gaston, A.G., 191
Gates, Otis, 251, 263–270, 313
decision making, 271
Gay rights, speaking out, 30
General Catalyst Partners, money
(raising), 243
General partners
definition, 278–279
limited partners, contrast, 278
Gmail, success, 295
Gooden, Linda, 285–288, 300
jobs, winning, 286
Gordon, Bruce, 11
feedback, 87
funding, search, 88
search fund decision, 86–87
Gordon, Earl A., 85–88, 95
résumé, 110e
Government (affordable housing
involvement), 280
Granite Broadcasting, 203
Great American Broadcasting,
BET stock sale, 249
Great American Hat Show,
creation, 222
Great Migration, 52–53
Green Book, The (Green),
43–44, 137

Green, Victor Hugo, 43–44, 137
Griffis, Charles (racial
  discrimination
  lawsuit), 133
Grossman, Roberta Bender, 291
Growth capital, availability
  (problems), 160
Gun brutality, speaking out, 30–31

H
Half Moon Management, 266–267
Hall, Carla, 152
Hamilton, Arlen, 160–164
  investments, 163
Harris, Kamala, 189
Harvey, William, 141
Health Insurance Portability and
  Accountability Act
  (HIPAA), 236, 239
Henry, Mary Kay, 15
Hiatt, Robert, 60
Higgins, Alfred, 39
High growth entrepreneurship,
  franchising (usage),
  138–154
Hollis, Michael, 50–52
Home2 Suites, acquisition, 76
Hotels, African American
  women ownership
  (percentage), 76
Housing Act of 1937, 274, 276
Howard University
  influence, 189–190
  Lewis donation, 84
  Malone contribution, 54–55
Hubbard, Gabriel, 272
Huckabee, Mike (Chick-fil-A
  Appreciation Day), 28
Hughes, Cathy, 39, 56,
  190, 215–220

Chemical Bank loan, 217–218
"Information is Power"
  theme, 218
"Quiet Storm" format, 217
radio stations, acquisitions,
  217–220
Human Rights Campaign, 31
Hutchinson, Gary, 312

I
Iacocca, Lee, 228
"I Have a Dream" speech
  (King, Jr.), 265
Illinois pension managers, diversity
  (increase), 23–24
Illinois State Board of Investment
  (ISBI) diversity policy,
  18–19
Illinois (race population), state
  pensions receipts
  (analysis), 33
Illinois Teachers' Retirement
  System, women/minority
  business allocation, 23
Iman (model), 61
Immelt, Jeffrey, 27
Information technology (IT)
  contracts, 286
  vulnerability, NIST
    definition, 253
Ingram, Dick, 21
Initial public offerings (IPOs)
  advantages, 244–245
  concerns, 252
  disadvantages, 245
  marketplace, 258
  process, 257
  profitability, absence
    (percentage), 262
  quiet period, 257

red herring, usage, 257
time/resources, commitment, 244
usage, 241, 244–245
Innovation, defining, 44–45
Innovator (intrapreneur
category), 290–291
Institutional investors, Rogers
criticism, 10
Internal rates of return (IRR),
production, 188
Intrapreneurs
categories, 289–292
creativity/drive, 299
definition, 285
entrepreneurs, contrast,
288, 288t–289t
support, examples, 308e
Intrapreneurship
benefits, 292–293
company benefits, 293–294
example, 299–301
models, 294–296
risks, 293
Intuit, intrapreneur support, 308e
Investment consulting
diversity, improvement, 17
minorities, entry, 11–13
opportunities, 15
public pensions, leverage, 20–22
women/minorities,
absence, 16–17
Investment, private equity
stages, 194e
Investors
angel investors, 173t
banks, 174t
black-owned banks, 175t
Community Development
Investment Funds
(CDIFs), 176t

corporate venture capital, 176t
directory, 172t–182t
fund-of-funds, 177t
non-bank lenders, 177t
non-for-profit venture
capital, 178t
private equity/buyouts, 178t
search funds, 179t
SPACs, relationship, 242–243
venture capital, 180t–182t
Investors, bias, 167–169
impact, 169
research, 168t
solution, 170–171
"It's About Damn Time fund"
(Hamilton), 163
Iwamoto, Taro, 299

J
Jackson, Jesse, 9, 12, 139
Jackson, Maynard H., 51–52
Jennings, Thomas (patent), 49–50
Jim Crow (impact/laws), 4, 13, 264
Jitney (Wilson), 49
Jobs, Steve, 296, 299
Johnson, Amanda E., 64e
case study, 55–59
partnership, foundations, 57–58
Johnson, Anthony, 2
Johnson, Bob, 1
Johnson Coleman, Sharon, 26
Johnson, George, 12
Johnson, John H., 1, 44, 167
Johnson, Magic, 142
Johnson Products Company, 246
impact, 10
minority business,
importance, 32e
Johnson, Robert L., 248–251, 291
SPAC money, raising, 242–243

Johnson, Ron (resignation), 210
Johnson, Sheila, 57, 248–251
Jones, Frederick, 41
Jones, Meredith, 21
Jones, R. Evan, 272
Jordan, Jr., Vernon, 51

K
Kennedy, William J., 51–52
Keys, Brady, 141
Kimberlin, Susan, 161–162
King, Jr., Martin Luther, 9, 30, 265
Kinney, Kathryn, 64
Knowles, Beyoncé, 60
Kutaragi, Ken, 295, 300–301

L
Lafontant, Jewel C. Stradford, 25–26
Lampkin, Stephanie, 163
Lang, Eugene, 37
Latimer, Lewis Howard, 41
Legal Rights Association, organization, 50
Leonardi, Claire, 192
Lerner, Josh, 12
Letter of intent (LOI), signing, 80
Levie, Aaron, 162
Lewis, A.L., 191
Lewis, Kim/Tim, 1, 163
Lewis, Reginald F., 80–85
Liggins III, Alfred C., 57
Limited liability company (LLC), PEVC structure, 186
Limited partners
    definition, 278
    general partners, contrast, 278–279
Limited partnership (LP), PEVC structure, 186

Local/global communities, reinvestment
Lockheed Martin Information Technology (LMIT)
    creation, 286
    revenue, growth, 287
L'Oreal, diversity report, 60
Lott, Juanita, 235–239
    angel investor funds, 237
    company sale, exit (appearance), 238
Love, John, 40
Lovette, W.A., 40
Low- and moderate-income (LMI) areas, funding, 206
Low Income Housing Tax Credit (LIHTC), 276–277

M
Malone, Annie Turnbo, 52–55, 137
Malone, John, 248
Management buyout, 241
Market gap, response, 45
Marshall, Thurgood, 189
Martinez, Iris, 23
Martin Marietta-Lockheed merger, 300
Match-pair test results, 169t
Mathews, Alan, 253
Mathias, Lauren, 22
Matzeliger, Jan E., 39
Mazany, Terry, 13
McCondichie, Eldoris, 3–4
McDonald's, racial discrimination lawsuit, 133
McGinty, Doris Evans, 190
McWorter, Frank, 2
Meachum, John Berry, 2
Meily, Rene, 82

Mented Cosmetics
  case study, 55–69
  content, example, 68e
  creation, 62–64
  investment matrix, 69e
  investor pitch deck, excerpt, 69e
  investors, attraction, 63
  market, approach, 62–63
  nude colors, 67e
  odds, understanding, 63–64
  opportunity, identification,
    56–58
  partnership, foundations, 57–58
  product development, 62
  soft launch, 63
Mergers, impact, 241–242
Merle, Renae, 16
Meyers, Sid, 225
Michaelson, Tony, 93
Miles, Alexander, 41
Milken, Michael, 82–83
Miller, Kristen Jones, 64e
  case study, 55–69
  partnership, foundations, 57–58
Miller, Melvin, 265
Milliner industry, 221–222
  turnarounds, 223–224
Millinery business, weakening, 223
Minorities
  business, importance, 32e
  investment consulting jobs,
    absence, 16–17
  jobs (providing), problem
    (Black entrepreneur
    solutions), 38
Minority Enterprise Small Business
  Investment Companies
  (MESBICs), 185, 190–191
Miranda case (1966), 25
Morgan, Garrett A., 41

Morgan-Thomas, Georgiette,
    221–231
  turnaround, 224
Morrison, Toni, 190
Morse, Laurence, 184–192, 198e
Multigenerational wealth,
    absence, 11
Murphy, Eddie ("White
    Like Me"), 158
Mutual Ownership Defense Housing
    Division (MODHD), 276
Myers, Jessica, 75–76
Mylavarapu, Swati, 162
MyYoMy (franchise), 146–147

N
National Association of Investment
    Companies (NAIC),
    role, 190–191
Netflix, founding, 46–47
Newman, Eric, 152
Nino's Southern Cooking
    (franchise), 146–147
Nintendo, console changes,
    295, 300–301
Nixon, Richard (Black Capitalism
    program), 190
Non-bank lenders, 177t
Non-for-profit venture capital, 178t
Nonprofit businesses (affordable
    housing involvement), 280
Non-start-ups, growth capital
    availability (problems), 160
North Star Dynamics, CRO
    questionnaire
    response, 306e
Nude
  colors (Mented Cosmetics), 67e
  redefining (beauty industry), 59
Nutraceuticals, usage, 301

NuViewMatics, CRO questionnaire
    response, 306e
Nyong'o, Lupita, 61

O
Obama, Barack, 311
Ohga, Norio, 301
Opportunist model, 294–295
Oracle acquisition, 237–238
Otsuka American Pharmaceutical,
    Inc. (OAPI)
  alliance, 301
  clinical trials, 302–303
Otsuka American Pharmaceutical,
    Ltd., founding, 301
Otsuka, Busaburo, 301
Otsuka Pharmaceutical, 301–302
  Bristol-Myers Squibb
    agreement, 299

P
Page, Clarence, 37–38
Pallmeyer, Rebecca, 25–26
Palmer, Zirl A. (anti-Black
    discrimination), 133–134
Parker, Alice, 41
Parks Sausage Company, IPO, 1, 246
Patterson, Kia (franchisee), 134–135
Payroll Protection Program (PPP)
  changes, 206
  loans, 204–207
Pension dollars, diversification, 21
Permatter, Isaac, 228
Personal funds, usage, 80
Petty, Herman, 141
Pharmaceutical industry,
    intrapreneurial
    innovation, 297–308
Philanthropy, faith
    (relationship), 140

Poro College, establishment,
    53–54
Price, JoAnn, 184–192, 198e
  NAIC, role, 190–191
Price, Lisa, 61
Private equity
  fund of funds, investment
    structure, 194
  fund performance,
    comparison, 195e
  funds, structure, 186
  market, 185–188
  stages, 194e
Private equity/buyouts, 178t
Private equity (P/E) investment
    funds, 80
Private equity/venture
    capital (PEVC)
  industry, 185
  market activity, 187–188
  partnerships, 187
  structure, 186
Producer model, 294–296
Project Diane, 64
Public companies
  Black-owned public
    companies, 246
  U.S. public companies, 245–246
Public pensions, leverage, 20–22
Purvis, William, 40

Q
Quiet period (IPO), 257

R
Race, speaking out, 30–31
Racial tension, attention, 31
Racism/jobs, reality, 38
Radio One, success, 39, 56, 219–220
Randolph, Asa Philip, 264

Raoul, Kwame, 23, 24
Rapid7
    consolidated balance sheets, 260e
    consolidated statements of cash
        flows, 261e
    consolidated statements of
        operations, 260e
    evolution, 253–254
    founding, 253
    funding history, 254–255
    growth, 257–258
    IPO consideration, 256–258
    IPO process, 257
    management, evolution, 254–255
    marketing materials, 259e
    performance, 255–256
    quiet period, 257
    stock price, punishment, 252
    venture capital investors,
        considerations, 256
Reaves, Davonne, 75–76
Red herring, usage, 257
Reeves, Mae, 223
Rehak, Jay, 20
Religious freedom bills,
        disapproval, 28
Renfro, Robert, 2
Request for proposal (RFP),
        usage, 263
Rexall Drugs, franchise
        purchase, 133–134
Roberts, Homer B., 125–126, 141
Robinson, Elbert R., 41
Rogers, Jr., John, 5–8
    CEO (Ariel Investments), 7–10
    controversy, 10
    criticism, reduction (decision), 10
    mission, 11–13
    parents, honoring, 25–26

Rogers, Sr., John, 9, 11, 25
Roosevelt, Franklin D., 276
Rosebud, Harriet, 222, 225
Rose, David, 162
Rudolph, Ryan, 272
Russell, H.J., 51

S
Sacca, Marc, 162
Saft, Harry, 225
Sammons, Walter, 40
Sampson, George T., 40
Sarbanes-Oxley Act, 236–237
Saunders, Brent, 27
Schill, Michael, 26
Schulman, Dan, 27
Schultz, Howard, 28, 31
Seafood franchise, investment,
        144–145
Search fund
    Gordon decision, 86–87
    source, 179t
Section 8 housing, 274
Security holes, management, 253
Seigel, Peter, 192
Seller financing, loan, 80
Siebert, Mark, 153
Simmons, Omar, 142
Simpson, Charles, 135
Singer, Isaac, 141
Sloan, Alfred P., 224, 290
Sloan, Carrie, 15
Small Business Administration
    (SBA)
    franchisor warnings, 143
    loans, 80
Small business, franchise
        conversion, 153
Smith, Robert F., 165

Social Security Administration,
    Gooden contracts, 286
Society, investor bias (impact),
    169–170
Sogah, Esi, 292
Southern food, news coverage, 152e
S&P 500 market activity,
    trend, 258, 262e
Spaulding, Asa, 192
Spearman, Kwame, 211–215
Special purpose acquisition
    companies (SPACs), 244
  Black entrepreneurs/investors,
    relationship, 242–243
  impact, 241–242
Spikes, Richard, 40–41
Standard, John, 41
Start-ups. See Black start-up
    entrepreneurs
  fundamentals, 44–48
Stewart, Thomas W., 40
Stites, Eric, 141
Strategic acquisition, 241
Sundown towns, 43–44
Susannah's Seafood Emporium
    (franchise), 144–145
  corporate information, 150e

T
Taft Broadcasting, 248, 249
Tattered Cover Book Store, 211–215
  backlash, 213–215
  business turnaround, 215
Tax Reform Act of 1986, 277
Technology Crossover Ventures
    (TCV), 255–256
The American Hat Factory
    (TAHF), 221–231
  acquisition, 225

competition, 227
equipment, 231e
hats, examples (photo), 229e,
    230e, 231e
manufacturing flow diagram, 230e
operations, 226–227
performance, 225
runway model (photo), 229e
Thomas, Corey, 255
  IPO case study, 251, 252–258
  IPO decision, 258
Thomas, Karen, 290–292
Threat Exposure Management
    (TEM) market, 252
TLC Group, establishment, 81–82
Toffel, Michael, 28–29
Tulsa (OK): Black Holocaust in
    America, 3, 9
Turnarounds
  activities, 204
  Black corporate turnaround
    specialists, 207–211
  Black turnaround
    entrepreneurs, 203
  business turnaround,
    example, 215
  milliner industry, 223–224
  successes, 228e
Turnbull, Clayton, 142

U
Uber, success, 47–48
Ullman, Myron, 210–211
United Housing, 251, 263–282
  affordable housing
    approach, 270–272
  background, 274–280
  business, profile, 269
  decision making, 271

finances (balance sheet/income statement), 273e
financial return potential, 270
history, 266–267
local community hirings, 269
partners, 272e
reputation, enhancement, 267–268
social mission, 268–269
United States
affordable housing
criticism, 278
history, 276–277
public companies, listing, 245–246
race, population breakdown, 33e
U.S. Forest Service Eastern Region, intrapreneur support, 308e
U.S. venture funds, capital under management, 195e

V
Value chain, identification, 45
Van Meter, Valerie, 12
Venture capital, 180t–182t
annual venture capital investments, 197e
Vulnerability Assessment
market, worldwide estimation, 259e
worldwide revenue share, 259e
Vulnerability Management, 253

W
Walker, Maggie, 2
Walker, Monica, 12

Walker, Sarah Breedlove (Madam C.J. Walker), 1, 40, 52, 54, 57
Warner, Jr., Rawleigh, 27
Weinheimer, Eric, 13
Welton, Maurice, 142
White, Robert L., 51–52
White, Shauna, 272
White, Thurman, 13
Why Should White Guys Have All the Fun? (Lewis), 83, 85
Wilkins, Herbert, 191
Williams, Carol, 56
Williams, Daniel Hale, 41
Williams, Jerome, 272
Williams, Venus, 142
Wilson, August, 49
Women
Chicago Teacher's Pension Fund investment, 20
investment consulting jobs, absence, 16–17
Woodson, Carter G., 189

Y
Yancey, Lovie (Black franchisor), 135–137
Y Combinator, Female Founders Conference, 161
Young, Andrew, 51, 189

Z
Zacharias, Walter, 291
Zell, Leah Joy/Sam, 22
Zerhusen, Thyra, 22
Zuckerberg, Mark, 30